P
THE GRE

"*The Greatest Knight* gives us a moving portrait of one man's struggle, ascent and final [peaceful] demise."   —*The Sunday Times* (UK)

"The term 'medieval biography' doesn't necessarily conjure up a lot of excitement among the general book-loving population. But . . . it really should. This blood, guts, gore and gallantry romp through medieval history, following the great knight William Marshall . . . is way more fun than it should be."   —*New York Post*

"A valuable biography of an important figure in a distant, violent, barely comprehensible era."   —*Kirkus Reviews*

"Big, readable, and enlightening . . . a rousing history."
—*Columbus Dispatch*

"England's greatest knight puts *Game of Thrones* to shame. A magnificent yarn, and Asbridge has astutely used it to tell the juicy and complicated tale of the ups and downs of the Angevin empire. Marshal was an astounding figure—his rags-to-riches journey, his prolific fighting career (even at 70 he essentially knocked an armored guy out with one blow), and his place at the table of history—all make for an irresistible tale. Asbridge takes the reader through an eye-opening account of the world of tournaments, of the structure of a lord's household, and the complicated, often symbiotically parasitic relationship between lord and knight, as well as the evolution of the Magna Carta."   —William O'Connor, The Daily Beast

"This is medieval history at its very best—a compelling story told by a historian whose knowledge is both thorough and extensive, and whose enthusiasm for the subject rings out on every page."

—Ian Mortimer, author of
The Time Traveler's Guide to Medieval England

"Captivatingly written and eye-openingly informative, *The Greatest Knight* is . . . a first-rate history told by a master of the craft. Read this book, and you'll never forget the name William Marshal—nor will you ever think of the Middle Ages in the same way again."

—Toby Lester, author of
The Fourth Part of the World and *Da Vinci's Ghost*

"History doesn't come more exciting than this. Thomas Asbridge has written a page turner about William Marshal, the Zelig of English history, a man who was indispensable to five kings, and had a hand in practically every important event during those turbulent and eventful reigns." —Danny Danziger, author of *1215*

THE
GREATEST
KNIGHT

Also by Thomas Asbridge

THE FIRST CRUSADE
THE CRUSADE

THE GREATEST KNIGHT

The Remarkable Life of William Marshal,
the Power Behind Five English Thrones

THOMAS ASBRIDGE

An Imprint of HarperCollins*Publishers*

For my brother
Per Asbridge

THE GREATEST KNIGHT. Copyright © 2014 by Thomas Asbridge. All rights reserved. Printed in the United States of America. No part of this book may be used or reproduced in any manner whatsoever without written permission except in the case of brief quotations embodied in critical articles and reviews. For information address HarperCollins Publishers, 195 Broadway, New York, NY, 10007.

HarperCollins books may be purchased for educational, business, or sales promotional use. For information please e-mail the Special Markets Department at SPsales@harpercollins.com.

A hardcover edition of this book was published in 2014 by Ecco, an imprint of HarperCollins Publishers.

FIRST ECCO PAPERBACK EDITION PUBLISHED 2015.

Library of Congress Cataloging-in-Publication Data has been applied for.

ISBN 978-0-06-226206-6

23 24 25 26 27 LBC 16 15 14 13 12

CONTENTS

PART IV OLD AGE: ENGLAND'S GREAT MAGNATE

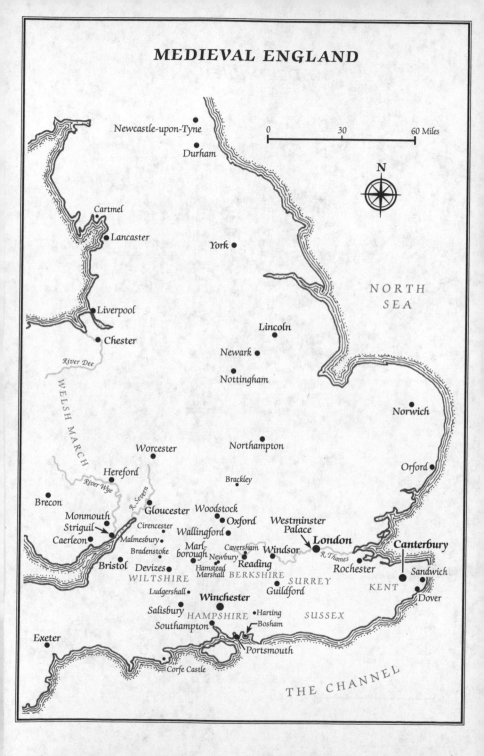

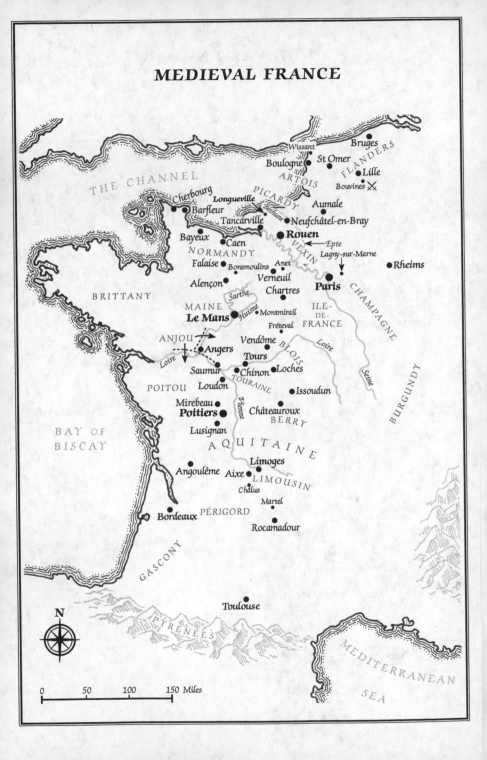

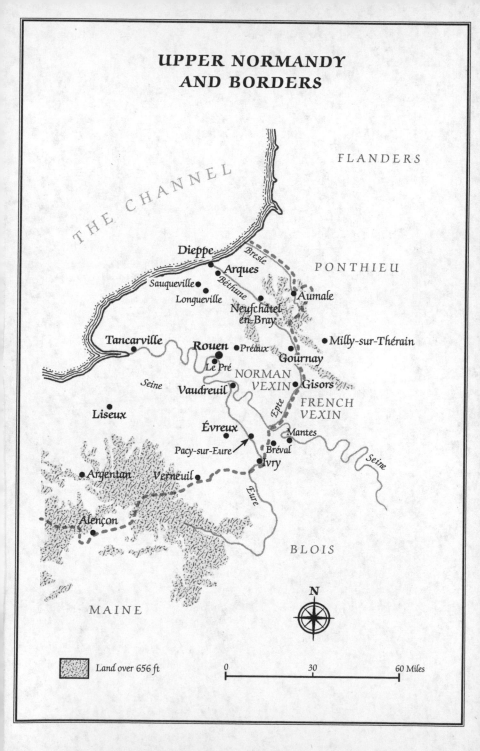

UPPER NORMANDY
AND BORDERS

FLANDERS

THE CHANNEL

Dieppe

Bresle

PONTHIEU

Arques

Béthune

Sauqueville

Longueville

Aumale

Neufchâtel
en-Bray

Tancarville

Rouen

Préaux

Milly-sur-Thérain

Le Pré

Gournay

NORMAN
VEXIN

Vaudreuil

Gisors

FRENCH
VEXIN

Seine

Epte

Liseux

Évreux

Mantes

Pacy-sur-Eure

Bréval

Ivry

Seine

Argentan

Verneuil

Eure

Alençon

BLOIS

MAINE

N

Land over 656 ft

0   30   60 Miles

PREFACE

On Wednesday, 6 February 1861, a young French scholar named Paul Meyer walked into Sotheby's auction house, then located just behind London's Covent Garden, at 13 Wellington Street. A prestigious sale was scheduled to begin at 1.00 p.m., with the official catalogue proclaiming that 'Some most valuable and important early manuscripts, chiefly on vellum' would be offered for purchase. These were works drawn from the celebrated Savile collection of rare medieval texts, assembled during the reign of Queen Elizabeth I, and not displayed in public for more than two centuries. Meyer – a dedicated student of the Middle Ages – was in England to attend this event, and what he saw that day changed the course of his career, sparking a forty-year obsession, a hunt to uncover a lost history and a discovery that would reshape our understanding of the medieval world.

A distinguished future awaited Paul Meyer. In time, he would achieve international renown as an academic and archivist, becoming the pre-eminent authority on early French manuscripts and the interpretation of arcane, handwritten texts. This rather esoteric expertise led Meyer to be called as a key witness in the notorious Dreyfus trial of 1898, where his testimony helped to clear the accused of espionage.* But in early 1861, he was just a twenty-one-year-old scholar, enrolled

---

* Meyer swore that the documents detailing French military secrets could not have been written by the accused, Alfred Dreyfus.

in Paris's esteemed centre of medieval studies, the École des Chartes, and still working on his somewhat un-inspiringly titled thesis: 'Research on the language spoken in France in barbarian times (fifth to ninth centuries)'.

Meyer had been sent to London by the staff of the Bibliothèque Impériale (soon to be re-dubbed the French 'National Library'), so that he might bid on their behalf in the Sotheby's auction, and hopefully acquire three well-known works of medieval French literature. Unfortunately, the library furnished him with only meagre funds, leaving little prospect of matching the wealthy private collectors and professional archivists sure to flock to the Savile sale. Meyer resolved to savour this exceptional opportunity nonetheless, and arrived at Sotheby's early in the morning, allowing himself time to stalk the exhibition room.

For a man of his background and training, this was akin to entering a treasure vault. Over the next two hours he scoured the tables, scribbling notes on each of the manuscripts presented. Many were copies of famous texts; some were wonderfully ornate and highly decorated, with vibrantly coloured illuminations. But one that drew his eye was neither familiar, nor at first glance especially remarkable. Listed as Lot 51, this unassuming work was bound in worn, dark brown leather (dating from the sixteenth century) and, in size, resembled a modern hardback book – its pages measuring nine-and-a-half inches by six-and-three-quarter inches. The Sotheby's catalogue described it simply as a 'Norman-French chronicle on English Affairs (in Verse)', written on vellum 'by an Anglo-Norman scribe' in the thirteenth century, and helpfully quoted the last four intriguing, yet unspecific, lines of its text:

Ci fini del conte lestoire	Here ends the Earl's story
Et dex en perdurable gloire	and may God grant that his soul
Vont que la sue ame seit mise	rest in eternal glory
Et entre ses Angles assise. Amen.	in the company of his angels. Amen.

Carefully opening the front binding, Meyer could perceive no obvious identifying marks, no title or indication of subject matter. He was confronted by a simple, but elegantly decorated text – with a minuscule script inscribed in black ink, set out in two columns, across 127 leaves (or pages), and a mixture of red and blue capital letters, each embellished with ornate, swirling, abstract designs. The first page showed some signs of water damage, but was still legible, so he examined the earliest sections of the work and jotted down a quick summary of his initial findings: 'Contains an original chronicle, which seems to report the conflict that broke out in England during the reign of Stephen, nephew of Henry I.'

Meyer began to suspect that this manuscript had remained untouched and unopened for at least 250 years. He would later write that this book 'strongly excited my curiosity', but this was in large part because he had no idea what it might be. In all his studies, he had never come across any mention of a medieval French verse account of this type. His interest was piqued. As he sat through the auction later that day, noting the bidding on Lot 51, it became obvious that the attention of others had also been drawn. The British Museum offered £200, then the archivist, Sir Frederic Madden, raised this to £250, but they had no chance of matching the famed book collector and antiquarian, Sir Thomas Phillipps – a self-confessed bibliomaniac, renowned for his outrageous profligacy. Phillipps bid the 'enormous price' of £380 (9,500 French francs by Meyer's calculation), adding Lot 51 to the other thirty-four Savile manuscripts he snapped up that day.

As the sale came to a close, the mysterious 'Norman-French chronicle on English Affairs' was packed away. Meyer would not see the text again for twenty years, and would only later realise that on that Wednesday in 1861 he had briefly handled a 'work of extraordinary importance' – the sole surviving copy of an unknown biography, detailing the life of an illustrious medieval knight. A man who rose through the ranks, serving the English crown, befriended the likes of Richard the Lionheart and Eleanor of Aquitaine, helped to negotiate the terms of Magna Carta and defended England from French invasion at the age of seventy. This storied warrior was William Marshal, and, unbeknown to Meyer, his body lay buried in London's Temple Church, less than a mile from Sotheby's.

In the years that followed, Paul Meyer's professional career flourished, but he became increasingly fixated by the intriguing 'Norman-French chronicle' he had seen in 1861. Two years after the London auction, he was formally attached to the manuscripts department of the Bibliothèque Nationale in Paris, and sent to comb the great British libraries in London, Oxford, Cambridge, Glasgow and Edinburgh, in search of manuscripts related to the culture and history of medieval France. He began to publish, earning a reputation for erudition and meticulous scholarship, even as archivists and academics across Europe continued to push back the frontiers of knowledge and chart the course of the Middle Ages. Yet in all this time, Meyer could not forget Lot 51.

At first, his enquiries began in a leisurely, almost random, manner – confident that a reference to the 'Norman-French chronicle on English Affairs' must appear somewhere amid the lists of manuscripts already archived in France, Britain and Germany. A slow search began, through thousands of entries, in each of the august institutions Meyer toured. But after years of increasingly painstaking research, he still had found no mention of any work that resembled the elusive verse text. Even more frustrating was the fact that Lot 51 appeared to have vanished into the Phillipps collection. Sir Thomas's extraordinary personal library contained some 60,000 manuscripts, acquired over many decades and deposited at his Middle Hill estate in Worcestershire. Since 1837, he had been slowly, but fastidiously, cataloguing these works – apportioning each text a unique reference number – and then proudly publishing an ever-expanding inventory via a small, private printing press. Few copies of these lists were circulated, yet Meyer tracked them down; but even here he could find no mention of his obscure manuscript, though other works bought in the Savile auction were noted.

Part of the problem seems to have been that Phillipps had decided, in 1863, to move his entire library to a large mansion in Cheltenham – a feat that took two years to complete. He was also nearing the end of his life, increasingly cantankerous and utterly determined that no one else should come near his precious books. When Sir Thomas died in 1872, at the age of seventy-nine, the situation hardly improved. The future of Phillipps' collection and estate was contested by his heirs; when Meyer contacted them with polite enquiries about a certain missing text, his letters went unanswered. It seemed that the 'Norman-French chronicle' had disappeared.

Nonetheless, Meyer persisted. He was now nearing his forties: an eminent academic, editor of his own highly regarded scholarly journal, *Romania*, and soon to be appointed as director of the École des Chartes itself. Phillipps' family finally relented in the autumn of 1880, granting Meyer access to the collection in Cheltenham. After a succession of visits, he narrowed the search down to 5,000 works and began checking each one by hand. At last, in 1881, he found the misplaced book – Phillipps had numbered the volume '25155', but it had never been properly catalogued, nor read. After two decades, Meyer had the 'Norman-French chronicle' in front of him once more. A quick leaf through its pages confirmed that this was indeed a unique copy of an otherwise unknown account, but its contents proved to be more significant that even he had imagined.

Meyer was probably the first person to read the manuscript in 600 years, but now that he was able to move beyond its initial pages, and absorb the 19,215 lines of rhymed medieval French verse, it became clear that this was neither a chronicle, nor a piece of fictionalised literature. His initial notes, hurriedly compiled in 1861, had barely scratched the surface, for the text moved far beyond the mid-twelfth century 'anarchy' of King Stephen's reign. In fact, it laid out – in glorious detail – the entire life story of a man named Guillaume le Maréchal, William Marshal. Meyer knew of scores of well-studied texts describing the careers of famous kings, queens and saints, but this was the first biography of a medieval knight, and had originally been composed in the mid-1220s.

Meyer began to work at a feverish pace, immersing himself in the study of the manuscript – which he now christened the *History of William Marshal* – while hunting down other references to Marshal. He clearly had been no ordinary knight, appearing intermittently in other contemporary chronicles and documents, identified as an important royal servant, and later, as the earl of Striguil and Pembroke. Towards the end of his life, Marshal had even been regent of England and re-issued *Magna Carta*. He was an established, yet shadowy presence in the annals of medieval history. The account discovered by Meyer suddenly added human flesh to the bones of this long-forgotten figure. It traced Marshal's path from relatively humble origins, through the pageantry of chivalric tournaments and the brutish realities of war, to the opulent royal courts of Europe, it followed him as he ranged across the medieval world – from his birthplace in England to the foothills of the Pyrenees and the distant Holy Land – and it charted his rise to prominence and the foundation of the Marshal dynasty.

The long hunt for Lot 51, the 'Norman-French chronicle', had been worth it – Meyer had made a crucial breakthrough, unearthing a text that shone revelatory light upon the culture and history of the Middle Ages. Within a year, he published an article, describing his search for the manuscript and initial observations on its text. He then dedicated another twenty years of his life to producing a full printed edition of the *History* in three volumes, published between 1891 and 1901 as *L'Histoire de Guillaume le Maréchal, comte de Striguil et de Pembroke*.

It is the manuscript of the *History of William Marshal*, identified by Paul Meyer and now residing in the vaults of the Morgan Library in New York, that allows the life of this peerless knight to be reconstructed. Drawing upon the evidence it preserves, and a range of other contemporary material, the details of William Marshal's extraordinary story can be pieced together. Yet, for all the insights that it furnishes, the *History* has to be read with a cautious and critical eye. The biography was commissioned by a member of Marshal's family, soon after his death, and written by an otherwise unknown Anglo-French scribe working in England, named John. The text was completed soon after 1226, and the extant version was a copy of this original, made in the course of the next twenty-five years.*

The biographer claimed to have drawn some of his account from personal experience and used a number of other documents and records, but he relied heavily upon the oral testimony of those who had known William Marshal – his close kin and trusted retainers. Marshal's friend and supporter of almost forty years, the knight John of Earley, was a particularly important source of information. Earley was not only able to recall what he had seen with his own eyes, but also repeated many of the tales of daring adventure that Marshal had himself been fond of recounting.

The *History* was a celebration of William Marshal's astounding achievements. As such, it offers an unashamedly biased account, presenting its hero as the perfect knight. In its pages William almost became the living embodiment of the mythical Arthurian knight, Lancelot – one of the central heroes of the popular literature written in Marshal's own day. Many of the *History*'s claims can be corroborated in other sources, but there were times when the biographer omitted uncomfortable details related to Marshal's rise to prominence, from his involvement in rebellions against the crown to his dealings with King John, England's infamous monarch. In some respects, the *History*'s inherent partiality can be useful, because it offers a glimpse of contemporary sensibilities. The biographer imbued his subject with laudable qualities and clearly expected readers to be thoroughly impressed by Marshal's character. Some of these qualities – like valour, martial prowess, loyalty and honour – are precisely what we might expect to find in an idealised medieval warrior; others – such as cunning, duplicity and avid materialism – are not.

*

---

* At least four other copies of the *History of William Marshal* appear to have been made, but these, along with the original, were lost over the centuries.

This book offers a new biography of William Marshal: the landless younger son who became perhaps the most famous knight of the Middle Ages, lauded as a peerless warrior and paragon of chivalry, a man who achieved untold power and status as a baron and politician, ultimately ruling England itself. In retracing his career, it follows in the footsteps of works by esteemed scholars such as Paul Meyer, Sidney Painter and David Crouch. But, for the first time, this account places Marshal's life into a far broader context.

William's astonishing story offers an unrivalled window on to the world of the medieval knight, allowing us to witness first-hand the emergence of the near-mythical warrior class that stood at the heart of medieval European history. This book traces the development of this elite martial cadre, from its training and rituals to the evolution of knightly arms, armour and fighting methods. And it reveals how a collision between the harsh realities of medieval war and politics and romanticised Arthurian myths spawned the notions of chivalry and courtliness, the codes that William Marshal came to epitomise and define.

It also follows Marshal, as he stood at the right hand of five kings, through a tumultuous era of military confrontation and cultural upheaval – a period that transformed England. William witnessed the rise and fall of the English monarchy's mighty Angevin 'Empire', fought embittered wars of conquest against the French that served, for the first time, to foster a distinct sense of 'English' identity and was party to the forging of Magna Carta, the original 'bill of rights', which reset the balance of power between the king and his subjects. This knight's tale thus traverses one of the most formative periods of our medieval past. It is the story of a remarkable man, the creation of the knightly ideal and the birth of a nation.

Part I

CHILDHOOD & YOUTH: BECOMING A KNIGHT

I

A TIME OF WOLVES

In 1152 King Stephen of England decided to execute a five-year-old boy. This child – William Marshal – had committed no crime. He was a hostage, given over to the crown as surety for his father's word, a pawn in the great game of power and politics then being played out within a realm wracked by civil war. When William's father promptly broke his pledge to the king, declaring that 'he did not care about the child, since he still had the anvils and hammers to forge even finer ones', Stephen was furious. In his rage, he ordered the boy 'to be seized and taken to the gallows for hanging', and young William was duly led away to face his fate.

Through the long years of his life, William Marshal seems never to have forgotten this moment of intense drama. It was, perhaps, his earliest childhood memory. For all the fame and success William later enjoyed, fêted even as the 'greatest knight in the world', he began as the boy forsaken by his father and condemned by his king. So why had William's young life been placed in such danger, and how did he survive?

THE LAND OF 'STRIFE AND DISORDER'

William Marshal was born in England around 1147, at a time of unrest. The kingdom was in the grip of a ruinous, fifteen-year-long conflict, as King Stephen struggled to resist his cousin Empress Matilda's attempts to seize power. Both possessed strong claims to the realm, so the country was divided in its allegiance and spiralling towards anarchy. One medieval chronicler described this as a period of 'great strife [and] disorder', in which England was 'plagued by war . . . and the law of the land was disregarded'. Great swathes of the landscape were left scarred and ravaged, such that one could 'go a whole day's journey' and yet find only empty villages and untilled land. Amid such desolation, the 'wretched people died of starvation'. One contemporary admitted that in these years many 'said openly that Christ and his saints were asleep'.

Yet for all the chaos and horror of this era, there were those who prospered during the civil war. With the collapse of crown authority, local warlords were left in many regions to impose some semblance of order, and this power was often abused by the predatory and the unscrupulous. One such was William's father, John Marshal, a nobleman of middling rank, with a lordship centred in England's West Country. By birth, John was not English (or Anglo-Saxon), but a French-speaking Norman. Back in the tenth century, his Viking ancestors – known then as the 'Northmen' – had settled in a region of northern France that came to be known as Normandy (literally 'the land of the Northmen'). They embraced some of the customs of their new homeland and even adopted French, or Frankish, names, but remained warlike and land-hungry. In 1066, their leader William, duke of Normandy – William 'the Conqueror' – led an invasion force across the English Channel and scored a stunning victory at the Battle of Hastings. This Norman triumph left England's last, short-lived Anglo-Saxon king, Harold Godwinson, and the cream of his ruling nobility, dead on the field. In its wake, William assumed the crown of England, while retaining control of Normandy. An Anglo-Norman realm was forged, and it was in this cross-Channel world that William Marshal would be raised.

In some respects, 1066 marked a decisive break with the past. William the Conqueror established a new and enduring royal dynasty, and England's 'native' peoples suddenly found themselves the subjects of foreign invaders. King William I distributed land north of the Channel to some 150 Norman warlords and officials, and together they pacified the realm through brute force and threw up an extensive network of imposing castles to secure their authority. John Marshal's father – Gilbert Giffard (literally meaning 'Gilbert Chubby Cheeks') – was one of these early Norman settlers, who came to England during the first wave of conquest or in its aftermath. By the time of William I's great Domesday survey of landholding in 1086, Gilbert held territory in the western county of Wiltshire. He also served as the royal master-marshal, an ancient military office, traditionally associated with the care and maintenance of the king's horses, which over time developed into an administrative post, largely concerned with the day-to-day running of the court.

When taken in context, the advent of the Normans was not as jarring as it might first appear. In a later era, Britain would be seen as an unconquerable island realm: William Shakespeare's inviolate 'sceptre'd isle', the 'fortress built by nature [against] the hand of war'. But in the early Middle Ages, England seemed fatally prone to invasion. Through the centuries preceding 1066, the Anglo-Saxons (themselves the successors of earlier Celtic and then Roman invaders) had faced repeated waves of Viking incursion and settlement that left much of northern England in Norse hands. A period of direct Viking rule eventually was witnessed under Cnut of Denmark in the early eleventh century, only for the brief reinstatement of Anglo-Saxon kingship, before William the Conqueror's arrival. As a result, the cultural, ethnic and linguistic identity of the 'English' was far from uniform, and the notion that the Normans crushed an otherwise untrammelled, pure-bred Anglo-Saxon society has little basis in reality.

The Norman colonisation of England proved to be remarkably successful. The Conqueror and his followers found a wealthy land, renowned for its natural resources and ripe for exploitation. More than one-third of the British Isles remained heavily wooded, but England boasted in excess of seven million acres of cultivated farmland in the late eleventh century, tended by a predominantly rural population of around two-and-a-half million people. A period of climatic change also saw the average temperature rise by about one degree centigrade, increasing agricultural yields (and even allowing vineyards to be planted in middle-England). For the ruling elite, at least, this was a time of plenty. A semblance of political continuity was also maintained after King William's death in 1087, as he was succeeded by two of his sons, William Rufus (1087–1100) and Henry I (1100–35).

It was during this latter reign that John Marshal began his career, gradually accumulating status, land and wealth. By 1130, John was in his twenties and had succeeded to the master-marshalcy, for which privilege he had to pay a fee of forty silver marks to the crown – quite a sum, given that an annual income of around fifteen marks would allow a noble to live in considerable comfort. The position brought no great power in or of itself, but marked him out as one of the great officers of the king's household. He had oversight of four under-marshals, a group of royal ushers, the keeper of the king's tents, even the supervisor of the royal fireplaces. More importantly, John had a degree of access to the king and his leading barons, which allowed him to curry favour and seek reward. He owned a cluster of houses close to the royal palace and castle in Winchester, as well as small parcels of land dotted across south-west England, but his prized family estate, which came to be known as Hamstead Marshall, lay in a verdant swathe of the Kennet valley, close to the border between Berkshire and Wiltshire. Around this same time, John secured himself a decent marriage to a minor Wiltshire heiress named Adelina, with whom he fathered two sons, Gilbert and Walter. So far his achievements had been unremarkable, his progress piecemeal. But

John Marshal's day was about to dawn, because the peace of the realm had already begun to unravel.

THE DESCENT INTO ANARCHY

On the night of 25 November 1120, William Ætheling – the seventeen-year-old heir to the throne of England – threw a raucous, wine-soaked party. A throng of young, well-heeled nobles had joined him aboard a fine newly fitted vessel, the *White Ship*, moored in the harbour at Barfleur, in Normandy. Notable among the revellers were William's half-siblings, Richard and Countess Matilda of Perche, as well as his cousin, Stephen of Blois (the man who, years later, would order William Marshal's execution). As the alcohol flowed, even the crew and oarsmen partook, and an atmosphere of drunken merriment and youthful exuberance took hold. When a group of clerics arrived to bless the vessel with holy water they were driven away with contemptuous shouts and mocking laughter. Earlier that day William's father, King Henry I of England, had set sail from Barfleur intent on crossing the Channel. Boisterous calls now went up on the *White Ship* for a race to be undertaken. Surely this sleek craft could outpace the king's vessel, beating him to the English coast? As hasty preparations for the departure were made, some seem to have thought better of this folly and disembarked, among them Stephen of Blois, apparently complaining that he was afflicted by diarrhoea. The great contemporary chronicler of this era, William of Malmesbury, described how the crowded *White Ship* was 'launched from the shore, although it was now dark' adding that 'she flew swifter than an arrow, sweeping the rippling surface of the deep'.

Within minutes disaster struck. Inebriated and inattentive, the steersman misjudged his course out of the natural harbour and the princely craft crashed at speed into a jutting rock exposed by the low tide. Two planks in the starboard hull shattered and the *White Ship* began to take on water. In the confusion that followed, William

Ætheling was bundled on to a rowing boat and looked set to escape, but the despairing wails of his half-sister Matilda prompted him to turn back and attempt a rescue. As it drew up alongside the foundering *White Ship*, William's small craft was quickly overladen by those clambering for safety and capsized. The young prince and all his peers drowned, 'buried', as William of Malmesbury put it, 'in the deep'.

It was later said that the *White Ship*'s captain, one Thomas FitzStephen, managed at first to swim away from the sinking vessel. But when he realised that his royal passengers had been lost, Thomas gave himself up to the cold water. Only two men survived the first horrors of this catastrophe by clawing their way up the *White Ship*'s mast to reach the yardarm – one was a minor nobleman, Geoffrey son of the viscount of Exmes, the other a butcher from Rouen named Berold. As the terrified screams of those below eventually died down to silence, both struggled to cling on to their desperate perch. Hours passed. The night was clear and frosty, and eventually Geoffrey lost his grip, plunging down to be swallowed by the sea. Berold alone, dressed in a commoner's sheepskins, saw the dawn and was rescued by fishermen; one survivor to tell the tale of this calamity.

William of Malmesbury would conclude that 'no ship ever brought so much misery to England; none was ever so notorious in the history of the world'. This dread-laden pronouncement was born out of bitter experience, for the chronicler lived through the decades that followed, witnessing an end to the stability of King Henry I's reign and England's descent into disorder. All of this, so William of Malmesbury believed, could be traced back to William Ætheling's sudden and untimely demise. The sinking of the *White Ship* was so calamitous because it deprived Henry I of his only legitimate male heir. The king had never had a problem fathering offspring – he sired more than twenty children – and his voracious sexual appetite prompted one contemporary to conclude that he was 'enslaved by female seduction'. Though two perished on the *White Ship*, many of the king's illegitimate issue prospered, chief among them his eldest bastard son Robert, who was gifted the earldom of Gloucester.

But there was no real prospect that Robert would inherit England's crown. Illegitimacy had not always been a bar to succession and power. Henry I's own father, William the Conqueror, was bastard born, yet became duke of Normandy and, in 1066, England's anointed monarch. During recent decades, however, a reforming Church had sought to tighten the strictures governing marriage, and proven legitimacy became paramount. Henry I's union with Edith of Scotland (who could herself trace her lineage back to the Anglo-Saxon kings of Wessex) produced only a boy and a girl, William and Matilda, and the king focused his grand dreams for peaceful dynastic succession upon the former. Young William came to be styled with the ancient Anglo-Saxon title 'Ætheling' in honour of his royal heritage and status as heir designate. He was to be the king who finally united the bloodlines of Normandy and Anglo-Saxon England.

When the *White Ship* sank and William drowned, these designs came undone. Nonetheless, the spiral into civil war that followed Henry I's own eventual demise, at the age of sixty-seven, on 1 December 1135, was not inevitable. Despite first appearances, England had no track record of clear, unchallenged succession; nor was there a fixed tradition of eldest sons inheriting the crown. England's recent kings had actually come to power through force of arms and speed of action, not unassailable right. Henry I himself stole England and Normandy from his elder brother, Robert Curthose, and then promptly imprisoned his sibling for the best part of thirty years. In fact, it would not be until the early thirteenth century that a king of England was succeeded by his first-born son, and even then the process was fraught and fragile. William Ætheling's accession was supposed to break this mould, yet the sequence of events initiated by his death might still have been halted. The real problem was that after 1135 neither of the two leading claimants to the throne possessed sufficient strength or sustained support with the realm to secure a lasting hold over England.

The claimants to the crown

One candidate was Henry I's sole surviving legitimate child, his forceful and ambitious daughter Matilda. It was to her that the king eventually turned after the sinking of the *White Ship*, declaring Matilda his heir in early 1127, and again in 1131, forcing oaths of recognition for her claim from his leading nobles. But in the medieval world, power and military might were inextricably linked. This was the age of the warrior-king, in which a monarch was expected to lead and command armies in person, and as such, the simple fact of Matilda's gender was a significant, though not insurmountable, impediment. She was also viewed as an outsider by many Anglo-Norman nobles. Wed as a young girl to Emperor Henry V of Germany, she had grown up in the imperial court, speaking German and learning the manners and customs of a foreign land. The union earned Matilda the right to assume the title 'empress', but produced no offspring.

Her second marriage to Geoffrey 'le Bel' ('the Fair'), the dandyish count of Anjou, was a strictly political union – though the couple did produce three sons in relatively short order – but the match was viewed in a dim light by many. Anjou was Normandy's longstanding rival; its people, the Angevins, were seen as a savage and shifty bunch, with an unhealthy appetite for indiscriminate violence and rapacious looting. It was little wonder then that Matilda struggled to press home her claim to England in 1135. She remained the unfamiliar empress, hampered by her sex and tainted by association with an Angevin, who most suspected might try to steal the crown for himself. The timing of her father's death also left her at a disadvantage, as Matilda was then around eight weeks pregnant with her third child.

Empress Matilda's claim was supplanted by a largely unheralded candidate, Stephen of Blois. Like his cousin Matilda, Stephen was a grandson of William the Conqueror, but in Stephen's case this ancestry was derived through the female line. His mother was the formidable Adela of Blois, daughter of the Conqueror and Henry I's

sister, a rare and remarkable woman, truly capable of wielding power
in a man's world. After the death of her husband on crusade in the
Holy Land, Adela looked to secure the future of her surviving sons.
One of the youngest, Stephen, was sent to his uncle King Henry I's
court in 1113, where he was granted the county of Mortain (in south-
western Normandy) and additional lands in England. In the years
that followed, Stephen prospered, accruing favour and influence,
earning title to further territories. By 1120, when he narrowly avoided
the disaster of the *White Ship*, Stephen was already a leading
member of the Anglo-Norman aristocracy. His status was further
enhanced when King Henry I orchestrated Stephen's marriage to the
wealthy heiress to the county of Boulogne (in north-eastern France),
one of England's most valuable trading partners. Nonetheless, no
one seems to have expected that he might stake a serious claim to the
crown in 1135. After all, in 1127 Stephen had been one of the first
nobles to swear an oath to uphold his cousin Empress Matilda's
rights.

When King Henry I died on 1 December, that promise was put to
one side. Emulating his late uncle's example, Stephen resolved to
seize power for himself. Moving with lightning speed, he crossed
immediately from Boulogne to London – England's commercial capital – securing the city's support, most likely in return for mercantile
privileges. Stephen then raced on to Winchester, the ancient seat of
royal power, where his younger brother, Henry of Blois, had become
bishop in 1129. With his connivance, Stephen was able to gain control of the royal treasury and then to persuade the archbishop of
Canterbury, head of the English Church, to crown and anoint him
king on 22 December. As 1136 began, rumour of this sudden takeover
raced across England and Normandy. To most, Stephen's position
must have seemed unassailable. In the eyes of his contemporaries he
was no longer an ordinary human being, but a man transformed
through sacred ritual into God's chosen representative on Earth.
Doubts might be harboured about his path to power, but once
Stephen had undergone the coronation, properly enacted by the

Church, there could be no question that he was the rightful king of England. Empress Matilda's cause appeared hopeless. Even her half-brother and leading advocate, Robert, earl of Gloucester (Henry I's bastard son), was forced to grudgingly acknowledge Stephen as the new monarch.

At first, John Marshal also offered Stephen his unreserved support, and by 1138 this show of loyalty had earned John a crucial commission: the castellany of Marlborough Castle. This was one of the most strategically significant strongholds in the West Country, positioned to control the main east–west thoroughfare between London and Bristol, and to police the open, rolling downlands of northern Wiltshire. A castellany was no permanent grant or gift; it merely empowered John to serve as custodian of Marlborough's royal fortress. Nonetheless, it established him as one of the region's leading figures, and further opportunities would soon follow.

The reign of King Stephen

The monarch who would eventually hold William Marshal's life in his hands thus came to power in 1135. The initial position of strength enjoyed by the new king might well have been sustained, had Stephen been a more forceful character. His forebears – from Henry I back to William the Conqueror – all seized and held power through might, not inalienable right. Yet though Stephen was a man of action and ambition, and would prove competent in the field of war, it soon became clear that in other respects he lacked the requisite qualities. Looking back from the later twelfth century, the courtier and commentator Walter Map described Stephen as being 'of notable skill in arms, but in other things almost an idiot', adding that he was 'inclined to evil', while to William of Malmesbury 'he was a man of activity, but imprudent'. The truth was that, in dealing with their subjects, successful medieval kings needed to balance a degree of ruthlessness with expedient largesse – Stephen could manage neither.

The first real test of his mettle came in the summer of 1136, when a minor rebellion broke out in the far south-west of England. Stephen moved quickly to contain this insurrection, laying close siege to the malcontents holed up in Exeter Castle. After three months their resistance was broken, and an abject surrender was offered. Every expectation was that the rebels would face stern retribution, ranging from the confiscation of lands and imprisonment, to physical mutilation, perhaps even death. In similar situations King Henry I had been merciless. Renowned by one contemporary as 'an implacable enemy to the disloyal', he proved willing to use gruesome punishments against his adversaries and rivals, such as blinding and castration; abhorrent measures that nonetheless caused him to be revered as a 'lion of justice'.

King Stephen lacked the stomach for such pitiless brutality. Following the counsel of Robert of Gloucester – who must surely have known that he was encouraging Stephen to undermine the crown's authority – the king showed astonishing leniency at Exeter, allowing the dissenters to leave unharmed, with their freedom and possessions. Most treated this as a grave sign of weakness, and from then on serious questions were asked about Stephen's competence, for it was obvious that this king could be challenged without fear of full reprisal. One chronicler noted that Stephen soon earned a troubling reputation as 'a mild man [who] did not exact the full penalties of the law'. By the summer of 1138 Robert of Gloucester felt confident enough to head up his own revolt, openly declaring support for the cause of his half-sister Empress Matilda.

As Stephen's grip on the reins of power faltered, Empress Matilda became emboldened. Her claim to the crown, so widely disdained in 1135, was resurrected, and in 1139 she crossed the Channel, establishing a power base at Bristol alongside the earl of Gloucester. From this point onwards, the realm split roughly down the middle, with the heartland of the king's supporters being in the south-east, and Matilda and Earl Robert holding the south-west.

THE CIVIL WAR

For the next fourteen years the kingdom was blighted by a destructive and intractable internecine conflict, in which neither side proved capable of achieving overall victory. Stephen clung to his status as England's anointed monarch, yet the weakness and innate incompetence of his reign had been exposed. Meanwhile, though Matilda's lineage suggested she was legally entitled to rule, her gender and marriage remained problematic, and her haughty and imperious demeanour seems to have alienated many in England, further damaging her prospects. The convoluted struggle between Stephen and Matilda was marked by some extraordinary twists in fortune, and punctuated by acts of fortitude and folly. It also offered a man of John Marshal's character, temperament and ambition manifold opportunities. When hostilities broke out, he was ideally placed to exploit the conflict, holding a position in the West Country between the two camps, frequently playing one side against the other.

The *History of William Marshal* described this period in some detail, but its account was sometimes garbled and always biased in John Marshal's favour. He was characterised as a 'courtly, wise and worthy man' and 'a brave and trustworthy knight'; just the kind of generous and admirable figure that other warriors might happily follow, even though he was 'no earl and no baron with fabulous wealth'. In reality, John's loyalties may have been far from certain, especially in the civil war's early stages, yet the *History* maintained that 'the worthy Marshal entirely threw his lot in with the rightful heir' Matilda from the start.

At times, the *History* inflated John's significance to an almost laughable degree. According to the biographer, 'King Stephen had the worst of it' during the war, primarily because John chose to support Empress Matilda, and John was said to have suffered 'many a combat and battle ... many a trial and tribulation on her behalf ... before things were settled'. In truth, the Marshal remained a relatively minor player in the grand scheme of the overall struggle, but it is impossible to know if this overblown representation derived primarily from William Marshal's own personal recollections, or whether his biographer himself consciously sought to embroider William's ancestry.

One dramatic story of John's heroism, recorded in the *History*, certainly had the flavour of a well-worn family legend that wove together strands of fact and fiction. It was set against the backdrop of a significant crisis in 1141. For a brief period that year, Matilda's faction appeared to be on the brink of victory, after Stephen was taken captive during a skirmish outside Lincoln. The king was led in humiliation to Bristol and placed in chains. In September, however, the tables were turned. Matilda and Robert of Gloucester had besieged Winchester, hoping to press home their advantage, but were caught by a relieving army loyal to Stephen. In the course of a frantic retreat westwards, the earl fought a gallant rearguard action at the Stockbridge ford of the River Test that allowed Matilda to make good her escape, but which led to Robert's own capture. A deal eventually was struck that saw King Stephen regain his freedom in exchange for Robert's own release. Not surprisingly, an atmosphere of intense suspicion and recrimination surrounded the whole affair, with both men having to provide hostages, including their respective sons, as guarantee that the terms of the trade would be honoured.

In the *History*'s account of Matilda's perilous flight from Winchester in 1141, John Marshal appeared as the central protagonist, and Earl Robert of Gloucester was erased. Thus John was depicted as the empress's only reliable advisor, counselling immediate retreat. It was he who told Matilda to stop slowing their flight by riding side-saddle 'as women do'; supposedly insisting (with a wry hint of bawdiness) that instead she 'put [her] legs apart' to ride like a man. And in the *History* it was John, not Earl Robert, who then fought a valiant last stand to cover her retreat, though at a ford in Wherwell, not Stockbridge, which was five miles to the south.

From here, however, the tale began to trace a more believable path, partially corroborated by other contemporary evidence. It appears that

John Marshal did indeed fight on behalf of Matilda's forces near the nunnery at Wherwell in 1141, and when overwhelmed by enemy numbers, took sanctuary within its abbey church. King Stephen's supporters promptly set fire to the entire structure and, as the flames spread, searing heat caused the church's lead roof to melt. According to the *History* this burning metal 'fell on the Marshal's face, with horrible consequences', charring his flesh and costing him an eye. Left for dead, John eventually stumbled out of the smoking ruin and, despite his grievous wounds, managed to walk to safety.

John Marshal's character

Intermittent and inconclusive fighting continued in the years that followed, with neither side able to achieve telling gains. But John Marshal thrived in the midst of this unrest. Even the *History of William Marshal* occasionally hinted at the darker facets of John's involvement in the civil war. His capacity for ruthless brutality was glimpsed in the description of a dawn ambush, unleashed against a lightly armoured enemy force near Winchester. The biographer proudly declared that 'no lion ever ran after its prey so [swiftly] as did those who were armed after those who were unarmed', adding that 'many a man [was] killed and maimed, many a brain spilled from skull and many a gut [left] trailing on the ground'. The stark reality was that the exploitation of weakness became commonplace during this anarchic period of English history. This was a time of wolves, when aggressive, despotic and devious warlords thrived. The author of the *History of William Marshal* may not have been comfortable admitting it, but John possessed all of these qualities in abundance.

Other chroniclers, who actually lived through the civil war, brought the Marshal's character into clearer focus. In the most antagonistic accounts he was portrayed as a 'scion of hell and the root of all evil, [who] troubled the kingdom by unceasing disorder'; a man who built castles 'of wondrous design', but then used them to impose his own tyrannical authority over the land, extorting money and property from the Church. Elsewhere John emerged as just one more brutish, grasping player in a desperately chaotic game. This was never more apparent than in one telling incident in the earliest phase of the civil war that was wholly ignored by the *History of William Marshal*.

In early spring 1140, Robert FitzHubert, a Flemish mercenary who had sought employ on both sides of the conflict, decided to seize a portion of land for himself. FitzHubert had a particularly unsavoury reputation, being described by one contemporary as 'a man of great cruelty and unequalled in wickedness and crime'. Rumour had it that he liked to strip his captives naked, slather them in honey and then leave them to be tormented by stinging insects. He was also heard to boast of having watched in glee as eighty monks trapped inside a flaming church in Flanders burned to death.

On the night of 26 March, FitzHubert led a stealthy assault on the stout royal castle at Devizes in Wiltshire, scaling the walls using makeshift ladders in the hope of capturing the fortress before any alarm could be raised. Night-time raids of this type were incredibly risky affairs, and rare in the Middle Ages, because coordinating such an offensive in near pitch-darkness was virtually impossible. The chances of an attacking force being detected, isolated and then butchered were high. On this occasion, however, FitzHubert succeeded. The guards were bypassed and the bulk of the garrison, then 'enjoying untroubled sleep', quickly overwhelmed. In theory at least, FitzHubert had been acting as the earl of Gloucester's agent up to this point, but now he promptly declared his intention to hold Devizes for himself – the mercenary planned to turn himself into a Wiltshire warlord.

However, Robert FitzHubert then made the mistake of contacting John Marshal. The latter's stronghold at Marlborough lay just fourteen miles to the north-east, across an open and eerie landscape, littered with ancient burial mounds and stone circles – remnants of a forgotten Neolithic age. FitzHubert proposed a parley with his new neighbour, though his precise intentions are impossible to divine.

Perhaps he hoped to propose some form of alliance, or expected to scare John into submission with threats of violence. The talks may even have been a ruse, simply designed to gain FitzHubert and his men access to Marlborough Castle, whereupon the fortress might be snatched from the Marshal's unsuspecting hands. Whatever scheme was entertained, it is clear that Robert FitzHubert badly misjudged John's character.

The latter readily agreed to a meeting, welcoming the mercenary and a portion of his men into Marlborough. Yet the moment they entered the castle, the trap was sprung. As the gates slammed shut behind them, the visitors were surrounded, disarmed and taken captive. Having outwitted FitzHubert, John threw him 'in a narrow dungeon to suffer hunger and tortures'. The Marshal seems to have hoped somehow to use his new prisoner as leverage in order to gain Devizes for himself. The treacherous mercenary was first handed over to the earl of Gloucester in return for a payment of 500 marks, then later dragged down to Devizes, paraded in full view of the castle's garrison and threatened with death unless his men within surrendered. When they staunchly refused, FitzHubert was duly strung up and, in the words of William of Malmesbury, 'hanged like a common criminal'. In the chronicler's opinion, this was a just end for such a 'sacrilegious wretch', while John Marshal, it was concluded, had shown himself to be 'a man of surprising subtlety'.

The union of the Marshal and Salisbury families

Through such machinations, John angled for advantage throughout the civil war. In reality, he was neither the grand hero of this protracted conflict, nor its arch villain – merely an ambitious, minor nobleman: canny, occasionally unscrupulous and certainly willing to exploit the turmoil around him in order to climb the ladder. Not all of the Marshal's schemes succeeded. In the mid-1140s, John came into conflict with one of Wiltshire's most powerful families: the lords of Salisbury. The head of this dynasty, Earl Patrick of Salisbury, ruled over one of the region's major fortified towns (now know as Old Sarum), and his loyalties had also shifted in the course of the 'anarchy'.

The quarrel between these two West Country warlords seems to have been sparked by John's attempts to expand his sphere of influence eastwards at Salisbury's expense, with the construction of a small fortress at Ludgershall. When an angry feud erupted, punctuated by raiding and bloody skirmishes, it became clear that the Marshal had met his match. The details of the entire affair are decidedly murky, but it seems that John was eventually forced to back down and agreed to make some form of submission to Earl Patrick. However, the episode did have one concrete, and quite momentous, consequence. John agreed to bind himself in alliance to Patrick of Salisbury's family through an arranged marriage.

The Marshal already had a wife in Adelina, but this problem was readily overcome. In the twelfth century, an increasingly censorious Western Church sought to tightly regulate the practice of marriage. To avoid any possibility of incestuous union, weddings between members of the same family, up to the degree of sixth cousins, were officially forbidden. In reality, this prohibition proved largely unenforceable, given the labyrinthine web of intermarriage and kinship that bound together Europe's aristocracy. For many, finding a spouse who was not, in some distant manner, a relation was virtually impossible. But this did mean that, when necessary, bloodlines could be perused and an illicit degree of consanguinity declared as grounds for annulment. This seems to have been the method employed to sever John's tie to Adelina (and she soon remarried a minor Oxfordshire noble). Meanwhile, the Marshal wed Earl Patrick's sister, Sybil. This union proved to be an effective means of reconciliation. It brought the feud to a decisive end, enhanced John's social standing and, before long, produced a succession of new heirs. In all, Sybil gave birth to seven of John's children: four sons and three daughters. The second-born of these, a boy, appeared around 1147. He was given the name William.

THE EXPERIENCE OF EARLY CHILDHOOD

Nothing certain is known of William Marshal's earliest years, beyond the simple fact that he survived them. In the mid-twelfth century that in itself was no mean feat. Estimates suggest that in this period at least a third of children died within a year of birth, and perhaps as many as another third failed to reach puberty. The vast majority of these children seem to have been lost to disease and illness, though their susceptibility to these causes of death were gravely exacerbated by deficiencies in diet, living conditions and medical care. Of course, as the son of a nobleman, William's lot was better than most, but that advantage was at least partially offset by the strife-ridden world into which he emerged.

Parents in the Middle Ages were only too aware that their children might die before reaching adulthood. They must have possessed a sense of mortality's proximity, even probability, starkly divorced from that experienced by mothers and fathers in much of the modern world. For this reason, it used to be fashionable to suggest that most medieval parents could not possibly have forged close bonds with their offspring. Through the basic expedient of emotional self-preservation, it was thought, parents would have maintained a detached relationship with their children, perhaps even routinely exposing them to neglect. At first glance, this conclusion appears to be supported by the evidence preserved in medieval coroners' records and collections of so-called 'miracle stories' – the popular tales of divine intervention, usually involving Christian saints, that were produced in their thousands in this period. This material throws up frequent stories of accidental death or injury involving children that suggest lack of care and supervision: those who fell down wells, drowned in rivers or were trampled by horses, for example. To this could be added instances of bewilderingly bizarre medical practice bordering on wilful mistreatment. The famous eleventh-century canon lawyer, Burchard of Worms, for one, complained that some parents sought to 'cure' children suffering from a fever either by leaving them exposed on a roof, or by placing them in an oven – the underlying suggestion being that this was deliberate infanticide. Should we then conclude that, in William Marshal's day, few parents cherished their children; that he would have experienced little more than disregard in his first years?

In truth, the nature of our surviving sources means that the emotional landscape of this era will never be fully reconstructed, and the quality and depth of love or grief experienced within families remains uncertain. Nonetheless, more recent research suggests that parents living nine hundred years ago did treasure their offspring in much the same way as we do today. After all, there is a real danger in extrapolating generalised conclusions from self-selecting evidence, like coroners' reports, that naturally dealt with life's bleaker occurrences, and miracle stories, which traded in the shocking and the dramatic. A broader search indicates that many parents felt fear and anguish when their children were ill, and suffered intense anguish if a child died. This emotion might be expressed by a mother tearing her hair from her head and beating herself, or by a father literally paralysed with grief. Indeed, from the twelfth century onwards, the Church sought to counsel parents against 'excessive' mourning for lost children, on the grounds that it implied a lack of faith in God's will – a move which must indicate that these emotions were widely experienced.

For all this, there were, it seems, subtle, but significant differences in the forms of attachment made with infants and children in this period, as opposed to our own. An array of evidence suggests that parents experienced a deeper and more profound sense of sorrow at the loss of an only, or sole surviving child. This appears to have been because offspring were highly valued, at least in part because of their potential to act as successors and continuators of a bloodline. Thus, the death of a last heir – particularly that of a male – was keenly felt.

The lord of Châteauroux

This sentiment found powerful expression in a striking tale related by
the twelfth-century polymath Gerald of Wales – a famous churchman
and author of the twelfth and early thirteenth centuries – who was fascinated by everything from history to geography and the natural world.
Gerald's story was centred upon the castle of Châteauroux, in the law-
less region of Berry (in central France) – a stronghold that would have
a close connection to William Marshal's own career. According to
Gerald of Wales, its ruthless castellan took one of his enemies captive
and, so as to ensure that he posed no further threat, had the poor
wretch blinded and castrated. These were vicious punishments, yet not
unknown in this brutal age; deeds guaranteed to strip a man of his own
potency and to snuff out any prospect of a vengeful heir being fathered.
Thus emasculated, the man remained a prisoner for many years, but
was given the freedom to roam the fortress, crawling and stumbling as
he went. In time, however, he 'committed to memory all [its] pas-
sageways and even the steps which led up to the towers', and through
all these long days, forgotten and ignored by those around him, the
man nursed his cold hatred.

This anger eventually boiled over and, when an opportunity presented itself, the mutilated captive took sudden and terrible action.
Seizing the lord of Châteauroux's only son and heir, the prisoner
dragged the boy 'to the topmost crenellation of one of the towers', lock-
ing all the doors behind him, and there 'he stood outlined against the
sky, threatening to throw the boy over'. The castle erupted in chaos as
'everyone screamed in anguish'. According to Gerald:

> The boy's father came running, and no one's distress was greater
> than his. He made every offer he could think of in an attempt to
> obtain his son's release. [But] the prisoner replied that he would
> not give the boy up until the father had first cut off his own testi-
> cles, [and though] the castellan went on with his appeals, they
> were all in vain.

Struggling with this horrific dilemma, the lord of Châteauroux eventually resolved to feign agreement and beckoned an onlooker to deliver
'a mighty blow [to his] lower body, to give the impression that he had
mutilated himself', while 'all those present groaned' at the sight. But
the blind man was not so readily fooled. He called out, asking the
castellan 'where he felt the most pain' and when the lord 'replied
falsely that it was in his loins', the captive stepped forward, readying
himself to push the boy over. The castellan had himself struck a
second time and, in answer to the same question, claimed that 'worst
pain was in his heart', but again he was not believed. By now, the blind
man had dragged his hostage 'to the very edge of the parapet'. Finally,
the lord realised he could hesitate no longer:

> The third time, to save his son, the father really did cut off his own
> testicles. He shouted out that it was his teeth that hurt most. 'This
> time I believe you,' said the blind man, 'and I know what I am talk-
> ing about. Now I am avenged of the wrongs done to me, in part
> at least … You will never beget another son, and you shall cer-
> tainly have no joy in this one.'

With that, the blind man 'hurled himself over the battlements …
taking the boy with him', and both died, their bodies broken by the
dreadful fall. Gerald of Wales concluded this grim tale by noting that
the lord of Châteauroux had a monastery built on the spot where the
pair landed 'to save his son's soul'; a religious house that, supposedly,
was still standing.

Much of this story may be fantastical. Certainly its details cannot
be verified in any other historical text and, in Gerald's telling, its style
echoes that popularised in miracle accounts – the difference being, of
course, that here its conclusion brought not divine salvation, but death
and despair. Nonetheless, Gerald expected the caustic, reciprocal violence that drove the action, and the central drama of a father's love for
his son, to ring true for his twelfth-century audience. This tale was
designed to be believable. It has sometimes been suggested, therefore,

that it demonstrates, in gruesome terms, precisely what a caring parent was willing to sacrifice for their child in the Middle Ages. Crucially, however, this insight needs to be refined. Gerald's story was grounded in notions of patrilineal inheritance (through the male line) and the immense value accorded to sole surviving heirs. The father's anguish, his willingness to suffer, and the depth of his eventual grief were all understood, precisely because the boy 'was his only son', never to be replaced. With his death a bloodline ended. As a younger son, William Marshal soon learnt that he might not be valued quite so highly.

THE SIEGE OF NEWBURY

It is likely that in his earliest years William enjoyed some of the comforts of childhood in an affluent noble household. This time was probably spent at the family estate at Hamstead Marshall, by now extended to include at least one timber-and-earth castle of the motte-and-bailey form – that is, with a raised earth mound (the motte) ringed by a ditch and a surrounding courtyard (the bailey) usually enclosed by a wooden palisade. Little would have been seen of his father John, but William seems to have forged a much stronger emotional connection with his mother, Sybil of Salisbury. This was not always the case, as noble and royal families frequently made use of wet-nurses, and it was common for these women to play a major role in a child's upbringing. Richard the Lionheart – William's contemporary and the future king of England – grew so fond of his wet-nurse, Hodierna, that he later rewarded her with gifts of land, and a small Wiltshire settlement, Knoyle Hodierne, came to bear her name. There may well have been opportunities for William to engage in the kind of simple, childish forms of play that would still be familiar to us today. Gerald of Wales, for one, recalled how, as a boy, he had played happily on the Pembrokeshire beaches of south-west Wales; there his brothers built sandcastles, while Gerald made sand-churches, seemingly already aware of his future career as an ecclesiastic. Children might also play with rudimentary toys, and these were often gendered, with boys receiving toy knights and doll's houses given to girls.

In 1152, however, at around the age of five, William Marshal's childhood was violently interrupted in the last gasp of the civil war. The ferocity of the conflict had abated in the late 1140s, as it became apparent that the deadlock between Stephen and Matilda would not be broken by force alone. Now in his mid-fifties, Stephen remained king, but his position had been further undermined by events on the Continent. There Empress Matilda's husband, Geoffrey of Anjou, used the distraction of England's disorder to invade Normandy. By 1145 he had seized all of Stephen's Norman lands and was declared duke of Normandy with the connivance of the French king. Geoffrey stopped short of leading his armies across the Channel to England in a direct intervention, but his occupation of Normandy nonetheless inflicted a mortal wound upon Stephen's dynastic ambitions.

Almost all of the king's remaining supporters held land in both England and Normandy, and knew full well that steadfast support for Stephen's line might cost them their valued Continental estates. A compromise was needed. The best prospect for a settlement was Matilda and Geoffrey's eldest son, Henry. This redheaded, fiery tempered youth possessed a strong hereditary claim to the English crown through Matilda's bloodline, and could rule as a male warrior-king in a manner that had always proved impossible for the empress. Henry had already visited England on three occasions, and when Geoffrey of Anjou conferred upon him the title of duke of Normandy, probably in January 1150, his prospects seemed virtually assured. All that remained was to push Stephen into a corner and either force a settlement or seize the crown outright.

It was in these final years of manoeuvring that John Marshal overstepped the mark and came into direct conflict with the faltering king. Ever ambitious to extend his lordship and to expand his sphere of influence, John built a new fortified outpost. His aim appears to have been to assert a degree of control over a significant crossroads, where the route from London to the west intersected that running north–south between Oxford and Winchester. The exact position of this new stronghold is highly debateable. The *History of William Marshal* located it in Newbury (then a small town), but given the lack of any archaeological remains there, the castle may perhaps be identified with a sizeable motte that can still be found nestled atop a natural slope, less than a mile east of John's existing castle at Hamstead Marshall.

Determined to hoard the last vestiges of his power, King Stephen decided to punish John's presumption. In 1152 he marched on Newbury and laid siege to the Marshal's new fortress with a sizeable army. John was not present at this point, and the lightly provisioned castle was under the command of his constable (the leading military officer of the Marshal's household). Stephen struck hard and fast, offering bounteous riches to whoever breached the defences. This first, furious assault faltered, however, when the garrison threw 'slabs of stone, sharpened stakes and massive pieces of timber' down on the advancing enemy as they clambered 'over the ditches and up the embankments', and a lull in the fighting followed.

Word of the siege now reached John Marshal, and he made a calculated decision. Using messengers, he established a line of communication with King Stephen and begged for a brief truce, probably on a promise of imminent surrender. Given his reputation, John knew that his word alone would not be enough to secure terms. So, just as King Stephen and Robert of Gloucester had done in 1142, the Marshal offered up one of his sons as a hostage; the guarantor of good behaviour. He did not choose his eldest son by Sybil of Salisbury and namesake to fulfil this role, but rather his second (and, at this point, youngest) son, William. The boy was duly handed over to the king's troops and Stephen withdrew a distance, so that the Marshal could parley with his constable and organise the castle's capitulation. But, of course, the king had been deceived.

The threat to William Marshal's life

The moment John gained access to Newbury castle he began hurried preparations for its renewed defence, installing 'valiant knights, men-at-arms and archers' – men who would be 'unwilling to surrender'. As the *History of William Marshal* admitted, John 'had no time for the idea of peace' and this put his 'child's life in danger, because the king [soon] realised that he had been tricked'. The author of the *History* managed to steer an exceptionally agile path through this whole episode, describing events in close detail, yet never openly admonishing either John Marshal or King Stephen. Instead, when criticism did come, it was directed against the supposedly treacherous and cowardly advisors in Stephen's inner circle – those described by the biographer as '*losengiers*' or 'deceivers' – who now 'stepped forward [and] advised the king to hang the child'. They were condemned as 'wicked and base men' for making this suggestion, yet remarkably, the biographer offered not a word of censure as he went on to describe how 'news of all this reached [John], but he said that he did not care about the child, since he still had the anvils and the hammers to forge even finer ones'. Enraged at this affront and deception, Stephen ordered the young boy 'to be seized and taken to the gallows for hanging'.

So it was that William Marshal came face-to-face with death at the tender age of five. John's apparently callous disregard for his son's life might seem deplorable and, even in the twelfth century, it would have elicited a degree of shock. The use of one's children as diplomatic hostages was commonplace in Western Europe; the act of forsaking a child in favour of military advantage was not. John had a proven track record of duplicity, so the very fact that King Stephen accepted young William as surety for his father's good faith shows that the provision of such a hostage was deemed a categorical guarantee of fidelity. William may not have been that most prized of offspring, the first-born legitimate son, but he was John's blood kin nonetheless. No one could have expected him to be discarded in this hard-hearted manner.

It is possible, of course, that John Marshal took a calculated risk with William's life. Ever since the events at Exeter, back in 1136, Stephen had been regarded as a clement monarch. Time after time, he had failed to act with ruthless resolve. Perhaps John judged that his ageing king would never bring himself to kill a boy in cold blood. If so, this was a terrible gamble. Siege warfare was a brutish, grinding business during the Middle Ages; one in which the battle for morale was everything. In this era, armies on both sides of a siege routinely perpetrated acts of atrocity in order to intimidate their opponents or to force surrender. A defending garrison might hang the mutilated corpses of captured attackers from the walls, or dismember bodies and fling limbs and heads back over the battlements. Besiegers often threatened to hang or butcher prisoners in plain view of a garrison and, as the case of Robert FitzHubert at Devizes attested, such threats were usually acted upon. Considering the events of 1152 in this context, it is clear that while John Marshal might have hoped, even suspected, that his son would survive, this outcome was by no means a certainty. In essence, the Marshal had decided that success at Newbury was worth more than young William's safety.

In the days that followed, it seems that William Marshal's life was endangered not just once, but on three separate occasions. He was threatened first with hanging, then led to a catapult to be cast into the fortress so as 'to strike fear into [the defenders'] hearts', and finally prepared for use as a human shield during a frontal assault on the walls, where he faced being 'squashed to a pulp'. William's mother, Sybil of Salisbury, was said to have 'experienced such great pain' and anxiety through this period, because she believed that her young son was doomed to endure 'atrocious suffering'. But throughout, Newbury's garrison remained resolute in their refusal to surrender. How then did the boy survive?

The only answer is provided by the *History of William Marshal*, the sole surviving source to preserve a record of these events. Its author evidently drew upon the oral tradition of William's own recollections of Newbury. According to this account, his simple, unmannered innocence stayed the king's hand, time after time: asking to play with a guard's spear, as he was led to the gallows; or happily preparing to hop into the catapult's sling, thinking it to be a child's swing. Charmed by this boy, Stephen halted the execution, apparently declaring that 'anyone who could ever allow him to die in such agony would certainly have a very cruel heart'.

Later, as the siege continued, William and the king were even said to have played a game of 'knights' together in the royal tent, using flower stems as mock swords. Though unharmed, the boy remained a crown hostage for many months, quite probably more than a year. Newbury eventually succumbed to the king's forces, though John Marshal avoided capture, and Stephen moved north-east to invest the major opposition-held castle at Wallingford. From this point on, negotiations to end the civil war began in earnest, and terms were finally agreed at Winchester on 6 November 1153: Stephen was to remain king, but would be succeeded by Empress Matilda's son, Henry, duke of Normandy. It was only after peace had been settled that William Marshal was returned to his family. Tellingly, the *History* noted that 'William returned to his father' and added that 'his mother was overjoyed to see him', yet made no reference to John Marshal's reaction.

The impact of William Marshal's early childhood

In spite of this apparent emotional detachment, John Marshal seems to have loomed large in William's memory. As a father, he may have been a distant figure – encountered only fleetingly during the boy's early childhood, and even then at arm's length – but there is an inescapable sense that John left an imprint. His image – as the grizzled, hard-bitten veteran of the civil war, his face disfigured by burns, one eye a ruin – was seared into the verses of the *History of William Marshal*, a text which often relied upon William's own memories.

In later life, William seems to have admired many of his father's supposed qualities, picturing him as a fearsome warrior and devoted royal servant, but also as a shrewd and ambitious warlord, beloved by his followers. How much William knew or understood of John's political machinations during the civil war, or his ruthless treatment of rivals such as Robert FitzHubert, remains unclear. On the surface at least, William appears to have forgiven his father for the cold-hearted decision he made during the siege of Newbury. As an adult, William evidently relished the story of his captivity and early brush with death, enjoying this self-deprecating tale of a boy discarded by his father, replete with instructive lessons about cunning and honour. It may almost have acquired the status of a foundation myth – in the course of his long career, Marshal would rise to unimaginable heights, yet he could always remind those around him that he had almost been executed by a king when just a boy.

There is no way of knowing whether the actual experience of being a hostage and facing the threat of death – or, perhaps more importantly, his subsequent reflection upon these events – left any enduring psychological marks. Perhaps the repeated telling of the tale represented some form of defence mechanism or coping device, but William may equally have judged his father's actions, and his own predicament, as a natural consequence of medieval war. It is notable, however, that in later years William never placed his own kin, nor even his knights and retainers, in such a position of forsaken peril.

2

THE PATH TO KNIGHTHOOD

The first years following young William Marshal's release from captivity passed in relative peace, as England finally moved beyond the destructive era of civil war. The truce agreed at Winchester held and, for a brief time, King Stephen was able to reassert some semblance of royal authority within his realm. Nearing sixty, Stephen was an old man by the standards of the day, yet even so, his death came unexpectedly. On 25 October 1154, he was struck down by what one contemporary described as 'a violent pain in his gut, followed by a flow of blood', and passed away that same night. The duke of Normandy's accession followed as planned, with the twenty-one-year-old Angevin crowned and anointed as King Henry II on 19 December 1154.

Possessed of boundless energy and ambition, Henry would become one of medieval England's greatest monarchs, and a central figure in William Marshal's life. Henry was said to have been a man of medium height, with close-cropped red hair (which lightened over the years) and piercing blue-grey eyes that were 'dove-like when he [was] at peace', but which gleamed 'like fire when his temper [was] aroused'. The young king founded a new royal line – the Angevin dynasty – and the majesty and magnitude of his realm eclipsed that of his Anglo-Norman predecessors.* This Angevin world, likened by some to a new empire stretching from Scotland to the Pyrenees, would be the setting for William's extraordinary career.

Virtually nothing is known of William's remaining childhood years. Having recounted the intense drama of Newbury's siege, the *History* passed over the rest of the 1150s in silence. But young Marshal must have settled back into life in England's West Country, alongside his family. By 1160, William was growing into the man he would become. His biographer later declared that 'it did not take long before [he developed] into a tall boy' (though, given that the average adult male height in the twelfth century has been estimated at five-foot-seven, he is unlikely to have stood above six feet) and added that 'his body was so well-fashioned that, even if he had been created by the sculptor's chisel, his limbs would not have been so handsome'. William was said to have had 'fine feet and hands', brown hair, a swarthy complexion and 'a crotch so large … that no noble could be his peer', though, almost certainly, this referred to the width of his hips and natural predisposition for the horse saddle. In short, the Marshal could easily have been mistaken for a noble Roman emperor of old. Seemingly conscious that the accuracy of this grandiose description might be doubted, the *History*'s author added that 'I can tell you this because I saw [William's features] and remember them well', though in truth he can only have encountered Marshal as a much older man.

Regardless of his appearance and physique, there can have been little expectation that young William would enjoy a storied future, filled with fame, glory and fortune. As the lesser son of a minor Anglo-Norman noble, he might hope to live a relatively comfortable life (by the standards of the day), but achieve little distinction. William's lowly

---

* Henry's father Geoffrey bore the nickname 'Plantagenet', probably because he habitually kept a sprig of broom (*planta genista*) in his helmet. However, the dynasty that followed him did not think of themselves as 'Plantagenets', and this term for the family line was not widely used until the seventeenth century.

position within his own family's hierarchy was made painfully apparent in a legal document drafted in 1158. In this charter, detailing the sale of Marshal land in Somerset, he was named alongside his mother, two half-brothers and his elder brother John. William appeared at the bottom of this list, and while his siblings gained certain benefits as part of the arrangement – a horse or some coin – he received nothing. It was John, the first-born child from the marriage to Sybil of Salisbury, who was expected to inherit his father's lands and the office of royal master-marshal (though by this stage the marshalcy was merely an honorific title, with the real work at court performed by a paid administrator).

Unusually for this period, the one thing William did take from his family was the appellation 'Marshal', even though the formal title would be held by his brother for decades to come. 'Marshal' seems to have been adopted as an early form of surname – a rare occurrence in an era when most were identified either by their place of birth, residence or lordship; through their relationship to a parent (King Henry II actually styled himself as Henry FitzEmpress, meaning 'son of the Empress', for most of his life); or through some notable physical characteristic (hence the famously corpulent King Louis VI of France became widely known as Louis the Fat).

With little more than his name to fall back on, William's prospects depended on his education. Some living in the twelfth century argued that an individual's fate and future were sealed at birth, with no chance of alteration. The famous holy woman Hildegard of Bingen maintained, for example, that a boy conceived on the twentieth day after a full moon was destined to become a robber and a murderer. But most placed increasing emphasis on the value of learning, training and apprenticeship. It became common in this period for noble-born boys to be purposefully removed from the comforts of home and packed off to live with a distant relative – a practice akin to toughening up children by dispatching them to a distant boarding school. As a boy, King Henry II himself had spent two years in Bristol under the tutelage of his half-uncle Earl Robert of Gloucester. The normal age for this separation was around eight, yet William Marshal was twelve or thirteen before any arrangements were made on his behalf. Some of this delay may be explained by a waning in his father John Marshal's fortunes. The end of the civil war curtailed John's ability to manoeuvre for advantage, and he failed to find lasting favour under the new monarch Henry II. John retained his marshalcy, but the cornerstone of his power in the West Country, the guardianship of Marlborough Castle, was reapportioned in 1158.

Eventually, in around 1160, John secured a position for his son in Normandy with the notable baron, William of Tancarville, though Sybil's maternal influence may well have been at work given that the lord of Tancarville was her kinsman. So it was that, as William Marshal entered his teenage years, he set off for northern France, seeking in the words of the *History* 'to win an honourable reputation'. On the day of his departure, William's family gathered together to say their farewells (though, as always, his father was absent). There was no elaborate and richly endowed entourage to accompany him on his way, just a solitary servant. According to his biographer, William's 'mother wept tears of distress' at this parting, as did his siblings. This journey away from the familiar world of his birth and childhood must have been unsettling – in the intensely localised society of medieval Europe, many lived out their days without ever travelling more than a day's journey from home. Yet William's future now lay in Normandy, some 150 miles to the south, and the journey there required him to cross the English Channel.

WITH THE 'FATHER OF KNIGHTS'

William Marshal lived through the era of the great Anglo-Norman and Angevin realms, in which English kings and their leading subjects held land on both sides of the Channel. This made travel between England and the Continent a frequent necessity of life and, in the years to come, William would sail over the Channel dozens of times.

Yet the voyage remained a dangerous and unpredictable affair. It often involved navigating more than seventy miles across open water (between the likes of Portsmouth and Barfleur), a far cry from the meagre twenty-one miles needed to traverse the Channel at its narrowest point between Dover and medieval French ports like Wissant (near modern-day Calais). The relatively rudimentary nature of medieval ship and sail design also meant that seafarers routinely found themselves at the mercy of the elements, praying for calm seas and favourable winds. Shipwrecks were alarmingly common – indeed, it has been estimated that, in the mid-twelfth century, more royal courtiers died from drowning than through fighting for the crown – so few made this journey without a degree of trepidation. On this first occasion, Marshal's crossing passed without incident, but he would not always be so fortunate.

William thus arrived in Normandy: a land far from home, but also the land of his forefathers. Despite his upbringing, there is little chance that he thought of himself – in terms of culture, identity and loyalty – as English. By birth, Marshal was a Norman. Certainly his first language would have been a Norman dialect of medieval northern French, though it is possible that his West Country heritage left a mark on his accent.* Much of his career, from this point forward, would be spent in Normandy, and he developed a deep affinity for the region and a particular familiarity with the area north and east of the River Seine, known as Upper Normandy, where the open, rolling terrain was not dissimilar to that of Wiltshire.

It was there that Marshal found the imposing Norman castle at Tancarville, perched on a rocky bluff above the northern banks of the Seine estuary. Today this is the site of a sprawling, derelict French château, its crumbling structures accumulated over the centuries,

---

* Some Anglo–Norman and Angevin nobles brought up in the west of England seem to have developed a noticeable accent, and were mocked as a result at the elitist Angevin court. By the later twelfth century a derisive story was circulating, suggesting that there was a cursed water spring in Marlborough and 'whoever tastes it speaks bad French', otherwise known as 'Marlborough French'.

through many disparate stages of building, but when William arrived it boasted a formidable stone keep. Its lord, William of Tancarville, was a figure of considerable standing and reputation – described by one contemporary as 'a man noble in race, unique in war-craft, splendid in strength, in worth a very death to the envious', He possessed two further strongholds in the duchy and held the office of chamberlain of Normandy in hereditary right.

William Marshal came to join his household with one particular purpose in mind. As a younger son, William might perhaps have followed the path set by the likes of King Stephen's brother, Henry of Blois, and pursued a career in the Church. The course set before young William led in a different direction. He had arrived at Tancarville, aged around thirteen, to acquire skill at arms: to learn the business of war and ultimately to join the ranks of Europe's new military elite by becoming a knight.

The evolution of medieval knighthood

Knights are central to our popular conception of the Middle Ages. The iconic image of a noble warrior, clad in resplendent armour, racing astride his charger to rescue an imperilled damsel is the classic medieval cliché. It would be easy to imagine then, that knights were an essential, constant and unchanging feature of this distant era; that everyone living in Western Europe 1,000 years ago understood exactly what a knight was, and knew precisely how one should behave.

Knights did play a crucial role in shaping this period of history, and some, though not all, of their practices and beliefs conformed to modern expectations. But the concept of knighthood only began to emerge in the second half of the eleventh century and it remained in its infancy even as William Marshal arrived at Tancarville and grew towards manhood. William lived through the precise period in which the ideas, rituals and customs of knighthood coalesced. Indeed, his own celebrated career as one of Europe's greatest knights helped to mould this warrior class.

In its most basic form, a medieval knight was simply a mounted warrior. Men had fought on horseback for more than a millennium, but in the course of the early Middle Ages, horsemanship came to be regarded as an essential aristocratic pastime – the badge of nobility. From the ninth century onwards, as the Frankish ruler Charlemagne (Charles the Great) and his successors sought to re-forge the Roman Empire in the West, men of power were expected to own and to ride horses. By around the year 1000 CE, the speed and manoeuvrability of horse-borne soldiers started to play an increasingly decisive role in warfare, and a more distinctive breed of fighter slowly emerged through the eleventh century.

Typically, these horsemen joined the military entourages of warlords, counts, dukes, even kings. At first most came simply for pay, but over time they began to hope for greater rewards for their service, including land. Written sources of the time reflected the appearance of these first 'knights' through the use of more specific language, though the terminology employed to identify these warriors was frustratingly vague and inconsistent. In Latin they might be described either as 'equites' (horsemen) or 'milites' (soldiers), in French as 'chevaliers' (horsemen) and in German and Anglo-Saxon as 'knecht' or 'cnihtas' (servants), from which the modern English word 'knight' was derived. Such imprecision reflected the embryonic nature of this military cadre. By the start of the twelfth century, the two concepts – of horsemen as aristocratic and of mounted warriors as a martial elite – were thoroughly intermingled. Certainly there was a natural assumption that any male noble (other than a cleric) would fight as a mounted warrior or 'knight', and by extension, an emerging sense that the very practice of knighthood might imbue a degree of nobility upon an individual. Nonetheless, aristocratic birth was not a prerequisite for entry into this warrior class.

Throughout the early twelfth century the essential markers of knighthood remained practical. These elite warriors were readily identified by their use of a specific range of equipment and weaponry. Every knight possessed a horse and a sword, but the majority also used a lance, armour and a shield. By the time William Marshal arrived in Normandy, knighthood was becoming an increasingly rarefied profession. The fundamental tools of the trade cost a small fortune to buy and maintain. Warhorses in particular were cripplingly expensive, with an initial outlay of around four or five times what an average knight might live on in a year.

Learning to ride a mount in battle and to wield weaponry with a measure of proficiency also took hundreds, perhaps even thousands of hours of practice – time not available to all. Not surprisingly, knighthood became the preserve of the privileged few. One had to be born to wealth or find a generous patron. By and large, William Marshal fitted into the second category. He came to Normandy seeking education and training, but also the patronage of a wealthy noble willing to bankroll his endeavours. Luckily for him, the lord of Tancarville was renowned for the size and the quality of his military retinue and known to contemporaries as a 'father of knights', and he welcomed William into the fold.

By the mid-twelfth century, Western society was developing a clearer sense of the rituals and obligations associated with knighthood. Two fundamental concepts would already have been at the forefront of William's mind when he set foot in Tancarville Castle. The nature and full significance of these ideas are not easily explained, because the two medieval French terms used to denote them – *mesnie* and *preudhomme* – have no exact translation in modern English. But these notions were at the forefront of William's mind through his teenage years and beyond.

The *mesnie* was the retinue of knights who gathered around a lord – the tightknit group of warriors serving as elite troops and trusted bodyguards. In many cases the knights in a noble's *mesnie* became like members of his extended family – steadfast supporters and valued advisors. The sense of an intimate community was conveyed by the word *mesnie* because it derived from the Latin term *mansio* (household) and could be used interchangeably with another Latin word *familia* (military household). Crucially, the concept of the *mesnie* imposed a degree of obligation on both parties involved. Knights served their lord, fighting in the field, showing allegiance and fidelity, but in return a noble was expected to shelter his warriors, protecting their status and advancing their careers. In real terms, this meant not only paying for a knight's living costs and funding the upkeep of their equipment, arms and horses; it could also involve rewards of land and title, even the arrangement of an advantageous marriage. This reciprocity also extended into the sphere of status. A knight's standing naturally was increased by entering the *mesnie* of a mighty baron or a member of a royal dynasty. But in the course of the twelfth century, increasing emphasis was placed upon the public display of military retinues as markers of power. In William's day, the size of your *mesnie* mattered and great nobles vied to be seen surrounded by tens, even hundreds of knights.

William harboured potent memories of his father's own *mesnie*. The *History of William Marshal* recalled that John Marshal 'surrounded himself with many worthy men', noting that the knights in his *mesnie* were 'in his pay', but adding that they were also 'all wearing livery supplied by him' and their mounts had 'horseshoes, nails, livery [all] paid for by him'. The *History* concluded that '[John] was able to do this' even though he was no mighty baron, because he understood the value of generosity and so 'knew how to attract and hold on to valiant knights'. The concept of the *mesnie* would play a crucial role in William Marshal's career as he served first in a number of retinues and then assembled his own.

His notion of knighthood, and that entertained by the society around him, was also profoundly shaped by the archetype of the *preudhomme* – the ideal warrior, literally the 'best kind of a man'. By the mid-twelfth century, worthy knights were increasingly expected to display the 'right stuff', to conform to an evolving code of behaviour. An admirable and respected warrior – a *preudhomme* – was skilled in combat and courageous, faithful, wise and able to give good counsel, but also canny, even wily, in war when necessary. He was the exact opposite of the type of serpent-tongued deceivers (or *losengiers*) who had tried to persuade King Stephen to execute young William back in 1152 – men of dubious loyalty and questionable judgement. William arrived at Tancarville hoping to become a *preudhomme*. Indeed, in many respects his life served to define that archetype.

The history of knighthood – real and imagined

William Marshal's sense of what might be expected of a knight, and how such a warrior might behave, were also informed both by actual recent history and an imaginary pseudo-historical past, woven out of myth and half-remembered fact. A century earlier, the knights who were his Norman forebears had been little more than mercenaries: men who used their martial skill to accrue wealth and land in the service of lords such as William the Conqueror, and whose conduct was primarily conditioned by self-interest. In the course of the eleventh century, however, the Roman (or Latin) Church became increasingly concerned by the violence and disorder caused by well-armed, mobile, mounted warriors across Western Europe. As a result, the papacy began to consider how the life of a knight might intersect with the Christian faith.

William lived in a medieval world that was almost universally Christian, where many aspects of daily existence were informed by religious doctrine. The Latin Church taught that every human soul would be judged at the moment of death, and either rewarded for Christian purity with the joys of heavenly paradise, or condemned for sin through an eternity of hellish torment. The notion that transgressive behaviour endangered the spirit exerted a powerful influence over the society into which Marshal was born. Knights were particularly prone to anxiety, being forced by their profession to fight and shed blood, yet conscious that this violence was inherently sinful in the eyes of the Church. The Latin papacy and clergy made some attempts to control and condition the behaviour of the warrior class, but at first these enjoyed only limited success.

In 1095, however, Pope Urban II alighted upon a potent idea: he issued a call to arms for a new form of holy war, in which Christian knights would redirect their aggression beyond the confines of Latin Europe, fighting instead to recover the sacred city of Jerusalem from Islam. When Urban proclaimed that participation in this expedition would actually earn spiritual merit, helping to cleanse the soul of sin, his words met with a rapturous response. Thousands of warriors set out for the Holy Land on this First Crusade, many of them – like Robert, duke of Normandy – drawn from the Anglo-Norman world. After long years of campaigning, and against all expectations, these crusaders achieved a near-miraculous victory in 1099.

The advent of the crusades had a powerful effect upon the concept and practice of knighthood, and this impact was still being felt in the 1160s. Through the twelfth century, there was a strong expectation that warriors would participate in a crusade, mirroring the 'glorious' achievements of their forbears; becoming not just *milites* (soldiers), but *militia Christi* (knights of Christ). In time, William himself would feel the call of this 'higher cause'. But these holy wars also prompted many to question how Christian knights should live and behave back in the West, encouraging the gradual evolution of codes of conduct. This sense that knights should aspire to be more than mere mounted mercenaries accelerated when Christian knightly orders sprang up in the wake of the First Crusade. Movements such as the Templar Order fused the ideals of knighthood and monasticism, and actively derided the existing paradigm of Europe's warrior class, literally branding themselves as the 'New Knighthood'. They proved to be extraordinarily popular, attracting thousands of recruits and a tide of charitable donations from nobles throughout Europe. Indeed, William's own father, John Marshal, gave the Templars a manor at Rockley, in Wiltshire, in 1157.

William Marshal arrived in Normandy, therefore, with a certain sense of the past achievements of the knightly class, and some awareness of the elevated standards to which this elite cadre might now be held. However, stories and sources that fused myth and reality must have exerted a powerful influence over his ideas. He had been brought up in an aristocratic culture that commemorated the great deeds of warriors in epic songs – the '*chansons de geste*' (literally the 'songs of deeds'). These publicly performed, medieval French poems wove tales of daring bravery and wondrous martial prowess around real historical events and figures. The popular *Chanson d'Antioche*, for example, offered a fictionalised account of the First Crusaders' siege of Antioch, in which the greatest knights cleaved their Muslim foes in two with a single sword blow. The most famous chanson of this period – the *Chanson de Roland* – drew upon the more distant Carolingian past of the eighth century, and immortalised the valorous death of Charlemagne's commander, Roland, during an ill-fated attempt to conquer Iberia from the Moors.

William also lived through the exact period in which Western Europe first developed an abiding fascination with the stories of King Arthur and his knights. The medieval legend of Arthur was constructed in the 1130s by Geoffrey of Monmouth, a monk of Celtic-Norman birth. His *History of the Kings of Britain* blended thin traces of reality with a fantastical, romanticised vision of the past: one that presented Arthur as a fabled hero to rival Charlemagne, traced the lineage of the first Britons back to Troy and incorporated the supposed prophecies of Merlin. Learned historians of the later twelfth century, like William of Newburgh, would deride Geoffrey's work as a 'laughable web of fiction' that was packed with 'wanton and shameful lying', but that did nothing to stop it becoming a medieval bestseller. His Latin text was soon adapted, embroidered and translated into vernacular languages – most notably in Wace's *Roman de Brut* – and an obsession with the Arthurian world spread like wildfire through royal and aristocratic circles.* Knights of Marshal's generation were undoubtedly influenced by these myth-

---

* A remarkable level of credence was also given to Merlin's prophecies and it became fashionable to foretell future events on the basis of these arcane pronouncements, with some treating them as almost akin to Scripture. According to Ralph of Diss, William Marshal's father, John, fell foul of this trend. John apparently made a public prediction, on the basis of 'pseudo-prophets', that Henry II would never return after his departure for the Continent in 1158. When the king duly landed back in England in January 1163, John lost royal favour.

historic stories: Richard the Lionheart would carry a sword that he named Excalibur on the Third Crusade (though he soon sold it when running short of cash), and great emphasis was placed on the 'discovery' of Arthur's and Guinevere's supposed tomb at Glastonbury in 1191.

TO BECOME A KNIGHT

William Marshal arrived at Tancarville around 1160, a young adolescent ready to start his education. His biographer offered only the barest details of the six or seven years that William spent training in Normandy, probably as a result of Marshal's own vague recollection of this distant period. He seems to have pictured himself as a rather lazy teenager whose main delights were food and sleeping. The *History* noted that 'people thought it a great pity that he retired to bed so early and yet slept so late', adding that many considered that William 'ate and drank too much' during his time at Tancarville. He even acquired the nickname '*gasteviande*', or 'greedy guts' – hardly the soubriquet of a hero-in-the-making; and though the lord of Tancarville supposedly predicted that Marshal would 'set the world alight', this looks like an attempt on the biographer's part to polish an otherwise underwhelming image.

Nonetheless, it was in this formative phase of his career that William first developed many of the skills that would set him apart in later life – the abilities that enabled him to rise through the ranks to become a distinguished warrior – so it is probably safe to assume that not all of his time was spent eating or asleep; and while the precise details of his transformation from untutored boy to adult knight may be lost, it is possible to reconstruct the outline of his experiences.*

---

* The notion that a trainee knight might be regarded as a 'squire' had yet to be formalised, so although the term 'squire' was sometimes used in this period, squires were often indistinguishable from servants, and not all such men went on to become fully fledged knights.

A *noble life*

William's schooling in Normandy would not have focused solely upon the hard grind of military training, but included broader instruction in a range of skills. Like any noble-born boy of this era, William had to learn how to fit into aristocratic society, assimilating the bluff etiquette of Anglo-Norman martial culture, while trying to grasp the subtle nuances of its mores. The hub of any aristocratic community, including that of Tancarville Castle, was the great hall. This was where a noble's household would gather each day for a communal meal, paid for and provided by the lord in affirmation of his patronage and largesse. These assemblies could be crowded, noisy, even chaotic, with a smoky chamber packed full of men, women and animals (dogs, birds of prey, even horses might be welcomed in the hall, though pigs and cats were frowned upon). In this setting, young Marshal received some favour, for his biographer wrote that William 'partook of the choicest dishes placed before his lord' – the equivalent of being seated at the top table.

A remarkable treatise on manners dating from the late twelfth century – Daniel of Beccles' *Book of the Civilised Man* – gives some insight into how nobles were expected to behave in a medieval great hall. In this public milieu, a measure of decorum was advised. Nobles were warned not to comb their hair, clean their nails, scratch themselves or look for fleas in their breeches. As a rule, shoes should not be removed and urinating was to be avoided, unless of course you were a lord in his own hall, in which case it was permissible.

The process of communal eating demanded particular etiquette. Some 200 years before the widespread use of the fork, knives were employed as the main utensil. Food was delivered to the table on shared 'messes', then picked up from these platters and placed on an individual 'trencher', though if one sought to appear polite, this action would be performed with only the thumb and the forefinger. Beccles' treatise counselled nobles to sit up straight when eating, refrain from placing their elbows on the table and face their superiors. Speaking with a full mouth, picking your teeth or nose were all frowned upon, and a cultured diner who wished to spit should turn away from the table, or look to the ceiling if they needed to belch.

As a member of the aristocracy, William enjoyed a richer and more varied diet than many of his contemporaries, though rough-ground bread, eggs, cheese and common vegetables like peas and beans, would still have been mainstays. Ale was drunk as a matter of course, because the fermentation process killed off germs (making it safer than water) and wine was likewise popular in more affluent circles. A noble of the lord of Tancarville's standing could afford to serve meat – such as mutton, pork, chicken and beef – and fish in his great hall on a regular basis, though the natural flavours of such fare were often overwhelmed by the heavily seasoned sauces favoured by medieval cooks. These employed the likes of sage, garlic, mustard and coriander, and might also include more exotic spices, such as pepper, nutmeg and saffron.

Alongside his experiences in the great hall, it is likely that the teenage William was exposed to aristocratic fashion. Given the local-ism of medieval society, trends in dress and hair were relatively slow to change, but styles came in and out of vogue nonetheless. The core ele-ments of a male noble's wardrobe were stockings or hose, fashioned from silk or wool, a shirt, often with detachable sleeves, usually worn under a tunic, with variations on a coat or surcoat (sometimes fur-lined) worn outdoors, topped off with a mantle or cloak. Popular fads of the day covered everything from the tightness and hue of one's sleeves to the precise length of cloak and the snugness of one's shoes – for a time the most fashionable footwear was so close-fitting that they could hardly be pulled on. Like the rich and powerful in any era, twelfth-century European nobles used clothing as markers of status, favouring expensive fabrics, coloured with rare dyes. But in the course of William's life it became increasingly popular for individual lords and families to sport distinctive colour schemes when in public, and before long these were adopted as a kind of uniform by a noble's *mesnie* – brightly visible symbols of collective identity.

Hair was another potent marker of status and identity in the medieval world. Centuries earlier, the Merovingian kings of Francia had been revered for the remarkable length of their locks, while monks used the tonsure (in which a section of the scalp was shaved) to indicate their dedication to religious life. When William the Conqueror invaded England in 1066, the prevalent fashion among the Normans had been to shave a large swathe of the back of one's head – a distinctive style much in evidence in the Bayeux Tapestry – while a generation later a craze for centre-partings that left the forehead scandalously exposed briefly took hold. By the 1160s the new Angevin royal dynasty was setting the pace, and Henry II was said to have preferred a simple, close-cropped hairstyle. Most of William's Anglo-Norman and Angevin peers would have been clean-shaven, though some may have sported moustaches. Many regarded a beardless face as an indicator of Frankish (or French) identity. Stories abound from the crusading world of Muslims cutting off their beards to disguise themselves as Franks, or of scruffy crusaders neglecting to shave during a long siege only to be mistaken for bearded-Turks and accidently butchered.

William Marshal's education

Alongside coaching in manners and dress, boys of William's status were routinely schooled in a range of aristocratic skills and pursuits. Most learnt to read, perhaps even to write, practising on wax tablets. Knowledge of Latin – the language of law, governance and the Church – was valued and cultivated. Henry II's famous son Richard the Lionheart was a remarkably skilled Latinist, able to crack jokes in the language at the expense of less fluent clerics. In this regard, William Marshal was unusual, as he never acquired a proper knowledge of Latin, though he may have achieved a very basic level of literacy.

Nobles were also expected to develop some proficiency in swimming, dancing and singing, and many gave over long hours to the day's game of choice: a simplified version of chess involving betting. Perhaps the most emblematic of all medieval aristocratic pursuits was hunting. This was one of the ultimate symbols of social status, because certain species of quarry and hunting grounds were reserved for the nobility or royalty. The sport was also deemed to provide valuable training for war, as it honed martial skills, including horse riding and archery. Most hunts were conducted from horseback, using dogs, falcons and hawks, and targeted the likes of deer, wild boar or wolves.

Many of the kings that William Marshal met during his life were obsessed with hunting. Henry II was described by one of his courtiers as 'a great connoisseur of hounds and hawks, and most greedy of that vain sport [of hunting]', though rumour had it he engaged in this rigorous pursuit so regularly only because he feared becoming fat. Of course, hunting was not without its dangers. Henry I's brother, William Rufus, had died in a hunting 'accident' in southern England's New Forest in 1100, supposedly struck by a stray arrow (though Henry's presence on the hunt and his seizure of the crown just three days later have caused some to question whether this was regicide).

Marshal himself appears to have shown only limited interest in the likes of dancing, music or even hunting. His first passion was for the art of war and, through the six years he spent at Tancarville, most of his time, day after day, would have been spent in arduous military training, hardening his mind and body, developing the raw physical strength and endurance necessary to function as a professional warrior in the Middle Ages. As one of William's contemporaries explained, a man had to learn to deal with the brutish rigours of combat. It was only after he had 'taken blows', seen 'his blood flow' and felt 'his teeth crack under the fist of his foe', yet still managed to fight on, that a man could 'engage in battle confidently'. On its own, though, sheer toughness was not enough. To enter the ranks of Europe's knightly elite, William also had to master three essential, interlocking skills: martial horsemanship, hand-to-hand combat and the ability to fight in medieval armour.

Medieval horses, arms and armour

In the twelfth century, successful knights were incredibly adept horsemen. Most of these medieval warriors had a natural affinity for horses – their daily lives were filled with the sounds and pungent smells of horse and stable, and many of their waking hours were spent in the saddle. The horse was a primary marker of knightly status, but also an intimate companion in combat, an animal in whom the rider placed his trust, perhaps even his life. Not surprisingly, favoured mounts were pampered, treasured, sometimes even named.

Men like William Marshal knew only too well that not all horses were born equal. Knights typically were expected to own at least three different types of horses – each bred and trained with a specific role in mind. In terms of cost and function, a vast gulf separated these various categories. For general riding and travel, William used a light 'palfrey', while a stout and stocky 'sumpter' carried baggage, weapons and armour. However, Marshal's most valuable mount was his *destrier* or warhorse – the animal ridden in combat. These cost anywhere from £40 to £100, sometimes even more. Working from the rates current in the 1160s, for the average price of one *destrier* William could have purchased either 40 palfreys, 200 packhorses, 500 oxen or a staggering 4,500 sheep.

Most twelfth-century warhorses measured between fifteen and sixteen hands (five feet to five-feet-four) and were bred not for straight-line speed, but a balance of fleet-footed agility, strength, endurance and martial temperament. The best stock was deemed to be Arabian, often imported via Spain or Italy, and mounts of this type were care-fully reared and conditioned. Through such training, the finest *destriers* could be expected to respond to a rider's every command, even without the use of reins (as hands might be needed for shield and sword in combat). Crucially, they would also be inured to the raucous tumult and terrifying violence of a medieval battlefield. Horse armour was not yet common, though it was in use by the end of the century, but a *destrier* might be cloaked in cloth covering or caparison, decked out in a knightly household's chosen colours.

By the time William Marshal reached the age of twenty, he must already have spent thousands of hours in the saddle. Certainly, he achieved a high level of skill in the art of horsemanship and, in the course of his later career, proved able to deftly control and manoeuvre his mount, outclassing many an opponent. Much of Marshal's fortune, both on the tournament field and in actual battle, would be founded on this equestrian expertise. But William also had to learn how to fight from horseback, handling a range of weapons.

The most important of these was the sword – the totemic weapon of knighthood. It played a central role in the ritual of knighting, and both the carrying of a sword, and the ability to show skill in its use, came to be intimately associated with this elite warrior class. In William's lifetime, the typical sword was single-handed, with a double-edged blade of around thirty-four inches, a broad point and an overall weight of some two-and-a-half pounds. Swords could be mass-produced for huge campaigns, like the crusades of the later twelfth and thirteenth centuries, but the finest weapons were masterpieces of metallurgy and smithcraft: wrought from a precise mixture of iron and steel to yield the perfect blend of strength and flexibility, capable of holding a razor-sharp edge that might slice through un-armoured limbs with a single stroke and extraordinarily well-balanced in the hand.

The first surviving manuals of European swordsmanship date from the early fourteenth century, so it is impossible to know precisely how William trained and fought with this weapon, but it is clear that he honed his ability to wield his sword both while mounted and on foot. This must have required the daily repetition of practice sword strokes through his teenage years and beyond – so as to develop strength and acquire muscle memory – and regular sparring to refine coordination and agility. By the time he became a knight, Marshal was an effective swordsman, but so far as the *History* was concerned, his primary gift was not flashy technique, but the brutish physicality that enabled him to deliver crushing blows. With sword in hand, William was, in the words of his biographer, a man who 'hammered like a blacksmith on iron'.

Marshal probably also trained with a number of other mêlée weapons popular with twelfth-century knights, including the dagger, axe, mace and war-hammer, but much of his time would have been devoted to mastering the lance. By construction this was a fairly rudimentary weapon – often simply a ten- to twelve-foot-long straight spar of hewn wood, usually of ash – but it was fiendishly difficult to use from horseback. The lance would be held under the arm (or couched) during a charge, and directing its point towards a target with any accuracy required immense skill. Lances often broke after one or two uses, but a successful strike could cause devastating damage to an opponent. In the course of his career, William would witness the lethal potential of this weapon with his own eyes and he would also be called upon to charge down one of the greatest warriors of the age, Richard the Lionheart, with lance in hand.

In addition, Marshal had to learn how to ride and fight while using the distinctive range of armour employed by twelfth-century knights. In the 1160s, most warriors wore a mail hauberk (or coat), formed of around 30,000 tightly packed, interlocking iron rings. This typically weighed in the region of thirty-five pounds, covered the upper body and arms, reached down to the knees, but was split-skirted both back and front, to enable use on horseback. William would have worn a padded jerkin ('aketon') underneath his hauberk – crucial for absorbing the blunt trauma of blows – and probably used mail leggings ('chausses'). Hauberks with sleeves that ended in mail mittens (or mufflers) were also becoming popular. As Marshal aged, military technology advanced, such that by the early thirteenth century, fitted plates of metal were beginning to be worn alongside or atop mail, but it would be another two hundred years before full plate (the classic 'knight in shining armour') became the norm.

In battle, William's head was protected by three layers of armour: a quilted, padded cap; a mail hood (that might be an integral part of his hauberk, or a separate 'coif'), often including a section of mail that could be raised and tied in place to cover the face (the 'ventail'); and an iron helm. While at Tancarville, Marshal likely used the basic conical helmets with central nosepieces that were still popular in the mid-twelfth century. But over time, these gave way to larger, more enclosing cylindrical great helms – flat topped, with a full face plate and perforated visor – that offered a high level of protection, but restricted vision and were intensely uncomfortable to wear over long periods of time. William's last piece of defensive equipment was a curved, triangular wooden shield, usually strengthened with either hardened leather or metal plating. This could be hung from the neck or shoulder using a leash, to free the arms and shelter the back.

Trying to move and fight while decked out in this bewildering array of gear – clad head-to-toe in mail, bearing shield, helmet, sword and lance – was no simple matter. Much of the weight of twelfth- and early thirteenth-century armour was distributed across the body, so Marshal would not have been desperately encumbered. He was able to walk, mount his horse unaided and certainly was capable of getting back to his feet if knocked over; but adapting to the load and feel of all of this equipment required years of training and physical development. William acquired the necessary strength and endurance, yet like any knight in this period, he only wore full armour when necessary, and generally travelled in much lighter gear.

Burdensome though mail, helm and shield may have been, they rendered William and his peers virtually invulnerable. Most sword and arrow strikes could not penetrate through these layers of defence, though lethal blows to the face and eyes were possible, and broken bones (especially from crushing lance attacks) were more common. Only crossbow bolts had the puncturing force to pierce mail and the padding beneath to reach flesh, and this helps to explain why the papacy sought to ban their use against Christians from 1139 onwards. In the majority of settings, however, knights could wage war with relative impunity, and for fully equipped members of this warrior class death in battle was a relatively rare, even shocking, occurrence.

The ritual of knighting

In 1166, when William Marshal was around twenty years old, he reached the end of his training and apprenticeship. The time had come for him to undergo the ritual of knighting. By the mid-twelfth century this ceremony was becoming increasingly formalised and elaborate – at least for those in the upper echelons of the aristocracy –

and its conventions had been imbued with symbolism and meaning. In William's day, publicly witnessed rituals were an essential part of the fabric of medieval society, and their power and efficacy were implicitly accepted. It was understood that the human soul might be purified through rites of Mass or penance, that a king or emperor could be created by coronation; and likewise, the ceremony of knightly 'dubbing' was believed to transform a young man into a different breed of warrior. Most rituals in the Middle Ages had a devotional or sacred dimension, and thus required the involvement of the Church. But despite the persistent attempts of the medieval clergy to intrude into the process of knighting by encouraging the likes of sword blessing, as yet the actual role of churchmen remained inconsistent and muted. For now, at least, knights were made, or invested, only by other knights.

For members of the wealthiest noble or royal families, the ritual of knighting could involve a high degree of pomp, pageantry and display. King Henry II's father, Geoffrey Plantagenet, reportedly underwent just such a lavish and elaborate rite in 1128. He was knighted at the age of fifteen, along with a small group of his peers, 'amid regal festivities'. The ceremony was held at Rouen – the capital of Normandy – as part of the preparations for Geoffrey's imminent marriage to King Henry I's daughter Empress Matilda. On the appointed day, Geoffrey began with a 'solemn bath' – an act of physical and spiritual cleansing – and his body was then clothed in the most opulent apparel. A 'crisp linen undershirt' was followed by 'a ceremonial robe interwoven with gold' and rich red in colour. Geoffrey then donned a 'cloak, dyed purple in the blood of oyster and murex' and pulled on a pair of luxurious silken shoes decorated with 'lion cubs'. His fellow aspirants were 'likewise dressed in linen and purple'. Decked out in their finery, the young men now emerged 'from a secret chamber into public view'. An awestruck crowd looked on as Geoffrey received a magnificent Spanish horse 'reputed to outpace many birds when it ran', as well as gifts of arms and armour, including a sword drawn from the royal treasury that was said to have been 'crafted by that master Wayland'. The ritual was followed by seven days of feasting, celebration and military games.

Of course, the vast majority of knighting ceremonies were neither so extravagant, nor so glamorous, though many did follow this pattern of group participation, and most involved an element of public witness. It was common for a gift (or gifts) to be given to a new knight, but often this was limited to a single new cloak – a piece of clothing that seemed to indicate an elevation in status. The only core element of the ritual that was virtually universal in the twelfth century was dubbing. Derived from the French word '*adouber*' (to arm), this meant literally to invest someone with a weapon, in most cases by belting (or girding) a sword to his body. For men like William, it seems to have been the receipt of these two objects, the knightly belt and sword, which signified their transformation into knights. The dubbing might be followed by one final act – the '*collée*' – a form of ritualised blow to the body that could vary from a light, almost genteel, tap on the shoulder, to a forceful cuff to the head. Its origins and meaning remain obscure, one theory suggesting that the strike was supposed to remind a warrior of his duties, another arguing that this symbolised the last blow a knight would receive without retaliation. It would be a century before the '*collée*' was typically delivered to the shoulder with the flat of a sword blade – the classic image of 'dubbing', now immortalised in modern imagination and still enacted by the English monarchy when conferring a knighthood.

Marshal's own elevation seems to have been a rough-and-ready affair. In what amounted to a battlefield commission, William 'was dubbed a knight' by his patron, the lord of Tancarville, in a simple ceremony held at Neufchâtel in north-eastern Normandy. The chamberlain gifted William a fine new cloak and then 'girded on his sword, with which he was to deal many a blow'. With this short, unadorned ritual, Marshal joined the ranks of Europe's martial elite. The speed and suddenness of his knighting seem to have been a direct result of events on the ground. For in 1166 Normandy was under threat and war was on the horizon. Thus, William of Tancarville called his young trainee to arms for a first taste of real battle.

'MIGHTY BLOWS AND FINE DEEDS'

In 1166 a heated border dispute broke out between the duchy and its eastern neighbours in the counties of Flanders, Ponthieu and Boulogne. The precise background to this conflict is disputable, but it led Upper Normandy to be placed on a war footing. The lord of Tancarville led Marshal and the rest of his troops fifty-five miles east to Neufchâtel-en-Bray, to join up with a number of other nobles, including the constable of Normandy. This may have been William's first visit to this border zone, but in the course of his career he would fight numerous campaigns in this area. The fortress of Neufchâtel was surrounded by a small town, and lay beside the River Béthune, some fifteen miles back from the duchy's main frontier at the River Bresle. The original intention seems to have been to assemble a war-band there, before moving forward en masse to counter an attempted invasion. In the event, enemy troops led a sudden, piercing raid into Norman territory and almost caught the lord of Tancarville and his allies off-guard. They were still billeted in Neufchâtel when news arrived that a direct attack on their position was imminent.

Showing a cool head, the chamberlain calmly gathered his men – said to number twenty-eight knights including William Marshal – and moved to intercept the enemy near a bridge on the town's outskirts. Marshal's blood was racing at the prospect of the coming fight and, as the Tancarville retinue rode through the streets, he tried to push to the front. The chamberlain was having none of it. Scolding William's youthful impetuosity, he apparently shouted 'get back ... let these knights pass'. Marshal 'withdrew a few paces, downcast and ashamed, his face the picture of gloom,' according to the *History*, 'since he thought he was indeed a knight', though he soon started edging forward again nonetheless.

Thoughts of rank were put to one side when a group of enemy knights were sighted up ahead, advancing along a street lined with houses and farmsteads. Both sides charged immediately and as 'they struck one another with great force' a frenzied mêlée began. Most medieval warfare was like a maelstrom – barely contained or ordered – with a hectic scrum of mounted knights wrestling their horses, each trying to plant a telling blow. In the first shock of contact 'lances were broken and shattered, shields were holed and crushed' and as a result, 'all they had to strike each other with were the stumps' of their lances, or their swords. A deafening wave of sound erupted, as the 'din and uproar created by the blows of combat' assaulted the senses, and the noise was such 'that you would not have heard God's thunder resounding'. As William's biographer remarked, 'the idle threats and boasts made back home' were forgotten in these moments, as the real fighting began.

Marshal proved his mettle that day. He was not thrown into hysterical panic by the first onslaught, nor paralysed by fear. Instead, 'having broken his lance', he was said to have drawn his sword and rushed 'right into the fray to lay about him'. Not surprisingly, the *History*'s author used this first military encounter to highlight his hero's martial prowess, and so William was depicted in grand terms, cutting 'a swathe through the throng' and 'dealing violent blows [that] were greatly feared'. When the dust settled, everyone on both sides of the fray supposedly agreed that he had shown himself to be the finest warrior present. But this was Marshal unashamedly painted as the 'valiant knight' – the man he would become – not William, the twenty-year-old, untested warrior, tasting war for the first time. Even so, it is possible to piece together some sense of how the fighting played out in Neufchâtel.

For much of this extended skirmish, Norman fortunes ebbed and flowed. On four separate occasions the enemy was driven back, only for them to regroup or be reinforced. At one point William became separated from the main party of Tancarville knights, having ridden into a small enclosure attached to a roadside farmhouse just as the Norman forces fell back. Seconds ticked by, yet no one seemed to notice the lone knight, isolated from his comrades. This dangerous moment could easily have ended in William's capture. As it was, he snatched up a discarded lance and charged back out into the street, unhorsing an unsuspecting foe while bellowing 'Tancarville! Tancarville!' for all he was worth. The Normans swept forward once again to answer this rallying cry and the fracas continued. Marshal had learnt the value of a surprise flank attack.

Later on, as the engagement drew to a close, he attempted to play the same trick again, but this time it had disastrous consequences. William charged back into the same enclosure only to find it filled with thirteen Flemish foot soldiers. Under normal circumstances this might have posed little problem. Even outnumbered and surrounded, Marshal was still in full armour and astride his warhorse. But things quickly took a turn for the worse when an enterprising Fleming grabbed a long, hook-tipped pole (normally used for pulling burning thatch from roofs) and began trying to rip William from his saddle. Caught on his shoulder, the iron hook began to bite and, clinging on as best he could, Marshal spurred his mount to make a hasty escape. The force of this sudden movement caused the hook to shred a section of William's mail hauberk, leaving a nasty gash below, but he managed to pull free. It was only as he retreated down the street that he realised his horse had been gravely wounded. With blood streaming from its body, 'its death was inevitable'. Not long after, the forces of Flanders, Ponthieu and Boulogne withdrew, leaving the Normans in control of Neufchâtel. William had survived his first day of fighting, but it had cost him his prized warhorse.

That evening, the lord of Tancarville threw a sumptuous feast to celebrate the Norman victory. No expense was spared, and even knights from other retinues were welcomed. The tables were laden with food and, out of gratitude for their salvation, the townspeople supplied 'valuable wines and very fine fruit'. On this evening of boisterous merriment William learnt an essential lesson – one that he would heed for the rest of his life. Still smarting at the death of his horse, he was nonetheless proud of his performance in the field. The hall was full of banter as knights traded tales of 'mighty blows and fine deeds', and William seems to have been well praised for his exploits. But then a knight apparently called out: 'Marshal, make me a gift out of friendship; [give me] a harness or failing that an old horse-collar.' Not realising that he was being set up for a joke, William innocently replied that he had never owned such things. 'What's that you say?' the knight replied. 'It is a trifling thing you refuse me', and then went on to recount how he had seen Marshal best numerous warriors that day. How could it be that William had no spoils to share? At this everyone broke into laughter. They understood that feats of arms were all well and good, but a knight making his way in the real world had also to accrue more practical, financial gains. William had fought with some skill and courage at Neufchâtel, but took neither booty, nor valued prisoners who could later be ransomed for cash. All he had to show for his efforts was damaged armour and a dead horse.

William's crisis

The conflict on Normandy's border soon petered out and, before long, northern France returned to a state of relative peace. The chamberlain duly brought his household knights back to Tancarville, but with no sign of any impending military action, he seems to have taken a decision to reduce the size of his *mesnie*. Much to William Marshal's horror, he now discovered that he had fallen out of favour. The cause of this rift remains unclear; the *History* skirted around the affair, noting only that the chamberlain 'showed little kindness towards [William], and the latter was very ashamed', but it must be likely that, as a junior knight of limited experience, Marshal was simply deemed surplus to requirements. He was not cast out of Tancarville exactly – his family connection to the chamberlain probably made such a brusque move unconscionable – but the patronage and shelter he had once enjoyed in the castle were withdrawn. Most critically of all, the chamberlain refused to furnish William with a new warhorse. He was a professional warrior without the most fundamental tool of his trade.

This was the first crisis of Marshal's adult life. He may have been a high-born knight, but he was also penniless and, as his biographer remarked, 'poverty has brought dishonour on many a nobleman and been the ruin of them'. William was left with only a light palfrey for riding and a single servant willing to follow him. He could have considered returning to England. By this stage both of his elder half-brothers had died and, in 1165, his father, John Marshal, had also passed away. As a result, William's elder brother John had inherited the remaining Marshal lands and his father's office. William might have begged for a permanent position in the Marshal household, but this would have meant a career lived firmly in his brother's shadow, awaiting John's grace and favour. That was not the life that William wanted. He chose instead to forge his own path. The precious cloak received at his knighting was sold for the rather paltry sum of twenty-two Angevin shillings (the equivalent of five-and-a-half shillings sterling), and with this money William was able to buy a 'hack' to serve as a packhorse. Swallowing his pride, Marshal strapped his arms and armour to his new mount and prepared to seek his fortune.

Part II

ADULTHOOD:
A KNIGHT IN SERVICE

3

A WARRIOR'S LIFE

In 1166, William Marshal was a professional warrior, newly elevated to the status of a knight, in desperate search of work. His first taste of combat at Neufchâtel had left him with an appetite for action, but also cost him his warhorse. Having lost the favour of the lord of Tancarville, William was now staring at a potentially bleak future of poverty and obscurity. Marshal was not the only twelfth-century knight to find himself in this predicament – short of money and gainful employ. This was the era in which knighthood emerged as a distinct class and calling, attracting thousands of young nobles and aspiring, upwardly mobile men to its ranks. The obvious, and increasingly pressing, question was: what were these warriors actually supposed to do? How were they to find an outlet for their military skills and their social ambitions?

In a culture that revered martial qualities, knights like William naturally hungered after opportunities to hone and to display their prowess. They had not spent long years training as warriors for nothing. More basic, practical requirements for financial reward and security also had to be addressed. Many knights might find long-term positions in aristocratic households, or *mesnie*, but unless Europe was to go up in flames, the need for such warriors in actual war was always going to be finite. The onset of peace in northern France in 1166 showed how any lull in fighting could leave members of the knightly class surplus to requirements. Under such circumstances, a spiral of lawlessness and discord could take hold, as lords actively sought reasons to put their prized warriors in the field – through border disputes or raiding – and predatory packs of 'freelance' knights roamed the landscape.*

The knightly tournament emerged in response to this dilemma, as organised contests in which medieval warriors could fight under controlled conditions, earning both renown and financial reward. The first small-scale tourneys appeared in the eleventh century, but after 1100 events became larger and more frequent, especially in north-eastern France, across regions such as Flanders, Hainault and Picardy. This area – nestled between the great German Empire and the small kingdom of France (centred around Paris) – had been particularly unruly in the eleventh century: the site of ruinous, thuggish feuding between rival warlords. By the mid-1160s, when William Marshal was knighted, tournaments were being held throughout Western Europe, including parts of the Angevin realm. These contests captured the aristocratic and knightly imagination, becoming the great craze of the day.

In the wake of the Neufchâtel campaign, news spread through Normandy that a tournament would be held just north of Le Mans. The *History of William Marshal* declared that 'any man seeking to win renown would go to tournaments, if he had the wherewithal'. Not surprisingly, William was attracted by the chance to prove his skills, but the question of a warhorse remained. The lord of Tancarville announced his intention to attend the event, leading a group of forty knights, and though Marshal was allowed to tag along, he was said to have been 'downcast' at the prospect of having to ride a mere palfrey into the fray. Finally, on the very eve of the tournament, the chamberlain relented – perhaps the prospect of seeing his young cousin

---

* The modern term 'freelance' actually derives from the famous fiction author Walter Scott's use of the phrase 'Free Lances' in 1820 to describe unattached medieval warriors or mercenaries – men whose lances were literally for hire – in his novel *Ivanhoe*.

shamed by fighting astride a lowly riding horse proved too much to bear.

William was given a *destrier*, but the very last one available. The steed looked the part, being 'strong, fine and well-proportioned', but it turned out that most of the Tancarville household regarded it as unrideable because the animal 'was so wild it could not be tamed'. William did his best, loosening the horse's bridle to make it more even-tempered, but he must have looked ahead to the next day with a degree of trepidation.

Entering a tournament was a gamble at the best of times. Success might bring William a measure of distinction and some much-needed financial reward. But the risks were not insignificant. Failure would only deepen his penury – knights, and their families, were known to have been ruined by the debts accrued through repeated tournament defeats – and William chanced injury or worse. Combat in these events was conducted in a 'controlled' setting, but there is no indication that tournament knights used specific, blunted weapons. They had to rely on their prowess and their armour to save them. Under these conditions, wounds and broken bones were commonplace, and even death was a possibility, especially if you were unhorsed and trampled by other mounts. Records indicate that in one particularly bad year, fifteen knights died tourneying in Germany. With all these risks and dangers in mind, holding his future in his hands, William embarked upon his first tournament.

THE TOURNAMENT

It would be tempting to impose a modern fantasy of the medieval world upon the twelfth-century tournament. To imagine William pitted against opponents in a well-ordered, almost genteel, joust, bevies of noble maidens agog at the sight of Marshal's prowess. But the world of the joust belonged to a different age, still more than a century in the future. Knightly tournaments in William's day were entirely different beasts: imbued with some pageantry and awash with colour, yes, but riotous, chaotic affairs, tantamount to large-scale war games, played out by teams of mounted knights across great swathes of territory. The origin of the term 'tournament' gives a sense of the spectacle involved – being derived from the French 'torner' (to revolve) – evoking a whirling swarm of knights, though contemporaries also referred to these events as a 'recreation', 'amusement' or, in Latin, simply as a 'ludus' (game).

Tournaments were a critical feature of knightly culture and lifestyle in the central Middle Ages. Kings often viewed these events with suspicion – allowing great lords to assemble with hundreds of warriors seemed like an invitation to insurrection, even open rebellion. To the Church they were dangerous and wasteful extravagances, and it did its best to stamp them out. A succession of papal pronouncements outlawed these 'detestable revels and shows' as fonts of pride and vanity, cautioning that anyone who died in such fighting would be denied a Christian burial. By the thirteenth century, clerics liked to suggest that slain tournament knights might either return as tormented spectres or languish in hell, condemned to an eternity in burning armour. But knights and their lords refused to listen. Across France, Germany, the Low Countries and northern Iberia they engaged in and sponsored tournaments regardless.

The vogue for these military contests took hold just as William reached adulthood. They were the closest thing to a professional sport in his world, only with higher stakes and a clear emphasis on the 'game' as training for real medieval warfare, and in time they would become a fundamental feature of Marshal's career. His first tournament, held between Sainte Jamme and Valennes, was fairly typical for its time. Played out not within some confined arena, but across an open area of landscape thirty miles wide, it involved hundreds of knights drawn from across the Angevin realm, as well as 'a numerous company' led by King William of Scotland and the revered warrior Philip of Valognes, described by the History as 'the handsomest knight of all'.

The mechanics of the medieval tournament

In common with so much of knightly culture and custom, the practical mechanics of the tournament – its rituals, rules and regulations – came together during William Marshal's lifetime. Events were held through most of the year, excepting the period from Lent to Easter, sometimes as frequently as every two weeks. Notice of an impending tournament would customarily be given well in advance, to allow time for preparation and travel, but an established schedule of well-known contests soon developed – the equivalent of a tournament circuit. Northern French events were usually held between two designated sites, as in Sainte Jamme and Valennes, located in the hinterland between established lordships and well away from major cities like Paris or Rouen. Most resembled a war game between two sides, with the likes of the English, Normans, Angevins and Poitevins on one team, and the 'French' from regions such as Flanders, Burgundy, Blois and Champagne on the other, and often the 'teams' would congregate at the specified settlements at least a day in advance.

The simple fact of hundreds, sometimes even thousands, of knights and their servants travelling from one tournament to the next, all requiring lodging and food, caused significant local disruption. The *History of William Marshal* described how an event held some years later in Champagne attracted so many participants, all coming from different directions, 'that the whole district was swarming with them and taken by storm'. Large, prosperous fairs were established at major tournament venues, with armourers, farriers, craftsmen, merchants and entertainers all coming to ply their trade. In time, events acquired many of the trappings of the modern music festival – the massed crowds and tented cities, the glorious spectacle and ostentatious display, even the notion of celebrity.

Most tournaments were fought on a single day, though some preliminary contests might take place on the last evening before the main event: training matches between pairs of swordsmen, or one-on-one jousts in which knights sought to unhorse their opponents with a lance. This was often an occasion for green warriors like William to get their first experience, though he did not do so at Sainte Jamme, perhaps because he was too busy trying to master his unruly warhorse. It also gave knights an opportunity to gain the measure of their opponents, though unscrupulous (or canny) old hands sometimes watched these fight in the hope of marking out weaker, inexpert quarry, ripe for capture the following day. For many, the eve of the tournament was a time for socialising. Wealthier lords and knights typically took lodgings, rather than resorting to the use of tents, and it was customary for the great and the good to visit one another, sharing stories and gossip, renewing friendships and alliances.

The day of the tournament itself began with a flurry of final preparations: the laborious process of pulling on mail hauberks, coifs and leggings, usually achieved with the assistance of a squire, the fine adjustment of shield straps and horse tack, a last check of lance, sword and perhaps mace, a test of helmet fit, though this cumbersome piece of armour would not be donned until just before the fighting began. Amid all of this clamorous activity, most knights found the time to consume some breakfast – a piece of early thirteenth-century chivalric literature cautioned tournament-goers not to forget to eat in the excitement of the moment. After 1200 it also became common for warriors to start the day with religious observance, prayer and the taking of Mass – all steps to gird the soul should the worst happen, though the famed thirteenth-century German knight Ulrich von Liechtenstein admitted that he prayed for luck more than anything else.

Around mid-morning, the various retinues of knights began to gather at one of two opposing 'lists'. These were the makeshift fences or pens where teams congregated, probably placed on this occasion just to the south-east of Sainte Jamme. William's biographer described how a more sober atmosphere took hold as the 'companies rode forward in tight and ordered formation' to join the Norman and English team. The time for joking, idle boasts and threats was past. Visual display was central to the tournament. Being seen to possess the finest, most resplendent arms and armour mattered to William and his peers;

indeed, the *History* noted that the Tancarville knights were up half of the night burnishing their mail.

The tournament field was also flooded with brilliant colours. The two main teams seem to have been distinguished by huge banners held aloft in their midsts, marked with distinctive colour schemes, patterns and devices, with that of the Norman–English team depicting two golden lions against a red background. The smaller component parts of each massed team – the individual military retinues, like that of Tancarville – also fought under their own identifying banners and by 1166 it was customary for knights to sport these colours and devices, either on shields or on cloth surcoats worn over their armour. The Tancarville colours of the day – and thus, those now worn by William – appear to have been white with a red border.

The use of banners and vivid designs had their origins in practical military necessity. These striking visual markers allowed warriors to instantly navigate their way through the frenzied confusion of medieval combat: to locate and follow their lord and fellow knights; and, just as importantly, to identify opponents and enemies. William soon discovered that, both on the tournament field and in real-life combat, there was enormous advantage to be gained from fighting in packs, not the tightly ordered ranks of a Roman legion, but looser, yet nonetheless coherent, groups of warriors, moving together and protecting one another. In the twelfth century, that type of coordination required unmistakeable visual cues. This seems to be how the notion of heraldry evolved in the later twelfth and early thirteenth centuries. Certainly by the end of William's long life, nobles across Europe were increasingly expected to adopt specific identifying colours and devices. Soon, the bewildering number of these 'coats of arms' was such that individuals were employed to memorise them and then move through the lists before a tournament, naming each contingent – these men were the first heralds.

Sound also had its part to play. Medieval commanders routinely made use of drums, horns and trumpets to deliver aural signals, aiming to achieve some measure of control over their troops, while also stirring hearts. In later decades, rousing music might accompany the preliminary stages of a tournament, inspiring knights as they prepared for the fight to come, though none seems to have been played at Sainte Jamme. However, William and his peers were already using specific war cries to rally and direct one another. At Neufchâtel Marshal had shouted 'Tancarville' to rouse his fellow knights, and that was probably the call his retinue used now. Most war cries were similarly simple, invoking single place names, kings or saints, though they could involve slightly more complex formulae. The traditional Norman rally cry was '*Dex aïe*' ('God our help'), while knights from the French town of Châtillon, near Paris, shouted '*Alom lour Châtillon*' ('Go get them Châtillon').

Once William Marshal and all the other knights had assembled at the lists outside Sainte Jamme, the two sides rode out to prepare for the main event of the day: the great mêlée. Knights on the opposing sides customarily took up positions, facing one another across an open field, often in single extended lines. Helmets were donned and a hush settled across the throng. Then, at a shout or horn-blast, the main charge began. This awe-inspiring spectacle of blurred colour and deafening noise reached a crescendo as the two sides crashed into one another with shuddering force, and the fighting began. These were the most dangerous moments of the day. William learnt over the years that to panic, lose control of your horse and fall in the middle of this wheeling mass of knights was to court death, and he witnessed many disasters first-hand. Success, even basic survival, required steely nerves, physical strength and masterful horsemanship.

During most tournaments, after the first phases of combat, the mêlée would break up into smaller contests, played out over many miles of countryside. In the course of this extended war game, contingents of warriors might try to use the landscape to their advantage, set ambushes, even attempt to hide. The whole affair could take hours, sometimes lasting till dusk. Like every participant, William's goal in all this was to capture opponents using a mixture of skill, brute force and guile, while avoiding being taken prisoner himself and protecting his lord. The crucial dynamic of the entire tournament was that success brought reward; not only reputation and honour, but also material gain, because captive knights were expected to pay a ransom in return for release – usually in cash – and might also relinquish their horse, arms and armour. Given that this was his first attempt, William did remarkably well at Sainte Jamme, securing 'two very valuable prisoners': one an unnamed knight whom he battered to the ground with the stump of a lance; and the prize of the day, Philip of Valognes, taken early in the general mêlée when Marshal deftly rode in and grabbed the bridle of Philip's mount. This neat trick – akin to snatching the steering wheel – was devilishly difficult to pull off, but gave William effective control over his adversary's horse, enabling him to 'drag [Philip] away from the tournament'. Thus immobilised, he submitted and promised to pay a ransom.

This tournament transformed William's fortunes, setting him on the path to financial security. 'Only that day', the *History* noted, 'Marshal had been a poor man as regards possessions and horses', yet he came away with four warhorses, as well as hacks, palfreys, sumpters and harnesses. After Sainte Jamme, the attitude of the Tancarville household altered. Impressed by the rich pickings he had accrued, 'they paid Marshal great honour and treated him so courteously, more so than before'. As William's biographer candidly admitted, material assets symbolised status; they marked Marshal out as a man of means and substance. As the *History* bluntly put it: 'You are what you have got, and no more than that.'

Tournaments played an essential role in shaping and defining the knightly class as a whole across Western Europe, and would become a critical feature of William Marshal's own career. Being full-scale war games, rather than mannered individual combats, these events offered valuable, perhaps even essential, training for war. As one contemporary chronicler put it when singing the tournament's praises: 'the science of battle, if not practised beforehand, cannot be summoned when necessary'. William's success at Sainte Jamme proved that tournaments also provided real opportunities for advancement. But, beyond these practical issues lay deeper, conceptual concerns. The tournament gave medieval knights and their lords a perfect opportunity to display their qualities: to show prowess through martial skill, to prove one's honour by respecting the rules of the game, to exhibit largesse by organising events or fitting out one's retinue and to affirm status by being seen either within, or better still at the head of, a large, finely equipped military entourage. In the later twelfth century, the tournament was where you showed yourself to be the archetypal *preudhomme* – the best kind of man.

All of this served to heighten the importance of visual display. Tournaments were events that demanded an audience; acts of valour and feats of arms had to be witnessed if they were to garner renown. There was more than a whiff of shallow narcissism and conceit about the whole affair, with as much, if not more, emphasis placed on being seen to do the right thing, as the action itself. To modern sensibilities this can all seem rather distasteful, and some contemporaries were equally unimpressed. The famed early thirteenth-century churchman and preacher, Jacques of Vitry, denounced tournaments as breeding grounds for deadly sins like pride and vanity. Nonetheless, in the *History of William Marshal*, the strong emphasis on spectacle and display seems utterly unselfconscious. For men like William, the need for an audience was a simple fact of knightly life.

Even so, twelfth-century tournaments were not really designed with spectators in mind. Some did attend events, but they were relatively few and far between; peering from the edge of the field, occasionally accommodated in rudimentary stands. Only once, at a contest much later in Marshal's career, did the *History* mention a group of noble-born ladies in attendance. For William, then, the tournament was no grand gladiatorial combat waged before a feverish throng; nor was it the formal joust of the later Middle Ages, performed within a contained arena for the entertainment of the crowd. For simple, practical reasons, early tournaments provided few thrills for onlookers. The preliminaries and the first grand charge were certainly worth a look, but after that, once the mêlée fragmented, the fighting moved out into the open landscape and was impossible to follow. In Marshal's day the critical audience did not stand outside the action looking in, they participated themselves. The key witnesses to all of this dazzling skill, manly daring and ostentatious pageantry were other knights. It was these peers who would stand testament to a warrior's worth, validating his achievements and broadcasting his fame.

The ideal of chivalry

The *History*'s account of the Sainte Jamme tournament contained one additional, seemingly minor, observation. In this tiny, incidental detail, the binding mechanic of the medieval tournament is glimpsed, and, by turns, a tantalising window opens on to the mental and moral landscape of William Marshal's thought world. The *History* recorded that after William snatched Philip of Valognes' bridle and dragged him from the field, 'Philip readily gave his pledge to the Marshal' and, trusting him, William 'let him go'. Philip had promised that, when the reckoning came at day's end, he would settle any ransom or forfeit due, and his word alone was deemed sufficient. Both men shared a deeply ingrained understanding that they had to honour the rules of this game; that by social and cultural convention, any failure to do so would be regarded as shameful. Such a transgression would cause disgrace and a loss of status, not only for the individual, but also for his retinue and kin.

In William's day, the *'chevaliers'* or knights who understood and observed these customs were following the principles of *'chevalerie'* – chivalry. In a literal sense, they knew how horsemen should act. These precepts might be bent, even manipulated, to one's advantage, but to be seen to break them openly would be to invite scandal and ignominy. The idea that knights ought to adhere to a higher code of conduct had been gradually percolating through Western society since the eleventh century. Embryonic notions of chivalry were stimulated and shaped by a wide array of interlocking forces, from Christian theology and the emergence of crusading and the Military Orders, to Western Europe's deepening fascination with the myth-history of knighthood. But it was on the tournament field that such concepts came into ever sharper focus, and from the mid-twelfth century onwards these war games were both the catalyst and the cauldron of chivalric ideals. It is no accident that at precisely this moment, authors of popular chivalric fiction began to write of Arthurian heroes like Lancelot fighting at tournaments.

For William and his contemporaries, chivalry was a rather loosely defined set of customs and expectations – a kind of collective sensibility – chiefly concerned with regulating conduct between knights and with establishing what obligations lords and knights owed to one another. As yet, 'chivalrous' knights showed little interest in wider social responsibilities; they were certainly not egalitarian upholders of justice or protectors of the poor. It would be decades before these rules became more clearly defined and delineated, and almost two centuries before the traditions of chivalry were refined and encoded in works like *Le livre de chevalerie* (*The Book of Chivalry*), authored by the famed fourteenth-century knight Geoffrey of Charny. By this time, foolish warriors might undertake acts of extraordinary folly in pursuit of these heightened chivalric ideals. In the 1330s, for example, a number of English knights went to war against France wearing eye patches, having sworn to ladies at court that they would not open one of their eyes until victory was achieved. Needless to say, thus encumbered, most died as a result.

William Marshal's career

William seems to have spent the next year, perhaps even longer, travelling around the tournament circuit, operating increasingly as something akin to a free agent, though still sporting the colours of Tancarville. His fortunes varied. At an event held between St Brice and

Bouère, to the south-west of Le Mans, Marshal was set upon by a group of five knights all intent on bludgeoning him into submission. 'They manhandled him terribly', according to the *History*, 'turning the helmet on his head by force from back to front', and though William eventually managed to break free, the reversed helm covering his face meant he was now riding blind and all but suffocating. The battered helmet proved so difficult to dislodge that Marshal badly sliced one of his fingers ripping it off and was gasping for air by the time he had freed his head. At a later tournament, he was captured by the Flemish knight Matthew of Wallincourt and had to forfeit one of his warhorses. William paid his ransom, but tried to persuade Wallincourt to show leniency by releasing his *destrier* – seemingly on the grounds that he was still just a young, inexperienced knight – but Matthew flatly refused. Marshal would remember this slight for decades to come. Despite these setbacks, on the whole William seems to have prospered. His biographer observed that through this period 'he led such a very fine life that many were jealous of him', adding that his fame began to spread through France.

Modern historians have typically indentified this period, in the mid-to late 1160s, as the start of William's abiding love affair with the knightly tournament. It has recently been suggested that, by 1170, William was already 'one of the most accomplished and devoted of the tournament champions of his day'. In fact, the evidence suggests that, for now, Marshal's engagement with the tournament scene was actually more intermittent. The clearest indication of this fact was his decision, either in late 1167 or early 1168, to return to England for the first time in nearly eight years. William was no longer the penniless supplicant seeking the favour of his elder brother John. He came home, instead, as a man of some reputation and independent means. But in doing so, he was turning his back on the tournament circuit, because these knightly contests had been banned in England by King Henry II for being too disruptive to the peace of the realm. Marshal was looking to take the next step in his career – to gain experience of real warfare. He soon learnt to his cost that it did not always conform to the chivalric etiquette of the tournament.

KNIGHT PROTECTOR

With favourable winds, William crossed the Channel without difficulty and rode straight for the West Country. According to the *History*,
he returned to England 'because that was the country of his birth and
because he wished to see his worthy kin'. But there is no evidence that
William made any effort to visit the surviving members of his immediate family at this point, nor does he seem to have paid his respects
to his late father, now interred at Bradenstoke Priory in Wiltshire.*
Marshal had a different kind of family encounter in mind; one that had
little to do with sentimentality or emotion, but was driven by the far
more pragmatic pursuit of patronage. He made straight for Salisbury,
seat of his powerful uncle, Earl Patrick – a man who had thrived in the
aftermath of the civil war, enjoying advancement under the new king,
and one who now retained the services of fifty to sixty knights.

William's brief, bitter taste of life as an impoverished, lord-less warrior in 1166 had left its mark. He had no intention of risking such a fate
again. His burgeoning martial reputation might have earned him a
position in any number of military households across Normandy and
England, but a more permanent post could only be cemented through
a close family bond. Earl Patrick was no sibling and potential rival, like
Marshal's brother John. He was an established noble; a man of
prospects, capable of acting as William's mentor, of shaping and
advancing his career. When Patrick duly offered him a position in the
Salisbury *mesnie*, a flourishing future looked certain. Shortly thereafter, the wisdom of William's decision to seek service with his uncle
was amply borne out. In early 1168 Earl Patrick was called to campaign
in south-western France, at the side of King Henry II himself. Marshal
had already met one monarch, King Stephen, as a child hostage. Now
he was to be drawn to the centre of the new Angevin dynasty.

---

* It would appear that William Marshal's mother, Sybil of Salisbury, had also died by
this point, though her death was not recorded in the *History*.

The Angevin dynasty

In the first decade following his coronation in 1154, Henry II proved himself to be an astute, dynamic and unfailingly ambitious ruler. Royal authority in England was quickly re-established, as Henry and his diligent officials reconstructed systems of law, justice and governance. Control over the minting of coinage was reasserted, while the determined enforcement of crown rights and strict imposition of taxation soon restocked the royal treasury. Impressively, all of this was achieved while holding on to Normandy and Anjou, and expanding Angevin influence into Brittany, in the far north-western corner of France. Throughout this period, Henry was able to rely on the steadying hand of his mother, Empress Matilda, who lived in semi-retirement near Rouen until her death in September 1167. But Henry II's power, the extent of his realm and the course of his reign were also defined by his marriage to another remarkable woman: Eleanor of Aquitaine.

In the words of one contemporary, Eleanor was 'a woman without compare' – strong-willed, sharp-minded and driven by a lust for life. Frustratingly, no chronicler gave any hint of her physical appearance, even though many described her husband Henry in detail. By birth she was heiress to the great duchy of Aquitaine, with lands stretching across western and south-western France, and dominion over the cities of Poitiers and Bordeaux. Eleanor's colourful career began long before she met Henry. In 1137, at around the age of fifteen, she was wed to King Louis VII of France, head of the royal Capetian dynasty. This seemed an advantageous union, promising as it did to unite the small French kingdom centred around Paris with the lands of Aquitaine, but Eleanor appears to have felt little warmth for her rather unprepossessing husband – a man whom she later likened to a monk because of his desultory sexual appetite.

In the late 1140s, Eleanor and Louis travelled to the Holy Land during the disastrous Second Crusade, but in Syria the queen was accused of having an incestuous affair with her uncle, Raymond of

Poitiers, ruler of the principality of Antioch. Eleanor brazened it out, refusing to be cowed, but the scandalous story spread across Europe. The gravest problem, however, was that the royal marriage failed to secure the Capetian line; two healthy daughters were born to the couple, but no male heir. Eventually, in 1152, the union was annulled on grounds of consanguinity, seemingly by mutual consent. Just eight weeks later – and much to Louis VII's horror – Eleanor married the more vigorous Henry of Anjou and Normandy, a man twelve years her junior, and an arch-rival of the Capetians. When Henry became king of England two years later, a vast new Angevin realm was created, with lands stretching from the borders of Scotland in the north to the foothills of the Pyrenees in the south.

For the first fifteen years, Henry and Eleanor's marriage flourished, as a veritable bumper crop of heirs was born. The couple's first child, William, died at the age of just three, but seven more children followed, all of whom survived to adulthood. The boy who became the Angevins' primary male heir was born on 28 February 1155 and christened Henry; three further sons – Richard, Geoffrey and John – and three daughters – Matilda, Eleanor and Joanne – came after. King Henry II was delighted. With this brood he could found an enduring dynasty and forge a web of diplomatic alliances through marriage, safeguarding Angevin interests.

Ruling such a huge and diverse empire presented formidable challenges. Chief among these was the enduring and embittered enmity of the Capetians, so recently inflamed by Henry's marriage to Eleanor. King Louis VII was born of a long-established royal line, but in terms of territory, wealth and military might, he inherited a relatively feeble kingdom. Centuries earlier, under the Carolingians, Francia or France had been a unified realm, but it had long ago fractured into numerous dukedoms and counties. The French monarchy retained only a small territory known as the Ile-de-France, with the city of Paris at its heart, and though the king was the nominal overlord of all the surrounding provinces, in practice his power was eclipsed by many of his supposed vassals.

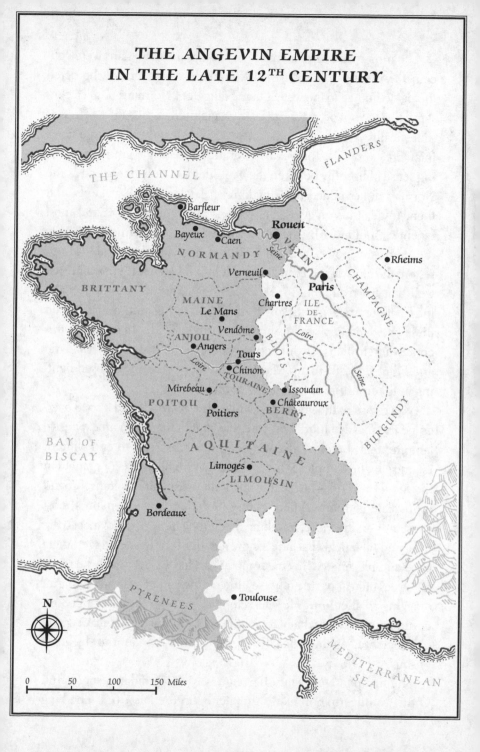

THE ANGEVIN EMPIRE
IN THE LATE 12ᵗʰ CENTURY

THE CHANNEL

FLANDERS

Barfleur

Bayeux • Caen

Rouen

VEXIN

NORMANDY

• Rheims

Seine

Verneuil

Paris

CHAMPAGNE

BRITTANY

MAINE

Chartres

ILE-
DE-
FRANCE

Le Mans

Vendôme

BLOIS

ANJOU

Loire

Angers

Tours

Loire

Chinon

Seine

Loire

TOURAINE

Mirebeau

Issoudun

BURGUNDY

POITOU

Châteauroux

Poitiers

BERRY

AQUITAINE

BAY OF
BISCAY

Limoges •

LIMOUSIN

Bordeaux

PYRENEES

• Toulouse

MEDITERRANEAN
SEA

N

0   50   100   150 Miles

The most irritating of all of these, as far as the Capetians were concerned, were the upstart dukes of Normandy, whose territory bordered the Ile-de-France to the west. These belligerent Normans posed a constant threat, not least because they claimed rights to a series of strategically significant frontier fortresses, barely forty miles from Paris, in an area known as the Vexin. Over the preceding century the abiding sense of hostility between the two sides had only deepened as the Norman dukes added the kingdom of England to their lands, and then, under the Angevins, the regions of Anjou, Maine, and most recently, Aquitaine. By the 1160s, the Angevins were unquestionably the dominant power in France. But King Louis had ambitions to restore the glory of the French monarchy, and Henry II knew only too well that his rival would seek to challenge, diffuse and deflect the might of the Angevins at every turn. The festering animosity between these two dynasties would simmer over the decades to come. As this contest intensified, it would come to shape the histories of England and France, and William Marshal would one day find himself fighting in the frontline of this titanic conflict.

As overlord of the grand Angevin realm, Henry II had also to overcome the massive hurdle of scale. He sought to govern an expansive 'empire' that stretched almost 1,000 miles from end to end without recourse to the complex infrastructure that we now take for granted in the modern world – the systems that allow expeditious transport and immediate communication. Henry's solution was to remain almost constantly on the move, travelling incessantly from one province to the next, and he quickly became renowned for his restless, and seemingly inexhaustible, energy. To contemporaries, Henry was a man who never sat 'except to eat or ride a horse', the equivalent of a 'human chariot dragging all after him'. He set a relentless pace for his itinerant court, covering in one day what it took others four to travel, and leaving one chronicler to conclude that 'he must fly rather than journey by horse or ship'.

The first phase of Henry II's reign was extraordinarily successful. Only two lingering problems threatened in the late 1160s. The king had become estranged from his former confidant and chancellor, Thomas Becket, after the latter's appointment in 1162 as archbishop of Canterbury, England's supreme prelate. Henry had expected his old friend Thomas to be a loyal and malleable ally, but Becket became a staunch defender of the Church against the predatory crown, seemingly inspired by his elevation. After a venomous quarrel, Thomas Becket went into exile in France in 1164, gaining the support of King Louis VII. Despite the papacy's attempts to effect a reconciliation, the dispute remained unresolved.

The other pressing issue demanding Henry II's attention was the unruly duchy of Aquitaine. The king spent part of 1167 reaffirming Angevin rule in the region, but in early 1168 news of a fresh uprising reached his ears. Determined to tame this valuable corner of France, the king laid plans for a new campaign to the south. Queen Eleanor would join the expedition, while Patrick of Salisbury was to be Henry's leading lieutenant. The earl duly crossed the Channel at the head of his military retinue with his newly appointed household knight and nephew, William Marshal, at his side.

IN THE WILD LAND OF AQUITAINE

The Aquitanian expedition took William Marshal far from home. Up to this point his life had been lived in southern England and Normandy, regions that, in the twelfth century, shared a strong affinity in terms of language, culture and landscape. Aquitaine was a different world. In its southern reaches they even spoke another tongue – not the French (or Langue d'Œuil) that William had grown up with, but Occitan (or Langue d'Oc). This huge province – the size of Normandy and Anjou combined – was one of the wealthiest areas of France: a land of rich soils, golden crops and fine wines.

Its people cherished culture and the arts, fostering new forms of music, poetry and song. Queen Eleanor's own grandfather, Duke William IX, had been one of the first troubadours, or courtly singers,

and it was not uncommon for local lords to be acclaimed both as warriors and composers. This was the world of mythic chivalry, from
which the Carolingian heroes of old had supposedly marched to holy
war against the Muslims of Spain. Local churches claimed to house
the body of Roland himself and the very horn with which he had
sought to summon aid against the Moors, while one of King Henry's
own favoured shrines – the cliff-top church of Rocamadour – displayed
Roland's legendary sword, Durendal.

Aquitaine's ducal capital, Poitiers, was the most astounding city that
William Marshal had ever seen. Perched upon a plateau, dominating
the surrounding landscape, it was home to a formidable stone walled
palace built on the orders of Queen Eleanor's grandfather, and boasted
two famous churches. One, dedicated to Poitiers' fourth-century
bishop St Hilary, was closely linked with the dukes of Aquitaine. The
other, Notre-Dame la Grande, was a late eleventh-century masterpiece, decorated with some of the finest Romanesque sculpture in
France. Not content with these architectural riches, Henry and
Eleanor had decided to leave their own mark, commissioning a massive new cathedral dedicated to St Peter in 1162. The construction of
this edifice had begun, so the city's lower slopes were a building site,
and the work would continue for decades to come.

Angevin authority held strong in this well-defended metropolis, but
William was to discover that the Aquitanians were a proud, fiercely
independent and quarrelsome people; little used to bending the knee
to anyone, and certainly not happy to bow down before an outsider
from the north like Henry II. Beyond Poitiers, in the neighbouring
regions of Poitou, Angoulême and the Limousin, lawlessness was
endemic. Here recalcitrant warlords expected to assert their own will
and many had built small castles to dominate the untamed landscape.
The Lusignans of Poitou were a case in point – a minor noble family
with a small parcel of ancestral lands, centred on a stout fortress just
fifteen miles south-west of Poitiers. They were hardly one of the great
aristocratic houses of the south, but the new head of the dynasty,
Geoffrey, was hungry for advancement. He was a fearsome warrior and

had an equally ambitious and acquisitive brother, Guy, by his side. In early 1168 they began raiding the region around Poitiers, riding through the royal domains in a 'violent manner', pillaging as they went.

This was precisely the kind of disorder that Henry II was unwilling to tolerate. When he arrived, with Earl Patrick's military household in tow, the king fell on the Lusignans like a hammer. William Marshal now received an object lesson in the gritty realities of medieval warfare. This would be no chivalric contest fought on an open battlefield. Instead, Henry's aim was to inflict maximum damage on the Poitevin rebels, using overwhelming force and brutal tactics to devastate their resources, thus crippling their military capabilities.

A mainstay of this type of campaigning was the *chevauchée* or destructive horse raid, in which packs of mounted knights conducted vicious sorties into enemy territory, ravaging the landscape by torching crops and razing settlements. The primary victims of these 'scorched-earth' attacks were local peasants, farmers and townspeople, and it was they who suffered now as William and his fellow knights ranged across Poitou 'destroying [the Lusignans'] towns and villages'. This was sadistic and remorseless work, but at times of war most twelfth-century nobles seem to have paid scant regard to the suffering endured by the 'lower orders' of society. No evidence survives to indicate how Marshal reacted to this first taste of open raiding – the *History* passed over this phase of the Aquitanian conflict in silence, and its details have only survived through a brief notice in a contemporary Norman account.

Savage as this type of warfare may seem to modern sensibilities, *chevauchées* were employed in the vast majority of military campaigns conducted in twelfth-century Europe. Veteran commanders like Henry II and Earl Patrick knew that they were the fastest and safest way to bring any enemy to his knees. As the *History* later observed, 'when the poor can no longer reap the harvest from their fields, then they can no longer pay their rent and this in turn impoverishes their lord'. The technique certainly worked for them in 1168. The Lusignans' 'rebellion' was crushed in less than a month, Geoffrey and Guy submitted, their castle was surrendered and Poitou returned to a semblance of order. But Henry also recognised that this type of sharp punitive enforcement could not provide a lasting solution, so he turned to his wife. She had given birth to their eighth child, the boy John, in 1166 and was ready to play a more active role in the governance of the realm. The hope was that, as a native of Aquitaine, Eleanor might be able to inspire a greater measure of loyalty and compliance within the province. She was installed in Poitiers, with Earl Patrick as her lieutenant, while the king left for the north to hold a peace conference with Louis of France.

Treachery on the road

In early April 1168, William Marshal was guarding Eleanor of Aquitaine's royal cortège alongside the rest of Patrick of Salisbury's retinue, as the queen travelled through the forest-cloaked hills of Poitou. The purpose of her journey is unclear, but there seems to have been little sense of apprehension within the party on that spring day. Patrick and his men were not dressed in armour and only a small number of knights were present. In all probability, Eleanor had been touring the recently subdued Lusignan lands and was now returning to Poitiers.

Without any warning the small column was attacked, seemingly from the rear, by a large party of heavily armed Lusignan warriors led by the brothers Geoffrey and Guy. The *History of William Marshal* described this as a calculated 'ambush', and although some aspects of its account can be verified in other contemporary chronicles, the exact causes of the sudden confrontation remain unclear and would later be hotly contested. Perhaps enraged by Henry's recent campaign, the Lusignans were probably hoping to capture some valuable hostages, thereby securing ransoms and gaining leverage in future negotiations. They may well have imagined that Queen Eleanor herself could be taken prisoner.

Earl Patrick recognised at once that his forces were heavily outnumbered and immediately 'sent the Queen on to the castle' –

probably in Poitiers itself. Patrick, William Marshal and the remaining members of the Salisbury *mesnie* now had to hold the road so that Eleanor could reach safety. Within moments a vicious skirmish began as Patrick, still un-armoured and riding only his palfrey, cried out for his warhorse to be brought forward and 'launched himself furiously into [the] midst' of the Lusignan troops. In the heated confusion of this first contact, the earl seems to have been isolated from the majority of his knights, as many of the Salisbury warriors, William included, were holding back, trying to hurriedly don armour. Nonetheless, Patrick seems to have survived the first burst of fighting unscathed and, as his *destrier* arrived, he leapt down and prepared to mount his warhorse and re-enter the fray. He was halfway into the saddle, his back turned to the enemy, when disaster struck. A Lusignan knight drove forward and skewered the earl with a piercing lance strike; un-armoured, as he was, the point of the weapon drove straight through his body. The *History* described, in horrified tones, how as a result of this terrible blow from a 'treacherous assassin' Patrick 'died on the spot'.

The world must have stopped for a fraction of a second, as the enormity of what had just happened dawned on both sides. It is exceptionally unlikely that the earl of Salisbury's death was ever part of the Lusignans' plans. Men of Patrick's standing were simply too valuable to kill in such an offhand manner and, in any case, everyone knew that properly armoured knights were virtually immune to severe injury. In those first moments, Geoffrey and Guy may already have understood that this dark deed would have grave consequences – certainly they would later argue that the incident had been a terrible accident, not deliberate murder.

But for the remaining Salisbury knights – William Marshal in their midst – that was exactly what it looked like. A wave of shock and blinding rage washed over them. According to the *History*, William 'almost went out of his mind with grief', despairing that 'he had not been able to reach the man who killed [Patrick] in time' to halt his attack. By now Marshal was wearing a mail hauberk, but he 'did not wait until he was fully armed'; instead, possessed by an almost berserk fury, he charged into the frantic mêlée, 'bent on exacting violent revenge'. William fought first with his lance and then, after his horse was killed under him, with his sword, scything down enemies and their mounts. His biographer likened him to a 'starving lion' ripping into its prey. But the number of opponents ranged against him eventually proved over-whelming. With the other Salisbury troops either beaten into retreat or battered into submission, Marshal took his last stand, backed up against a hedge, like 'a boar before a pack of wolves', desperately trying to hold back a ring of foes at sword-point. It was only when a Lusignan knight circled round to attack from behind – shoving a lance through the hedgerow that 'went clean through [William's] thigh and out the other side' – that he was felled.

When Marshal finally collapsed, the Lusignans warily closed in to take him prisoner. The lance was pulled from his thigh, and 'once it was out, blood ran from his wounds down his leggings and breeches', leaving 'the whole ground beneath him … covered in blood'. As the physical pain of his injury hit home, a dreadful realisation must have settled over William. In this far-flung, unfamiliar corner of the Angevin realm he had lost everything; the lifeless body of his lord and uncle lay just yards away. The raw anguish of that loss can only have been deep-ened by the certain knowledge that, with his patron's demise, his own future lay in ruins. All his hopes of security and success had come to nothing. Marshal was a largely unknown and severely wounded knight, and the prisoner of a desperate band of rogue Poitevins – men who could surely guess that they would now be labelled outlaws. As the Lusignans prepared to take flight they made no move to tend to William's injury. Instead, his blood-soaked body was unceremoniously strapped to an ass and led off into the wilds of Aquitaine.

4

THE MAN WHO WOULD BE KING

William Marshal was fortunate to survive his encounter with the Lusignans and the long, painful months of captivity that followed. Much of the time he was roughly treated, even by the standards of the day – led, astride an ass, on a seemingly endless journey through 'the length and breadth' of Poitou's densely forested hills by his fugitive captors, the grave wounds to his thigh untended. The *History of William Marshal* described how none of the Lusignans 'spared him a thought as they jolted along through the wooded land like men with much to fear', because there 'was no safety for them in any spot'. As wanted outlaws, their first concern was to evade Angevin retribution, so they remained constantly on the move, never staying in one place more than a night. Their prisoner, William, had little value – no one expected his ransom to be paid and a knight of such modest status was of limited use as a bargaining chip. They were not so vicious as to butcher him in cold blood, but would make scant effort to save his life.

In the first days after Earl Patrick's death, William therefore had to fight for his own survival. At first, he fashioned strips of his own clothing into makeshift bandages, hoping to arrest his bleeding. Later he begged the Lusignans for a scrap of sackcloth and 'swabbed and plugged his wounds with it', but these dressings were soon 'completely soaked in the blood that welled from his body', and Marshal had to wash them as best he could and then reuse them. It is a remarkable testament to William's physical resilience that he did not succumb either to blood loss or infection. Years later, these desperate days became a half-remembered blur of agonising pain and incessant discomfort, but Marshal's recollections were punctuated by two notable incidents.

The first had the air of an embroidered chivalric tale, though it could be true. According to the *History*, one of the Lusignans' allies offered them sanctuary for the night and the 'noble-hearted, kind lady' of the house apparently took pity on William: 'she brought a loaf of bread from her room, removed the inside with her fingers and then filled the crust ... with fine linen bandages'. Once this gift had been smuggled to Marshal he was better able to dress his wounds and his condition slowly improved. The second story is curious and comical, but perhaps offers an authentic sense of William's intensely competitive personality. Weeks had passed and Marshal was all but 'cured of the wounds which had given him such great pains'. He seems to have become more familiar with his captors and was allowed some freedom to move about the camp. On this particular night, some of the Lusignan warriors were passing the evening playing '*la pere geteient*' – a simple game in which each man tried to throw a heavy stone as far as possible. William could not resist asking for a turn, but although his effort supposedly won the contest, it also caused his wounds to 'burst open again', leaving him in excruciating agony and delaying his recovery.

For William, this whole period must have been a nightmare of bleak uncertainty; his mind darkened by a growing suspicion that he had been forgotten and discarded by his Angevin overlords. But then, abruptly, Marshal's fortunes improved beyond all expectation. News arrived that Queen Eleanor was willing to pay a ransom in return for his release. No surviving evidence explains this sudden decision: perhaps William had caught Eleanor's eye during the first stage of the Aquitanian campaign, or it may be that she had heard of his heroics during the roadside ambush. For whatever reason, William was now freed into her care and, better still, once fully healed he was offered a place in the queen's own military retinue. This was a spectacular transformation – the forsaken captive had become knight to one of the most eminent women in the world. William soon found himself dressed in fine clothes and newly armed, furnished with horses and money. As Marshal's biographer put it, he could hardly believe his luck, reckoning he was now 'in the gold'.

TO SERVE THE YOUNG KING

Almost nothing is known of the next two years of William Marshal's life. The *History* suggested that 'he moved about through many lands' seeking 'fame and fortune', but it is also clear that he remained a member of Eleanor's household. Perhaps William did attend tournaments in this period, but in all likelihood he stayed in Aquitaine, helping to impose Angevin authority in the region.* By the time of his release, Earl Patrick's body had been buried with great honour in the church of St Hilary in Poitiers, but the feud with the Lusignans had not been laid to rest with him. Fighting continued across Aquitaine until the summer of 1169, but Poitou and the surrounding provinces were eventually subdued, though Geoffrey and Guy of Lusignan remained free.

One thing is certain: by 1170, Marshal had cemented his reputation with Queen Eleanor as a valiant and skilful warrior and was regarded as a trusted member of her entourage. He may well have come to the notice of her husband, King Henry II himself. William now had the favour of the Angevin royal family. In the space of just four years, he had gone from being a penniless knight, shunned by the Tancarville

---

* According to the courtier Walter Map, Marshal's old patron, William, lord of Tancarville, was appointed as Eleanor's military commander in Aquitaine after Patrick of Salisbury's death, but if true, it is strange that this detail was not recorded in the *History of William Marshal*.

household, to an esteemed warrior serving Europe's most powerful dynasty.

The full scale of William's mercurial ascent became clear when he accompanied Eleanor of Aquitaine back to England in the summer of 1170. The queen had travelled to London to attend the coronation of her son, Henry, on 14 June in Westminster Abbey – an event that would shape Angevin history and change the course of William Marshal's own career. Henry II was determined to avoid both the uncertainty that had followed his grandfather King Henry I's death and a return to the ruinous days of civil war witnessed during King Stephen's reign. The succession plans for the new Angevin dynasty were to be clear and indisputable, and the king's eldest surviving son and namesake stood at the very heart of these designs. In 1170 the young Henry was just fifteen years old, but already tall and incredibly handsome. Contemporaries admired his broad shoulders, long elegant neck, pale freckled skin, striking blue eyes and golden red hair. It was as if a great mythical hero of the ancient world had been brought to life; one who possessed Paris' good looks, Hector's bravery and the unrivalled martial skill of Achilles – at least, that was the view espoused by one of Henry II's fawning courtiers.

Henry the Young King

This dashing prince became one of the central figures of William Marshal's life and, for the next decade and more, the pair would be virtually inseparable. Henry had been groomed for power from an early age. At first, his father, Henry II, was content to use him more as a pawn in the great rivalry with Capetian France. To secure an advantageous truce with King Louis VII in 1160 guaranteeing Angevin rights to the disputed territory of the Norman Vexin, King Henry married his son – then barely just five years old – to Louis' daughter Marguerite (a product of Louis' second marriage to Constanza of Castile). Marguerite was even younger than the boy Henry – two years old at most and little more than a baby. The wedding was a scandal, being in direct contravention of Church law, and it was later joked not only that Marguerite had been presented in a cot, but that both children wailed through the ceremony.

Nonetheless, as the years passed, Henry II began to prioritise his son's education – sending him to be schooled for a time in Thomas Becket's household – and to involve him in acts of governance. In January 1164, young Henry (then eight) attended a great assembly of magnates and churchmen at Clarendon. The meeting confirmed a document listing the 'customs and privileges of the crown' (what became known as the 'Constitutions of Clarendon') and care was taken to record that this controversial legislation had been drawn up 'in the presence of Lord Henry, and of this father, the lord king'. By this time, Henry was already entertaining the idea of having his eldest son crowned and anointed while he himself lived, so that the boy's status as heir could not be disputed. Indeed, financial records show money being spent in 1162 to prepare a special diminutive crown and set of royal regalia. However, after Thomas Becket's alienation from King Henry, the scheme had to be put on hold because the rite of coronation had long been deemed the archbishop of Canterbury's prerogative.

The clearest expression of Henry II's master plan for the Angevin Empire came in January 1169 at a grand peace conference with King Louis VII, convened at Montmirail, to the east of Le Mans. In a wide-ranging treaty, King Henry specified without equivocation that his eldest son would succeed him as king of England, duke of Normandy and count of Anjou. Provisions were also made for two of Henry II's other sons: Richard, the next eldest, was to inherit the duchy of Aquitaine, his mother Eleanor's homeland, while Geoffrey was designated as heir to the duchy of Brittany. In return for Louis' confirmation of these arrangements, the Angevins paid him homage for their Continental French lands and Henry agreed to another marriage alliance with the Capetians, this time involving young Richard's betrothal to another of Louis' daughters, Alice.

It seemed after Montmirail that the Angevin house had been put in order, though some questions remained. No territory had been allocated to Henry II's youngest son John, then barely two years of age, earning him the nickname 'Lackland', and the intended balance of power between Henry's heirs was also unclear. Even so, the king appeared to have shown commendable care and foresight. By this stage he had also started marrying off his daughters to secure valued political alliances. In 1168 Matilda wed Henry the Lion, duke of Saxony, cousin of the German emperor – even though she was twelve and he almost forty. Plans were also afoot to finalise the younger Eleanor's betrothal to the Iberian King Alfonso VIII of Castile.

Through all this, Henry II was the arch dynastic architect, forever juggling, scheming and manipulating to advance the current interests and the future stability of his mighty Angevin realm. The royal seal set upon this design was to be young Henry's coronation in the summer of 1170. If the king had harboured any lingering doubts about the wisdom of this definitive act of pre-designation, they were pushed to one side after a close brush with death, when the royal fleet was caught by a howling March storm in the Channel. Four hundred courtiers drowned in this catastrophe – among them the king's personal physician Ralph of Beaumont. The ceremony was set for mid-June, so Queen Eleanor came north to attend, with William Marshal and the rest of her retinue in tow. Henry II circumvented the ongoing issue of Thomas Becket's absence and exile by convincing Roger, the archbishop of York, to preside over the ritual. Realising that this break with tradition would probably elicit papal condemnation, the king ordered England's ports to be shut, forestalling any message of objection from Rome.

On 14 June young Henry was crowned and anointed as king of England in Westminster Abbey, before his father and mother, and an assembly of the realm's greatest barons and nobles. William Marshal may well have been present as part of Eleanor's household, and his biography later recalled the 'rich pageantry' of the day. The only significant absentee was Henry's young wife, Marguerite of France, who had remained in Normandy. Some contemporaries thought that her exclusion was accidental – the result of unfavourable winds, or an unintended consequence of the Channel ports' closure. More likely, it was a calculated move, designed to leave an opening for future political machinations, perhaps even for the eventual annulment of the marriage. This certainly appears to have been King Louis VII's interpretation, for he was said to have been furious to learn that the ceremony had been held without his daughter.

A new English monarch had been proclaimed: Henry the Young King; the man destined to become Henry III. The practice of preemptive coronation was common elsewhere in Europe and customary among the Capetians. It established an heir's inalienable right to succession. But this was its first use in England since the ninth century, and it was not without its problems. There were now two anointed Angevin monarchs; two human beings who had been transformed by a sacred Christian ritual and thus held the same office. It was obvious to all in June 1170 that the teenage Young King was the junior partner – the associate monarch – waiting in the wings, but that situation could not be expected to hold indefinitely.

For now, Henry II was ready to put his son to work. The Old King (as contemporaries began calling him, even though he was barely forty) was set to return to France, eyeing a reconciliation with Thomas Becket, and he wanted Young Henry to hold the reins of power in his absence. A special royal seal-die was created for the new monarch. This was one of the medieval world's most critical instruments of government – a carefully engraved mould, designed to leave a unique, authenticating imprint on the wax seals attached to crown documents. Most English royal seals had two sides (thus requiring a two-part die) and typically showed a monarch both seated in state, and on the reverse, astride a horse, thus evoking the interlocking ideals of king and warrior. Young Henry's seal had only one side and, unusually, depicted him without a sword in his hand – one of the key symbols of regnal authority. Henry II might be leaving his son with a seal-die of his own, but it was one that offered a graphic affirmation of the Young King's limited, associate status.

King Henry II also took care to surround his son with trusted counsellors. Those tasked to watch over the Young King's governance of England were all known familiars of the Angevin regime; men like William of St John, Hugh of Gundeville and Ranulf FitzStephen. But Henry II also made one additional appointment. William Marshal was chosen to serve as the Young King's tutor-in-arms and a leading member of the new monarch's *mesnie*. This was a significant opportunity, not the same as joining Henry II's entourage itself, but another step closer to the centre of power. Marshal was now to serve at the right hand of England's next king; the glittering young royal described by the *History* as 'the finest of all the princes on earth, be they pagan or Christian'.

William was perhaps twenty-three-years old; the Young King, his new lord and pupil, eight years his junior. The age gap was not so wide, but Henry was just emerging from his youth, while Marshal carried himself as a seasoned warrior. He had seen battle and death, fought in grand tournaments and earned a certain degree of renown. As such, he was judged a suitable mentor for Young Henry – a figure who could act as his teacher, friend and confidant.

To whom did William owe this marked honour? On the evidence preserved in the *History of William Marshal*, the decision seems to have been Henry II's. The biographer recorded that 'the king put [William] in the company of his son', adding that Henry II 'promised to do the Marshal much good in return for his care and instruction' of the Young King. The *History* even noted that William graciously decided not to haggle over terms of service at this point. However, the biography also made it clear that Marshal came to London with the queen, and her hand in this affair must be suspected. Historians have long argued that Eleanor was already obsessively concerned with Aquitaine and the career of her younger son Richard, but this view is strongly informed by hindsight. In 1170 the queen had every reason to maintain close contact with, and potential influence over, her eldest son, the heir designate to the Angevin heartlands. The appointment of her household knight, William Marshal, as the Young King's military tutor offered just such a connection. Only time would tell where Marshal's loyalties really lay.

King Henry II duly left Young Henry with William Marshal in England and crossed over to Normandy before the end of June. In the course of the summer the king met with Thomas Becket and, in official terms at least, their bitter quarrel was finally put to rest, though barely submerged tensions remained. The Angevin realm appeared at last to be at peace. Then, around 10 August, the Old King fell ill with a persistent fever and was confined to bed near Domfront in southwest Normandy. Perhaps years of incessant travel and the strain of managing his vast realm had finally caught up with him, and though a new doctor had surely been appointed to his household, Henry may now have missed the ministrations of the late Ralph of Beaumont, his former personal physician. As weeks passed, the king's condition deteriorated, and he seems to have made a heartfelt appeal to the Virgin Mary, hoping for a miraculous cure. It seemed that his careful provisions for the Angevin succession had been made not a moment too soon. Fearing that he was close to death, the Old King issued detailed instructions for his burial, and drew up a final will confirming the Treaty of Montmirail and Young Henry's rights to England, Normandy, Anjou and Maine. News of the king's grave infirmity crossed the Channel, only to be followed in September by rumours that Henry II had died. The Angevin world held its breath. It seemed that a new young king was about to come to power, and William Marshal would be at his side.

AN UNQUIET HEIR

Henry the Young King came tantalisingly close to power that autumn. Waiting anxiously in London through mid-September, Henry and the entourage of clerics and knights like William Marshal around him, must all have been quietly preparing for his accession – for the moment when the reign of King Henry III would begin in earnest. But in the end, news of the Old King's recovery arrived and the moment of danger and opportunity passed. Given that Young Henry was only fifteen and possessed very limited experience of rule, these tidings were perhaps greeted, first and foremost, with a sense of relief. After all, the Young King still had a long and golden future ahead of him; his day would come.

Though Henry II ultimately survived this illness, the experience evidently left him shaken. Having despaired of his life, the king immediately set out on a 300-mile pilgrimage to the shrine of the Virgin Mary at Rocamadour, in Aquitaine. This remote cult site housed a famous effigy, the Black Madonna – thought to be a particularly powerful focus of the saint's presence. It was also the supposed burial site of Mary's own household servant Amator (who, legend told, had travelled from Palestine to France, living out his days as a hermit in the local cliff-side caves). In spite of his convalescent state, the Old King made the long, arduous journey to venerate the Virgin and show gratitude for his recovery, distributing alms to the poor as he went. Perhaps he even followed local custom of ascending the steep flights of steps leading to the cliff-top shrine on his knees. With his act of devotion complete, Henry returned to the business of state.

Young Henry was to remain in his father's shadow, as heir to the realm and associate king, for years to come. Historians have traditionally offered a withering assessment of Young Henry's career after the summer of 1170. He is typically portrayed as a handsome but feckless dandy – the extravagant playboy who, once denied the chance to rule in his own right, submerged himself in the dissolute cult of chivalry, with William Marshal as his guide. Though published as long ago as 1973, Professor Lewis Warren's seminal biography of King Henry II has retained its influence, and Warren's appraisal of the Young King in this work was thoroughly damning. Henry was dismissed as 'shallow, vain, careless, empty-headed, incompetent, improvident and irresponsible' – quite a list of failings. This estimation has held in almost all quarters of academic perception and (if he is remembered at all) in popular imagination, and as a result Young

Henry remains a misunderstood and often overlooked figure to this day. He is England's forgotten king.

But a closer and more impartial study of Henry's life, and his association with William Marshal, reveals that the accepted view is overly simplistic – at times even misrepresentative – and deeply shaded by hindsight. In fact, the best contemporary evidence indicates that the Young King was an able and politically engaged member of the Angevin dynasty, and throughout this period he seems to have worked in close concert with William Marshal. To begin with, in the early 1170s, Henry helped his father to steady the realm during two years of intense crisis by governing England in the Old King's absence.

Having recovered from his grave illness in the autumn of 1170, Henry II must have imagined that the worst was over, but this crisis was soon overshadowed. Towards the end of that year Thomas Becket, the long-exiled archbishop of Canterbury, returned to England. Some weeks later, four knights attending the Old King's Christmas Court in Normandy overheard their monarch angrily decrying Becket's continued disobedience. Misinterpreting these angry words as a signal for direct action, they crossed the Channel and made for Canterbury. Perhaps their first intention was to arrest the archbishop, but once they had Becket cornered inside the great cathedral by the altar, heated words were exchanged. With their swords already drawn, the enraged knights began hacking at the defenceless prelate and Thomas died beneath a furious cascade of blows that left his brains strewn across the floor.

The scandal of this horrific murder caused outrage across Europe and marked a defining moment in Henry II's reign. Not surprisingly, the Roman Church responded to the slaying of one of its leading prelates with vituperative condemnation. The emergence of a powerful international cult dedicated to Archbishop Thomas was more remarkable. In life Becket had been a divisive figure; in death he was revered as a pious martyr. Reports of miracles associated with his resting place in Canterbury were soon legion, and by early 1173 he had been formally canonised as a saint. The Old King survived this storm through a mixture of apologetic diplomacy and absenteeism – setting off to conquer Ireland, while closing the ports behind him so that no orders of excommunication could be delivered. By 1172 a measure of calm had returned and, in May that year, Henry submitted to the formal judgement of a papal legate in Normandy and performed a public penance.

All of this meant that Henry II did not return to England until the summer of 1172 and, throughout this extended period, the Young King ruled in his stead without apparent difficulty. There is some evidence that he was already struggling to live within his means, given that he had no independent wealth or income of his own. The *History of William Marshal* recalled that in these years, while William was tutoring Henry in the art of combat, the Young King was 'spending lavishly', but observed that this was only to be expected from 'a king and a son of a king'. In late 1171 Henry crossed to Normandy to hold his own Christmas Court near Bayeux for the first time. One contemporary noted that the Young King was 'anxious that the festival should be celebrated with great magnificence' – this was his chance to display the largesse expected of any lord of knights, let alone a crown monarch. A 'multitude' attended this opulent gathering; so many that when William of St John jokingly declared that only those named William could dine beside him, 110 men were still left in the room, Marshal presumably among them.

On King Louis VII's insistence, Young Henry underwent a second coronation in August 1172, this time with his young wife Marguerite of France in attendance, and Archbishop Rotrou of Rouen presiding over the solemn ritual performed in Winchester Cathedral. Despite the fact that they had already been married for more than a decade, it was probably only from this point onwards that Henry actually began to live with his wife. His status as king had now been proclaimed twice, yet he still had no lands of his own, and with the Old King's health and political position rejuvenated, Henry had little prospect of inheriting the realm in the near future. The disjuncture between his royal title and actual position began to grate.

The Young King has often been represented as a rather petulant figure in this period – the impatient, disobedient teenager, unwilling to wait his proper turn. But this ignores the mounting financial and social pressures that Henry had to shoulder as he approached his eighteenth year and full adulthood. He now had a wife and queen of his own to support, and although Marguerite had been allocated valuable dower lands and a hefty cash dowry, these remained in the hands of the Old King, beyond Henry's grasp. Even contemporaries who usually favoured Henry II acknowledged that the Young King 'took it badly that his father did not wish to assign him any territory where he could dwell with his queen'. Young Henry also had to think of his household knights – the men who naturally anticipated reward for their loyal service.

After his first coronation in 1170, Henry gathered a close-knit group of retainers around him. Five knights formed the core of the Young King's *mesnie* from this period onwards: three were originally from Normandy – Adam of Yquebeuf, Gerard Talbot and Robert Tresgoz; two from England – Simon Marsh and, of course, William Marshal. By the cultural norms of the day, a man in Henry's position was expected to offer these supporters protection, advancement and ultimately land; any failure or inability to do so could be seen as a cause of shame, dishonour and impotence. Knights in this period, Marshal included, routinely nagged their lords for favours, seeking everything from property to the hand of wealthy heiresses. This was all an accepted part of climbing the social ladder. But for now the Young King had little to give.

On the whole, these pressures remained hidden in the *History of William Marshal*, but other contemporary sources suggest that, by the end of 1172, some of Young Henry's retainers were encouraging him to take action. One chronicler noted that 'certain persons began whispering' to Henry that he ought 'to rule jointly with his father' or even 'rule alone, for having been crowned, the reign of his father had effectively been brought to an end'. It is impossible to know whether William Marshal joined this 'whispering' campaign, but word that some knights in Young King's *mesnie* were fomenting intrigue certainly reached Henry II, because around this time he intervened, removing the warrior Hasculf of St Hilaire 'and other young knights' from his son's 'counsel and household'.

The Old King had no intention of sharing real power with his son. As far as his father was concerned, Young Henry was a king in name alone; a figurehead to be paraded and, if necessary, manipulated. He would be paid a generous (though not inexhaustible) allowance – thousands of pounds per year – but not given actual, independent authority. The lad was expected to wait in the wings obediently and indefinitely. This approach to the business of rule was a hallmark of the Old King's reign.

Henry II was a phenomenally skilful monarch and politician, but he was also a compulsive hoarder when it came to power, reluctant to let a single ounce of authority to slip from his grasp. Perhaps this was sheer greed, or maybe Henry simply thought it inconceivable that another could bear the Herculean task of governing the empire. Certainly, for the majority of his career, he acted like a chess player sitting before a vast board, determined to direct every single piece with his own hand. When pressed, the Old King might turn to a 'trusted' subordinate: Young Henry ruled England in his stead after the crisis of 1170; his younger sons, Richard and Geoffrey, would be expected to oversee Aquitaine and Brittany as the decade progressed. But Henry II remained stubbornly unwilling to cede unfettered authority over England or any part of the Angevin heartlands of Normandy and Anjou. In 1150, when Henry II was just sixteen, his own father – Geoffrey Plantagenet – had seen fit to grant him full rights to the duchy of Normandy. Now, twenty years later, the Old King could not bring himself to do the same for his eldest son.

Walter Map, one of Henry II's courtiers, later argued that the Old King had been taught by his formidable mother Empress Matilda to instil loyalty through the harsh denial of favour. She was said to have told him that 'an unruly hawk' could only be tamed if kept hungry. The secret, she believed, was to repeatedly offer the creature meat, but always snatch the reward away at the last second. By this means, the bird of prey would become 'keener and more obedient and attentive'. The danger of course, as Map knew only too well, was that a starving hawk might turn on his master.

The road to rebellion

The first signs of a gathering storm could be detected by late 1172. In November, Young Henry and Queen Marguerite travelled to Paris to meet with her father King Louis VII of France, and he was said to have treated both as his children. The Young King and his wife then held their own Christmas Court, with William Marshal and the rest of his household, at Bonneville in northern Normandy, while Henry II and Eleanor of Aquitaine met at the great Angevin fortress of Chinon more than 200 miles to the south. In all likelihood, Young Henry was already preparing to challenge his father's authority, perhaps even scheming with his Capetian father-in-law. The Old King must have had some sense of his son's festering discontent, but he failed to predict the explosion that was about to rip the Angevin realm asunder.

Henry II summoned his wife and four sons to a meeting on 25 February 1173 at Limoges, capital of the Limousin region in central Aquitaine. Leading dignitaries from southern France and Iberia, including the count of Toulouse and the king of Aragon, were also brought together. The Old King intended this grand Angevin gathering to serve as an affirmation of dynastic superiority and regional dominance. Instead, it sparked the greatest rebellion of his reign. The problems began when Henry II proudly announced to the assembly that he had secured a propitious marriage alliance for his youngest son John, then just five years old. The boy was to be betrothed to a daughter of the French magnate Humbert, count of Maurienne, and gifted possession of three of the most important castles in Anjou – Chinon, Loudon and Mirebeau. This was a crafty manoeuvre. With John obviously in no position to administer these fortresses in person, they would revert to the Old King himself and be kept from the clutches of Young

Henry, the nominal 'count of Anjou', for years to come. His eldest son was bound to be displeased, but the Old King must have calculated that Henry would be forced to swallow his anger in this public setting. He was mistaken.

Young Henry made a clear display of outrage, resolutely declaring that this plan offended his rights as count of Anjou and would never be accepted. What is more, he demanded that his father now hand over full possession of either Anjou, Normandy or England itself. The Old King's bluff had been called, and the grave rift between father and son was suddenly clear for all to see. Both men were left fuming and unable to speak to one another 'in a peaceable manner'. That evening, however, Henry II discovered that a greater game was in play. During a private audience, the count of Toulouse informed him that two of his other sons, Richard and Geoffrey, and, unthinkably, even his wife Queen Eleanor, were rumoured to be plotting his overthrow. A conspiracy had evidently been brewing for weeks, perhaps even months – one that threatened to shatter the Old King's beloved empire.

Henry II took immediate action. He seems to have discounted the story of Eleanor's connivance because he left Richard and Geoffrey in her care – after all, as chroniclers would later attest, no queen in the annals of history had ever betrayed her husband in such a treacherous manner. But Young Henry was another matter. His meeting with Louis of France back in November now took on a different complexion. The Old King hurriedly set out for the north, taking Henry and Marguerite with him, and discreetly ordered that his castles be readied for war. The Young King must have had his military household with him at this point, William Marshal included, but it is unclear whether Henry was in any way compelled to accompany his father. According to one local chronicler, Henry II pretended to be embarking on a hunting excursion, but given that the party then travelled almost 150 miles, this excuse cannot have held for long. In all likelihood, the Young King was simply informed that he would be escorting the king, for as yet, no decisive breach had occurred.

Young Henry finally made his move at Chinon, stealing from the castle in the dead of night, accompanied only by his '*privata familia*' (the very closest members of his household), including William Marshal. In the chaotic rush of this sudden escape Marguerite was left behind, and amid the confusion, even some of the Young King's most trusted servants did not realise, at first, what was happening, though it might be assumed that leading knights, like Marshal, were party to the flight. Once away from Chinon and racing through the night, it became obvious that Henry intended to openly rebel against his father, and every one of his followers had a choice to make. Where did their loyalties lie: with the Young King, their lord; or with his father, Henry II, the great Angevin monarch? The wrong decision could spell the end of a retainer's career, perhaps even his life. Richard Barre, the bearer of Young Henry's royal seal, turned around immediately and returned to Chinon, taking the seal with him. Rather humiliatingly, the household staff responsible for Henry's baggage (including his clothes) did the same, but when they presented themselves before the Old King he sent them straight back to his son, along with a gift of 'silver cups, horses and rich cloth'. Young Henry might now be an adversary, but he was still an Angevin with a royal dignity to preserve. Needless to say, his seal was not returned.

After these departures the Young King demanded a formal oath of allegiance from his remaining followers. Having some sense what was to come, he was determined to surround himself only with those of proven fidelity. Some, like his steward William Blund, refused to swear and were allowed to return unharmed to Chinon. Most, like William Marshal, remained. They now set out with Henry to meet with Louis of France some 180 miles away, on the outskirts of Paris. As far as the Young King was concerned, these men had affirmed their steadfast devotion; but in Henry II's eyes they were now guilty of the most heinous crime of treason against the crown. A formal list of these 'diabolical' traitors was later drawn up and the five leading members of Young Henry's *mesnie* were all named. This roll call of dishonour survives to this day – copied by the great twelfth-century historian Roger of Howden, into his account of King Henry II's reign. So it was that the great William Marshal made his first known appearance in a contemporary chronicle, and the man who would one day become England's peerless knight was named an enemy of the state.

'A WAR WITHOUT LOVE'

King Henry II may have sensed that some form of confrontation with his eldest son was all but inevitable even before the meeting at Limoges began. But he could not possibly have guessed that Young Henry's rebellion would spark a massive uprising that would see his authority challenged in almost every province of the Angevin Empire. In the immediate aftermath of the Young King's flight from Chinon, his brothers Richard and Geoffrey travelled to the Ile-de-France to join him, and Eleanor's complicity in the whole affair was revealed. The queen appears to have made a calculated decision to challenge her husband's authority, but her motives remain uncertain. Some have suggested that she was spurred to action by feverish jealousy over Henry II's infidelities, most notably his affair with the beautiful English woman 'Fair' Rosamund Clifford – later legends even suggested that Eleanor had Rosamund assassinated in 1176. But this explanation probably owes more to chivalric fiction than reality. Now in her fifties, the queen may have been worried about being excluded, but not from Henry's bedchamber. Like her husband, Eleanor was a political animal; one seemingly determined not to be sidelined as she aged. Her primary concerns in 1173 were probably to cement her own position in Aquitaine and to advance her sons' careers, especially those of Young Henry and Richard.

In the spring of 1173 the 'rebels' gathered at a great assembly in Paris organised by King Louis VII. The Young King was proclaimed Henry III, England's rightful ruler, and using a new royal seal helpfully provided by the French monarch, he set about binding a number of powerful allies to his cause. Documents were drawn up promising rich rewards of lands and income to the likes of Young Henry's cousin Philip of Alsace, count of Flanders – one of the most powerful magnates in northern France, who at the age of thirty-one, was fast earning a reputation as a fearsome warrior and a canny political operator. Philip's brother, Count Matthew of Boulogne, was similarly drawn into the conflict, as were the count of Blois and King William of Scotland. The Young King was building a powerful alliance, but to what purpose, and at whose behest?

Most historians have suggested that either Eleanor or Louis VII orchestrated the entire affair, discounting out of hand the possibility that Young Henry – the 'feckless' playboy – might have been the architect of his own fate, even though he was now eighteen. It is true, of course, that Henry's visit to Paris in November 1172, and his connection to Louis through Marguerite, all pointed to the Capetian king as an active ally. Louis was, at the very least, a co-conspirator in the rebellion, but that did not make him its instigator. The queen's influence is perhaps even more intriguing, given that she may have retained an agent within the Young King's entourage – none other than William Marshal, her former household knight. But frustratingly, Marshal's precise role in these events remains unknown. As a leading member of Young Henry's *mesnie*, William must have been an influential voice and perhaps encouraged this bold move to action. On balance, Young Henry appears to have played a significant role in planning and then executing the confrontation with his father. Certainly, he is unlikely to have been a mere puppet manipulated by others.

Young Henry sought more than a mere token of land or increased allowance when he challenged his father. His goal was nothing less than the overthrow of the Old King's regime and the seizure of his Angevin heartlands, and this attempted coup enjoyed remarkably widespread support. The Young King and his allies incited insurrection across the realm – such that Henry II soon faced attacks along the Scottish border, unrest within England itself and revolt in Aquitaine – while they focused their own resources on an invasion of Normandy. By the summer of 1173 the entire realm was in the grip of a destructive civil war and it seemed that the dark days of King Stephen's reign were about to be repeated.

Contemporaries characterised this bitter, internecine struggle as 'a war without love'. But some eyewitnesses were also aware of its underlying causes and sympathised with Young Henry's predicament. The cleric Jordan of Fantosme, then living in southern England, noted perceptively that 'a king without a realm is at a loss for something to do; at such a loss was the noble and gracious Young King'. In spite of being broadly supportive of Henry II's position in his chronicle, Jordan actually laid much of the blame for the conflict at the Old King's feet. After describing Young Henry's coronation, he addressed a direct complaint to Henry II, stating that: 'After this crowning and this transfer of power you took away from your son some of his authority, you thwarted his wishes so that he could not exercise power. Therein lay the seeds of a pitiless war.'

Very little is known of William Marshal's conduct in this conflict beyond the fact that he remained loyal to the Young King. The author of the *History* seems to have been determined to offer a balanced – but also remarkably vague – account of the rebellion, and perhaps he was reflecting Marshal's own equivocation as he looked back on this treacherous struggle. The biography mourned the fact that 'many noblemen died' in the conflict, stating that the land was 'ravaged by the war' and that 'on both sides there were excesses'. The physical damage to the landscape during this 'savage' conflagration left 'many a castle and many a town ... razed to the ground', and the scars were obviously evident many decades later, because the *History* noted that 'in many places there are still the remains of what the war left'.

Neither the Young King, nor Henry II, was explicitly blamed for the war in the *History of William Marshal*, with the latter described as 'very wise and courtly'. This was the same agile avoidance of criticism witnessed in the account of young William's time as King Stephen's hostage in 1152. Just as he had done then, the biographer laid the blame upon the *losengiers* (deceivers) who offered evil counsel to both father and son. The *History* indicated that there was a difference of opinion within the Young King's inner circle, with some advising Henry 'to turn against his father and use force to reduce him', while others cautioned that 'it would be very wrong to act in this way'. Marshal's own opinion was never explicitly stated. Perhaps this meant that William stood as a voice of reason and reconciliation in this period; or it may well be that this was merely the sanitised version of events that he chose to recall. In the course of the war, Marshal was surely called upon to fight in the front line and to offer military counsel, but he remained inexpert in certain aspects of martial conduct – most notably siege-craft – and this raised the importance of others with more experience of command, like Philip of Flanders and King Louis VII.

The *History of William Marshal* described only one significant deed in any detail during the rebellion – at the height of the conflict, William supposedly knighted the Young King. Prior to this, the *History* made no mention of the fact that Henry had not attained knightly status, and its claim has to be doubted. It would have been very unusual for the young royal not to undergo a dubbing ceremony before his coronation, and a well-placed contemporary recorded that Henry was indeed knighted by his father's hand in June 1170. The 1173 'knighting' in the *History* seems to have been constructed both to inflate Marshal's reputation and to subtly impute that William ennobled the Young King in the midst of an otherwise dishonourable conflict. Henry's retinue supposedly encouraged him to be dubbed, because his lack of knightly status was 'not to everyone's liking', adding that 'we would all be a more effective force if you had a sword girded on'. William's biographer then hammered home his hero's standing and renown. Even though there were high-ranking 'counts and barons' present, Henry allegedly chose Marshal to perform the ritual because he was 'the best knight who ever was or will be' – a significant overstatement of his reputation and achievements at this stage. As a result, William 'gladly girded on his sword and kissed him, whereupon he became a knight'. In his biographer's opinion, Marshal had just transformed the Young King's status, even though he himself 'had not one strip of land to his name or anything else, just his chivalry'.

The great rebellion

The Young King and his allies made their first move in June 1173, launching a coordinated invasion of Normandy. Aiming to capture the ducal capital of Rouen through a pincer movement, King Louis of France led an attack towards the border fortress of Verneuil from the south, while Young Henry advanced from the north-east at the head of a large coalition force, including his brothers, Richard and Geoffrey, and the counts of Flanders and Boulogne. By this point William Marshal's former patron, the lord of Tancarville, chamberlain of Normandy, had also sided with the Young King, bringing one hundred knights to the cause.

Young Henry enjoyed initial success, seizing the castle of Aumale on Normandy's eastern frontier almost immediately (probably as a result of its commander switching sides) and then marched on to besiege Neufchâtel-en-Bray. This was a strange reversal for William Marshal. Seven years earlier, he had fought his first military engagement at this town, battling alongside the lord of Tancarville to defend Normandy from invasion. Now, as William returned in the company of his old master and beside the Young King, he had become the invader.

Marshal had certainly seen at least one siege in his life to date, having been present as a hostage when King Stephen sought to capture Newbury Castle in 1152, but the investment of Neufchâtel was probably his first direct experience of this form of military engagement. Like the mounted raid, or *chevauchée*, the siege was an essential feature of medieval warfare. In William's world, castles were almost ubiquitous. The ruling elite used strongholds to maintain strategic, economic and administrative control of territory, and virtually every town or city was, to one degree or another, fortified by walls or a citadel. Disputed regions, like the borderlands of Normandy, were guarded by a dense network of forts, and most of these were constructed of stone by the mid-twelfth century. As a result, most territorial wars revolved around hard-fought contests for control of castles, and

William Marshal would himself engage in countless sieges (both as aggressor and defender) in the course of his long career.

Two strategies were open to William and Young Henry when they arrived with their allies at Neufchâtel in the summer of 1173. As Marshal knew only too well from first-hand experience, the town contained a stout stone fortress, surrounded by suburbs, which would not be easily overcome. Neufchâtel could have been subjected to an encirclement siege: surrounded by a tight cordon and cut off from resupply, such that its garrison would eventually be starved or intimidated into submission. This was an exceptionally effective technique – though it often boiled down to a bleak, and sometimes savage, test of will – but it was time-consuming and potentially hazardous for an attacking force, who might easily find themselves isolated or confronted by a relieving army.

Needing to push on at speed towards Rouen, the Young King's army adopted an assault-based strategy at Neufchâtel. Facing the castle's formidable defences, the allies deployed a number of siege-engines (probably fairly rudimentary stone-throwing weapons, capable of propelling ten- to twenty-pound projectiles) and unleashed a fierce aerial bombardment. These volleys might inflict some damage on the walls, potentially causing a breach, but they also provided valuable cover under which direct attacks using battering rams and scaling ladders could be launched. Fighting in one of these offensives was a risky affair – garrisons used every available means to stem an attack, from unleashing scouring volleys of arrows and crossbow bolts, to pouring boiling pitch and burning sand down on advancing troops. William and Young Henry emerged from this first siege unscathed, but Count Matthew of Boulogne was less fortunate. In the midst of a frontal assault, he took an arrow in the knee and, when the wound became infected, he was left struggling for his life.

While the fighting continued above ground, a secondary battle was being waged beneath the surface. The allies sent in sappers to undermine Neufchâtel's battlements, and these siege specialists proceeded to dig tunnels beneath the walls, carefully buttressing their excavations with wooden supports as they went. Once complete, these mines would be packed full of branches and kindling, set alight and left to collapse, thus bringing down the wall above, though on this occasion it appears that no tunnels were actually fired. Facing the combined onslaught of sapping and frontal attacks, Neufchâtel's garrison decided that further resistance was futile and duly capitulated. This significant success was soured, however, when Matthew of Boulogne succumbed to his injury. His death sent a shockwave through the Flemish contingent and left his brother Philip of Flanders too grief-struck to continue with the war. When he withdrew, Young Henry's advance faltered. This setback was compounded by King Louis' marked lack of success to the south, where his army was driven from Verneuil and forced into humiliating flight. The first phase of the rebellion had ended in failure.

Throughout the war, King Henry II proved himself to be a canny and adroit commander. Facing a swelling tide of unrest, and confronted by enemies on many fronts, he remained calm and cautious. Trusting that those barons and castellans still faithful to the crown could hold the provinces, the Old King staunchly refused to be drawn into precipitous action. Like any medieval military leader, Henry was exceptionally wary of pitched battles, because these open confrontations were highly unpredictable. Most twelfth-century generals avoided full-scale clashes of this type unless they enjoyed absolutely overwhelming numerical superiority, and as a result, battles were remarkably rare in this era. Indeed, through all his long years of campaigning, William Marshal would only fight in one engagement that could be properly classed as a battle, and even that was set within the context of a siege.

In 1173, King Henry II committed his forces only when an overwhelming threat presented itself and stayed back from the front line whenever possible. Instead, he used his well-stocked treasury to employ some 20,000 ruthless Brabançon (Flemish) mercenaries to fight in his name. Henry recognised that his capture would be catastrophic. The fear was not execution – such an act of cold-blooded regicide would have been virtually unimaginable – but the removal from power through enforced 'retirement'. Some seventy years earlier, Henry II's great-uncle, Robert Curthose, had been plucked from the board in this way and then frittered away the rest of his days in prison. The Old King had no intention of following in his footsteps.

After the abortive invasion of Normandy, the two sides were deadlocked, and attempts at reconciliation that summer foundered. It was probably around this time that Queen Eleanor tried to leave Aquitaine and join her sons. Rumour had it that she disguised herself as a man in an attempt to evade capture, but she was seized nonetheless and taken into custody. With Queen Marguerite also under close guard, Henry II now had two valuable hostages. A lull in the fighting followed, indeed a truce may even have been proclaimed between Christmas and Easter, though if so the Young King seems to have broken it by attempting a daring, but ultimately fruitless midwinter attack on southern Normandy. It was not until the spring of 1174 that hostilities recommenced in earnest.

Young Henry's rebellion was faltering and his father-in-law, King Louis, had proved to be a largely ineffective ally. Meanwhile, Henry II and his royalist supporters were making significant headway in Anjou, Maine and Aquitaine. The Young King needed to land a telling blow, but the plan he now concocted with Count Philip of Flanders involved considerable risk. Young Henry was to attempt a full-scale invasion of England itself; almost a repeat of 1066, but this time with landfall made in East Anglia. Royalist strongholds in the north were already under attack from King William of Scotland, and there were others in England who favoured Young Henry's cause. A fleet was prepared on the Flemish coast and in mid-May the first ships sailed. This advance force of just over 300 men successfully established a beachhead and later seized control of Norwich. Now primed to strike, all the Young King needed was a favourable wind. Henry waited on the coast of Flanders for weeks, and William Marshal must have been beside him during these long days of anxious anticipation. But through June and early July the wind stubbornly refused to change.

By this time the Old King was back in Normandy, and urgent messages of alarm from England had reached him. Henry II now had no choice but to attempt an immediate sailing, regardless of the weather. Taking Eleanor and Marguerite with him, he set out from Barfleur around 7 July 1174. The sea was roughening and the wind was 'blowing directly against them' according to one close contemporary; understandably nervous, the crew doubted that a crossing could be made. It was said that Henry stood on the deck 'in front of everyone', and 'lifting his eyes to Heaven', prayed to God that he might make 'a safe landing'. Was his story about to end in disaster on the water, just like that of William Ætheling in 1120?

By some accounts it was not until dawn the next day that the coast was spotted. The royal ship had been blown off course, but somehow found its way to Southampton, allowing Henry to disembark unharmed. From there he sped to Canterbury and the new shrine to the martyred Thomas Becket. The motives behind Henry's sudden pilgrimage that July are difficult to untangle. He was driven in part it would seem, by a heartfelt desire to give thanks for his safe passage and perhaps an authentic sense of remorse for Becket's murder. But the Old King had also made a calculated decision to mark his arrival in England with an extreme and public act of atonement – one that could leave his subjects in no doubt that their true, pious and God-fearing monarch had returned. So it was that, on 12 July, King Henry II came walking barefoot to Canterbury Cathedral, 'with streaming tears, groans and cries', begging for absolution. Stripped to the waist, before a hushed crowd, Henry was beaten with rods by a gaggle of prelates. Once scourged of his sin, the king promised an annual endowment of £40, so that 'lamps [might] burn perpetually around the martyr's tomb' in veneration of St Thomas.

In the immediate aftermath of this visit, news arrived of a startling victory for royalist forces in the north; William of Scotland had been captured near Alnwick and his insurrection crushed. To many this seemed like an act of divine providence. With the pendulum now swinging in his favour, Henry II rapidly quashed the remaining pockets of resistance in England, securing the kingdom. Back on the Continent, the Young King realised that his chance had passed and the invasion was called off. While his father remained preoccupied in England, Young Henry and William Marshal joined Count Philip and King Louis to launch a second invasion of Normandy in late July. If they could seize Rouen then something might still be salvaged from the wreckage of the rebellion. Mustering every remaining ounce of manpower, they laid siege to the great ducal city with a 'vast and terrible' army, and began to assemble engines of war. But Rouen was heavily defended, strongly fortified and, lying on the banks of the River Seine, could not be fully encircled. The allies proved unable to tighten the noose and, moving with his legendary speed, Henry II re-crossed the Channel and relieved Rouen on 11 August. The Young King had been outplayed. Torching their siege machines and tents, the rebel armies began a despondent retreat. The war was over.

In the end, Young Henry had been unable to overcome his father's cool-headed resolve and seemingly inexhaustible resources. As one of the Old King's supporters smugly declared, the rebels had learnt 'that it was no easy task to wrest the club from the hand of Hercules'. Had luck been with him, or if Louis of France had proved to be a more dynamic collaborator, then victory might well have been possible. As it was, the Young King was forced to make peace on his father's terms. At a gathering near Tours, on 30 September 1174, he witnessed a formal treaty finalising the settlement, and so too did William Marshal. Henry II was magnanimous in victory. His eldest son was to receive an allowance of 15,000 Angevin pounds per annum, and rights to two Norman castles (when his father saw fit to release them). Richard and Geoffrey were similarly promised incomes and lands. Most of those who had supported the Young Henry's cause were permitted to keep their lordships – though unsanctioned castles were destroyed across the realm – and the majority of prisoners were released. The Old King had brought his cubs to heel, and few could doubt that he would now watch them with a far more wary and vigilant eye. Only Queen Eleanor remained unforgiven. Perhaps Henry judged her to have been the spider at the centre of this treacherous conspiracy; it may be that he was simply appalled by her unbidden betrayal. She was taken into close confinement and would spend the next decade and more in captivity in England.

The Young King caged

Young Henry was not imprisoned as such, but nonetheless he was forced to live the next year-and-a-half in the equivalent of an open cage, travelling under his father's watchful gaze at almost all times. At a succession of formal gatherings, the Young King was made to reaffirm his allegiance, and a renewed oath of fealty for himself and his men given near Bayeux was witnessed by Rotrou, the archbishop of Rouen. On 8 May 1175, father and son crossed over to England and remained within the kingdom for the rest of that year.

William Marshal evidently recalled this period as one of almost restful inactivity, as the *History* stated that the Young King and his knights now resided in a 'fine and beautiful place', and gave themselves over to the recreations of hunting and hawking. William's biographer maintained that it was only after months of such idleness that Henry and his household became restless. Recognising that 'a long period of rest is a disgrace to a young man', the Young King supposedly sought leave from his father 'to go over the Channel for my sport' – that is, to begin attending the kind of knightly tournaments that were still banned in England. Historians have generally accepted this account and therefore concluded that, in the wake of the failed rebellion, both Young Henry and William Marshal became detached from the world of high politics and military conflict. By early 1176, both men are supposed to have thrown themselves into the obsessive pursuit of tournament glory, with barely a thought for the real world beyond. In reality, this was at best only half the story.

An array of detailed evidence allows us to track the movements of the Young King's household within England, and it turns out that, far from putting up their feet in some rural idyll, Henry and his knights travelled hundreds of miles during the course of 1175, zigzagging across the kingdom, usually at the side of the Old King. Young Henry can be placed in London, Oxford, Canterbury, Woodstock, York, Windsor and Winchester, often attending major assemblies with the likes of the Scots, the Irish and papal legates. It is possible that Henry II was deliberately parading his son through England simply to proclaim his own supremacy and flaunt his wayward heir's new-found docility. But perhaps he was also trying to gauge his son's allegiance, wondering already whether the Young King's political and military career might be rejuvenated. Certainly, Henry II was not content to merely release his son into the tournament world, even in 1176.

The Young King did eventually grow restless under this close surveillance. By early 1176 he was suggesting that he and Marguerite might undertake the long pilgrimage to Santiago de Compostela in north-western Iberia. But Henry II judged this to be a ruse cooked up by 'evil hangers on' to buy Young Henry a measure of freedom, and vetoed the journey. After Easter, however, the Old King relented somewhat. His heir would be permitted to travel south, but only so that he might assist his brother Richard – now the well-established count of Poitou and duke of Aquitaine – in quelling another outbreak of provincial unrest. Thus, in the summer of 1176, William Marshal accompanied the Young King on his journey to Poitiers, returning to fight once again in the region that had witnessed Patrick of Salisbury's 'murder' and his own despairing captivity. Much of the focus in 1176 was on suppressing Angoulême, to the south of Poitou, but it was back in the city of Poitiers itself that Young Henry's hostility to his father bubbled to the surface once more.

Once out of England, and free of Henry II's constant supervision, the Young King began to expand his household. Over time he drew a number of skilled clerics and administrators into his service, including a relative of the Salisbury and Marshal families, Gervase of Tilbury (who served as his personal chaplain), and the theologian Ralph Niger. At first, however, his primary focus was to recruit knights. The inner circle of his *mesnie*, like William Marshal and Robert Tresgoz, remained, as always, by his side. But Henry sought new warriors, and he took the defiant step of welcoming in French and Norman knights who were deemed 'enemies' of the Old King – presumably men who had been named traitors during the rebellion. Perhaps Henry was simply seeking to reassert his independence, but his father construed this as wilful insubordination.

The Young King must have imagined that he was safe in Poitiers, far from Henry II's gaze, but he was mistaken. In August, a scandalous discovery was made. A member of Young Henry's own household, his chancellor Adam, was caught attempting to send a message detailing his lord's questionable actions back to the Old King in England. Within the context of a medieval *mesnie* – the intimate fellowship in which iron-cast fidelity was expected – this was a grave act of treachery; one that incriminated both the spy Adam and his master Henry II. The Young King convened a summary court to try his chancellor – on which William Marshal likely sat – and a death sentence was passed. Only the bishop of Poitiers' imploring intervention saved Adam from the gibbet. Moved to mercy, Henry had the renegade stripped naked and whipped through the city streets, before packing him off to Normandy.

It was probably only from this point onwards, in the late summer of 1176, that Young Henry began increasingly to turn away from the dynastic struggles of the Angevin realm, sickened by his father's meddling. It would be almost three years before he set foot in England again. That December he held his own Christmas Court in Normandy with Queen Marguerite. By then she was pregnant with their first child, and perhaps this sparked new schemes and ambitions, but they were extinguished when the baby boy died at birth in the summer of 1177. Twice in that same year, the Young King reluctantly followed Henry II's orders to lead military forays into the region of Berry, east of Poitiers. But his heart was elsewhere. Together with William Marshal, he had turned to the tournament. For now, at least, both men would seek to make their mark on the world of chivalry.

5

TOURNAMENT CHAMPIONS

William Marshal was drawn into the world of the tournament from late 1176 onwards and, for the next three years, both he and Henry the Young King became increasingly obsessed by these knightly contests. With his political ambitions stymied, the tournament offered Henry a new arena in which to earn the respect of his peers, to achieve a degree of renown, even celebrity, which might somehow offset the rankling sense of dissatisfaction that still gnawed at this king without a kingdom. For William and his fellow household knights, meanwhile, these chivalric games offered a chance to redeem some of the frustrations of the last five years – time spent in the loyal service of a lord and king, loved and honoured, yet ultimately incapable of advancing their careers. Triumph in these contests would serve not only to affirm their prowess after the defeats endured during the rebellion; it could also bring them rich material rewards. It is little wonder that Henry and his knights were soon in the thrall of the tournament.

This period of intense dedication to the tournament circuit had a transformative effect on William Marshal's career. Up to this point, he had shown himself to be a competent knight and loyal retainer, moving through a series of military households and coming to the notice of the Angevin dynasty. In spite of the glory that the *History of William Marshal* was already prepared to associate with his name, in real terms William remained relatively little known or recognised outside select social circles, such as the Young King's entourage. Marshal's tournament successes wrought a dramatic change, bringing him international renown and considerable wealth, and cementing his already close connection with Young Henry. William became the pre-eminent figure within the Young King's *mesnie* and, for the first time, truly began to stand out within a much larger peer group of knights, drawn from across Western Europe. Now around thirty years of age – a hardened warrior in peak physical condition – he proved able to prosper in these chivalric contests when others enjoyed only mixed fortunes, or in the worst cases, faced financial ruin, suffered injury or even death.

This was not simply luck, though there must have been an element of good fortune, because William succeeded across such a large number of events, spread over more than five years. He evidently turned tourneying into an art, almost an industry. Indeed, as an old man, William would claim that he captured no less than 500 knights during his tournament career. So what made him a winner, and what do his achievements in this hugely competitive environment reveal about his qualities and nature as a man? The answers lie within the *History of William Marshal*, but as always, the text has to be read with care.

The biographer dedicated a large portion of his work to this phase of William's life, giving over some 2,300 lines of the *History* to describing his tournament exploits, when just thirty-six had been expended on the six years Marshal spent training at Tancarville. This probably reflected William's own enthusiasm for his glory days as a tournament champion. This period seems to have been etched into his memory as one of the happiest phases of his life: a time of few responsibilities, but many victories, and a source of countless stirring tales. Needless to say, the *History* often presented William as the all-conquering hero of these contests, but a nuanced picture of Marshal's progress through the tournament world can be reconstructed. It reveals a knight who was skilled in feats of arms and horsemanship, but also resolutely acquisitive, devious, proud and even preening.

LEARNING TO WIN

Victory on the tournament circuit did not come early or easily. Historians have generally assumed that the Young King burst on to the tournament scene in the mid-1170s, with William Marshal at his side, and immediately achieved widespread success. But this impression largely derived from the idea that Marshal had already mastered these contests and somehow remained a revered champion. In fact, William's earlier tournament career was probably quite short-lived (perhaps ending nine years earlier, in 1167) and his track record was solid, but not necessarily spectacular. Marshal likely understood the game and its rules better than anyone else in Henry's household. But he was no tournament superstar, not yet at least.

Far from being an instant sensation, the Young King's retinue were more of a comedy sideshow at first. Indeed, the *History of William Marshal* admitted that for eighteen months, Henry's knights 'never came to a single tournament site without being humiliated and ill-used', and his warriors were routinely 'captured and ill-treated'. French knights apparently became so accustomed to battering the Young King's team that they started agreeing the divisions of ransoms and booty among themselves on the eve of each tournament. Henry's men had a stirring battle-cry, using the traditional Norman shout of '*Dex aïe*' ('God our help'), their horses, arms and armour were all impressive enough and, given that he could draw on the Old King's bankroll, the team contained the 'pick of fighting men', all used to 'high exploits'. The real problem was discipline and, at first, William Marshal appears to have been an arch offender. His biographer conceded that, at an early event, 'Marshal left the king and spurred his horse in the direction of another company', and thereafter happily

'launched himself into the fray'. This was all well and good in terms
of displaying individual prowess – William duly sent many a foe 'on
their way with his mighty blows' that day – but he had also abandoned
his lord, Henry, and the Young King rightly chided him for it on his
return.

Over time the team improved. Marshal learnt to curb his head-
strong enthusiasm, and the *History* subsequently made constant
reference to the fact that he always remained 'close by the king', protecting him with blows that were 'exceedingly mighty and dangerous'.
Henry's knights gradually honed their skills and, with more experience,
they began working together as a compact and coherent body of horsemen – recognising, as the biographer bluntly put it, that 'a man who
breaks ranks too early is a fool'. The Young King and his household
were also mentored by Henry's old ally, Philip of Flanders, by now an
established patron of the tournament circuit and an acclaimed participant to boot. Philip was something of a scoundrel: ruthless,
unprincipled and unswervingly ambitious. He had hitched his wagon
to the Young King's cause when he saw advantage, but he was an unre-
liable ally. The *History of William Marshal* did its best to paint him in
a heroic light, as a 'worthy man, who in wisdom surpassed' all contemporaries, but remarkably it was also quite candid and accepting of
his devious conduct on the tournament field.

Count Philip's tournament tactics mirrored his approach to real life.
He bent the rules, employed wily, even underhanded, methods, and
pursued victory and gain with singular focus. His preferred technique
in knightly contests was to arrive with his retinue at the lists (or assembly points), but publicly declare his intention merely to spectate rather
than participate. Only after the grand charge and first phase of the
mêlée had left his opponents 'weary, disarrayed and disorganised',
would Philip spur his warriors into action, suddenly entering the
tournament after all. Using this trick, the count's retinue was able to
cut a swathe through the field, leaving scores of knights 'knocked to the
ground ... injured [and ultimately] captured'. This ruse echoed the
use of a reserve troop in real battle – the highly effective tactic of

holding a portion of one's force back from the fray until the fighting reached its peak, and then timing its deployment so as to strike a decisive blow. In the context of a tournament such duplicity might today seem like blatant cheating, but Philip's peers appear to have accepted his ploy as a canny manipulation of the rules. The *History* lauded him as 'wise and brave', and what is more, it went on to reveal that William Marshal himself embraced this tactic.

Acting as Young Henry's tournament captain and strategist, Marshal advised the retinue to imitate Philip of Flanders' methods. At the next event, they arrived 'giving no indication that [they were] going to tourney that day or carry arms into the fray', and then abruptly launched a blistering attack 'when the other side were unable to defend themselves'. It proved to be an overwhelming success. The muddy field was left strewn with enemy banners and flags, and for once, 'the King's men made great gains'. William's biographer gleefully declared: 'After that the King never came to a [tournament] without availing himself of this sort of trick or deception.' Much as the *History* might chastise loathsome *losengiers* (deceivers) in the real world, here it seems that a degree of dishonesty was fair game.

THE DAYS OF GLORY

By the end of 1177, the Young King's retinue – with William Marshal at its heart – was enjoying ever more success on the tournament circuit. Victories began to mount, and ransoms and spoils started to flood into the household's coffers. Henry, Marshal and the retinue as a whole were now seen in a different light. No longer easy victims, they were garnering a reputation as accomplished, steely-eyed practitioners of the art, and fast becoming one of the most feared and respected teams in northern France.

William and Henry had now known each other for seven years; the boy-king had grown up to become a tall, stunningly handsome twenty-three-year-old. These two men had fought and lost a war together, and the bond forged between them in 1170 had only strengthened. They were not (and could not be) equals, given Henry's rarefied royal blood, but they were firm friends; and these years fighting side by side on the tournament field seem to have been the happiest that they shared. Of course, the *History* would be expected to emphasise Marshal's especially esteemed position within Young Henry's *mesnie*, so we might wonder whether the suggestion that 'the king loved [William] dearly, more than any other knight he knew in any land', should be taken at face value. But other external sources confirm Marshal's pre-eminent status – most importantly, Henry's surviving *acta* (issued documents), in which William consistently appeared in pride of place, as the first witness drawn from the military household.

The *History* painted a vivid picture of the exuberant joy shared by William and the Young King at their daring exploits, evoking an unmistakeable sense of unfettered bravura and camaraderie. This was never clearer than at a 'grand and excellent' tournament held on the Norman-French border between Anet and Sorel. Henry's retinue performed well in the early stages of this event, timing their charge to perfection so that they 'drove right through' the French ranks. With their opponents in full flight, most of the Young King's household set off in pursuit, but Marshal remained at his lord's side. Together they 'rode downhill until they came out clean in the middle of the main avenue in Anet'. The town seemed deserted until they turned a corner and were suddenly confronted by the sight of the mounted French warrior, Simon of Neauphle, blocking the way ahead with a well-armed party of infantrymen. The *History* related that: 'The King said, "We shall not get through, and yet there is no question of going back." The Marshal replied, word for word: "So help me God, there's nothing for it but to charge them."'

Hammering headlong down the street, the throng of foot soldiers scattered before them, all desperately trying to avoid being trampled to death. A way through opened up, but William was not content merely to make a getaway. He rode in towards Simon of Neauphle, deftly snatched his horse's bridle and, holding on with all his might, began dragging his opponent along behind him, as Henry followed. This was one of Marshal's favourite techniques – it had earned him plenty of captures back in the 1160s – and he now rode off to the lists, with Simon in tow, intent on declaring the French knight his prisoner. Simon had other ideas. As they raced through the town, with William 'paying no attention to what was going on behind', the French knight leapt out of his saddle to grab an overhanging gutter, and was thereby plucked from his mount. Marshal remained oblivious, but the Young King witnessed this spectacular feat, yet said nothing.

When they reached the lists and William instructed his squire to 'Take this knight into custody', Henry cheerily enquired in reply: 'What knight?' and then revealed Simon's 'splendid trick'. The *History* presented this as a comical moment: Marshal 'burst out laughing' as both men savoured the joke, and the tale was heartily retold for weeks to come. The episode has the feel of a favoured, and perhaps embroidered, anecdote, but the kernel of truth – William's intimate friendship with Young Henry – seems authentic.

A 'hero' rises

The *History* recorded many of William's own individual, and equally colourful, exploits, as he gradually mastered the tournament circuit. By the late 1170s Marshal began to attend events on his own as a way of gaining experience, reputation and reward. The first of these 'freelance' ventures seems to have been a tournament held at Pleurs, in the Champagne region, east of Paris. The biographer maintained that, because this was judged to be too far for the Young King to travel with his 'heavy baggage' train, Henry gave 'his bosom friend' William leave to go with only one other knight in his company. In reality Marshal may well have had to pester his lord for permission to depart, and he does not seem to have borne Young Henry's colours or device at this event, because his biographer indicated that, once the contest had begun, 'many looked at him hard [but] had no idea who he was'.

The tournament at Pleurs attracted some of France's most illustrious barons and knights: Philip of Flanders was present, as were Duke Hugh of Burgundy and Count Theobald of Blois. Two of Europe's finest warriors – James of Avesnes and William des Barres – also attended. These two men were Marshal's direct peers in the 1170s, knights who garnered widespread renown for their skill-at-arms. William revelled in the day, fighting 'like a lion amongst oxen', and according to the *History*, as he clove a path through his opponents, 'he struck and hammered like a woodcutter on oak trees'. In reality, though Marshal evidently relished the fracas and more than held his own, the lack of protection from a disciplined retinue left him exposed. Targeted by numerous attacks, he received such a pummelling from sword and mace blows that his helmet was crushed down 'to his scalp'. All in all, Marshal seems to have regarded it as a splendid day, with many knights displaying noteworthy prowess. William had impressed his peers and begun, in the words of his biographer, 'to establish his reputation', but his actual winnings may have been fairly modest.

The fighting at Pleurs gradually petered out by mid-afternoon, but the main field retained a chaotic, fairground atmosphere, as knights and their stewards milled around, sharing stories, securing ransoms and hunting down lost equipment. A lengthy, chivalrous debate ensued about who should receive the ceremonial award gifted to the day's worthiest knight. To affirm their courtly modesty many declined, Philip of Flanders included, and it was eventually decided that William Marshal should be given the award. The only problem was that he was nowhere to be seen. Two knights and a squire eventually tracked him down to a local forge. There they found Marshal on his knees, his head lain upon an anvil, as a blacksmith struggled to pry his 'smashed and battered' helmet off with an assortment of 'hammers, wrenches and pincers'. It all made for a laughable scene – one that William evidently remembered with great affection. He was duly presented with his prize and, though he too humbly declared himself undeserving of the award, he accepted it nonetheless.

In the months that followed, William's tournament career flourished. At an event held at Eu, on Normandy's eastern frontier with Picardy, he captured ten knights and twelve horses in a single day, and the *History* reported that 'the tide of his valour and reputation now began to rise, lifting him to high eminence'. Marshal's fortunes depended in part on the quality of the warriors surrounding him in the Young King's *mesnie*: knights hand-picked and recruited through William's contacts, and paid for out of Henry's allowance. But William also possessed innate qualities and acquired skills that set him apart. Marshal's raw physicality allowed him to absorb battering blows that might fell others, while his strength lent jarring force to the attacks he delivered with either lance or sword. Few could match the assured agility of his horsemanship and a canny, guileful strategic awareness meant that he was able to outthink opponents.

As a flurry of successes followed, William was soon fêted as a champion – revered within the enclosed, hothouse atmosphere of the tourney circuit – and courted by the great and the good. The *History* recounted how, on the eve of a great contest at Épernon in the province of Blois, Marshal was welcomed as a guest by the local magnate, Count Theobald. The custom was for 'high-ranking men' to visit one another's lodgings through the evening, sharing stories, gossip and wine. By this time, Marshal's standing was such that even the most powerful men in France were happy to be seen in his company. On this particular night, however, things almost went awry.

William had ridden into Épernon on 'a tall and valuable horse', which he left in the care of a young local lad. But, just as he was basking in the attention of Count Theobald's gawking guests, a violent commotion was heard in the street outside. Marshal leapt to his feet and, 'without taking his leave', sprinted outside to discover a thief riding off on his precious steed. The scoundrel must have thought that he would easily make good his escape under the cover of darkness, mounted as he was; but he had not counted on William's determined pursuit. Racing down the street, Marshal tracked the clatter of the horse's hooves. Even when the thief darted down an alley and hid behind a cart full of branches, William managed to catch the faint sound of the beast stamping its feet. Closing in, he grabbed a piece of wood from the cart and battered the thief so hard that one of his eyes popped out. The horse was recovered, and though the Count of Blois called for a hanging, Marshal supposedly showed mercy, arguing that, with his head half caved in, the wretch had 'suffered enough'.

Victory on an industrial scale

In spite of his biographer's continued emphasis upon William's upstanding behaviour and the honour he accrued in knightly contests, there can be no doubt that for warriors like Marshal the attraction of tournaments was not simply related to abstract notions of chivalry. Reputation mattered enormously to be sure, but the great beauty of the tourney, as far as Marshal and his peers were concerned, was that it allowed knights to earn renown and, at the same time, amass booty, ransoms and wealth. The author of the *History of William Marshal* had a fascinating attitude to this question of material gain. On the one hand, he insisted that his hero gave no thought to riches, stating that: 'Not for a moment did [William] have gain in mind, [and] he was so focused on noble exploits that he had no concern for making profit.' But at the same time, he could not bring himself to wholly conceal the fabulous wealth Marshal now accumulated, because these material assets were such an essential component of William's meteoric progress.

The biographer may have struggled with these issues, but Marshal himself apparently saw no shred of incompatibility between chivalry and materialism. In his world, these two fundamental concerns were inseparable. The mechanics of the medieval tournament meant that the taking of prisoners and plunder served both as the visible affirmation of prowess and the source of practical gain. Indeed, as William won more and more victories, he began to treat the tournament circuit almost like a business. In the late 1170s he struck a deal with Roger of Jouy, a Flemish knight who had been recruited into the Young King's household.

William's biographer did not really approve of Roger, characterising him as 'a brave and doughty man, renowned for feats of arms,
venturesome and clever, but inclined to be greedy', but Marshal seems
to have been more interested in Roger's well-known ability to win copious amounts of loot. The two men forged a formal agreement to fight
side by side in tournaments so as to make 'greater gains', and then split
their winnings evenly. They even employed one of the Young King's
household servants – his kitchen clerk, Wigain – on the side, to keep
a tally of their victories. Years later, William's biographer saw one of
these account sheets covering the period between Lent and
Whitsuntide (which probably equated to no more than two months of
tourneying at most), and seemed both appalled and impressed to discover that in that time, Marshal and Roger took an extraordinary 103
knights prisoner. The 'companions' worked together for two years and
must have made a fortune.*

Even with this flood of money coming in, William shepherded his
assets with meticulous, almost miserly assiduity. During a second tournament between Anet and Sorel, two horses were snatched from him
when he was caught momentarily on foot and thus unable to mount
a defence. It was an opportunistic capture, but hardly criminal. That
evening, Marshal haggled mercilessly for hours to secure the horses'
release and later gloated that he had cannily managed to buy back one

---

*While the *History* seems to have been mildly troubled by this profiteering, outside
the immediate context of tournaments, Marshal's biographer often took a more positive attitude to material gain. Perhaps the most striking example of this came in an
incident drawn from the early 1180s, when William was journeying through northern
France. He encountered a furtive couple on the road and intervened to ensure that
the young woman was not being forced to travel under duress. It transpired that the
pair were eloping lovers – a noble-born maiden and a runaway monk – hoping to start
a new life together far from home. When the monk made the mistake of revealing a
moneybag packed with £48 (funds with which the couple were hoping to finance their
future), Marshal promptly confiscated the cash and sent them packing to a life of
penury. The biographer clearly expected his medieval audience to applaud this behaviour – to view the lovers as transgressive social outcasts, subject to summary justice.
Indeed, he even commended William's unusual generosity in not stripping the pair
of their clothes and horses.

of the mounts for only £7, even though it was actually worth £40. In the course of this episode, William also made calculated use of his reputation to browbeat one of the 'cowardly' knights involved, Peter of Leschans, forcing him to admit his supposed thievery in front of his uncle, the distinguished knight William des Barres. Marshal's status meant that his word could not be challenged, even by des Barres (who did his best to smooth over the embarrassing affair). In the opinion of his biographer, William was merely putting the upstart youngster in his place, but it is hard to avoid the conclusion that Marshal was actually exploiting his position in a rather unscrupulous manner.

Through this critical stage of his career, thriving on the tournament field, William's character edges a little further into the light. He comes across as a man imbued with rare physical prowess and clear fortitude; one who understood, and carefully adhered to, the knightly code of honour prevalent in his day. Some of his actions might sit uncomfortably alongside modern conceptions of 'chivalry' – from the use of crafty battlefield tactics, to the instances of prideful self-promotion and ceaseless materialism – but there can be little doubt that Marshal's contemporaries lauded him as a paragon of chivalry. His conduct and achievements evidently exemplified the behaviour expected of a *chevalier*.

The father of chivalry

The Young King Henry also emerged as a celebrated luminary of the tournament world in the late 1170s. But unlike his friend and retainer William Marshal, Henry's fame did not derive primarily from his own skill-at-arms, nor was his worth measured in ransoms and spoils. The Young King fought at the heart of his retinue, of course – though it was naturally expected that his household would shield him from the fray – and the reflected glory of his warriors' achievements on the tourney field did augment his own reputation. But above and beyond all this, Henry was hailed for his largesse and patronage.

Contemporaries compared the Young King to Alexander and Arthur, the great heroes of old, and hailed him as a 'father of chivalry'. They did so because after 1177 Henry assembled one of the most impressive military households in all of Europe, packed with warriors drawn from across the Angevin realm and beyond. The visible proof of Henry's eminence was the quantity and quality of the knights in his *mesnie*. The author of the *History of William Marshal* lauded the Young King's determination to always keep 'worthy followers in his service', because his seemingly inexhaustible generosity set a new standard in northern Europe. The likes of Philip of Flanders followed Henry's example because 'they saw very well that neither king nor count could raise his standing except through the worthy men he had with him'.

This was all well and good for the leading knights of the day, and it was their view – or, more particularly, William Marshal's view – of the tournament circuit that the *History* reflected. These warriors had everything to gain from Young Henry's bounteous munificence. He gave them all the 'horses, arms and money' they wanted – and, better still, 'he did not haggle' – and they worshipped him in return. But elsewhere, this massive inflation in the market for knights had consequences. Men such as Philip of Flanders and Hugh of Burgundy must have inwardly groaned at the Young King's unfettered generosity, because it meant that they, and other rival patrons, had to pay through the nose to recruit the best warriors. Eventually, the massive expenditure also put Henry's own finances under pressure. More than ever before, his retinue left a trail of debt to armourers, farriers and innkeepers as they criss-crossed northern France. By 1178, the Young King was dangerously addicted to the pageantry of the tournament circuit. He 'journeyed through many a land to win fame and glory', according to the *History*, 'for he could never have enough of risking and giving generously', and was 'incapable of refusing anything to any man'.

Nonetheless, the grandiose display of largesse, honour and status worked its magic. As the 1170s drew to a close, the Young King ascended to the very pinnacle of the tournament scene. For the knights and nobles of northern France, increasingly obsessed with the ideals of chivalry, Henry became almost a cult figure. He was the talk of every tourney and contest, the focus of awestruck rumour and feverish gossip – the golden celebrity of his day. In the words of the *History*, 'every man would have liked to be like him'. This iconic standing was felt in England too, where a chronicler portrayed Henry as an inspiration to both his class and his generation, calling him 'the glory of all knighthood' and the 'flower and mirror of youth and generosity'.

The Young King's fervent dedication to the world of chivalry and tournament might seem like the frivolous excesses of an indulgent playboy. Yet that was not the full picture. Tourneys were mere games of prowess, but they were played by many of the most powerful men in the West – barons and magnates driven by a deepening fixation with chivalric culture. By the late 1170s, it was clear that displays of military might and knightly eminence had an impact that stretched beyond the confines of the tournament field. This lent Young Henry's stardom an edge, because as the famed 'father of chivalry', he inevitably came to enjoy a measure of influence in the real world. As a teenager he had sought power through rebellion; now he had made his name, and affirmed his regal status, in a different arena.

These achievements could not be ignored by Henry's father, the Old King. Historians have often suggested that Henry II viewed his son's lavish tournament career as merely 'wasteful and trivial'. But by 1179 his attitude was unquestionably more positive. This was apparent to Ralph of Diss, the well-connected dean of St Paul's Cathedral in London, who offered this balanced estimation of the Young King's activities:

[Henry] passed three years in tournaments, spending lots of money. While he was rushing all over France, he put aside the royal majesty and was transformed from a king into a knight, carrying off victory in various meetings. His popularity made him famous; the Old King grew happier counting up and admiring his victories [and later restored] his possessions that he had taken away.

Henry II may not have tolerated tournaments in England, but he could hardly ignore the near-fanatical popularity of these contests across the rest of Europe. The Old King's Capetian rival, the ageing Louis VII of France, had made little or no effort to represent himself as a patron of chivalry. That left a significant gap, within which the Young King might usefully operate, wielding influence and forging a network of connections to advance Angevin interests. In all likelihood this had been apparent from an early stage, and the Young King's relationship with the likes of Philip of Flanders (his former ally) probably had a political subtext from the start. When the 'high-ranking men' visited one another on the eve of tournaments, not all their talk can have been of sport and prowess. Certainly, by 1179 at the latest, Henry II was intent upon harnessing his eldest son's celebrity. In mid-Lent that year, the Young King returned to England for the first time since 1176, and later attended his father's Easter Court at Winchester. Young Henry was back in the fold.

THE GRANDEST TOURNAMENT

By the summer of 1179 it seemed that the Young King's career had been rejuvenated: the defeats and disappointments of his rebellion were now in the past, the irksome sense of paternal containment and manipulation largely erased. Young Henry's tournament career might have been bankrolled by his father's generous allowance, but the mark he had made on the world was his own. Now twenty-four-years old, he was the doyen of Europe's knightly aristocracy. Henry's star had risen alongside that of his friend and leading household warrior, William Marshal. In the decade since he entered Angevin service, Marshal had climbed the ladder to an entirely new level. Such was his fame and wealth that William began to attract a retinue of his own, becoming in the terms of the day a 'knight banneret' – a warrior in service to a lord, yet permitted to carry his own banner. Now in his early thirties, Marshal proudly bore his new colours and device: a red lion rampant, against a halved green and gold background. These arms, echoing the lions of the Norman banner, would remain with William for the rest of his career. Both he and the Young King were in the prime of life, and the events of late 1179 would give them the perfect opportunity to display their quality.

King Louis VII of France was now around fifty-nine-years old, and his grip over the Capetian realm was faltering. A third marriage had finally produced the long-awaited male heir his dynasty needed and, by 1179, this boy, Philip, was fourteen and plans were in hand for his imminent coronation. But that summer the young French prince endured something of an ordeal. During a boar-hunt in the wild forests near Chartres, Philip became separated from his companions and was soon hopelessly lost. By day's end, he was still wandering aimlessly – alone, afraid and exposed to the elements. Luckily Philip spotted the faint glow of a woodsman's campfire and the peasant kindly led him to safety. But the prince fell gravely ill thereafter and his survival was soon in doubt.

Fearful for the future of his Capetian royal line, Louis VII took the extraordinary step of making a pilgrimage to the shrine of Thomas Becket in Canterbury, hoping that his pious appeals for saintly intercession might save young Philip's life. The king was by now a rather elderly and frail man himself. He managed the long journey, crossing the Channel in late August to be greeted on the Dover sands by Henry II himself, and escorted to Canterbury. Given their longstanding rivalry, contemporaries were astounded by this unprecedented, peaceful visit. After three days, Louis returned home. The Angevin King Henry had endowed the shrine with lamps after his public flogging in 1174; the Capetian monarch now promised Canterbury's monks an annual supply of 100 barrels of fine French wine with which to slake their thirst. Louis' prayers seemed to have been answered when Philip made a full recovery, but the trip left the king shattered, and soon after his arrival back in Paris he suffered a massive stroke. Paralysed down one side of his body and barely able to speak, the Capetian monarch was forced to withdraw from public life, remaining an invalid until his death in September 1180.

To secure the succession, it was now imperative that Philip be crowned and anointed while Louis VII yet lived, so a grand ceremony was scheduled for 1 November 1179 in the royal city of Rheims. This would be the greatest assembly of the decade, with representatives of

all of Western Europe's leading dynasties and noble houses in attendance, and to top it all, a massive tournament was also organised to
celebrate Philip's investiture. That autumn the close correlation
between practical power and chivalric spectacle was laid bare. With
the creation of a new French king, the chessboard of politics was about
to be reordered, and naturally, all the key players were angling for
influence and advantage. Leading figures such as Philip, count of
Flanders, and Duke Hugh of Burgundy would attend the coronation,
eager to establish themselves as the young Capetian monarch's preferred mentor.

At this critical juncture, King Henry II looked to his eldest son to
represent the Angevin house. With the Old King's sponsorship, Young
Henry would travel to Rheims and the coronation tournament in the
most magnificently regal style imaginable. Standing beside William
Marshal, his illustrious champion, the beautiful Young King would
astonish the world with his chivalry and, it was hoped, gain an
unbreakable hold over his brother-in-law Philip of France. This was
not the first time that Henry II had spent a fortune to create the aura
of opulent majesty. Twenty-one years earlier, when the Old King still
enjoyed the trusted service of Thomas Becket, he had sent his then
chancellor to negotiate Young Henry's marriage to the infant
Marguerite of France. The low-born son of a Cheapside textile merchant, Becket was determined to appear every inch the noble diplomat
during this critical embassy to Paris in 1158, so he demanded the most
extraordinary entourage. Onlookers were left agog at the sight of the
passing procession, with Thomas accompanied by 200 knights, a small
army of infantrymen, clerks and stewards, eight wagons (two of which
were packed with barrels of the finest beer) each drawn by five massive horses, and twelve packhorses bearing Becket's own luxurious
possessions, each of which had a small monkey riding upon its back.

The Young King travelled in similar majesty in 1179, but this was
not – as some historians have suggested – simply extravagant frivolity;
this was chivalric display with a political purpose, enacted at Henry II's
urging and paid for out of his pocket. The Norman chronicler Robert

of Torigni, writing at this time, noted that the Young King travelled to the coronation bearing 'gifts of gold and silver' and in the company of 'a large knightly retinue', but specified that 'by his father's orders, [Henry] had brought with him such provisions for the journey, that he accepted free quarters from no one, either on the road or during the festivities'.

The *History of William Marshal* provided further details of the Young King's entourage that autumn. He was accompanied by a select band of eighty leading knights, but no less than fifteen of these warriors, including William Marshal, were 'knights-banneret' and therefore trailed by around ten household warriors of their own. Young Henry paid each of these additional knights twenty shillings a day for the full duration of the journey. Even excluding all the other associated expenses, the cost of paying this war-band has been estimated at over £200 per day, and the group seems to have been maintained, at least, for the best part of a month. Bearing in mind that, at this time, the royal income from the entire county of Worcester was £200 per year, it is obvious that the Young King's magnificence came with a crippling price tag. As the *History* ruefully observed, 'it was a source of wonder where this wealth was to be found'.

Yet costly as it was, the splendour marked the Young King out as the guest of honour at Philip II of France's coronation. The count of Flanders was also present, and he was privileged with the task of carrying the ceremonial royal sword as young Philip processed into Rheims Cathedral. But it was Henry who took pride of place. He moved through the crowds, talking 'with all the nobles present', and claimed the supposed prerogative of Norman dukes by bearing the royal crown as William, archbishop of Rheims (Philip II's uncle), performed the coronation. Henry's close connection to the new French king was clear for all to see.

After a round of feasting, the grandiose celebrations moved to a large area of open terrain east of Paris, at Lagny-sur-Marne – a setting which today, rather incongruously, hosts the site of Disneyland Paris. The tournament held at Lagny in November 1179 was on a scale 'never seen before or since' according to the *History*. No less than 3,000 knights attended – more than enough to wage a crusade in the Holy Land. Such was the throng that 'the entire field of combat was swarming with [warriors]' and 'not an inch of ground was to be seen'. William Marshal was one of the most renowned participants, and he may well have been given a special commemorative parchment listing all of the leading knights present, because his biographer appears to have used such a document when drafting his account. The *History* thus recorded a long and detailed roll call of all those from France, Flanders, England, Normandy and Anjou.

Almost every knight received a short epithet, so the biographer described the great William des Barres as a 'wise and valorous knight', while noting that the Norman warrior John of Préaux 'was as good as gold when it came to taking blows'. In fact, John was just one of five Préaux brothers who appear to have served in the Young King's *mesnie*. Not surprisingly, many of Young Henry's household knights received special mention. Like Marshal, the Flemish warrior Baldwin of Béthune was a knight-banneret. He had recently entered Henry's retinue and soon became one of William's closest confidants. Simon Marsh was styled as 'a courageous, valiant and indomitable knight', Gerard Talbot, as a man 'truly fit to be king' and Robert of Tresgoz as a 'valiant knight and a witty man' while the newer arrival, Thomas of Coulonces, was said to be exceedingly worthy. These were the men who were William Marshal's everyday associates – his friends, compatriots and sometime rivals.*

The tournament at Lagny was remarkable for its size and splendour, but not necessarily for its sport. Indeed, as a martial contest it may even have been somewhat disappointing. With such a horde of knights packed on to the field, the mêlée was extraordinarily chaotic. Some of the knights unhorsed were trampled and injured. Amid the

---

* An English knight named 'Ansel the Marshal' also appeared in this long list. This may have been William Marshal's younger brother. The *History* described him as 'a noble, amiable man, brave and loyal', but made no mention of his lineage.

swirling fray, the Young King briefly became isolated from many of his knights and William Marshal had to intervene, wrestling Henry's horse free from a group of opponents. In the resulting scuffle, the Young King's helmet was 'torn from his head', which was 'a source of great annoyance', but otherwise the event passed without major incident. More than ever, the point of this tourney was to be seen at the head of – or within – a resplendent household; and to have been part of a unique spectacle, awash with the colour of hundreds of unfurled banners, and resounding to the thunderous din of 3,000 charging, battling knights.

Lagny marked the apogee of William Marshal's tournament career and the Young King's dedication to the cult of chivalry. Both men had been elevated to positions of prominence in these years of glory. With his fortunes resuscitated, Henry was once again ready to assume his royal mantle and claim the realm he had been promised. In that pursuit he would turn to his friend and loyal retainer, William, a man now starting to be regarded as one of Europe's greatest knights.

ENGINEERING A CRISIS

William Marshal's career, and that of his lord and friend Henry, the Young King, continued to blossom in the early 1180s. The animosity and suspicion that had once coloured Young Henry's relationship with his father thawed, and the pair actively cooperated to deepen Angevin influence within the Capetian court. Count Philip of Flanders began to distance himself from the Young King, seeking instead to take the new French monarch Philip II (or Philip Augustus) under his wing. In these early years of his reign, King Philip remained a timid, sickly teenager, prone to vacillate in his allegiances. At first he favoured the count of Flanders, and together they led a rather heartless assault against his mother, the French queen. Later, the pendulum swung in the Angevins' favour: a peace treaty with the new Capetian monarch was settled at Gisors in the Norman Vexin, and Young Henry found himself fighting a short-lived, but ferocious military offensive against both Philip of Flanders and the duke of Burgundy. William Marshal may well have participated in this campaign, but it was not recorded in the *History* and only briefly described in other sources. The Young King emerged victorious, and Henry II began to show signs of deepening respect for his eldest son.

Nonetheless, the question of Young Henry's status remained unresolved, and by the autumn of 1182 his patience was running thin. In a move calculated to alert the Old King to his wavering allegiance, Henry made a formal visit with his wife Marguerite to King Philip in Paris, and then issued a demand for the duchy of Normandy. The same problems that had underpinned the Young King's rebellion a decade earlier now resurfaced. In the words of one chronicler, Henry sought territory 'in which he and his wife might take up their abode', but also added that the Young King wished to own land 'from which he might pay his knights and servants for their services'. This suggests that, in spite of their tournament successes, William Marshal and the other members of Henry's *mesnie* may well have been pressurising their lord for further reward. As always, the Old King prevaricated, merely promising Henry a renewed allowance of 100 Angevin pounds per day (plus a rather measly ten for Queen Marguerite) and the service of an additional 100 knights.

What made this all the more galling was that the Young King's brothers, Richard and Geoffrey, were thriving. Both were now grown men, governing the territories of Aquitaine and Brittany in their own name. Richard, in particular, was garnering a formidable reputation. He would come to be known by the nickname 'Cœur de Lion' or the 'Lionheart' and later play a critical role in William Marshal's career. Deprived of his mother Queen Eleanor's influence and guidance since 1174, Richard had nonetheless held his own in the south. In physical terms he bore some resemblance to his elder sibling, though it was always Henry who possessed the easy good looks. A chronicler who knew Richard personally wrote of his 'tall, elegant build', adding that 'the colour of his hair was between red and gold [and] his limbs were supple and straight'. But in temperament, Richard differed from the Young King. He shared more of his father's mercurial energy, was at once cultured and learned yet readier to resort to violence, even casual brutality, and he showed little interest in the knightly pageantry of the tournament. Some of these qualities perhaps emerged in response to the incessant demands of pacifying Aquitaine, but Richard had proven himself to be up to the task. Through hard-nosed military campaigning, siege warfare and destructive raiding, he was busily thrashing his independent-minded subjects into submission, and finding the time to eye territory to the north in neighbouring Anjou, the county to which Young Henry held rights.

As the Young King's brothers grew in stature, an obvious, but troublesome question came more into focus: would the Angevin Empire endure beyond Henry II's death? Or would Brittany and Aquitaine become fully fledged, independent territories? This divisive issue served only to inflame Young Henry's nagging anxieties. For close to three decades, his father had stood as overlord of the realm, at the head of the Angevin world. When the Young King finally came into his inheritance, he naturally expected to enjoy this same, pre-eminent status. He was, after all, his father's eldest son and primary heir – an anointed king. Surely it was only right that he should stand above his younger brothers; be able to call on their allegiance and expect their subservience. Just as naturally, Duke Richard and Count Geoffrey held a rather different view of the future; one in which any formal sense of empire would die with the Old King, leaving them free to govern their domains – the lands which they sweated over and shed blood to hold – as autonomous lords. The wrangling over this thorny issue, and Young Henry's renewed focus on the issue of his position, would draw William Marshal back into the arena of high politics.

The path to a second rebellion

In Young Henry's eyes, the Old King remained frustratingly evasive on the subject of the empire, equivocating just as he did over the duchy of

Normandy. Henry II was now almost fifty – a man entering his twilight years – yet he showed no sign of loosening his grip on the levers of power. By the second half of 1182, the Young King had waited long enough. He wanted clear answers and definitive action. It is not known whether he sought the advice of leading retainers like Marshal and Robert Tresgoz, or formulated a plan of action on his own, but Henry certainly resolved to place his father in a position where choices could no longer be avoided or postponed. First, Young Henry declared that he was considering a crusade to the Holy Land. Crusading was viewed as an act of knightly virtue and Christian piety. It was customary for those planning such a campaign to make a ritualised crusading vow – a formal promise to God of their intent – and to 'take the cross' by sewing a simple cloth crucifix on their cloak or clothing as a visible symbol of their crusader status and an affirmation of their resolve. In the autumn of 1182, Young Henry announced his intention to take these two steps and thus make a formal commitment to crusade in the East.

In some respects, this decision was hardly surprising. Calls for aid from the embattled Latin Christian settlers in the Levant were becoming increasingly desperate. Henry also had a close family connection to the Christian rulers of the Holy Land: his great-grandfather, Fulk of Anjou, had become king of Jerusalem in 1131, establishing a bloodline that still held. Jerusalem was now ruled by Fulk's enfeebled grandson, King Baldwin IV – a tragic figure who had contracted leprosy as a child – while, by contrast, the Muslims of the Near East were uniting under the rule of Saladin, a fearsome Kurdish warlord. The future survival of the crusader states thus hung in the balance.

The Young King's crusading impulse also had clear precedent. King Henry II had himself frequently promised to lead a crusade to the East, though as yet those vows remained unredeemed. As a king struggling to govern the great Angevin realm, Henry constantly protested his inability to leave Europe, and instead sent money to help pay for Jerusalem's defence. Count Philip of Flanders had actually followed through on a crusading vow taken in 1175, travelling to the Levant in the summer of 1177 at the head of a sizeable military contingent and fighting in Syria. At one level then, Young Henry's suggestion that he too might answer the call to crusade made perfect sense. But his declaration also sent the Old King a clear message. Should his requests remain unanswered and the future of the Angevin Empire unresolved, the Young King might be forced to seek a different future in the Holy Land – perhaps even to pursue a claim to the Jerusalemite crown. That would leave Henry II's precious plans for the succession in ruins and shatter the finely tuned balance of power with Capetian France.

With his crusading project still under discussion, Henry the Young King eyed a more direct means to force Henry II's hand, one that would play out far closer to home. As the Old King refused to give him lands of his own or to confirm his pre-eminence, Young Henry might have to take power for himself and thereby prove that he stood above his brothers. Aquitaine seemed to be a likely target. The sprawling province remained prone to unrest, and much of its populace saw Richard as a brutish tyrant. Even English chroniclers admitted that he 'oppressed his subjects with unjustified demands and a regime of violence' and acknowledged that 'the great nobles of Aquitaine hated him because of his great cruelty'. Indeed, one shocked contemporary stated that Richard routinely 'carried off his subjects' wives, daughters and kinswomen by force and made them his concubines', later handing them on to his men to enjoy.

William Marshal had a well-established familiarity with this region dating back to 1168, but the Young King also knew the depth of the Aquitanians' antipathy from first-hand experience. The spring and summer of 1182 had seen Richard fighting yet another string of campaigns in Angoulême and, further south, in Périgord. Henry II had come to his son's aid and later summoned the Young King to join the war effort. Young Henry obliged, marching through Aquitaine with William Marshal and the rest of his military household, to arrive at the siege of Puy-St-Front in Périgord on 1 July. In the face of this overwhelming concentration of Angevin might, the locals reluctantly sued for peace.

However, the Young King also used this visit to establish links with a number of local nobles, surreptitiously forging a loose network of connections and alliances, testing the water. It was clear that many Aquitanians were eager to throw off the yoke of Richard's rule, and Young Henry could easily present himself as the man who might bring justice to the province, especially in aristocratic circles. After all, he was the grandiose hero of countless tournaments, a famed paragon of chivalry and the lord of renowned knights like William Marshal. It was perhaps with a view to cultivating this image of regal magnificence and honourable piety among a wider audience that Henry travelled to Limoges – the scene of his first open rift with the Old King in 1173 – to visit the revered Abbey of St Martial. There he received a joyous welcome from 'the monks, the clergy and the people' and then made a special gift to signal his devoted patronage: a majestic cloak, wrought of the finest materials, and richly embroidered with the legend *Rex Henricus* – King Henry.

In spite of the summer's campaigning, open resistance to Richard's authority resurfaced in the autumn of 1182. Young Henry sensed his opportunity. A number of Aquitanian nobles were already encouraging him to intervene and release them from oppression. If he answered their call, he could argue that he was pursuing a just cause, snatch the duchy from Richard and leave his father no option but to acknowledge his standing. The question was whether the Young King had the stomach to wage open war against his brother.

But then, just at the moment that Henry was weighing up these momentous choices – when he most needed the steadfast support and measured guidance of his trusted household knights – a dreadful rumour reached the Young King's ears. He had been cuckolded. One of his warriors was bedding Queen Marguerite, his wife. And most shockingly of all, the man accused of this heinous crime was none other than William Marshal.

6

THE QUESTION OF LOYALTY

William Marshal's betrayal remains shrouded in uncertainty and mystery. It was only recorded in his biography, the *History of William Marshal*, yet given that its author decided to include a record of these events, and to address the accusations, it seems certain that a grave rift did occur. According to the *History*, a faction within Young Henry's military household became jealous of William's preferred status: envying the renown he had gained, the wealth he had accrued and, perhaps above all, his constant proximity to the Young King.

Five conspirators supposedly decided to engineer Marshal's downfall, hatching a 'treacherous plot' to 'sow discord between [William] and his lord'. The biographer stated that he could only name two of the men responsible. They were Adam of Yquebeuf, a Norman knight who, like Marshal, had been a core member of Henry's *mesnie* since the early 1170s, but who had not enjoyed the same storied tournament career; and a newer arrival, Thomas of Coulonces. Both had fought at the great Lagny tournament in 1179. William's biographer refused to reveal the identity of the remaining three plotters because their relatives were still alive when the *History* was written in the 1220s, but he did later specify that one of them – perhaps even the ringleader – was the Young King's seneschal (the officer in charge of administering the

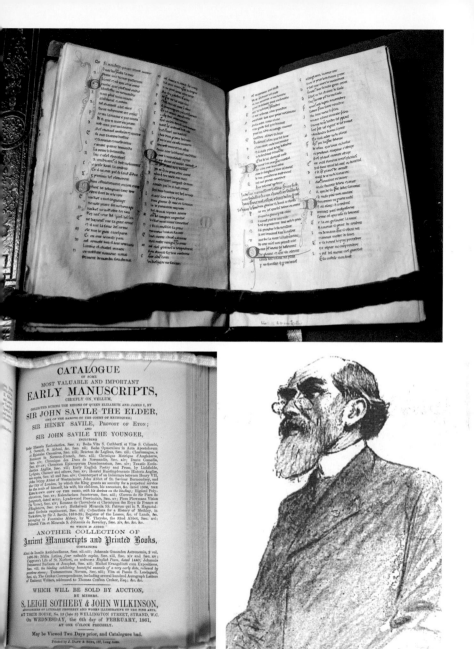

On Wednesday, 6 February 1861, a young French scholar named Paul Meyer (shown, in later life, above right) attended an auction of rare medieval manuscripts at Sotheby's in London (the cover of the original auction catalogue is shown above left). On that fateful day, Meyer stumbled upon the unknown thirteenth-century text that he would later dub the *History of William Marshal* (top), though it would be twenty years before he saw the manuscript again.

Born around 1147 in southern England, William Marshal passed some of his childhood years on the family estate at Hamstead Marshall, where the remains of a number of motte and bailey castles can still be seen (left, one of the possible sites of the 'Newbury' siege of 1152, when young William's life was threatened by King Stephen).

William was also related, through his mother, to the powerful Salisbury dynasty, who held a formidable fortified town in Wiltshire (Old Sarum, left). In around 1160, William was sent to train as a knight at Tancarville in Normandy (below, the remains of the château above the Seine, with the medieval tower visible on the far left).

The equipment used by knights in the mid-twelfth century was not so dissimilar from that employed by warriors at the Battle of Hastings in 1066 (shown above, in the detail from the Bayeux Tapestry). The three essential elements were a *destrier* (or warhorse), a one-handed, double-edged sword (the example shown right probably dates from the thirteenth century) and a mail hauberk (or coat of armour) fashioned from linked metal rings (below).

Once elevated to the status of a fully fledged knight, William gained some experience of warfare and the tournament circuit, before entering the military retinue of his uncle, Earl Patrick of Salisbury, and journeying to the southern French province of Aquitaine. There, he would have seen this masterpiece of Romanesque sculpture, the west facade of Notre-Dame La Grande in Poitiers.

In 1168, William Marshal entered the service of medieval Europe's most powerful dynasty – the Angevins – headed by King Henry II of England. At first, William was inducted into the knightly retinue of Henry's wife, Eleanor of Aquitaine. The manuscript image (left) is one of a number associated with the queen. By 1170 William had earned sufficient favour to be appointed as tutor-in-arms to Henry's and Eleanor's eldest son and heir, Young Henry (shown below at his coronation in 1170 and supposedly being served by his father at the subsequent banquet).

The mid-thirteenth century Morgan Picture Bible (above) sought to depict the chaotic brutality of war, though in reality much of the combat between knights during William Marshal's lifetime was neither as bloody, nor as lethal, as this image would suggest, because warriors were usually well protected by their armour.

Styles of armour, shields and helmets were all refined in this period. Note the use of mail covering the arms, hands and legs, and the mail coif with tied *ventail* (covering the lower face), seen in the kneeling knight (right). This figure, bearing the symbol of the cross on his surcoat and banner, kneels in supplication before departure on crusade – a reminder that knights were encouraged to offer service to the Church and to adhere to codes of conduct.

By the second half of the twelfth century the ideals of chivalry and courtesy were gaining currency, while new forms of so-called 'Romance' literature explored the lives of noble knights, often in the setting of Arthurian myth-history. These ideas and stories were also expressed in art, as seen in these two 'Romance' caskets, fashioned from ivory and carved bone, and probably used to hold aristocratic ladies' jewellery. The late-twelfth-century example (above) depicted scenes from the tale of Tristan (an idealised knight) and his lover Isolde, while the artistically more sophisticated casket from the fourteenth century (below) shows the 'Siege of the Castle of Love', with mounted warriors jousting and battle waged with flowers.

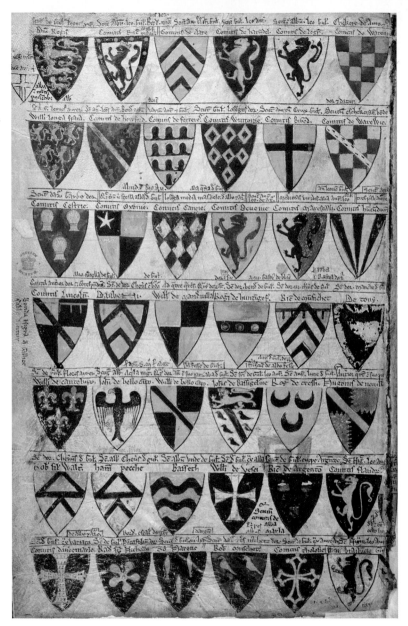

In the later twelfth century it became customary for leading nobles and knights to sport distinctive colour schemes and devices, emblazoned on banners and clothing, during tournaments, and the growing popularity of these 'coats of arms' gave rise to the notion of heraldry. By the late 1170s, William Marshal had adopted his own 'coat of arms' – a red lion rampant, against a halved green and gold background – depicted here in this mid-thirteenth-century Roll of Arms (third row, second from the right).

household), and this office was held by Peter FitzGuy in the 1170s, so this may be the third man.

The accusations levelled against Marshal took two forms. First, it was suggested that William was brazenly acting above his station, stealing the limelight and thereby usurping honour and renown due to the Young King. Not only had Marshal assembled his own military retinue, he was also said to have employed a herald, Henry 'li Norreis' ('the Northerner'), who would proudly strut through the lists before a tournament proclaiming the war-cry *'Dex aïe lei Marschal'* ('God for the Marshal') – a rather cheeky and ill-advised extension of Young Henry's own chant *'Dex aïe'*. The description of William's second supposed crime was more direct. It was said that he had been 'fornicating with the queen' (*'il le fait a la reïne'*), or more literally, that he had been 'doing it to the queen'.

The five conspirators apparently moved with great care once they decided to blacken Marshal's name. Deeming it too risky simply to go directly to the Young King, they slowly began spreading their rumours within the household, trying to insinuate, without themselves being caught in an open allegation. Peter of Préaux, one of the five Préaux brothers in the *mesnie*, heard these early whispers and immediately warned William 'to be very much on his guard', urging him to take pre-emptive action by speaking to Henry 'before the [Young King] should show him any hatred', but Marshal refused to do so. Eventually, Adam, Thomas and the other plotters found a proxy to do their dirty work – a young intimate of the king named Ralph Farci. Ralph was invited to a small gathering, plied with copious amounts of alcohol and, in the course of the evening, the tale of Marshal's crimes was retold. The seed had been sewn. That same night, while still drunk, Ralph took the rumour to Henry, and though the Young King refused at first to believe such scurrilous hearsay, when each of the five conspirators came forward to say that 'the matter was well known, heard of by people and actually seen', the story began to gain purchase.

Young Henry still seems to have harboured doubts. He reacted neither with blind rage, nor violence. Instead, he simply began to treat

William with cold detachment. In the rarefied atmosphere of a royal household, where public demonstrations of favour were critical to a retainer's status, this sudden change in disposition was damaging enough. As the *History* reported, 'the king was very upset and ill-disposed towards the Marshal', refusing to speak to him. It was soon obvious to all that William was no longer 'cherished by the king or in such a position of influence', and evident that instead, Henry 'hated him with all his heart'.

The case against William

Could William Marshal really have been guilty of these crimes? The accusations of prideful arrogance and vain display are more than plausible, though William's actual intent may not have been malicious. Marshal was not the only knight-banneret to serve in the Young King's entourage, but he was now one of the fêted celebrities of the tournament circuit, and he seems to have relished the renown and fame that victory brought. Having risen at an extraordinary pace from relatively humble origins, it was almost inevitable that, to some, he might seem a social upstart – a mere knight, trying to step out beyond Young Henry's shadow.

William lived in an aristocratic society fascinated by knightly culture and chivalric ideals. In this world, there was a natural tension between a lord or king and his knight. Each might display estimable virtues – the Young King was revered for his largesse; Marshal for his prowess. But which quality took precedence? If a knight was actually a better warrior than his lord, did that make him more worthy of praise? This question did not just apply to William and Young Henry. It was one of the simmering social dilemmas of the day, and would be repeatedly rehearsed and explored in the chivalric 'Romances' – the popular fiction of the late twelfth century. These epic stories of knightly endeavour and courtly intrigue, often set in the Arthurian world, evolved out of the earlier *chanson de geste* and were just then starting to grip the imaginations of noble courts across Europe. Not surprisingly, their fictionalised plots and characters often reflected their audience's real-life concerns, and one of the central dynamics of Arthur's relationship with Lancelot was the question of pre-eminence between a king and his leading knight. The accusation that William was somehow competing with his lord and comporting himself with unseemly grandeur was understandable given this obsession with the contest for renown. In fact, it is perhaps a testament to the strength of Henry and Marshal's friendship through the 1170s that this inherent tension had not caused an earlier rift.

What of Marshal's illicit affair with the queen? Is it conceivable that William could have carried out such an act of betrayal? The affair might have been driven by lust or love, with Marguerite perhaps irresistibly drawn to Marshal by his famed prowess. After all, in the world of courtly literature, the tension between characters like Arthur and Lancelot often culminated in adultery – with Guinevere choosing the great knight over her husband the king – and this plot was echoed in a number of Romance stories already circulating in that period. The power of sexual desire to shape human behaviour was well understood in this period. The medieval Church sought to promote the sanctity of celibacy, warning that sex out of wedlock was a deadly sin. Even within marriage, intercourse was proscribed: being permissible only in pursuit of procreation, not physical pleasure, and strictly forbidden on feast days or fast days – of which there were more than 200 per year.

But for all that, many of the men and women living in twelfth-century Europe had a surprisingly frank and natural approach to sex. Regular lovemaking was thought by some to be essential for the maintenance of good health, and sexual pleasure was also encouraged, especially for women, because it was widely believed that procreation could only occur when a woman experienced an orgasm. Bawdy entertainments were also popular. It was in William Marshal's lifetime that the humorous poems known as *fabliaux* came into vogue. They typically dealt with tales of sexual conquest or misadventure, made use of toe-curlingly explicit language and, by the 1180s, were all the rage in the aristocratic circles of northern France.

It is also the case that, in William's world, male adultery was commonplace – indeed, most noble-born men were expected, as a matter of course, to have mistresses, and some chroniclers actually expressed amazement at the very idea that a lord might stay faithful to his wife. King Henry II had a number of well-known mistresses, including 'Fair' Rosamund Clifford and the Welsh noblewoman Nest Bloet. It was also rumoured that Henry took King Philip II's half-sister Alice of France as a mistress, even though she had been betrothed to his son Richard. Nobles serving in the king's household were not expected to see their wives, instead official royal whores catered for their sexual needs.

Adultery initiated by a noble-born woman, however, was a different matter – a rare and scandalous occurrence. Nonetheless, it was not unheard of – Queen Eleanor herself had been accused of pursuing an incestuous affair with her uncle during the Second Crusade. The treatise on courtly manners authored by Daniel of Beccles towards the end of the twelfth century offers a glimpse of the mores of the day. Beccles was not at all surprised that noble ladies might be possessed by lust – like many contemporaries, he believed that women possessed an insatiable sexual appetite; he also thought it only natural that they would find well-endowed men irresistible. In light of this, he helpfully offered two pieces of advice to knights trying to fend off the sexual advances of their lord's wife: first, pretend to be ill; second, never, under any circumstances, tell your lord. Walter Map also related the rather salacious story of a queen who lusted after a handsome young knight at court named Galo. One of the warrior's friends tried to solve the problem by suggesting to the queen that Galo was actually a eunuch, but she promptly sent one of her ladies-in-waiting to seduce him with strict instructions to 'put her finger on the spot [and] bring back word of whether he was man or no'.

It is obvious that lust and adultery were real possibilities in the setting of an aristocratic household; even an illicit affair with a married woman of royal birth might not have been utterly unimaginable in this period. But no other shred of evidence suggests that William Marshal and Queen Marguerite were in any way familiar with one another, nor is there any hint that either of them had a reputation for licentious behaviour. The *History of William Marshal* maintained a discrete silence regarding the more raucous celebrations that must have followed many tournaments – what the historian David Crouch described as the '*après-tournoi*' entertainments. In fact, almost nothing is known of William's sexuality in the 1170s and 1180s – there are no traces of mistresses or illegitimate children. The same is true of Marguerite; beyond the one child she conceived with Henry in 1176, she remains a virtually invisible cipher. All of this makes the accusation of an adulterous affair hard to believe.

The muted nature of the Young King's reaction was perhaps even more telling. In similar circumstances, his one-time ally, Count Philip of Flanders, had responded with merciless fury. In the summer of 1175 Philip accused a knight named Walter of Fontaines of committing adultery with his wife, Isabel of Vermandois (Young Henry's cousin). Walter denied the charges and offered to prove his innocence, but he was never given the opportunity. Instead, supposedly driven by his 'fury', the count had Walter beaten with cudgels to within an inch of his life. A makeshift gallows was then erected above a foul-smelling latrine trench. Walter was stripped, bound and strung up by his feet, with his head left dangling into the cesspit until he died of suffocation.*

Henry the Young King's response in late 1182 seems remarkably mild by comparison. The shock of the accusations levelled against one of his closest friends and confidants – the man under whose watchful gaze he had grown up over the last thirteen years – must have been devastating. The *History* admitted that Henry's 'hatred for the Marshal was violent and bitter', and that as a result '[William] withdrew from

---

* Walter's summary execution caused local outrage, and the scandal may have had some connection with Philip's decision to take the cross for a crusade in 1175. However, the accusation of adultery also enabled Philip to seize control of Isabel's family lands in Vermandois, so it may be that the whole story of the affair was manufactured.

his lord's company, not coming anywhere near him'. Nonetheless, Marshal was not immediately banished or publicly punished – a stark contrast to the brutal treatment meted out to the Young King's vice-chancellor Adam for his treachery in 1176. It is also notable that other members of Henry's *mesnie*, past and present – including men such as Baldwin of Béthune – remained on close terms with William, though this might be explained by William's elevated status and fame. The only other hint of a reaction related to Queen Marguerite, as she was subsequently removed from Young Henry's court and sent to her brother Philip of France in Paris. At first glance this seems to indicate a serious marital rift, but in fact her dispatch to the Capetian capital took place only in February 1183, and might easily be explained by the fractious political climate at that particular moment. On balance, there has to be a very strong possibility that the whole accusation of an adulterous affair was a fabrication, and seen as such by the Young King, though the charge of dishonouring Henry by supplanting his position remained. With the surviving evidence, however, the exact truth of these events remains hidden.

Into exile

In the late autumn of 1182, William and the Young King attended their last tournament together, held north of Paris, between Gournay and Ressons, but it was a lamentable affair and the estrangement between the two former friends was obvious to all. Both men seem to have been ill at ease with the public exposure of their quarrel: Henry was left 'blushing with shame and the Marshal likewise ... full of anger and shame'. Philip of Flanders reportedly counselled the Young King not to 'let the Marshal slip away from him', but Henry refused to make any effort at a rapprochement. William's accusers had achieved their goal – he had fallen from favour. Once the tournament was done, Marshal absented himself from the *mesnie*, going into a kind of voluntary exile. Soon after, the Young King travelled to visit the great Cistercian abbey of Fontevraud, near Chinon – a monastery favoured by the Angevins.

There he issued two charters that survive to this day, one in its original form, the other in a later medieval copy. Both documents bear the names of Henry's leading household knights. William Marshal's name – so often in pride of place at the head of this type of witness list – is absent, and tellingly, his position has been usurped by none other than Thomas of Coulonces. The second named conspirator, Adam of Yquebeuf, is also listed just behind Gerard Talbot, Robert Tresgoz and John of Préaux. The Young King's household had been reordered.

William Marshal made one final attempt to clear his name at the massive Angevin assembly held by King Henry II at Caen, in Normandy, that December. The annual Christmas Court was always a time of celebration and lavish feasting. These gatherings offered a perfect opportunity for the public affirmation of royal eminence and largesse, and gave a chance for the thronged aristocracy to see and be seen – to marvel at the unrivalled regal spectacle, while flaunting their own status. The assembly in 1182 was especially ostentatious, with nobles gathered from across the Angevin realm, and guests from Germany and Gascony in attendance. All four of Henry II's sons were present, as was his daughter Matilda and her husband Henry, the Lion of Saxony, with a grand retinue of 1,000 knights.

The Christmas Court was also a time when nobles might present their grievances or seek royal justice – indeed, at this same gathering, Marshal's old patron the lord of Tancarville openly complained to the Old King that his role as chamberlain of Normandy was being usurped. By this point, news of William Marshal's alleged crimes had already been brought to the attention of Henry II, but it was to the Young King himself that William came during the feast. Marshal seems to have been oblivious to the swirling currents of political tension pulsing just beneath the surface at Caen. The Court that year was alive with intrigue and machination – a greater game was afoot – but William was concerned only to achieve some measure of reconciliation with Young Henry.

Marshal's sudden appearance at Caen was unexpected. The *History* noted that he was 'made very welcome by the high-ranking people', though his enemies were 'greatly displeased'. William clearly felt the eyes of the crowd upon him, because by now the accusations against him were 'public knowledge'. He presented himself before the Young King and requested an opportunity to prove his innocence through trial by combat. William offered to fight no less than three opponents, one after the other, stating that if bested he would willingly go to the gallows. He even suggested that his accusers could try cutting off one of the fingers from his right hand to see if that would make him 'admit defeat'. But Young Henry remained unmoved, bluntly refusing any such trial or test. With that, Marshal's fall from grace was complete. He was now effectively banished from the Young King's military house-hold. Realising that he might face arrest, imprisonment or even attack, William requested and received letters of safe conduct from Henry II, and these saw Marshal safely to the borders of the Angevin realm. His exile had begun.

In early 1183, William Marshal found himself without master or *mesnie* for the first time in fifteen years. Now around thirty-six, he was suddenly out in the cold. News of the scandal – or at least of the 'strife between the Marshal and his lord' – spread across northern France, but William's famed prowess as a tournament champion meant that other nobles, outside the Angevin world, were still willing to recruit him into their own households. The *History* was rather coy about Marshal's behaviour in this period. His biographer was happy enough to admit that a bidding war to secure William's services broke out, with Philip of Flanders offering £500, Duke Hugh of Burgundy matching that sum and the lord of Béthune proposing to pay £1,000, and throw in the hand-in-marriage of his beautiful daughter to boot. According to the *History*, Marshal declined all of these offers, remaining in effect a free agent, but this may have been a convenient blurring of the truth, designed to maintain the impression of William's unbroken loyalty to Young Henry. In fact, William probably entered the count of Flanders' entourage for a brief time, as charter evidence indicates that Marshal accepted the substantial endowment of one quarter of the income drawn from the Flemish town of St Omer from Philip, presumably as remuneration for joining his tournament team.

There is certainly no suggestion that William struggled to make ends meet in early 1183, and was said to have 'led a very fine, sumptuous and magnificent existence in France'. This was no return to the frightening uncertainty of 1166 and his short-lived ostracism from the Tancarville household. Marshal also struck up a close friendship with another prominent figure from the tournament circuit, the great James of Avesnes. Once the annual break in chivalric games began with the coming of Lent, the pair made a pilgrimage to Cologne in Germany, where a great golden casket, thought to contain the bones of the Three Magi who visited the infant Christ, could be venerated. It seems likely that William only returned to France in mid- to late April 1183. At some point thereafter he apparently met the Young King's chamberlain, Ralph FitzGodfrey, on his travels. The *History* described Ralph literally seeing Marshal approaching along on the road and galloping up to greet him. The chamberlain had spent weeks scouring the towns and cities of northern France looking for William, and he bore an urgent message from the Young King. The accusations against William had been discredited and he would now be welcomed back into Henry's household. But Ralph urged him to come with all possible speed, because the Young King was in the middle of a bloody war in Aquitaine.

THE FINAL GAMBIT

Seemingly unbeknown to William, the inexorable march towards this conflict had begun almost the moment he left the Christmas Court at Caen. Henry II and his sons moved on to the city of Le Mans in late December and the Old King recognised, amid the tense and fractious atmosphere, that he must finally take some decisive action to clarify the balance of power between his heirs. At first he ruled in favour of Young Henry. On 1 January 1183, Richard and Geoffrey were required to pay homage to the Young King, thus acknowledging the subjection of Brittany and Aquitaine to his ultimate overlordship. Geoffrey readily acceded to his father's demand and, though Richard grumbled, eventually he too agreed, but only on the proviso that Young Henry first guaranteed his rights to Aquitaine in perpetuity. With the hard-won terms of this pact in place, Henry II must have thought that his eldest son would be mollified. The pre-eminent status that he yearned for could now be confirmed.

In fact, any semblance of peace was about to unravel before the Old King's eyes. Standing before his father, brothers and a large crowd of Angevin courtiers, Young Henry placed his hands on a copy of the Holy Gospels and 'swore that from that day forward ... he would remain loyal to King Henry [II]', but he also confessed that 'he had pledged to support the barons of Aquitaine against Richard' and that these magnates now wished to declare him as the new duke. This was a public declaration of war against his brother, the Lionheart. Young Henry had summoned the courage to force a confrontation, backing the Old King into a corner from which he would have to choose which of his sons to support. The Young King must have hoped that this gambit might not only force his father to confirm Young Henry's status as Angevin overlord, but also bring him actual territory of his own, either won through arms in Aquitaine or earned through his father's concession of Normandy. But Young Henry was playing a dangerous, unpredictable game.

At first, a frustrated Henry II made desperate efforts to hold the family together, compelling his quarrelling sons to accept a new pact at another assembly at Angers, but this was little more than a facade. The Old King's position was incredibly finely balanced. Should he support his eldest son and primary heir, the renowned paragon of chivalry; or back Richard, the hardened warrior with a proven track record of wielding power in the real world? Our ability to judge Henry II's intentions is impaired by vague or contradictory evidence at this point. Contemporaries seem to have been confused and uncertain of the Old King's position, quite probably because he kept his cards close to his chest. As one of the most experienced, subtle and canny politicians of the age, Henry was moving with care and caution. According to the English chronicler Ralph of Diss, the Old King did reveal his tacit approval of Henry's cause, after Richard 'exploded with anger', refusing any further talk of peace. '[Falling] into a rage', Henry was said to have 'threatened difficulties for Richard' – suggesting that the Young King 'was going to tame Richard's pride' – and urged Geoffrey to 'stand faithfully by his brother as his liege lord'.

In fact, it may be that the Old King had simply resigned himself to the fact that his two eldest sons were going to come to blows and that, in some sense, the contest for Aquitaine would serve as a test of their skill and ambition, and he planned to support whoever emerged victorious. In public, at least, Henry II announced yet another assembly – to be held, this time, just north of Poitiers – the notional plan being for the Aquitanian aristocracy to air their grievances against Richard. But none of his sons was interested in further negotiation. Geoffrey travelled to the Limousin, supposedly to arrange a truce, but immediately declared his support for the Aquitanian cause and sided with the local baron, Viscount Aimery of Limoges.

The Young King followed in February 1183, and it was at this point that his wife, Queen Marguerite, was sent to Paris. Some eight months earlier, Young Henry had made a point of visiting Limoges and offering his patronage to its famous abbey dedicated to St Martial. Now the city became the rallying point for his forces. Little remains of the heart of medieval Limoges in the modern city (barring some recently unearthed remnants of the crypt of St Martial's), but in 1183 the area was dominated by the great abbey and the viscount's neighbouring citadel. This latter structure had been largely demolished on Richard's orders in 1181, so work now began apace to rebuild its walls using wood, earth and scavenged masonry.

With the battle lines being drawn, other local magnates started to offer Young Henry their support, including Geoffrey of Lusignan – the man who had attacked Earl Patrick of Salisbury's entourage in 1168. Viscount Aimery also summoned mercenary forces from Gascony. It is difficult to know who had the Young King's ear during this critical period, as the conflict that he had engineered gathered pace. Denied the counsel of his old friend and retainer William Marshal, he must have turned to the remaining intimates within his household and perhaps also to his younger brother, Duke Geoffrey of Brittany. If so, he was in grave peril of being led astray.

Now in his mid-twenties, Geoffrey was a devious, scheming sycophant. In the words of one contemporary, he was 'smooth as oil' and 'a hypocrite in everything'; his 'syrupy and persuasive eloquence' gave him the 'power of dissolving the apparently indissoluble'; indeed, he was a man who could 'corrupt two kingdoms with his tongue'. This unsavoury character had given every impression of acquiescence at Le Mans on 1 January, but he must surely have been angling for his advantage; judging that by backing Young Henry, for now at least, he might gain future advantage. Geoffrey could draw on the martial resources of Brittany, and he instructed Breton mercenaries to cross into Aquitaine and threaten Poitiers, but he was not to be trusted.

A *family at war*

By early February it was obvious to Richard that his brothers were about to mount an offensive. Fuming at his father's inaction, the Lionheart left for Poitiers to prepare for a direct military confrontation. Richard was not a man who played at war, but a brutal, efficient and relentless commander, already tried and tested through years of campaigning. In short order he crushed the Breton mercenary force, executing all prisoners, and then on 10 February he led his troops out of Poitiers on a forced march south-east. For two days and two nights they rode incessantly, covering seventy-five miles, to reach the outpost of Gorre, only twelve miles west of Limoges. There, Richard made short work of a party of the Gascon mercenaries serving Young Henry's faction: most were slain, the rest taken captive. Having made his lightning strike, the Lionheart retreated a short distance down the Vienne river valley to the fortress of Aixe. There his prisoners were either drowned, put to the sword or blinded. The statement was clear. This was the manner in which Richard would wage war, should his brothers be foolish enough to persist in their aggression.

In mid-February King Henry II finally came south to intervene. He must have already begun summoning military forces from across Anjou and Normandy, but was as yet supported by only a small contingent of knights. The Old King arrived at Limoges intending to speak with Henry, apparently still undecided as to whose cause he would support. But as his party rode up to the makeshift citadel, arrows were suddenly loosed from within. One struck and wounded a knight standing close to the king; another flew directly towards Henry II's chest. At the last second his horse reared up and the missile struck the beast in the head. The Old King had been inches away from severe injury, quite possibly even death. In the ensuing chaos, the royal household hustled Henry II to safety and he travelled directly to Richard's castle at Aixe. His choice had been made for him – he would now back the Lionheart.

It is impossible to know whether this was a deliberate attempt at assassination, or even if it was, whether Young Henry was in any way complicit. The Old King's death would certainly have cleared the way for Henry's accession, but such a direct attack was incredibly risky. The excuse later given was that the garrison had believed they were under attack, yet as King Henry had been riding beneath his red and gold royal banner, it is difficult to believe such a mistake could have been made. That evening the Young King came to Aixe to parley and offer his apologies for the shocking incident, though his cause was not helped by the fact that the archers responsible remained unpunished. Obviously angry and suspicious, it was plain to see that Henry II now favoured Richard.

There was a hiatus over the next two weeks, as the Old King and Duke Richard assembled their forces, ahead of an attack on Limoges. Suddenly confronted by the stark reality of his position, Young Henry's nerve seems to have faltered. This was a war largely of his own making, yet it now dawned on him that, with the alienation of his father, outright defeat had become a real possibility. The exorbitant costs of the Gascon mercenaries drafted in by Aimar also began to bite, and the Young King was quickly running out of money. He was out of his depth. Before long, he resorted to the shameful expedient of looting the abbey of St Martial of its gold and silver just to meet his expenses. The last two weeks of February also witnessed a confused series of diplomatic exchanges between Henry and his father, some carried out face to face, others via envoys. Throughout, the Young King vacillated: offers of peace were made, but then rescinded, Henry restated his intention to crusade to the Holy Land – and seems to have actually taken the cross at this point – but when the Old King agreed to finance his expedition, he backed away from the plan.

No resolution had been achieved by 1 March and, with their armies now in place, Henry II and Richard moved in to besiege the citadel in Limoges, using a mixture of encirclement and assault. Surrounded and outnumbered, the Young King had little choice but to mount a defence. The siege proved to be a grim affair for both sides. Late winter weather meant that it was still cold, and the rains lashed the besieger's tents – in misery, some of the Old King's troops asked to depart after just two weeks. Nonetheless, Young Henry's prospects looked bleak. It was probably at this point, in March 1183, that the Young King's seneschal – one of the leading men to have accused William Marshal the preceding autumn – revealed himself to be a 'traitor'. Having judged Young Henry's cause to be hopeless, he abandoned his lord and *mesnie* and went over to the Old King. According to the *History*, this act of treachery caused Henry to realise that the allegations against Marshal had been nothing more than 'harmful lies'. This may have been the case; perhaps the whole plot really was revealed and dis- credited. It is also possible that, with his back against the wall, the Young King simply decided to put any lingering grudge or suspicion to one side. Whatever the truth may have been, Henry now needed a man of William's prowess and quality in his retinue, and so his cham- berlain Ralph FitzGodfrey was instructed to locate Marshal with all possible haste.

Ralph was perhaps dispatched at the same time as Young Henry slipped away from Limoges – either by breaking through Henry II's encirclement, or (more likely) by using the cover of a brief parley truce as an opportunity to abscond. Geoffrey of Brittany, Viscount Aimar and the lord of Lusignan were left to hold the citadel, while the Young King ranged across the Limousin and Angoulême, desperately seeking out supplies and spoils. Once again, he looted monasteries, plundering Grandmont, north of Limoges, and the abbey of La Couronne, but the booty taken kept his war effort alive. The citadel at Limoges stubbornly held out through April, and by early May the Old King had called off the siege. Having weathered the worst of the storm, it looked as though the tide was now beginning to shift in Young Henry's favour. His support within Aquitaine remained strong, despite the attacks on local religious houses. Neighbouring powers like Duke Hugh of Burgundy and Count Raymond of Toulouse were also beginning to line up behind the Young King, preferring the prospect of his rule to the known ferocity of Richard's regime.

It was probably at this point, sometime in May, that William Marshal finally returned to the Young Henry's side. Using the political connections forged on the tournament circuit, Marshal had secured letters of support and safe-conduct from King Philip of France, the archbishop of Rheims and the count of Blois so that he could traverse the war zone. Even Henry II eventually gave William leave to be reunited with the Young King, perhaps hoping that he might steer his wayward son on a more moderate course. In fact, Marshal's arrival at Limoges may have encouraged Henry to go on the offensive; certainly by 23 May he had marched down the Vienne river valley to occupy the now un-garrisoned castle at Aixe, and then moved on south. After the cheerless uncertainty of the early winter, his prospects had been transformed. The Young King was still in deep financial debt to his mercenary forces, but Richard and the Old King were now on the back foot.

But then, on 26 May, Young Henry fell ill with a fever at Uzerche, some thirty-five miles south of Limoges. At first he was able to keep

moving, passing the small castle of Martel two days later, and travelling on to plunder the Old King's favoured shrine at Rocamadour. By
early June, however, he was back at Martel and so weak that he had to
be confined to bed. His fever remained high, but he also contracted
'a flux of the bowels' – what today would be termed dysentery. Like
Henry II in 1170 and young Philip of France in 1179 before him, Young
Henry's life was now in danger.

Realising that he was no longer in any position to wage a war, the
Young King sent an envoy to his father, asking that he come to Martel
so that they could be reconciled. Fearing for his son's condition, Henry
was said to have considered setting out on the journey, but in light of
the treachery witnessed at Limoges that February, his advisors counselled him to decline. A ring of 'forgiveness and peace' was sent in his
stead. As the days passed, Young Henry's condition deteriorated.
Wracked by pain, his body became severely dehydrated, even as his
physicians struggled to bring him back to health. William Marshal and
the rest of the Young King's closest household knights waited with him
at Martel, their anxiety deepening. There was no doubt that Henry was
now gravely ill, but at only twenty-eight, he surely had the strength and
resilience of youth on his side.

By 7 June, however, it was clear that for Young Henry there would be
no recovery – no last-minute reprieve. He was dying. That day he made
a private confession to the bishop of Cahors, prostrating himself naked
on the floor before the prelate's crucifix to renounce his attempt to seize
Aquitaine and to receive the ritual of Mass. Four days later, on 11 June,
Henry was at the point of death. The Young King now repeated his confession in public, before William and the other members of his *mesnie*,
and then received absolution for his sins and the last rites.

On that final day, the man who had been destined to become King
Henry III of England dictated his last testament. His body was to be
buried alongside his forebears, the great dukes of Normandy, in the
cathedral at Rouen. A heartfelt appeal was made to his father Henry II
'to deal mercifully' with his mother Eleanor of Aquitaine, his wife
Queen Marguerite of France and his knights 'to whom he had made

many promises which he had been unable to fulfil'. Turning to Marshal, 'his most intimate friend', Henry bid him take up the cloak upon which he had affixed his crusading cross, and begged him 'to carry it to the Holy Sepulchre (in Jerusalem) and with it pay my debts to God'.* After that his face became 'sallow, wan and livid'. The Young King's dying moments became a tableau of penitence. A hair shirt was placed on his emaciated body, a noose around his withered neck. With this rope he was dragged from his bed and laid upon the ash-strewn floor, with large stone blocks placed beneath his head and feet. Clutching the Old King's ring of peace to his chest, he fell unconscious and died soon thereafter.

The cult of the Young King

For William Marshal and those others huddled inside the castle at Martel, the mixture of shock and disbelief at Young Henry's passing left them 'quite out of their minds and greatly disturbed'. The Old King, too, was said to have been gripped by the 'deepest grief' when he heard the dreadful news, and 'bursting into tears, he threw himself to the ground, greatly bewailing his son'. The beautiful, golden-haired Young King had died a pointless, squalid death. With his demise, the resistance in Aquitaine soon collapsed. Regardless of the anguish he must have felt, William Marshal was forced to confront the unseemly issue of Henry's debts. Challenged by one of the Young King's mercenary commanders – now angry at the prospect of not being paid – William had to pledge himself against the money owed, though King Henry II later settled the arrears.

Nonetheless, Marshal and the other loyal members of the Young King's *mesnie* did their best to follow their late lord's final wishes. Given the summer heat, careful preparations had to be made before

---

* The deathbed charge laid upon William Marshal was confirmed by Roger of Howden and the local contemporary chronicler Geoffrey of Vigeois, who described William as the Young King's *'carissimus'* – his most intimate or treasured associate.

Henry's corpse could be moved. The internal organs of the royal dead were often interred separately, so the Young King's brains, eyes and bowels were removed, and later laid to rest at Grandmont Priory, even though this was one of the religious houses he had ransacked. The rest of his body was packed with salt, stitched into a bull's hide and then placed within a lead coffin. William and his fellow knights were now ready to begin the long funeral procession to Rouen, more than 300 miles north of Martel. The Young King's bier was 'carried on the shoulders of his comrades through villages, castles and towns, with people running from everywhere to look'.

As the slow-moving cortège passed through the landscape of Aquitaine, Anjou and then Normandy, an atmosphere of feverous collective grief took hold, especially among ordinary townspeople and the peasantry. Young Henry was idolised as the great flower of chivalry, and many mourned the loss of a man who, it was believed, would have ruled as a king of justice and mercy. In part, the power of this conviction, and the sheer, unexpected force of the sentiment that now began to sweep across the Angevin realm could be explained by the fact that Henry had never actually held or exercised full regnal power in his life. He had been able to play the role of the chivalric figurehead without ever having to enforce laws or raise taxes. With his hands unstained by the grubby work of governance, he became the perfect king of the imagination.

Even so, the cult of the Young King that quickly sprang up in June 1183 went beyond mere political adoration, and began to parallel the charged devotional outpouring that had followed Thomas Becket's murder in 1170. Claims for the late Henry's sanctity were made as William and his comrades marched his corpse north: illnesses were supposedly cured as the funeral procession passed, lepers came forward to touch the bier and a great shaft of heavenly light was said to have shone down on the coffin at night. When the procession reached Le Mans, the crowds became so overwrought that the bishop halted the funeral party and had the Young King's body quickly interred within the local cathedral – the resting place of Henry's paternal grandfather, Geoffrey Plantagenet. This may have been a rather unscrupulous attempt to relocate Young Henry's cult to Le Mans (after all, there were fortunes to be made from pilgrim traffic). The Old King was said to have been enraged by the hasty burial, issuing the dean of Rouen with a special royal warrant so that the corpse could be recovered. In a rather gruesome final act, Henry's body was duly dug up in mid-July, carried to Rouen Cathedral and laid to rest 'with due honour . . . on the north side of the high altar'. William Marshal had buried his first king. It would not be his last.

The cult surrounding the Young King proved short-lived. With Henry II still in power and Young Henry now cast as the vanquished rebel, there were few Angevin nobles or clerics willing to risk their careers by repeating stories of his 'miracles'. In fact, Young King Henry received a scourging press from most late twelfth-century chroniclers. For these historians, writing during the reigns of the Old King and his successors, Henry was easy game – a wayward princeling who died young and left no great court historians to sing his praises. In their accounts, he became little more than a mutinous traitor. Walter Map claimed to have known Henry as 'a friend and intimate', but condemned him nonetheless as 'a false son to his father' who 'befouled the whole world with his treasons'. Gerald of Wales offered some degree of balance, accusing the Young King of 'monstrous ingratitude', while acknowledging that he had been 'an honour to his friends, a terror to his enemies and beloved by all'.

Only a few of Young Henry's closest contemporaries offered a more immediate impression of his achievements and character. The famed troubadour, Bertrand of Born, composed a *'planh'* (lament) on Henry's death, praising his largesse, courtesy and chivalry; styling him as the 'sovereign of all courtly knights' and the 'emperor of champions'. Perhaps the most heartfelt memorial was offered by Henry's chaplain, Gervase of Tilbury. He wrote that the Young King was 'a solace to the world while he lived' and that 'it was a blow to all chivalry when he died in the very glow of youth'. Gervase concluded that 'when Henry died heaven was hungry, so all the world went begging'.

The Young King was a tragic figure – a man who seemed to forever see true greatness just beyond his grasp; cut down long before his time, with all his promise squandered. He had been William Marshal's greatest patron and, despite their brief estrangement, one of his closest friends. Henry had transformed William's career and marked him as a man. Marshal would cherish the Young King's memory for the rest of his days, but for now his first task was to fulfil Henry's crusading vow by travelling to the Holy Land.

JOURNEY TO THE HOLY LAND

Honouring Young Henry's request was no simple matter – it involved a journey of more than 2,000 miles, almost to the edge of the known world – but William undertook this last act of service nonetheless. His pilgrimage seems, first and foremost, to have been driven by selfless dedication and authentic religious devotion. With the Young King defeated and dead, there was little advantage to be gained from upholding his memory, and that summer William found himself in a precarious position, deprived of a lord and patron. Had William's first priority been to secure his future, he would have focused on finding a new post in a military retinue, either within the Angevin realm or alongside the likes of Count Philip of Flanders. This was certainly the route chosen by most of his peers – the former members of Young Henry's household. Over the next few years, knights such as Baldwin of Béthune, Robert Tresgoz and Gerard Talbot managed to ingratiate themselves with the Old King. They were accepted into royal service and began the slow process of seeking favour, climbing the ladder to preferment.

Marshal chose a different path. After the Young King's burial in Rouen, William made a firm commitment to travel to the Near East by taking the crusaders' cross himself. In many respects, this was a step away from royal service and an interruption to his career – one that prevented him from seeking personal advancement. Now in his

mid-thirties, Marshal was at a critical juncture in his life, facing fateful choices. He had been party to two failed rebellions against Henry
II and had endured scandalous accusations about his conduct in late
1182. His prospects were not assured. But William had also watched
Young Henry's agonising death with his own eyes, and the experience
seems to have left its imprint. He was clearly determined to carry out
Henry's dying wish, by bearing his cloak to Jerusalem, and later events
would suggest that Marshal was also moved to ponder his own mortality and faith.

This is not to suggest that William was simply the saintly retainer,
his eyes fixed only on the distant Holy City. He was willing to make
some sacrifices in 1183, but he was also a realist. Once the Young King
had been laid to rest, Marshal sought an audience with Henry II.
According to the *History*, he came before the Old King simply 'to take
his leave', that is to seek royal permission for his pilgrimage, and this
consent was duly granted. But this was also a crucial opportunity for
William to gauge his standing with the king and to achieve a measure
of reconciliation. Henry evidently knew that his eldest son had charged
Marshal with a crusading obligation before his death, and seems to
have respected William's fidelity, while also recognising his martial
renown. As a result, the Old King promised to hold a place for Marshal
in the royal household, probably in response to William's request for
such a guarantee. Henry even gave Marshal 100 Angevin pounds 'to
assist him on his pilgrimage', though he also took 'two fine horses'
from William – supposedly as surety of his return from the East – and
together these 'magnificent' steeds were apparently worth 200 Angevin
pounds.

Marshal had laid the groundwork for a prosperous future in
Western Europe should he return from the Levant, but in spite of the
Old King's commitment, William seems to have considered the
possibility that he might remain in the Holy Land. In mid-summer
1183, he travelled back to England 'to take leave of his friends, his sisters, his immediate family and all his other kinsmen', calling upon
one of his sisters, Matilda, who had married the minor southern

English landholder, Robert of Pont-de-l'Arche.* William may also have visited his elder brother John Marshal, who had retained the hereditary royal marshalcy, but otherwise enjoyed little crown favour under Henry II. The journey to England was certainly a detour for William Marshal and seems like the act of a man placing his affairs in order ahead of a prolonged, perhaps even permanent, absence.

Many knights of William's age, background and station had forged new careers in the Levant. For much of the twelfth century, the crusader states established after the Latin Christian (or Roman Catholic) conquest of Jerusalem in 1099 offered manifold opportunities for men of Marshal's class. By travelling to defend the Holy Places, these knights could do 'God's work' and at the same time find advancement, even lands of their own. The Burgundian knight, Reynald of Châtillon, was a case in point. He had fought on the Second Crusade in the contingent of King Louis VII of France in his mid-twenties, but remained in the East. In spite of being a relative unknown, Reynald married Princess Constance of Antioch, heiress to the northern crusader state, in 1153, and ruled as prince of Antioch for eight years. Captured by Muslims, he spent fifteen years in prison in Aleppo before being ransomed (a period of incarceration that rather put Marshal's own experience in 1168 in the shade). By the time he was freed, Constance had died and a new ruler of Antioch had been declared, but Reynald soon secured another advantageous union, this time with the heiress of the great desert lordship of Transjordan (east of Palestine). This brought him command of the formidable fortresses of Kerak and Montreal, and put him in the front line of the holy war with the mighty Sultan Saladin.

Another knight who made his fortune in the East was Guy of Lusignan, one of the two brothers who had ambushed Earl Patrick of Salisbury and William Marshal in Poitou in 1168. At some point in the 1170s, Guy had travelled to Palestine, perhaps in part to atone for

---

* One of William Marshal's other sisters, Margaret, married first Ralph of Somery, and later Maurice of Gant.

Patrick's death, but like Reynald he achieved sudden advancement through marriage in 1180, wedding Sibylla of Jerusalem, the sister of King Baldwin IV. In light of Baldwin the Leper King's desperate ill health, Guy now had his eyes on the crown of Jerusalem itself – a staggering transformation of fortunes, given that just fifteen years earlier he had been an Aquitanean outlaw on the run from Henry II. With such precedent, it would be surprising if William did not entertain at least some thoughts of a Levantine future.

William's pilgrimage to Jerusalem

Marshal does not appear to have travelled to the Holy Land with a knightly retinue of his own. The small entourage he had assembled by 1179 seems to have been disbanded by the time of his exile in December 1182, and it is quite possible that he was accompanied by only one or two servants, including his squire – a low-ranking warrior named Eustace Bertrimont, who would remain a member of William's household for many years to come. No detailed record of Marshal's journey eastwards has survived, but it is almost certain that he would have sailed to Palestine, for while the First Crusaders had marched overland to reach the Near East, the vast majority of pilgrims and crusaders now travelled by ship. William may have embarked from a Channel port or, perhaps more likely, from a southern-French centre of pilgrim traffic like Marseille. His crusader status – signalled by the cross sewn on to his clothing – afforded him a degree of protection and freedom to travel unhindered in Christian lands.

Given that the Young King was buried in Rouen in mid-July, and that William first travelled to England, the earliest likely date for his departure for the Levant was September 1183 and, in all probability, he set out before the Mediterranean sea-lanes closed for winter in early November. In one sense, Marshal was travelling 'out of season', or at least against the prevailing stream of traffic. In the years after Jerusalem's recapture, tens of thousands of Western Europeans had seized the opportunity to visit the Holy Places, some travelling, like

William, as crusaders, others simply as pilgrims. Typically, these men and women would sail to the East in early spring and then return in the autumn. With fair winds, the voyage across the Mediterranean could take as little as twenty days, but a journey of four to six weeks was not uncommon. Most arrived in Palestine at the thriving port of Acre, a bustling, cosmopolitan hub of trade and commerce; one that even welcomed Muslim merchants and travellers in spite of the ongoing holy war.

William's first priority was to complete his pilgrimage to Jerusalem and fulfil his promise to Young Henry. That brought him inland, through the Judean hills, to the Holy City itself – a great, walled metropolis and the epicentre of the Christian faith. Marshal's ultimate destination was the Church of the Holy Sepulchre, believed to have been built on the site of Jesus Christ's death and his resurrection. For William, like all medieval Latin Christians, this was the most sacred space on Earth. It was here that the First Crusaders had come on 15 July 1099 – fresh from massacring Jerusalem's Muslim population – to give thanks to their God for victory. Exactly fifty years later to the day, a grand reconstruction programme, initiated by King Fulk (Henry II's grandfather) and his half-Armenian wife Queen Melisende, had been completed. It was this magnificent structure, with a spectacular domed rotunda enclosing the supposed site of Christ's tomb, that Marshal entered, finally discharging his duty to the Young King.

During his time in the East, William became friendly with members of the two celebrated Military Orders – the Templars and the Hospitallers. These religious movements combined the ideals of knighthood and monasticism, and their adherents were regarded as the ultimate holy warriors, forming the elite core of the kingdom of Jerusalem's armies. Given his own background and the martial renown he had garnered in Western Europe, the association with these revered knightly orders was natural. According to the *History*, the Templars and Hospitallers 'loved the Marshal very dearly because of his many fine qualities' and he must have been equally impressed by their legendary discipline and skill-at-arms. In Jerusalem itself he would have visited the Templar compound (now part of what is the Aqsa Mosque) on the Haram as-Sharif or Temple Mount, where he would also have seen the Dome of the Rock transformed into the Latin 'Templum Domini', topped by a huge cross rather than a crescent. It is very likely that William also visited the massive hospital in Jerusalem, where up to 2,000 poor or sick Christians could be treated.

Marshal may also have seen the most treasured relic in Palestine – the True Cross – a golden crucifix believed to contain a piece of the very cross upon which Christ had died. This sacred object had been miraculously 'discovered' after Jerusalem's conquest in 1099 and came to be regarded as the vital totem of Latin military might, being carried into battle at the heart of the kingdom's forces. Many believed that, with the True Cross in their midst, victory was assured.

A knight in the East

William Marshal spent two years in the Holy Land, but virtually nothing certain is known of his actions in this period. The *History* recorded that William performed 'many feats of bravery and valour' during his stay, achieving as much as 'if he had lived there for seven years', adding that these 'fine deeds' were 'still known about today' and widely discussed. But Marshal's biographer then declared that he could not describe these marvellous exploits because: 'I was not there and did not witness them, nor can I find anyone who can tell me half of them.' This leaves much of this phase of his life as a frustrating blank.

As a result, most historians have been content simply to pass over William's time in the East in a few sentences, concluding at best that 'a crusade was the supreme adventure' and that William 'undoubtedly performed [great deeds] against the forces of the redoubtable Saladin'. In fact, considerably more can be deduced. Through the use of an array of other contemporary sources, it is possible to construct a detailed account of the kingdom of Jerusalem's history in these precise years between the autumn of 1183 and early 1186. This picture is revealing because it demonstrates that Marshal arrived in a Latin realm that was on the brink of disaster, and that the looming shadow of this catastrophe was obvious to all. More importantly, and perhaps surprisingly, in spite of the simmering tension with the Muslim world, William happened to reach Palestine in a period of relative calm just before the destructive storm of 1187 broke.

The kingdom of Jerusalem was in an embattled state in 1183. That June, Saladin had finally managed to overcome Muslim rivals in the northern Syrian city of Aleppo. This gave the sultan control of an arc of territory running south to Damascus, and then on to Egypt and the great city of Cairo, effectively surrounding the kingdom of Jerusalem. However, his ambitious plan to unite the Muslim world remained incomplete, as he had yet to subdue the Iraqi city of Mosul, and Saladin was determined to assemble a grand coalition of Islamic forces before attempting a mass invasion of Latin Palestine. This meant that, although the sultan did prosecute two exploratory attacks on Christian territory in the autumn of 1183 and the summer of 1184, his real focus lay elsewhere.

It is just possible that William Marshal saw almost immediate action in September 1183, after Saladin marched his forces into Galilee in the northern reaches of the kingdom of Jerusalem. A large Latin army was assembled in response to this incursion and pilgrims waiting in Acre to sail back to Europe were even pressed into service. It may be that William joined this draft as a new arrival in the second half of September, but it is perhaps doubtful that he reached the Levant so quickly. Baldwin the Leper King's illness meant that the Latin forces were commanded by none other than Guy of Lusignan. Given that this was Guy's first experience of leading a large field army he did an admirable, if unspectacular job, advancing in close formation to threaten Saladin's forces, yet staunchly refusing to be drawn into a hasty confrontation. Barring some limited skirmishing, there was no determined combat and, faced with a stalemate, Saladin withdrew. Thus, even if Marshal did participate in this campaign, he would hardly have been party to a titanic confrontation.

Saladin moved on that autumn to besiege Reynald of Châtillon's massive desert castle at Kerak, on the route linking Damascus with Arabia and Egypt, and the sultan returned to attack the fortress for a second time in the summer of 1184. On both occasions, Latin armies marched to break the siege, and it must be likely that William joined one or both of these expeditions, but neither resulted in fighting, as the Muslim sultan retreated as soon as the Christians approached. In this period, Saladin moved with extreme caution, testing his enemy and building his own forces. There were no other notable campaigns in Palestine during Marshal's time in the East. By the spring of 1185, Saladin was more interested in battering distant Mosul into submission and, to forestall a war on two fronts, agreed a twelve-month truce with the kingdom of Jerusalem. The resultant lull in fighting dismayed newly arrived crusaders, including a party of frustrated European knights, who appeared in early 1186 only to be strictly forbidden from launching an attack on Muslim territory for fear of inciting a massive reprisal.

The only other military offensive in these years was a small-scale, illegal raid, conducted by Guy of Lusignan in October 1184 against Bedouin nomads living near the fortress settlement of Darum (on the kingdom of Jerusalem's southern border with the Sinai). These Bedouin often provided the Latins with valuable intelligence about Saladin's movements, and were therefore afforded official protection by the Jerusalemite crown, so Guy's unsanctioned plundering expedition infuriated King Baldwin IV. Given their past history in Poitou, it would be easy to imagine that William Marshal still harboured considerable ill-feeling towards the Lusignan 'murderer' of 1168. In fact, one of the few additional details recorded in the *History* about Marshal's time in the Holy Land was that he was on good terms with Guy of Lusignan, so it may be that William was party to this rather disreputable raid.

Clearly, William had precious little opportunity to perform the 'many feats of bravery and valour' alluded to in the *History*. In military terms at least, Marshal was probably left somewhat disillusioned by the

experience of his crusade; certainly he can have had few tales of glorious daring to relate on his return to Europe and this may well explain
his biographer's cursory treatment of these years.

At the world's end

In spite of the lack of decisive military confrontation, William can
have been in no doubt that the kingdom of Jerusalem was plunging
inexorably towards disaster. While Baldwin the Leper King clung on
to life – his twenty-three-year-old body ravaged by crippling deformity
and blindness – Marshal would have witnessed the destructive squab-
bling over the succession, and the office of regent, to which Guy of
Lusignan was party. When Baldwin IV died in April 1185 and was succeeded on 16 May by his seven-year-old nephew and namesake,
Baldwin V (Sibylla's son by her first marriage), the crisis only deepened. The realm descended ever further into political chaos and the
Latins became paralysed by factionalism.

It was against this backdrop of spiralling Christian disunity and
mounting Muslim strength that a last desperate appeal for aid from
Europe was mounted. In the early summer of 1184 a high-level dele-
gation was sent to the West, led by the head of the Latin Church in
Palestine, Patriarch Heraclius, and the masters of the Templars and the
Hospitallers. Given William Marshal's proximity to both King
Henry II and the Military Orders, it is possible that he offered some
advice or mediation as the embassy was preparing to depart. Patriarch
Heraclius' party travelled first to the pope in Rome, then made an early
winter crossing of the Alpine passes to reach King Philip of France in
Paris. The mission arrived in England in early 1185 and was greeted
with honour by the Old King. On 10 February, Heraclius consecrated
a new Temple Church in London – its circular architecture designed
to evoke a sense of physical union with the rotunda of the Holy
Sepulchre. Then, on 18 March, Henry II convened a weeklong council, just one mile to the north at Clerkenwell, to debate the Angevin
response to Heraclius' pleas for assistance. The patriarch had brought

the keys to the Holy Sepulchre and the Tower of David, Jerusalem's citadel, as well as the Latin kingdom's royal banner, to offer in ritual submission, but in the end Henry II proved unwilling to mount a new crusade for fear of abandoning his own realm to the predations of the Capetian French.

By this time, it was apparent to those living in the kingdom of Jerusalem that a catastrophe was looming. Shortly before his death in around 1185, Archbishop William of Tyre wrote that it now seemed inevitable that the 'palm of victory, which had so often been earned' by the Christians, would soon pass to their Muslim foes, and he expressed his deeply held fear that Jerusalem could not be saved. If William Marshal had considered forging a new life in the Levant in 1183, he likely discarded those plans in the face of this mounting evidence of imminent collapse.

Yet for all the frustration and dread that must have coloured his visit to the East, Marshal's pilgrimage had a lasting spiritual impact. The surviving sources for William's life afford few glimpses into his interior world, so it is difficult to gauge the depth of his faith. He lived through an age in which Christian devotion was virtually universal in Europe. Few would have paused for even a second to consider whether they believed in God, because his existence was considered an undoubted reality, affirmed for all to see through miraculous inter-vention on Earth. This is not to suggest that the Christianity of medieval Europe was blindly ignorant and unthinking, merely that for most, religious adherence was a natural, almost innate, feature of daily life. Profound questions were being asked about the ways in which Latin Christian faith might be defined or best expressed, and the efficacy of the Church – and the papacy in particular – was open to challenge because of obvious abuses and materialism.

Many knights like William Marshal were plagued by doubts about the inherent sinfulness of their worldly profession, because Christian doctrine condemned most forms of bloodshed and violence. William appears, in large part, to have rejected such misgivings. He seems to have believed at a fundamental level that, so long as his conduct as a warrior conformed to the broad precepts of chivalry, his knightly career presented no particular barrier to religious purity. Marshal showed little interest in deep issues of theology, and entertained no aspirations to sanctity. Instead, he appears to have been moved by a conventional concern to live what he considered a decent Christian life, one that might earn him a place in Heaven after his death. He had come to Jerusalem to fulfil a promise to the Young King Henry, having just witnessed his tortured death. Not surprisingly, William gave some thought to his own mortality before he left the Holy Land. Most pilgrims and crusaders who visited the Holy City returned to Europe with some token of their journey – many First Crusaders had returned carrying palm fronds in imitation of Christ. William bought two large lengths of precious silken cloth in Jerusalem to serve as his funerary shroud. These were carefully wrapped, packed away and borne back to the West in secret, awaiting the eventuality of his death. Marshal also made a binding commitment at this point to end his days within the Templar Order, though this too was done in secrecy. For now, not a word of either of these provisions was spoken, even to his closest confidants. These were his private, heartfelt preparations for his own day of judgement.

After an absence of some two years, William Marshal returned to Western Europe at some point between the autumn of 1185 and the spring of 1186. A little over a year later, the cataclysm that had been threatening finally struck. The boy King Baldwin V died in 1186 and was succeeded by Guy of Lusignan, through his marriage to Sibylla of Jerusalem. By 1187, Saladin had forged an alliance with Mosul and was ready to mount a full-scale assault on Palestine. That summer the sultan invaded Galilee once again, at the head of some 40,000 troops, and this time Guy marched to confront him in open battle. On 4 July, Saladin scored a crushing victory that left thousands of Latin Christians dead and the remainder in captivity. King Guy was taken prisoner and the relic of the True Cross was seized by the sultan's horde. Reynald of Châtillon was executed by Saladin's own hand, and some 200 knights of the Military Orders were also put to death. Later that year, Jerusalem itself was recovered for Islam and the sultan ordered the huge cross atop the Dome of the Rock to be ripped down and smashed. When the tidings of these catastrophes reached the pope, he promptly died of shock and grief. In the weeks and months that followed, the devastating news raced across Europe, triggering a new call to arms for the campaign known as the Third Crusade – one that the Angevins could not ignore.

Part III

MIDDLE AGE:
A LORD OF THE REALM

7

A KING'S WARRIOR

William Marshal returned from the Holy Land in either late 1185 or early 1186, and presented himself before Henry II in Normandy. The Old King held to his promise and appointed William to the royal household. Having spent long years in the entourage of a king with no realm to rule, Marshal now found himself, on the brink of his fortieth year, at the very heart of the Angevin world. William's days of grand martial display on the tournament field were over. His duty now was to offer direct service to Henry II, commanding troops in the field and fighting when necessary, proffering sage counsel and steadfast support. This immensely privileged position placed Marshal at the side of the most powerful man in Europe, bringing with it a new level of influence and access to crown favour.

The appointment soon brought rewards in the form of land and title, and enabled William to start building up his own inner circle of loyal personal retainers and knights. Marshal's status also meant that he had to maintain a near-constant presence at the royal court. William's former lord, the Young King Henry, had enjoyed an extravagant lifestyle, but had also felt the nagging burden of his debts. The regal splendour of the Old King's court left his late son's profligacy in the shade. Henry II lived in majesty, surrounded by hundreds of fawning courtiers, each thirsting for advancement. As a hardened warrior, William Marshal had risen to the top of Europe's tournament circuit. The question was whether he could now adapt to this new environment, navigating his way through the rarefied atmosphere of the Angevin court?

THE ANGEVIN ROYAL COURT

Henry II's court was a grand travelling circus. Confronted by the challenge of governing a sprawling Angevin Empire that straddled the Channel, the Old King had chosen not to proclaim any one city as his capital. Instead he became the archetypal itinerant monarch, forever touring his domains, administering crown justice in his 'court' and manifesting royal might throughout the provinces. Without a stable seat of power, it became customary for virtually the entire machinery of government to follow in his wake as he criss-crossed the realm. Thus the court became bloated with an army of officials, clerks, servants, retainers and barons – the largest institution of its kind in Europe. This heaving entourage could fill fifty ships when it crossed from England to France. One courtier likened it to a 'hundred-handed giant', declaring that 'no such court like it has been heard of in the past or is to be feared again in the future'.

William had gained some experience of the Angevin court from his time with the Young King, but the sheer scale and chaotic hustle of this throng must have been bewildering. Marshal was also exposed to the opulence of Henry II's crown residences, where he could enjoy comforts unimagined by the masses. The ancient seat of royal power in England was Winchester and its palace housed the king's inner-sanctum – his 'Painted Chamber' – where the Old King would recline upon his state bed to receive distinguished visitors. It was said that one wall of this room had been painted, in mocking reference to Henry's wayward sons, with a fresco depicting a great eagle being ripped to pieces by its four offspring.

The newer royal palace at Westminster, then on the outskirts of

London, was challenging for pre-eminence. Its centrepiece was the massive Great Hall constructed at the end of the eleventh century – at 240 feet in length, easily the largest hall in north-western Europe. Most of the royal complex at Westminster burned down in a fire in 1834, but the Great Hall remains standing to this day and its looming expanse is still overwhelming. Henry II maintained a string of other palaces across his domains. His preferred residence in Normandy was the royal estate at Quévilly, across the Seine from Rouen, complete with its own private hunting park. Elsewhere, the palace at Clarendon, in Wiltshire, consisted of a series of private royal apartments surrounding a central stone and flint-walled hall, its roof held aloft by Purbeck marble pillars and its walls covered in plaster dyed blue with powdered lapis lazuli, sourced from as far afield as Afghanistan.

The twelfth century marked the start of a decisive shift across Europe towards the use of stone, rather than wood, in building and construction. This brought numerous advantages, not least the ability to create fireplaces and chimneys that were much more efficient and effective than central fires and open roofs. But stone structures literally cost hundreds of times more than their wooden precursors, and only the king and a handful of his wealthiest magnates could countenance such expense. Financial records show, for example, that the late twelfth-century timber hunting lodge built at Kinver in central England cost just over £24. By contrast, Henry II's majestic stone tower at Orford (on England's east coast), complete with a private royal bedchamber and an en-suite privy, cost £1,000. Most staggering of all was the mighty stone keep at Dover Castle – known as the Great Tower – that boasted its own advanced plumbing system, with lead pipes drawing fresh water from a well dug hundreds of feet into the chalk below. Its construction was just being completed when William joined the Old King's household, for a total cost of some £6,500.

Within these luxurious settings, Marshal was treated to the finest foods, drinks and entertainments. Some of the more exotic fare – such as crane, swan and peacock – required a refined palate, and the scale of consumption was mind-boggling. Royal accounts show that in 1180 the court went through 1,000 pounds of almonds in London alone. William and his fellow courtiers also drank vast quantities of beer and wine, with the latter being transported in giant 252-gallon wooden casks. One contemporary remarked that English wine 'could only be drunk with your eyes closed and your teeth clenched', so it was fortunate that Henry's Aquitanean estates gave him access to the celebrated vineyards of Bordeaux and Poitou.

The itinerant Angevin court attracted minstrels, musicians and storytellers, happy to regale the crowds with mannered tales of chivalric prowess, drawn from the myth-historic world of King Arthur and his knights. Less earnest amusements were also on offer. One courtier noted that Henry II's entourage was followed by a disreputable gaggle of hangers-on, ranging from harlots, dicers and confidence tricksters, to barbers and clowns. A famous jester, known as Roland the Farter, earned particular renown because he was able to jump in the air, whistle and pass wind at the same time. In England and Normandy at least, court prostitutes were carefully regulated, and Ranulf of Broc and Baldric FitzGilbert held the office of 'marshal of the whores' in these two localities.

William's life at court was also unusual in that it regularly continued well into the night and the hours of darkness. In the twelfth century most people had to confine the bulk of their activities to the daylight hours as wax or tallow candles were simply too expensive to burn on a daily basis. The Angevin court consumed an extraordinary quantity of candles, and each member of the royal household received a fixed allowance. Walter Map was playing on this theme of nocturnal activity when he described Henry II's courtiers as the 'creatures of the night', alluding to what he regarded as their more unsavoury habits and damning them as men 'who leave nothing untouched and untried'.

The courtly life

The Angevin court offered William manifold luxuries, delights and enticements, but it was also a place of danger and insecurity – a viper's nest of gossip, intrigue and duplicity, where a single misstep or ill-chosen word could threaten ruin. Indeed, one courtier likened it to a Hell, littered with 'the foul trailings of worms [and] serpents, and all manner of creeping things'. The prize, yearned after by all, was access to the king – to his ear and favour – because royal patronage could transform one's fortunes. The example set by Thomas Becket in the 1150s proved that Henry II had it in his gift to turn a relative unknown, of middling or even low birth, into one of the richest and most power-ful figures in the realm. In theory, at least, the court was highly stratified, with only the elite inner circle – of which Marshal was now on the fringe – permitted regular contact with the Old King. But the alarming feature of Angevin court was its unpredictability. Its sheer size, constant mobility and ever-changing personnel made it, in the words of Walter Map, a 'perilous whirl ... fluctuating and variable', in which it was simply impossible to remember everyone's name and station.

William Marshal's task in 1186 was to mark the most important players – the great magnates and clergymen, the leading clerks and officers – and to move with exceptional caution. At knightly tourna-ments he had been expected to conform to the emerging code of chivalry. Now, success depended on his ability to interpret and absorb the unwritten rules of the court; to be able to follow the precepts of 'courtesie' ('courtesy', or quite literally 'how to behave at court'). Those found in the upper echelons of the Angevin court were generally either of knightly or clerical background. As a member of the warrior class, William did have some natural advantages. His acknowledged status as a *preudhomme* – a man of virtue, worthy of respect – weighed in his favour and, at times of military conflict, he could continue to reaffirm his value to the king through feats of arms. This would prove to be particularly significant during the turmoil of the Old King's final years.

Even so, most leading courtiers were prized first and foremost not for their physical prowess, but their measured advice and trusted guid-ance on matters of state. To earn Henry's respect and gain his ear,

Marshal needed to prove his worth as a counsellor and confidante. The ideals of '*courtesie*' current in the 1180s meant that, to achieve this goal, William had, above all, to be impassive; capable of maintaining an icy, ironclad grip on his feelings. Excessive public displays of emotion (especially anger) were frowned upon as indicators of an intemperate and unbalanced personality, and any advice proffered by such a figure might be easily discredited as hasty or unwise. Rivals for the king's affection often sought to goad the unwary through insults – some veiled, others blatant – in the hope of provoking an enraged outburst. Not surprisingly, many hot-blooded knights, born to the battlefield, struggled to achieve this mannered control.

William had experience of mixing with men of power – as a tournament champion he had been on speaking terms with the likes of Philip of Flanders and Theobald of Blois since the late 1170s – and the scandal of 1182 had given him a bitter taste of courtly machinations, but nothing can have prepared him for the scale and complexity of the challenge he now faced. Nonetheless, over time he learnt to navigate the quagmire of courtly customs and politics, and proved to be a remarkably successful courtier. He possessed a rare ability to thrive both in war and at court. Marshal seems to have gradually developed a form of emotional armour, allowing him to present an imperturbable public face. This glacial calm would serve him well in the latter stages of his career.

William also appears to have diffused the tension of 'courtly' confrontations by recounting disarming anecdotes from his past. This was where the oft-repeated tales of his time as a child hostage, or his various tournament triumphs, came into their own. Each carefully crafted story affirmed Marshal's laudable qualities: his ability to charm King Stephen in 1152 or to earn the triumphal spear at the Pleurs tournament around 1177. But at the same time any hint of prideful boasting was countered by notes of humour and self-deprecation: the young boy spurned by his father or the champion found with his head on a black-smith's anvil. In relative terms these were simple, but effective, stories – hardly the masterpieces of veiled subterfuge employed by men such as the likes of Walter Map, where everything was implied and nothing said openly.

It would be naive to assume that William's conduct as a courtier was thoroughly admirable. In truth, it was probably impossible to climb through the ranks as he did without a degree of obsequious duplicity and scheming ambition. To thrive in the shark-pool of the Angevin court one had to manage an array of shifting alliances, and engage in a delicate dance of nuanced flattery and guarded insinuation. As his career advanced, William would take great care not to make powerful enemies and to avoid alienating those who might further his interests in the future. Indeed, one of Richard the Lionheart's favourites, the plain-speaking William Longchamp, would later accuse Marshal of just such conniving equivocation. Nonetheless, at moments of crisis, when the hardest choices had to be made, William would prove to be a remarkably loyal retainer and servant of the crown. Ultimately, it was perhaps his well-earned reputation for unfailing fidelity that brought Marshal to the notice of successive monarchs.

The psychological strain of holding a mask of placid 'courtly' composure, while constantly weighing the intentions of rivals, must have been immense. There was perhaps some relief to be had from finding former associates at court; men who had followed a similar path from the Young King's military entourage to Henry's household, such as Robert Tresgoz, Gerard Talbot and Baldwin of Béthune. Marshal certainly cultivated close friendships with a handful of trusted confidants like Baldwin. He also forged an important alliance with another rising figure in the Angevin court, Geoffrey FitzPeter. Like William, Geoffrey was the younger son of a minor West Country crown official, but he had pursued the clerical, rather than knightly career path, and was fast achieving distinction as an administrator and bureaucrat. However, it was perhaps only in the company of his own inner circle – his *mesnie* (military retinue) – that Marshal could actually drop his guard, and as the years passed, this must have served to deepen his relationship with, and dependence upon, these retainers.

WITH THE KING'S FAVOUR

As William Marshal found his bearings within the Angevin court, grat-
ifying evidence of Henry II's favour was soon forthcoming. During his
thirteen years of service in the Young King Henry's entourage,
William's hopes of gaining advancement through title and land had
been constantly thwarted. His own fortune and fame had depended,
in large part, upon continued success on the tournament circuit, but
these chivalric contests could be dangerous and unpredictable. They
were a young man's game and Marshal was now entering his forties.

Luckily for William, the Old King was not merely a monarch in
name. He wielded real power and could shower his favourites with
gifts. Nonetheless, even an august ruler of Henry's stature could not
simply dole out estates and honours on a whim. In 1066, when
William the Conqueror's Norman forces ransacked England and dispatched the vast majority of its Anglo-Saxon aristocracy, virtually the
entire realm had reverted to the crown. In the first wave of Norman
settlement and colonisation, these newly seized territories could then
be parcelled out as King William saw fit, along with an array of titles
and offices. When the pickings were this rich it was easy to satisfy
ambitions, and the Conqueror was able to retain a vast quantity of land
for himself and still have more than enough left over to transform his
leading retainers into great magnates.

More than a century had passed since those heady days. Patterns of
landholding, lordship and entitlement had become established and
then ingrained, while the king's own estates had been slowly whittled
away. Laws and customs had evolved to protect many of the nobility's
rights, though there was a constant tension between the interests of the
crown and the expectations of his aristocracy. By the later twelfth
century, in most cases, land and title could not be stripped and redis-
tributed without good cause. There had been opportunities for fresh
conquests in Wales and Ireland, and some remained, but for the most
part, kings wishing to reward loyalty and allegiance had either to work

on the margins through legal channels, or to forfeit a portion of their own royal lands.

It was this latter approach that Henry II employed in 1186 when granting William Marshal his first estate at Cartmel in north-west England – a handsome parcel of Lancashire land, set between the majestic shores of Lake Windermere (at the foot of the Lake District) and the windswept-coast at Morecambe Bay to the south. This was a modest enough start, but it brought William an annual income of £32 and gave him a firm foundation from which to build. Around this same time, the Old King made use of another significant royal pre-rogative to bring Marshal further reward. It was traditional for young male and female noble-born heirs to become wards of the crown if their lands were held directly from the king. Henry II had it in his gift to confer guardianship of such wards as he saw fit, and two were now bestowed upon William.

The first of these brought Marshal wardship of Heloise of Lancaster. Since her father's death in 1184, she had been heiress of Kendal, one of the major lordships in northern England, with lands stretching across Westmoreland, Lancashire and the West Riding of Yorkshire and control of a number of castles. Given that Kendal lay just fifteen miles north-east of Cartmel, there was an obvious connection with William's new estate. In formal terms, Marshal had a duty as her guardian to protect Heloise's interests and to care for her person, and the *History* was keen to emphasise that he discharged this role, keep-ing the 'lady of Lancaster, [a woman of] great elegance ... from dishonour for a long time'. At a practical level, however, this wardship was a valuable gift. So long as Heloise remained unwed, William could control and exploit her lands for his own benefit. As guardian, it was also his responsibility to arrange her marriage and this meant that he could either wed her himself or use the promise of her hand to secure other advantages.

This might seem like a desperately seedy and mercenary arrange-ment, but in many ways it suited all parties. Heloise obviously had little say in her future, but she was at least shielded from harm and could expect to retain a direct claim to her family lands, while Henry II was able to discharge his responsibility for the lordship of Kendal and reward his new household knight. Of course, the main beneficiary was William. He now had the promise of significant advancement, but also the opportunity to shape his own future. Marshal could have jumped at the opportunity that now stood before him, marrying Heloise, uniting his Cartmel estate with the Kendal lands and assuming the role of a noteworthy northern baron. That seems to have been the Old King's expectation. As it was, William proved content to bide his time. So long as the lady of Lancaster remained living and healthy the option of a marriage remained, but he decided for now to leave the door open to other, even rosier, prospects.

Marshal's second ward was a young lad, around fifteen years of age, named John of Earley. In many respects, John's background was strikingly similar to William's own, being the orphaned son of a minor West Country nobleman (the late royal chamberlain William of Earley). John was given into Marshal's care to receive a military education and, in the first instance, to serve as his squire. The two forged an exceptionally close bond and, as the years passed, Earley became one of William's most trusted retainers and closest friends. Indeed, John's personal recollections and eyewitness testimony would later prove to be crucial sources of information when the *History of William Marshal* came to be written. From 1186 onwards, John of Earley's fidelity and near-constant presence became a prominent feature of William's life.

John of Earley was also one of the cornerstones of the *mesnie* that Marshal now began to assemble around him. Two other prominent knights entered William's entourage in this period – William Waleran and Geoffrey FitzRobert. Both were from Wiltshire, one of the counties of Marshal's childhood, and together they would enjoy long and successful careers at William's side. Marshal had begun a slow, but significant transformation. He had lived the bulk of his life as a knight in service, but he was now becoming a lord in his own right, with knights who looked to him for protection and promotion. The burden of responsibility had begun to settle.

Luckily for William, and his new knights, his career was flourishing. He was climbing the social ladder, though as yet he had not come close to its highest rungs. The *History* suggested that, from 1186 onwards, Henry II 'showed great affection towards' Marshal and appointed him 'his chief advisor', but this was a significant overstatement of William's position and importance. As a leading household knight, Marshal was part of the Old King's inner circle at court and he quickly became a notable commander in the field and a source of counsel on matters of martial strategy and military planning. But in the day-to-day business of governance and power politics, William still stood on the periphery. A range of documentary evidence from the Angevin court indicates that in eminence, Marshal still ranked well below men like Ranulf Glanville – justiciar of England (the man charged with governing the kingdom in Henry's absence) – and the great magnate William Mandeville, earl of Essex.

By the later 1180s, William Marshal clearly aspired to reach the level of these men. He decided not to marry Heloise of Lancaster, though he 'acted as a most courtly guardian', she remained, in the *History's* polite terms, merely 'his dear friend'. This suggests that William was both confident of his ability to rise higher in the king's favour, and exceptionally ambitious. A small fragment of an otherwise unknown royal letter written in 1188, and only rediscovered at the end of the twentieth century, offers a momentary, but nonetheless remarkable, glimpse of Marshal's impatient hunger for advancement and the methods he was willing to employ in its pursuit. By this stage, the Old King was hard-pressed by an ongoing conflict with the Capetian French and preparing to wage a major campaign on the Continent. He duly sent a missive to William Marshal entreating him to 'come to me fully equipped as soon as may be, with as many knights as you can get, to support me in my war'. Henry then acknowledged, with extraordinary candour, that 'you have frequently complained to me that I have bestowed on you only a small fee', and went on to promise Marshal the great castle of Châteauroux in Berry 'with all its lordship and whatever belongs to it' by way of recompense.

This text indicates that William was not above demanding due reward for his service, indeed it suggests that he routinely grumbled, wheedled and perhaps whined to the Old King in order to get his way. Given the fierce competition for crown largesse, it may well be that this type of incessant petitioning was commonplace among courtiers, but this evidence still reinforces the strong impression that Marshal's conduct did not always conform to modern fantasies of lofty chivalric behaviour.

THE OLD KING FALTERS

In some respects, William was also fortunate to arrive in Henry II's court at a time of burgeoning confrontation, when an especially high premium was placed on martial skill. The Old King was now in his mid-fifties and starting to show intermittent signs of the debilitating illness that would ultimately rob him of his life. Yet he remained stubbornly determined to preserve his grip over the Angevin Empire and content to manipulate his children if he believed it would advance his dynasty's best interests. The balance of power within the royal family had been reset during William Marshal's absence in the Holy Land. With Young King Henry's death in 1183, Richard the Lionheart – the count of Poitou and duke of Aquitaine – suddenly became Henry II's eldest surviving son and primary heir. Queen Eleanor remained in captivity in England, though the conditions of her confinement had loosened briefly in late 1184 and early 1185, when she was permitted to attend the Christmas Court at Windsor and then make a fleeting visit to Normandy.

Richard's major rival looked for a time to be the Old King's son, Geoffrey, count of Brittany. But, in August 1186, he fell from his horse during the grand mêlée of a French tournament and was badly trampled by the horses of his own household knights. Severely wounded, Geoffrey died later in Paris, leaving behind a wife who was already two-months pregnant. She eventually gave birth to Geoffrey's only male heir, Arthur. This left Henry's and Eleanor's youngest son, John, who was now entering his twenties, as the only adult challenger for power.

Fate had thus conspired to place Richard in a similar predicament to that long endured by his elder brother Young Henry. He had become the new restless heir in waiting, thwarted by his father and threatened by his sibling. By the late 1180s, the Lionheart's priority was to secure an unequivocal confirmation that he would inherit the English crown. But Richard was also determined to hold on to the prized province of Aquitaine, having poured years of his life into subduing the duchy. Unfortunately, the Old King was still smarting from Young Henry's two rebellions and had not the slightest intention of anointing another heir during his own lifetime. His policy was to withhold power and equivocate on the issue of the succession in the belief that the resultant mixture of hunger and anxiety would compel loyalty. Just as he had with Young Henry, the Old King expected Richard to wait obediently in the wings, and he was only too happy to drop hints that John should be handed Aquitaine, or perhaps even groomed for the crown, if that kept the Lionheart in his place.

But in falling back upon this familiar strategy, King Henry had miscalculated. The world had moved on, even if his thinking had not. No longer the virile young monarch, Henry was likely to struggle to defeat a major uprising. Richard was also a more ruthless and experienced opponent than his elder brother. Above all, the Old King underestimated Philip Augustus, the Capetian king of France. The rather skittish, feeble teenager of 1180 had grown into his crown and was fast maturing into a lethal adversary. Like Henry II, Philip understood that efficient governance could fill the royal coffers, giving him the wealth to challenge Angevin dominance in France, and he also shared the Old King's gift for political machination. Not for nothing would one contemporary describe him as 'wily and as cunning as a fox'. To Philip, the power held by the upstart lordlings from Anjou was an unconscionable insult to the ancient royal majesty of his Capetian house. Their possession of the Norman Vexin and their influence over the contested region of Berry to the south-west were particularly galling. He was determined to reassert the might of the French monarchy, and willing to break promises, betray friendships and wage bloody wars to achieve this goal.

King Philip recognised that Richard the Lionheart's frustrations might be turned to his own advantage. He was also intent upon resolving the issue of his half-sister Alice's status. She had been betrothed to Richard in 1169 and taken into Angevin custody, yet no marriage had taken place and it was strongly rumoured that the French princess had become Henry II's lover. In all probability, Philip's concern over her fate was not driven by filial affection, but the cold realities of dynastic politics. Alice's marriage to Richard would bring a dowry that might enable Philip to leverage access to the Vexin. The union could also produce heirs and thus bring the Capetians a stake in the Angevin realm.

Angevin-Capetian rivalry (1187–88)

King Philip made his first serious attempt to test Henry II's resolve in 1187, launching a major incursion into Berry – the semi-independent territory that dangled invitingly between Aquitaine and the southern reaches of the French kingdom. The campaign scored an early success when the frontier fortress of Issoudun submitted to French authority, but the great prize of this region was the powerful lordship of Châteauroux. Its young heiress, Denise, had been Henry II's ward ever since her father died leaving no male heir in 1176, and the great castle of Châteauroux and all its dependants remained in Angevin hands.

Philip laid siege to Châteauroux with a substantial force in the early summer of 1187, but was repulsed by its garrison. That June, the Old King and Richard hurriedly joined forces to launch a counter-attack and, as the Angevin and Capetian armies moved into position, it looked for once as if a major pitched battle was unavoidable. Nothing is known of William Marshal's movements at this point, though in all likelihood he was present in the Old King's military retinue. Envoys shuttled between the two camps and Richard seems to have played a significant role in brokering a last-minute peace deal with Philip. On 23 June a two-year truce was finalised and both sides withdrew. However, the Lionheart then shocked his father by suddenly switching sides, riding back to Paris with Philip in a very public demonstration of friendship. It seems that the two men had plotted a temporary rapprochement of their own, finding that it served both their interests to unnerve the Old King. The message implied by Richard's display of affection for the French monarch was obvious. If deprived of Aquitaine or his wider inheritance, the Lionheart would follow the example set by Young Henry in 1172, by breaking with his father and siding with the Capetian enemy. Henry II seems to have been wholly unprepared for this treachery and immediately sent a stream of messengers to his son, begging him to return. Richard was eventually drawn back into the Angevin fold, but it was apparent that in future his loyalty would only be secured at a price.

It was at this precise moment, with the balance of power between Henry II, Richard and King Philip delicately poised, that Latin Christendom was struck by disaster. Just two weeks after the confrontation at Châteauroux was averted, Guy of Lusignan, king of Jerusalem, was lured into battle in Palestine. His army was annihilated by Saladin at the Horns of Hattin on 4 July 1187 and, three months later, Jerusalem fell into Muslim hands. This calamity sent a shockwave through Western Europe and, with the preaching of a massive new crusade to avenge these injuries and reclaim the Holy Land, thousands of knights took up arms. According to the *History of William Marshal* 'the number of those taking the cross was so great ... that there was no man convinced of his worth who did not abandon wife and children to become a crusader.'

Amid this groundswell of crusading enthusiasm, it proved impossible for the great crown monarchs of the West to ignore the call to holy war. Richard took the cross at Tours in November 1187 – the first major lord to do so north of the Alps – and both Henry II and Philip Augustus followed suit in January 1188, after an impassioned sermon by the new archbishop of Tyre, recently arrived from Palestine.

Jerusalem's fall and the launching of the Third Crusade served merely to complicate the interplay between the Angevins and Capetians. The Lionheart's apparent enthusiasm for the expedition alarmed both the Old King and Philip, because Richard's precipitous departure might overturn Henry's plans for the succession and leave the issue of Alice's marriage unresolved. Meanwhile, Richard himself was unsettled by the fact that his younger brother John had made no move to take the cross – surely a sign that he hoped to seize power in the Lionheart's absence. The papacy strictly prohibited any attacks on a crusader's lands while he was fighting in the East, but neither Henry II, nor Philip Augustus, trusted the other to respect this law. Their mutual suspicion was so entrenched that detailed plans had to be laid for a simultaneous departure, because neither king would leave Europe without their rival in tow. The resultant delays meant that it would be three years before the main Angevin and Capetian crusading contingents reached the Levant. Other crusaders set out with greater speed. The Poitevin lord, Geoffrey of Lusignan, left France in the autumn of 1188 and went on to earn renown fighting in the crusade's first titanic confrontation – the great siege of Acre. Europe's elder statesman, the mighty German Emperor Frederick Barbarossa began an overland march at the head of a massive army in May 1189 and many expected him to seize overall leadership of the campaign.

Any hope that the Angevins and Capetians might set aside their differences in the interests of the holy war were shattered in June 1188, when King Philip broke the supposed two-year truce, launching a second invasion of Berry that this time brought the surrender of Châteauroux. Around the same time, Capetian forces prosecuted a series of destructive raids into Norman territory. The *History of William Marshal* described this as 'war on a vast scale', decrying the fact that 'the land was laid waste and shamefully damaged'. Richard moved to defend the major fortresses of neighbouring Touraine, such as Loches, while launching punitive raids of his own into Berry, but the bulk of the region was now in French hands. At the news of this

French aggression, Henry II 'summoned a huge army', including thousands of Welsh mercenaries. It was at this point that William Marshal received his call to arms and the promise of Châteauroux once it was retaken. Together with the king, he crossed to Normandy on 11 July and took up a defensive position in the northern duchy, prompting Philip Augustus to pull back to the French heartlands.

The Old King seems once again to have been caught flat-footed by the Capetian offensive, because rather than responding with an immediate attack of his own, he dispatched a diplomatic mission to the French court. The party was led by the eminent archbishop of Rouen, Walter of Coutances, but also included William Marshal. In reality, the deputation looks to have been little more than a stalling tactic, designed to give Henry time to muster his armies. Once in the presence of the Capetian king, Archbishop Walter bluntly demanded reparations for the damage recently inflicted on Angevin territory, and Philip unsurprisingly demurred, declaring his intention to hold Berry and recover the whole of the Norman Vexin. Nothing may have come from the embassy, but it marked Marshal's first deployment as a high-level envoy, further signalling his rising status.

William also appears to have played a leading role in devising Angevin military strategy that summer. Both sides in the conflict had already employed the tactic of mounted raiding or *chevauchées*, with which Marshal had first become familiar in Poitou back in 1168. In spite of the *History*'s voluble criticism of the Capetians' recent use of these ravaging assaults, the biographer now happily recorded that William advised the Old King to launch a sudden, devastating incursion into French territory, suggesting that, caught unawares, the Capetians would 'suffer greater damage'. According to the *History*, Henry responded enthusiastically: "'By God's eyes!" said the King "You are an excellent man and have advised me very well; it will be done exactly as you say.'" On 30 August, the Angevin forces crossed into French territory near Pacy-sur-Eure and marched south-east. The biographer noted that their 'hearts were set on causing great destruction [and] they made no secret of burning the whole countryside as far as

Mantes'. The Old King rode further south to Bréval, where he 'burned and destroyed everything he came to and never held back for anything', taking 'fine, handsome booty' as he went. When he heard of the assault Philip Augustus was said to have been 'full of grief'.

This form of scorched-earth warfare, targeting enemy resources, might have been commonplace in the twelfth century, but it still left terrible scars on the rural landscape and local population. Perhaps most chillingly of all, it is clear that these raids were not random acts of chaotic rampage. Instead, William and his peers had turned the *chevauchée* and its associated forms of assault into methodical campaigns of destruction and calculated brutality. Count Philip of Flanders was said to have offered the following advice: 'Destroy your foes and lay waste their country, by fire and burning let all be set alight, that nothing be left for them, either in wood or meadow, of which in the morning they could have a meal.' Contemporary sources also detailed the techniques involved, noting the use of scouts and scavengers to ransack settlements and seize 'money, cattle, mules [and] sheep', while specialist 'incendiaries' or 'fire-starters' torched villages and farmsteads, leaving 'the terrified inhabitants [to either be] burned or led away with their hands tied'. Incursions of this type were specifically designed to inspire dread and panic, and were said to send 'a surge of fear [sweeping] over the countryside'.

Marshal went on to prosecute a second ravaging expedition along the eastern frontier of Touraine, near the fortress of Montmirail, and on this occasion the *History* recalled that the Old King instructed William to 'burn and destroy the entire region, sparing nothing'. The biographer then gleefully described how Marshal and his men marched through landscape 'burning, robbing and plundering as they went'. Scant effort was made to justify these atrocities, though the *History* did make the remarkable suggestion that this raid might be considered 'a great act of chivalry' if it brought the enemy to his knees, because peace might then be restored. William and his contemporaries evidently felt little or no compunction about this grim feature of medieval warfare.

In spite of the ferocious tactics employed on both sides, the campaigning through the late summer and early autumn proved inconclusive. Henry II withdrew to Le Mans in Maine and began to experience more frequent bouts of illness, with some form of tumour developing in his groin. As winter approached, the fighting petered out and the Old King, Richard and Philip Augustus sought to settle their differences through a series of diplomatic exchanges and gatherings. The Capetian king used this period to re-establish contact with Richard, and seems to have stirred up the Lionheart's discontent and suspicions, urging him to turn on his father. The rift might still have been repaired, had Henry made a decisive move to declare Richard his heir in England, but the Old King was plagued by doubts about his intentions and now began to regard young John as his one faithful son.

This rupture at the heart of the royal family would have far-reaching consequences. Had Henry and his offspring stood shoulder to shoulder, King Philip's dreams of reasserting Capetian authority would surely have been foiled. As it was, the fissures within the Angevin dynasty gave the French king a crucial opening – one that, in the words of the *History*, would prove 'injurious to all the heirs to the realm of England'. The decisive break came on 18 November 1188, at an assembly at Bonsmoulins (in southern Normandy). William Marshal travelled to this peace conference with Henry II and witnessed the Old King's dismay when Richard and Philip arrived together. This public display of their renewed amity confirmed Henry's worst fears and 'he knew then for certain that he had been betrayed'. On that day, the Lionheart went down on his knees before King Philip and paid him homage for Normandy, Aquitaine, Anjou, Maine and Berry – an act of ritual subservience that confirmed their alliance. Denied power by his father, Richard was now willing to unite with the enemy and seize the Angevin realm by force.

The Old King had been roundly outmanoeuvred. He had been the scourge of international affairs for more than thirty years – a scheming mastermind, able to read his opponents and plot their downfall. Now, weakened by ill health and advancing age, he seemed paralysed by shock and fury; backed into a corner from which he could see no escape. Henry's brusque refusal to confirm the Lionheart as heir to the English crown in the wake of Bonsmoulins made a direct confrontation all but inevitable. In these foreboding days of winter, the Old King turned to his inner circle, calling 'Marshal and the others whom he loved and trusted the most [and asking] them for their advice in the matter'. As a result of this meeting, William was sent on an urgent mission to follow Richard and recall him to his father's side, so that their feud might finally be settled. The Lionheart had been brought to heel in the summer of 1187 and the vain hope was that open conflict might yet be averted. William tracked Richard as far as Amboise (east of Tours), but discovered that the Lionheart had been up half the preceding night urgently preparing more than 200 letters calling his supporters across the Angevin realm to arms. With the wheels of war in motion, Marshal 'sent word to the king [of this] cruel act of treachery'.

The Old King's isolation

Henry II retreated into the Angevin heartlands of Maine and Anjou through the winter and early spring, seething with rage, but immobilised by illness. Sensing the Old King's weakness, many of his supporters began to melt away. A number of notable barons absented themselves from Henry's Christmas Court at Saumur in December 1188, and in the New Year Henry tried to flush out any turncoats by issuing a general summons to his nobles, instructing them to come 'without delay and to offer no pretext for not doing so'. Ranulf Glanville (justiciar of England) remained loyal, but fearful of leaving the kingdom unprotected, sent his well-regarded clerk and deputy Hubert Walter in his stead. Others simply ignored the request.

With each passing week, the list of Henry's friends and supporters grew shorter. His youngest son John stood firm alongside a diminishing circle of barons, as did the king's military household. Marshal remained by Henry's side through Lent, witnessing his slow decline, moving with the fractured remnants of the royal court between the mighty fortress of Chinon and the city of Le Mans. At one point, William was sent on another embassy to Paris, this time to see if a wedge could be driven between Philip Augustus and Richard by offering to agree a separate peace with the Capetian king on terms of his naming. When Marshal arrived in the city, however, he found that the Lionheart's 'wise and crafty' representatives, including the 'artful' William Longchamp, were already closeted with the French monarch, and had to return empty-handed.

With the onset of spring, Henry began to prepare for an invasion, strengthening the defences of Le Mans and placing his remaining troops on a war footing. By this stage, those retainers who continued to show unfaltering loyalty were fast rising in the Old King's esteem and favour. William had moved from the edge of Henry's inner circle, to stand among a handful of men like William Mandeville, still trusted to offer counsel and lead troops in the field. The king chose to reward this fidelity. The previous summer, Marshal had been promised Châteauroux, but that castle remained in French hands. In its place, Henry offered William another crown ward, one whose wealth and prospects left Lady Heloise of Lancaster in the shade. This eminent heiress was Isabel of Clare, 'a worthy and beautiful girl', the eighteen-year-old daughter of the late Earl Richard Strongbow of Striguil. Her hand in marriage would bring Marshal a powerful lordship, with lands on the Welsh March (border), and title to other territories in west Wales, Normandy and Ireland. He would become, at a stroke, a great baron of England.

The Old King's pledge makes it clear that he now placed a high value on William's service. There can be no doubt that Marshal's star had risen at a formidable rate in the three years since he returned from the Holy Land, partly through his own qualities, but also because the tumult of this period had given him ample opportunity to shine. Nonetheless, a nagging question remains. Was this royal gift simply an unbidden act of gratitude from an ailing king, or the mercenary price specified by Marshal in return for his continued allegiance? Henry's

1188 letter proved that William was not above pleading for, and perhaps even demanding, recompense; and there can be no doubt that he aspired to join the upper ranks of England's aristocracy. Nonetheless, it would have been obvious to Marshal, even in the first months of 1189, that the Old King's power was faltering, his reign drawing to a close. William must have known that he was fighting on the losing side of this conflict; that the promise of Isabel of Clare's hand might well prove worthless once a new monarch came to power, with Henry's pledge disregarded and the heiress reapportioned. Perhaps Marshal was gambling on the embattled Old King's ability to struggle on long enough for an actual wedding to be arranged, but if so, this was a rather forlorn hope. Had self-interest been paramount then the obvious choice would have been to abandon Henry, as so many others had, and seek promotion from either Richard or Philip Augustus. As it was, Marshal remained at Henry's side.

By early summer the Old King had recovered enough strength to consider attending yet another peace conference. With the Third Crusade about to begin, the papacy was distraught at the prospect of further war in France when, it believed, all eyes should be on the Holy Land. A papal legate thus arranged a meeting for early June 1189 between Henry, Richard and Philip near La Ferté-Bernard (some twenty-five miles north-east of Le Mans, on the border of Maine), hoping to orchestrate a reconciliation. It turned out to be a predictably bad-tempered affair. 'Both sides came fully armed on horseback', according to the History, and the chronicler Ralph of Diss admitted that after hours of pointless quarrelling 'they withdrew as enemies'.

It seems likely that Philip and Richard never had any expectation or intention of reaching an accord, but agreed to the meeting merely to draw the Old King out into the open. Instead of peacefully retreating eastwards out of Maine as custom required, they launched an immediate offensive, sending thousands of troops pouring into Angevin territory. La Ferté-Bernard fell in short order, only to be followed by a series of other strongholds, many of which seem to have willingly surrendered to the Lionheart. Henry II was said to have been 'furious about losing his lands', but now had no option but to beat a hasty path to Le Mans, the great city of Maine.

Le Mans is most famous today for its twenty-four-hour car race, but at the heart of this bustling modern city lies a well-preserved medieval quarter – now known as the 'Cité Plantagenet'. Much of this picturesque warren of cobbled streets and huddled, timber-framed buildings dates from the later Middle Ages. But two remnants of the Le Mans to which Henry and William retreated in June 1189 are still in evidence, and they help to explain why the Old King chose this city as the site of his last stand.

The first is the towering cathedral of St Julien, begun in the eleventh century and dedicated by Henry himself in 1158. This was the burial place of Geoffrey Plantagenet, Henry's father, and it stands as a potent reminder of the intimate associations between Le Mans and the Angevin dynasty. This was the city of the Old King's own birth and childhood, a bastion of his family's pride. It was also a redoubtable, perhaps even impregnable fortress, enclosed within a towering circuit of ancient Roman walls. One long stretch of these mighty, red-stone fortifications remains in place, replete with a succession of looming towers, a well-defended gate and a deep moat. Standing at the foot of these battlements it is easy to understand why Henry sought sanctuary in Le Mans, and in 1189 he could also fall back on the formidable stone keep that lay within. In addition, the city enjoyed a strong degree of natural protection in the twelfth century, being located in the fork between two rivers: the broad Sarthe and its tributary, the Huisne, flowing in from the east. Only the latter could be crossed with ease, via its one major bridge, and Le Mans' south-eastern walls were further guarded by a marshy ravine.

The Old King had taken further steps to reinforce Le Mans that spring: digging a series of deep ditches to form an outer perimeter, driving sharp stakes into the riverbed at any possible fords of the Huisne and even pulling down some of the houses that had sprung up between the city walls and the two rivers. All of this helped to engender a strong sense of security when Henry, William Marshal and the rest of the Angevin army arrived near dusk on 10 June. According to one contemporary, the Old King even went so far as to promise the citizens of Le Mans that he would never abandon the city.

The defence of Le Mans in 1189

Once safely installed in Le Mans, Henry II summoned William and instructed him to conduct a tour of the outer defences at first light. As dawn broke the next day, Marshal rode out at the head of a small, lightly armoured scouting party. The rolling landscape south of the city was cloaked in a dense fog, so it was difficult to see any great distance as they crossed the River Huisne. Before long, however, they spotted a group of French scouts picking their way northwards. One of William's fellow knights, Robert of Souville, urged an immediate return to the city to raise the alarm, but Marshal refused, unsure of whether the enemy force they had seen represented an advance guard or merely a long-range patrol. Determined to get a better view, he rode to the crest of a low hill and it was only then, as the fog slowly lifted, that 'the whole army of the king of France' came into view 'riding in vast numbers' alongside Richard the Lionheart's forces. They were no more than half a mile away and heading 'straight for Le Mans'.

William raced back to the Old King and the decision was taken to cut down the bridge over the Huisne. Philip and the Lionheart made camp to the south of the river, just out of arrow shot, and the rest of the day passed in a tense stand-off, as both sides readied themselves for the battle to come. Henry seems to have been convinced at this point that the impassable waters of the Huisne would thwart any major enemy assault, though the precautionary decision was taken to torch the remaining buildings south and west of the city walls should the river somehow be crossed. Marshal was less certain of their security. At daybreak on 12 June he insisted on donning full armour with the assistance of his squire, John of Earley, while a number of others – the Old King included – remained un-armoured.

Marshal was detailed to hold the main southern gate, while Henry made the day's first patrol alongside his youngest son John, and a party of knights including Robert Tresgoz, Gerard Talbot and Baldwin of Béthune. Once down by the Huisne, they discovered the French vanguard milling around on the southern banks, examining the wreckage of the bridge that had been 'broken to pieces' and scanning the slow-moving river for any possible crossing point. According to the *History*: 'Nobody imagined that there was a ford there, but they tested the waters with their lances and discovered the best ford in the world.' Ten mounted knights immediately ploughed into the river, drove forward and launched themselves up the opposite bank. Caught completely by surprise, the warriors in the Old King's troop charged forward to stem their advance, but with more French knights now streaming across the Huisne they were soon driven back and forced to lead Henry to safety.

With the Huisne breached, it now fell to William Marshal to hold the southern gate, as the Capetian forces streamed through the jumbled streets of Le Mans' outer suburb. As 'the French rode up to him to launch a fierce attack', a vicious skirmish erupted, not unlike that he had fought at Neufchâtel more than twenty years earlier. Rallying what Angevin knights he could, Marshal tried to hold his ground, but the mêlée surged back and forth. In the midst of this 'hard-fought onslaught', one of the Old King's knights, Hugh of Malannoy, was driven, man and horse, into the ravine south of the city. William also came face-to-face with a leading member of Richard the Lionheart's retinue, Andrew of Chauvigny, 'a man renowned for his deeds of great valour'. Marshal tried to employ his old tournament trick, seizing Andrew's bridle and dragging him towards the gate and possible captivity, but Chauvigny managed to wrestle free, though he broke his arm in the process.

By this stage the suburbs had been torched and with flames spreading fast through the crowed houses, the sense of chaos only intensified. At some point a general retreat was sounded, and William drew back within the southern gate, but elsewhere Philip's and Richard's troops were able to pour in before entrances were barred. To make matters worse, strong winds were whipping up the fires of the burning suburbs, and the raging conflagration eventually spread to the city itself. With smoke pouring into the streets and enemy forces now at large inside Le Mans, bedlam reigned.

Henry II, Marshal and William Mandeville seem to have regrouped in the north of the city, probably not far from the Cathedral of St Julien. Any thought of retreating within the keep was quickly rejected. In spite of the Old King's grand proclamation just two days earlier, a decision was made to relinquish the city and ride hard for the north in the hope of escape. The *History* glossed over the details of this bitter setback, noting only that the remaining Angevins left 'as one body', but other chroniclers like Roger of Howden indicated that in the course of this harried flight, Henry left many household servants and knights behind, and hundreds of his Welsh mercenaries were hunted down and butchered.

The remaining members of the royal household now formed a close bodyguard around the Old King – the last line of protection 'against death or capture' – determined to see their monarch and his son John to safety. They had covered some two to three miles when it became apparent that another party of knights was in hot pursuit, racing along the road behind and closing fast. Marshal and another household warrior, William des Roches (literally William 'of the Rocks'), reined in and turned to bar their path, only to find none other than Richard the Lionheart bearing down upon them. As des Roches moved to intercept one of the duke's knights, William charged forward to confront Richard himself. The great tournament champion was about to meet the Lionheart in single combat.

Only the *History of William Marshal* described this encounter in close terms, though the broad details of its account were confirmed in other contemporary sources. One thing seems certain. This was to be no fair fight. So intent had Richard been upon hunting down his father, that he had begun his chase wearing only a doublet and light helm. This added speed to his pursuit, but left him dreadfully exposed to attack. Worse still, the Lionheart was armed with only a sword. Marshal, by contrast, had a shield and lance. The biographer described how:

> [William] spurred straight on to meet the advancing [Duke] Richard. When the [duke] saw him coming he shouted at the top of his voice: 'God's legs, Marshal! Don't kill me. That would be a wicked thing to do, since you find me here completely unarmed.'

In that instant, Marshal could have slain Richard, skewering his body with the same lethal force that dispatched Patrick of Salisbury in 1168. Had there been more than a split second to ponder the choice, William might perhaps have reacted differently. As it was, instinct took over. Marshal simply could not bring himself to kill an un-armoured opponent, let alone the heir-apparent to the Angevin realm, King Henry II's eldest surviving son. Instead, he was said to have shouted in reply: 'Indeed I won't. Let the Devil kill you! I shall not be the one to do it', and at the last moment, lowering his lance fractionally, he drove it into Richard's mount. With that 'the horse died instantly; it never took another step forward' and, as it fell, the Lionheart was thrown to the ground and his pursuit of the king brought to an end.

The Old King made good his escape that day, but his power had been shattered nonetheless. Once at a safe distance, Henry was said to have ridden to a hilltop and looked back on the burning city of Le Mans in shame, cursing God for the ruin of his reign. In the days that followed, Marshal was sent on north to Normandy with a platoon of fifty knights in a half-hearted attempt to rally support for the king, while John seems to have stayed in Maine and Henry himself arced back south towards the security of Anjou's mighty castle, Chinon. The hopelessness of the Old King's predicament was only confirmed when Tours – site of the Angevin treasury – fell to Richard and Philip. Now a broken man, Henry's infirmity returned in force. 'Sorely troubled by his illness and his pain which grew worse with every passing day', he took refuge in Chinon and ordered William to return to his side.

The last days of Henry II

Marshal's moment of decision had arrived. There could be no more lingering hopes of recovery for the Old King, with the Angevin realm crumbling and his royal authority smashed beyond repair. Many who had remained faithful up to this point now abandoned Henry; some went directly to Richard, others merely waited, watching from the wings for a new regime to begin. William was perfectly placed to do the same, far from the king's side. In 1183, the Young King Henry's death had been swift and unheralded, leaving Marshal and his fellow household knights little or no time to consider their positions. No one seems to have thought to transfer their allegiance during those grim days at Martel, but there was every reason to do so now, confronted by the Old King's slow and certain decline. If Marshal laid himself before the feet of the Lionheart and begged forgiveness for their recent encounter, he might yet salvage some reward and secure his future. But to do so, would be to forsake his reputation for honour and loyalty. During the flight from Le Mans he had been forced to act on impulse; now he had to time agonise over his decision.

In the event, William rode to Chinon to stand by his king through his last, desperate days, arriving by the start of July 1189. With no choice but to accept defeat, Henry agreed to a final meeting with Richard and King Philip near Tours on 4 July, so that terms could be settled. The Old King was barely able to sit astride his horse, but Marshal rode with him, and tended to his needs in the hours before the conference began as they waited in a nearby Templar commandery. Henry was in such agonising pain that 'he could neither suffer it nor endure it', and wracked by the sense that his ravaged frame was rebelling against him, he apparently told William, 'I feel I have neither body, heart, nor limb to call my own', and Marshal could only watch as the king 'first turned a violent red and then became a livid colour'.

When Henry II finally arrived at the agreed meeting place, the grave extent of his infirmity could not be disguised. The Lionheart looked on, impassive and suspicious of some ruse, but Philip Augustus was genuinely shocked by the sight of his hated rival, now reduced to such abject frailty. The Capetian offered up a cloak so that the Old King might sit upon the ground, but Henry insisted on standing, starring down his opponents even as he conceded their terms. Richard was finally confirmed as Henry II's successor throughout the Angevin realm and the French monarch was promised a tribute of 20,000 silver marks to seal the peace. The Old King's one request was that the allies supply him with a list of 'all those who, deserting him, had gone over to [Philip and Richard]'. As the conference came to an end, Henry was said to have mustered the energy for one final, parting barb. Leaning forward to seal the accord by conferring the ritual kiss of peace upon his son, the Old King whispered, 'God grant that I may not die until I have had my revenge on you.'*

King Henry was carried back to Chinon on a litter and confined to bed, but he could find no peace. The Old King now became fixated by the desire to make a last account of his supporters. The keeper of the royal seal, Roger Malchael, was sent to Tours to demand the list of turncoats promised by Philip. When Roger returned he was hurriedly ushered into a private audience with Henry, but could hardly bring himself to reveal the bleak truth, saying:

'My lord, so Jesus Christ help me, the first name written down on this list here is that of your son, count John.' When King Henry heard that the person he most expected to do right, and who he most loved, was in the act of betraying him, he said nothing more except this: 'You have said enough.'

This final act of treachery crushed the Old King's spirits. He soon collapsed into a 'burning hot' feverish stupor, and 'his blood so boiled within him that his complexion became clouded, dark, blue and livid'. Unmanned by agonising pain, he 'lost his mental faculties, hearing

---

* According to Gerald of Wales, Richard the Lionheart later recounted Henry II's spiteful comment to Philip Augustus and the Capetian court.

and seeing nothing', and though he spoke 'nobody could understand a word of what he said'. On the night of 6 July 1189, with only a handful of servants in attendance, Henry's will finally gave out. In the words of the *History*: 'Death simply burst his heart with her own hands', and a 'stream of clotted blood burst forth from his nose and mouth'.

In a last indignity, the household staff detailed to watch him looted his corpse, stealing 'his clothes, his jewels, his money as much as each of them could take', and this 'rabble' left the great monarch strewn, half out of bed, wearing only his 'breeches and shirt'. When Henry's body was later discovered, the whole castle was thrown into commotion. Marshal and the remaining members of the royal household rushed to the room and hurriedly covered their dead king with a cloak, sobered by the sight of this once mighty figure brought to such a wretched end. The chamber was then placed under close guard and clergymen arrived to wrap the Old King in a shroud and sing Mass.

In the days that followed, William helped to carry Henry II's body to the nearby abbey of Fontevraud, and the corpse was laid out in state to await Richard's arrival, so that the son might pay his last respects to the father he had forsaken. Marshal stood vigil, his grief mixed with a dreadful unease. A new king would now be proclaimed, a man whom William had unhorsed outside Le Mans and resisted to the bitter end. There could be little doubt that the Lionheart would exact his revenge, stripping Marshal of his status and condemning him to exile or worse. William was about to learn the true cost of loyalty.

8

DEFENDER OF THE REALM

Richard the Lionheart arrived at Fontevraud around 10 July 1189. As he entered the great abbey church and saw the body of his father, his face was said to have been an emotionless mask, such that 'nobody could say if he felt joy or sadness in his heart'. He stood impassive for long minutes, staring down at the man who had been his mentor, ally, monarch and enemy. In a very real sense, Richard had hounded the Old King to his death. With his eyes focused solely upon the dogged pursuit of power, the Lionheart had betrayed his family, sided with the Angevins' avowed foe and waged open war upon his kin. Now all his cherished ambitions had been fulfilled and Henry's corpse lay cold and lifeless before him. It was perhaps in these moments of quiet reflection that the full burden of kingship settled on his shoulders, as he felt the weight of all that he had done, and began to glimpse the trials that lay ahead.

At last, Richard turned from the body and 'asked for the Marshal to come to him immediately'. With only the Old King's chancellor, Maurice Craon in tow, the two men rode out into the verdant countryside surrounding Fontevraud. The *History* preserved a dramatic record of this tense encounter. After a long pause, Richard finally broke the silence, apparently saying: 'Marshal, the other day you intended to kill me, and you would have, without a doubt, if I hadn't deflected your lance with my arm.' This was a dangerous moment. Should William accept this comment, he would allow the Lionheart to save face, yet at the same time admit to having sought his death. According to the *History* at least, he chose the harder path, replying: 'It was never my intention to kill you ... I am still strong enough to direct my lance [and] if I had wanted to, I could have driven it straight through your body, just as I did that horse of yours.' Richard might have taken mortal offence at this blunt contradiction. Instead, he was said to have declared: 'Marshal, you are forgiven, I shall never be angry with you over that matter.'

The Lionheart may have been testing or toying with William during this meeting, but it is likely that he had decided how to deal with Marshal even before he arrived at Fontevraud. Richard would soon be crowned king. He had a fragile realm to defend and a crusade in the Holy Land to fight. He could ill afford to discard a man of William's quality. Over the last month, Marshal had proven his resolute loyalty to the king and his martial prowess. He was precisely the kind of supporter that the Lionheart would need in the months and years ahead. Perhaps there was, at first, a lingering grudge over their confrontation outside Le Mans, but Richard was shrewd enough to recognise that this had to be put to one side. If he was to prevail as king, such resentments could not govern his actions.

Resolved to draw William into his own circle, the Lionheart offered to confirm the Old King's pledge of the wealthy heiress, Isabel of Clare's, hand in marriage. But he took care to emphasise that Henry II had only promised Isabel to Marshal; the actual gift of her guardianship would come as a result of Richard's own patronage. As the Lionheart's leading modern biographer, Professor John Gillingham, noted, with this act Richard 'in effect, made William a millionaire overnight'. Marshal was then entrusted with an urgent mission: instructed to travel to England, 'take charge of my land and all my other interests', and bear a secret message to Queen Eleanor. Once they returned to Fontevraud, William received a number of royal writs (letters of instruction), including one confirming his appointment as Isabel's guardian, and he then set out for the north almost immediately.

The Lionheart dealt with many of his late father's barons and retainers in a similar fashion. Those who had remained faithful to the last were rewarded. Baldwin of Béthune, for example, received the valuable lordship of Aumale in Normandy, William des Roches, who had covered Henry II's retreat from Le Mans with Marshal, was accepted into Richard's military household and Hubert Walter was appointed as bishop of Salisbury. Less favour was shown to those who had turned away from the Old King in his last months, though Richard's younger brother John was left unpunished. The Lionheart also took care to repay his own leading lieutenants for their service, such that Andrew of Chauvigny received the honour of Châteauroux. Richard went on to meet with Philip Augustus near the great castle of Gisors in the Norman Vexin. The pair had parted as allies, but with the Lionheart now leading the Angevin dynasty, they would soon be forced to confront one another as deadly adversaries. For now, terms of peace were agreed, with the French king returning all recently captured territory, including Berry, and Richard pledging 40,000 silver marks as compensation for their recent campaign.

THE REWARDS WAITING IN LONDON

William Marshal raced north through Anjou and Maine, but paused en route in Normandy to take possession of Isabel of Clare's lands at Longueville near Dieppe (in the duchy's north-eastern reaches), before crossing the Channel – a sure sign that he was now determined to reap the benefits of Richard's patronage while he could. Once in England, William travelled straight to Winchester, where Eleanor had already been released after fifteen years in captivity. This must have been a strange encounter. When they last met, Marshal had only recently left the queen's own service and was a mere household knight in his mid-twenties. Now, William was around forty-two and well on the way to becoming a great baron, while Eleanor was an elderly, yet still sprightly, woman in her late sixties. As always, their connection – seemingly so fundamental to Marshal's early career – can only be glimpsed. The content of the Lionheart's intriguing message to his mother is lost to history, and frustratingly William's biographer merely recorded that the message was safely delivered.

Marshal then made his way 'to the fine city of London' to claim his bride. As a royal ward, Isabel was residing in the White Tower of London, under the protection of Henry II's justiciar Ranulf Glanville. At first Glanville was reluctant to release the heiress into William's care, presumably on the grounds that Richard had yet to be crowned and thus lacked the official authority to apportion a guardianship, but Marshal pressed his case and the justiciar eventually relented. So it was that William finally met his future wife, Isabel of Clare, the lady of Striguil. At around sixteen years old, she was less than half Marshal's age, but by birth and eminence she was his superior. Her celebrated father, Richard Strongbow, had been one of the great Marcher lords who helped Henry II to conquer territory in Wales and Ireland, and had himself earned the hand in marriage of an Irish princess, Aoife (Eve) of Leinster, Isabel's mother. Isabel had been a crown ward since 1185, so even though Marshal was now being foisted upon her, the prospect of marriage after four years of uncertainty may well have felt like a release.*

Isabel held title to one of England's major lordships. At its heart lay a swathe of territory in the southern borderlands with Wales, including the formidable stone castle of Striguil (now known as Chepstow). Elsewhere, Isabel had rights to major manors at Caversham (near Reading) and Long Crendon (to the east of Oxford), the Norman estate of Longueville and significant claims to land in west Wales and Ireland. Her hand in marriage was an inestimable prize – one that would transform William into a leading magnate of the realm. The

---

* Richard Strongbow of Clare, earl of Striguil had died in 1176. His son and heir Gilbert (Isabel's brother) then died at the age of twelve in 1185, leaving Isabel as heir.

History conveyed a clear sense of his excitement, noting that 'now that he had her in his possession he had no wish to lose her', and so immediately made plans for their wedding.

Given Marshal's flourishing prospects, there were now plenty of powerful men willing to cultivate his favour. One such, Richard FitzReinier – a city sheriff – gave him lodgings, probably in the environs of St Paul's Cathedral, and even offered to cover the expenses of the marriage ceremony. William now had a brief moment to draw breath in London. By 1189, the city was set firmly on the path to becoming England's unquestioned capital and was already one of Europe's greatest urban centres – with a population of around 40,000, only Paris was bigger. Its growth reflected a much broader trend of urbanisation. Indeed, Marshal lived through a period in which scores of new towns were created in England, including Newcastle upon Tyne, Liverpool and Portsmouth, and the subsequent rise of the 'burgess' or merchant class of townsfolk would transform the balance of power in medieval society in the decades and centuries that followed.

Lying astride the River Thames, London was perfectly placed to serve as a centre of trade and commerce, just as Western Europe was emerging on to the world stage as a major economic power. William thus found himself in a vibrant and increasingly cosmopolitan city that summer – a place where everything from Egyptian gemstones, to Chinese silks and Arabian gold could be purchased. Like Le Mans, London had been a Roman settlement and an enclosing circuit of ancient walls dating from that period still stood on the northern banks of the Thames, though they were crumbling along the water's edge. For the first time in a millennium a magnificent new stone bridge was even then being built across the broad river; commissioned at enormous cost by Henry II in 1176, it took more than thirty years to construct, but would stand until 1831. In one sense London was a centre of Christian devotion, boasting more than a hundred churches by 1189, so William had his pick of sites in which to marry. There were those, however, who condemned the city as a den of vice, with one contemporary complaining that 'whatever malicious thing can be found anywhere in the world can be found [in London]', adding that it was packed with 'actors, jesters, smooth-skinned lads, Moors, flatterers, pretty boys ... quacks, belly dancers [and] sorcerers'.

William and Isabel were wed in late July. In all likelihood, they followed the normal custom of undergoing a simple ceremony on the church steps – perhaps even those of St Paul's itself – with Marshal presenting his bride with a token symbolising his dower gift, possibly a ring or even a knife. Only then would the couple have entered the building, prostrating themselves before the altar to receive Mass and, after Communion, William would have exchanged the kiss of peace with the attendant priest, and then finally turned to embrace his new wife.

Before Richard the Lionheart arrived in England and the incessant whirl of court life began anew, the couple were able to steal a few weeks together, lodging at the nearby manor of Stoke d'Aubernon, eighteen miles south-west of London – a 'peaceful spot, well-appointed and a delight to the eye'. To begin with, at least, William and Isabel's marriage was simply a political match, but they seem to have developed a relationship based on real affection and mutual respect. In time, they would have no less than ten children, including five sons, the eldest of whom was born within a year. It is also true that, even in an age when male infidelity was commonplace and broadly reported, there is no evidence that Marshal ever took a mistress. On balance, there is a good chance that their union was happy and intimate. Even so, William's career in royal service led to long periods of separation, and by mid-August that summer he was drawn back into the maelstrom of power politics.

In defence of the realm

Richard landed in England on 13 August 1189, having already been confirmed as duke of Normandy in Rouen. His coronation followed on 3 September in Westminster Abbey, just two miles upriver from the city of London. Richard's elevation marked the very first occasion when medieval chroniclers described the ceremonial creation of an English king in precise detail. Though the *History* strangely made no mention of it, William Marshal is thus known to have played an important role in the ritual that day, and he was also joined in the abbey by his brother John Marshal and cousin, William FitzPatrick of Salisbury. John, in particular, appears to have benefited from his younger brother's rising fortunes. Having himself enjoyed little promotion under Henry II, the elder Marshal had in recent years become an associate of the Lionheart's brother, Count John, though that connection had done little for his prospects. It is not clear whether William actively lobbied for favour to be shown to his elder sibling, but John certainly enjoyed a short-lived renaissance in his own career after 1189.*

The coronation ceremony began with a solemn procession, accompanied by sonorous 'chants of praise', that saw Richard taken from the royal palace to the abbey doors, and then through to the altar. Bishops, abbots and clergy led the way, carrying 'holy water, the cross, tapers and censers'. They were followed by the leading crown officers and the great barons of the kingdom, each carrying portions of the royal regalia and robes of majesty. John Marshal came bearing 'a huge pair of golden spurs'; William Marshal carrying the royal cross-tipped sceptre (one of the key symbols of authority) and William of Salisbury with the royal rod of gold, topped by a dove. Richard's brother, John, bore a golden sword, drawn from the royal treasury, while William Mandeville had the honour of carrying the 'great and massive crown, decorated on every side with precious stones'. As William Marshal and the assembled throng looked on, Richard knelt before the altar and swore sacred oaths to protect the Church and rule with justice. The central drama of the ritual was performed by Archbishop Baldwin of Canterbury. The Lionheart was stripped to his undershirt and breeches, his chest bared. The prelate then poured

---

* William Marshal's younger brother, Henry Marshal – who had entered the Church – also enjoyed rewards in this period, being appointed as bishop of Exeter.

holy oil upon Richard's head, chest and arms, each site representing knowledge, valour and glory. Once clad in his regal raiment and holding the great symbols of office, the vast crown was finally placed upon his head.

In the eyes of all those present, indeed in all of Christendom, Richard the Lionheart had been transformed from a mere man, into a divinely ordained king. He walked in state from the abbey to begin his new life as monarch of England, just five days short of his thirty-second birthday. The afternoon and evening were given over to glorious celebration. Richard quickly changed out of his heavy robes and massive crown, donning lighter dress and a simpler diadem to attend a long and luxurious feast. Royal accounts show that no fewer than 1,770 pitchers and 5,050 plates were bought for this occasion.*

King Richard I now had one overriding priority. He was determined to sail to the Holy Land and wage war against Saladin in the Third Crusade. Like thousands of warriors across Europe, the Lionheart had taken the cross, answering the pope's impassioned call to arms. The rumbling conflict with the Capetians and the power struggle with his father had both caused long delays, but from this point onwards the Lionheart focused his own energies, and the considerable resources of England and the Angevin realm, upon the crusade. It would still be the best part of a year before the Angevin and Capetian armies began their journey, but there was a new sense of urgent purpose to the preparations.

Many of Richard's leading knights joined him on the expedition, including Baldwin of Béthune and Andrew of Chauvigny. But William Marshal, one of the greatest warriors of his generation, did not. There is no certain explanation for this apparent anomaly. William had, of course, already made one crusade to the East, but that was also true of men like Philip, count of Flanders and Duke Hugh of Burgundy, yet they set out on the Third Crusade nonetheless. King

---

* The festivities were marred by the outbreak of anti-Jewish rioting in London and Westminster, inspired in part, it would seem, by misdirected crusading fervour.

Richard certainly had a different role in mind for Marshal, but it may be that his decision to leave William behind was also shaped by an element of pride and jealousy. The Lionheart gloried in war and carefully cultivated his own martial reputation. The battle for Jerusalem promised to be the ultimate proving ground of prowess – the arena in which a legend might be forged – so perhaps the prospect of Marshal's participation as a potential rival for renown proved unattractive. It is certainly the case that Richard developed a deep loathing for another Third Crusader and distinguished tournament champion, William des Barres. The pair had already clashed during the Angevin-Capetian war of 1188, since des Barres had joined Philip Augustus' military retinue. In early 1191, when the crusading fleet was moored in Sicily, they met once again in single combat, during a hastily organised joust. When the Lionheart proved unable to unhorse William, he became consumed by rage, 'uttered threats against him' and banished des Barres from his sight. For all his regal bearing, Richard was not a man who liked to be bested.

The *History* hinted at the fact that Marshal's failure to participate in the Third Crusade had been the cause of comment, even a degree of shame. The biographer pointedly observed that William did not take the cross because he 'had already made the journey to the Holy Land to seek God's mercy ... well acquitting himself of his mission', and added, somewhat elliptically, that: 'Whatever anyone else might tell you, that is how matters were arranged.' Other men were mocked for not joining the holy war, even accused of cowardice and a reluctance to fight. In some circles it became common to humiliate non-crusaders by giving them 'wool and distaff', the tools for spinning, to suggest that they were fit only for women's work – a distant precursor to the white feather.

William Marshal would be remaining in England while many of his peers sought fame and distinction in the East, but he would not be idle. Richard's commitment to the holy war meant that the new king would be absent from the realm for many months, perhaps even years. Having fought to win the Angevin realm, the Lionheart was hardly willing to abandon it to its fate. Two overwhelming threats loomed large in his calculations that autumn. With their temporary rapprochement over, it was obvious that King Philip of France would seize upon any opportunity to snatch Angevin territory. For this reason, the two kings would be setting out for Palestine together.

Richard found the prospect of leaving his younger brother John behind in Europe equally troubling. John was now in his early twenties. His life had been spent in the long shadow of greater kin: from his overbearing father Henry II, to his dashing, chivalrous brother, Young Henry; and, perhaps above all, the Lionheart himself, the fearless warrior. John had a proven appetite for power, but lacked the martial genius, charm and judgement of his siblings. With the Old King's encouragement, he had already made one attempt to steal Richard's lands, invading Aquitaine in 1184, while William Marshal was in the Holy Land. Famously known to contemporaries as 'Lackland', because he had received no portion of territory in Henry II's grand settlement of 1169, John had finally been allocated the province of Ireland in 1177 – a region partially subdued by Henry II after Thomas Becket's murder. John led a campaign to Ireland in 1185, but achieved little of worth. He had also betrayed the Old King in his dying days.

Richard thus faced an intractable dilemma. As yet, he remained unmarried and childless. This made John – the only other adult male in the family – an obvious choice as his successor. Their late brother Geoffrey of Brittany's son, Arthur, possessed a strong claim to the crown through birth, but he was just two years old. John might be ineffectual and untrustworthy, but he was still the only man alive who stood a chance of holding the Angevin realm in one piece, should Richard fail to return from the Levant. The Lionheart was about to embark on the greatest war of the century; there was a very real possibility that he might meet his death in this titanic conflict. The inherent danger of the expedition also meant that he could not risk bringing John on a crusade. In dynastic terms, to do so would be pure folly; and yet the prospect of leaving his brother behind, to scheme and plot in his absence, made Richard seethe with anxiety.

The new king constructed the best solution he could. Rather than follow Henry II's example, by thwarting John's ambitions for land – potentially igniting his hostility – the Lionheart provided him with ample territory. John's possession of the county of Mortain, in south-western Normandy, was confirmed. He was also endowed with a significant concentration of lands in west and south-west England. Some of this came through marriage to another wealthy heiress, Isabella of Gloucester, who held title to major castles in Bristol and Gloucester itself, and the Marcher lordships of Glamorgan and Newport. John was also given control of the crown fortresses at Marlborough and Ludgershall, and later the counties of Devon, Cornwall, Dorset and Somerset. In England alone, he was set to earn £4,000 per year. In spite of this generosity, Richard's underlying suspicion was laid bare when he required John to swear he would not set foot in England for three years (though this provision was soon broken).

The king hoped to sate John's hunger, but he also resolved to keep him on a tight leash. The kingdom of England would be left in the hands of Richard's most trusted and able supporters – the guardians of his realm and reign – one of whom would be William Marshal. Queen Eleanor would oversee the interests of England and, in a broader sense, the Angevin Empire as a whole. Within the kingdom itself, royal power would be wielded, as was customary, by the justiciar of England, though the previous incumbent, Ranulf Glanville, was replaced by William Longchamp, Richard's brusque, Norman-born chancellor. Longchamp was imbued with an extraordinary array of powers and offices, being also appointed as bishop of Ely, keeper of the royal seal and guardian of the Tower of London. But his position was buttressed and balanced by the creation of four 'co-justiciars'. In this way, not all power would reside in the hands of just one man; instead, the governance of the realm would be managed and supervised by a small inner circle of magnates. William Marshal was appointed as one of these co-justiciars – a heavy burden, given that he had no real experience of administration. His ally from Henry II's court, Geoffrey FitzPeter, was also chosen, alongside William Brewer

and later Hugh Bardolf (both administrators and former servants of
the Old King). As a clerk, Geoffrey had no experience of war, but a
proven gift for bureaucracy. Having been allotted the hand in marriage of a Mandeville heiress, Beatrice, in around 1185, Geoffrey's
fortunes rose considerably with the death of the great baron, William
Mandeville, earl of Essex, in December 1189. Through his wife's
claim, FitzPeter inherited lands across a large swathe of eastern and
south-eastern England, in counties such as Essex, Suffolk and
Cambridgeshire – like his friend William Marshal, Geoffrey thus
became a leading magnate.

Through the first half of 1190, Marshal and his fellow justiciars
helped to oversee King Richard's furious preparations for the Third
Crusade. This would be the most efficiently organised expedition to
the Holy Land ever launched, underpinned by a massively complex
logistical operation and financed in large part by a swingeing tax,
known as the Saladin Tithe. By that summer, the Lionheart and his
rival, King Philip Augustus of France, were ready to begin their grand
campaign. Marshal crossed to the Continent to see the great crusading armies assemble at Vézelay in Burgundy, and bid farewell to his
king on 4 July. Richard later set sail from Marseille, his avowed goal
to wrestle the Holy City of Jerusalem from the hands of the mighty
Muslim sultan, Saladin. It would fall to William Marshal to ensure
that the Lionheart still had a kingdom to rule on his return.

THE LORD OF STRIGUIL

In 1190, William Marshal began his new life as lord of Striguil – a
powerful baron of the English realm. The tournament champion
and household knight had become a major landholder, endowed
with wealth and prospects. That year, his new wife Isabel gave birth
to their first child, a boy, named for his father – 'Young' William.
Marshal had realised the ultimate aspiration of the twelfth-century
knightly class. Born a younger son of limited expectations, his

skill-at-arms, determined ambition and steadfast loyalty had lifted him from the warrior ranks. Alongside Isabel, he now had a lordship of his own and a real chance to found an enduring dynasty – to leave his mark on the medieval world.

Though contemporaries did occasionally afford him the title, William had not yet formally earned the right to be named earl. In fact, the earldom of Pembroke in west Wales, to which Isabel retained a claim, had been in crown hands since the 1150s. Nonetheless, as Marshal took up his seat on the Welsh March he could be more than proud of the lands in his possession. Along with more established Marcher lords – such as the earls of Chester to the north and the Briouze family in Herefordshire – William was now a major figure in the region. The centrepiece of his lordship was an expanse of fertile land in lower Gwent, west of the great Severn Estuary, that brought both possession of stone castles at Striguil and Usk, and farming income from the wool trade. King Richard had also sold William rights to the lucrative office of sheriff of Gloucester. This gave Marshal temporary control of Gloucester Castle and the verdant Forest of Dean, and a notable concentration of power and influence in the southern borderlands.

This was, and still is, one of the most stunningly beautiful corners of the British Isles – a green land of rolling hills and open skies. The tranquil River Wye meandered through William's territory until it eventually emptied into the Severn, and some five miles upstream on the Wye's west bank, lay the secluded monastery of Tintern, founded by one of Isabel's ancestors in 1131. Tintern was the first house established in Wales by the great monastic superpower of the twelfth century, the Cistercian Order. Such was the austere asceticism of these holy brethren that they were not even permitted to dye the wool of their habits, and so were known to contemporaries as the White Monks. William and Isabel became patrons of Tintern, forging a close association with the abbey.

Throughout this period, Marshal's main residence was the majestic stone castle of Striguil, perched on a rocky bluff above the western banks of the River Wye, a little more than a mile from its confluence with the Severn. This fortress still stands relatively intact today, though it was much enlarged and improved in later centuries. It is one of the few places where one can still touch the fabric of William's world. When Marshal arrived, the stronghold consisted of a rectangular stone keep, or Great Tower, probably surrounded by a timber palisade. Work to improve and enlarge the castle began almost immediately, in either late 1189 or early 1190, with the construction of a formidable, double-towered stone gatehouse, 110 yards downslope from the keep. This technologically advanced entryway boasted two portcullises and a pair of massive, ironclad oak gates (dated through dendrochronology to 1189). Remarkably, this twelfth-century gate remained in place until 1964, when it was replaced with a replica, but the original can still be seen hanging in the castle's small hall porch. In later years, William added an inner wall (between the keep and gatehouse), with a pair of three-storey towers, and probably established the stone-built perimeter curtain-wall, creating a truly impressive fortification. *

William Marshal's household

After 1189, William Marshal was in a position to assemble a full-scale baronial household of his own. He had spent his life in service to others, but now at Striguil, he himself could truly become a 'father of knights'. Using the evidence preserved in the History of William Marshal alongside additional documents, it is possible to piece together a richly detailed picture of the warriors who entered William's military retinue and the clerks who helped to administer his lands. This offers a rare and illuminating insight into the inner workings of an aristocratic household, and gives us a glimpse of the men who would surround Marshal in the years to come, helping him to survive the rigours of war and the intrigues of court politics. For close to three

---

* William Marshal was also able to use Striguil as a minor port because of its position on the banks of the Wye and its close proximity to the River Severn.

decades, William had known the life of the retainer, serving no less than five patrons, fulfilling the roles of warrior, counsellor and confidant. As a lord, it was now Marshal who sought out the essential support and allegiance that only the loyal members of his *mesnie* could provide. Some of those who joined William's ranks would remain with him to the very end of his days, others would come and go, and a few would betray his trust.

Marshal also had to shoulder the financial burden of patronage – feeding, clothing and arming his knights – while cultivating the bonds of trust and interdependence within his household through social conventions such as feasting and the semi-ritualised bestowal of the kiss of peace to his followers. As the historian David Crouch observed, a man of William's standing also had to assume two distinct personas: becoming 'a great oak to his men, spreading his sheltering branches over them' in his paternal guise; but presenting a far sterner face to the outside world, such that his reputation inspired 'such terror that the fear of him keeps ... the men under his protection' safe from the predations of rivals. Much of Marshal's behaviour through the rest of his career would be coloured by these obligations and expectations.

Four established members of the Marshal household followed William to Striguil. John of Earley, his ward and squire, was soon to enter his twenties and would be knighted, probably by Marshal's own hand. The servant Eustace Bertrimont, and the young Wiltshire knights William Waleran and Geoffrey FitzRobert can also be placed in the Marshal entourage, with the latter being married to Isabel of Clare's illegitimate half-sister, Basilia, who had already been twice wed and widowed, and was fast approaching her forties.

Some of the significant knights drawn into William's circle were local potentates in their own right, with family connections to the Clare dynasty. The most prominent of these was Ralph Bloet (whose brother had married Isabel's aunt), the guardian of Striguil castle until 1189. When Marshal took possession of his lordship, Ralph lost control of this fortress, though he retained his own English lands in Wiltshire and Hampshire. He also enjoyed significant influence in the Marches through his marriage to the Welsh noblewoman Nest Bloet (King Henry II's former lover), a member of the 'royal' dynasty of Caerleon. Ralph was probably younger than William Marshal, but of a similar generation, having fought in Ireland alongside Strongbow in 1171; his local knowledge and connections were clear assets, so it is likely that William courted his services. William was also joined by Philip of Prendergast, a knight of Irish and Welsh ancestry, who had married Basilia's daughter, Maud, more than a decade earlier.

Other household knights had no direct link to Striguil or the West Country, but seem to have forged a connection with Marshal during his career. Roger d'Aubernon was the son of Engelrand of Stoke d'Aubernon, lord of the peaceful Surrey manor where Marshal and Isabel had spent their 'honeymoon'. Alan of St-Georges hailed from the Rother valley in Sussex, at the foot of the South Downs. He may have come to William's notice through the Marshal family's connection to Sussex and the nearby coastal village of Bosham. In all, William Marshal appears to have maintained a core group of between fifteen and twenty knights in his retinue. Between eight and ten of these would have accompanied him at any one time, while others rotated through key postings, holding lands and offices in Marshal's name. The West Country knight, Nicholas Avenel, for example, took the position of under-sheriff in Gloucester in William's stead.

Marshal also employed a number of clerks and chaplains within his household. He was probably accompanied at almost all times by a personal chaplain. This priest, who was responsible for William's spiritual care, travelled with a portable altar, vestments and sacred vessels, and was thus capable of hearing confession and performing the ritual of Mass. A chaplain named Roger was in Marshal's service by 1190, and was later joined by Eustace of St-Georges (probably a kinsman of the knight Alan). Clerks, on the other hand, played an administrative rather than devotional function. These well-educated men oversaw the day-to-day administration of William's estates, managing his accounts and correspondence, and Marshal's own limited literacy only served to heighten their importance. William's first chamberlain, for example, a man named Walter Cut, was essentially the keeper of Marshal's purse, with responsibility for his coin.

William must have turned to some of his clerks for advice, particularly on issues of governance and politics. He formed a particularly close attachment to Michael of London, who may well have been recruited during Marshal's sojourn in that city in July 1189. Michael held the title of *magister*, or master, which meant he had spent nine years studying grammar, rhetoric and logic, as well as more advanced subjects like astronomy, in a cathedral school, perhaps that of St Paul's. Alongside the knight John of Earley, Michael seems to have been one of William's closest associates, following virtually his every footstep for the best part of a quarter of a century.

Other clerks represented Marshal's interests on semi-permanent detachment. From the mid-1190s onwards, Master Joscelin was employed in London, overseeing affairs in Westminster and the city. He lived on a small Marshal-owned estate in the Thames-side suburb then known as Charing (positioned between the city walls and the royal palace), but was required to provide Lord William and his knights with ample lodging whenever they stayed in London. Over time, this London satellite of Marshal's affairs seems to have developed into a form of clearing house. Master Joscelin could use his access to London's markets to purchase whatever William required, and store these goods on the Charing estate while they awaited transportation. Similarly, the valuable wool produced in the Welsh Marches might be brought to the city and traded for a lucrative profit – a process that must have been eased by Marshal's connections with the Flemish city of St Omer, given that Flanders was now the centre of the European wool industry. William had learnt early on that a knight could not prosper through acts of prowess alone. Just as he had taken care to reap the financial rewards of his tournament victories in the late 1170s, so now he looked to nurture the wealth and resources of his new lordship. It would not be long before Marshal amassed a considerable fortune.

In his first year as lord of Striguil, William also established a religious house of his own – the Augustinian priory of Cartmel. Marshal endowed the new institution with lands and property from his small Lancashire estate – making it clear that this was a very personal act of devotion – and the text of the charter that confirmed this transfer has survived. In the Middle Ages, documents of this type usually contained a list of witnesses – those willing to attest to the accuracy and legally binding nature of the deed. As such, they offer a snapshot of a nobleman's 'affinity' – his inner circle of vassals and contacts. The Cartmel charter was witnessed by eleven members of William's household (many appearing for the first time in connection with their new lord), and by his ally Geoffrey FitzPeter, brother John Marshal and cousin, William FitzPatrick, earl of Salisbury.

But the fascination of this window on to Marshal's world does not end there. In the main body of the charter, William sought to explain why he was creating this priory, the first monastery formed through his patronage. Foundations of this type had become extremely popular in aristocratic circles over the preceding century, so the act itself was not unusual for a man of his status. The establishment of Cartmel clearly served as a public affirmation of Marshal's charitable piety, but it was also a way to give thanks to God and earn spiritual merit that might ease the path to Heaven. William sought to apportion this redemptive force in his charter, stating that the priory had been created 'for my soul and the soul of my wife Isabel, and those of my ancestors and successors and our heirs'. Marshal also paid tribute to his royal patrons, the men who had lifted him to fortune: Henry II and Richard I were named, but only Young King Henry was described more intimately as 'my lord' – a man who had left an imprint on William's heart and soul.

THE PROTECTORS OF ENGLAND

As a powerful magnate and co-justiciar of England, William could not afford to focus solely upon the interests of his own lordship; the realm was his to protect. Unfortunately, William Longchamp, the man chosen by King Richard to hold the reins of power in England, soon proved to be something of a disaster. Longchamp was justifiably paranoid about Count John's intentions, but he also had a worrying tendency to hoard power and a natural gift for alienating and infuriating his peers. In truth, Longchamp was probably driven more by heartfelt loyalty to the Lionheart than personal ambition, and simply doubted the ability of others to defend his monarch's interests. But, because he had no time for the unctuous niceties of courtly politics, his co-justiciars quickly assumed the worst and took against him.

William Marshal's own antipathy for Longchamp was laid bare in the *History*, where the chancellor was described as a man who lacked wisdom, enjoyed 'spending the king's wealth' and 'imposed his own laws everywhere'. Marshal probably played a significant role, alongside his fellow co-justiciars, in drafting a letter of complaint to Richard in late 1190 setting out Longchamp's failings. This missive reached the Lionheart in Sicily in February 1191, where he was waiting for the Mediterranean Sea lanes to open, and sounded a serious note of alarm. In response, the king sent the trusted prelate Walter of Coutances, archbishop of Rouen, back to England with a pair of royal writs authorising him to depose Longchamp should the need arise.

Archbishop Walter reached England in the summer of 1191, and by that time Count John had crossed the Channel and was pushing to have William Longchamp removed from office so as to open his own path to power. The count wished to be formally recognised as Richard's heir, and perhaps hoped to assume the role of regent in his absence. John knew that the chancellor and chief-justiciar would block his every step, but the same could not be said of William Marshal. As co-justiciar, William was expected to defend England against the creeping influence and devious aspirations of Count John. It is also likely that Marshal's elevation as lord of Striguil was actually part of a wider strategy, conceived by Richard, to contain and counterbalance John's own significant power in the Welsh Marches and the West Country. William may have achieved his position precisely because King Richard trusted him to watch and resist John's every move. But the Lionheart had misjudged his man.

Marshal had a reputation for unbreakable fidelity, but he was not the bluff, plain-speaking Longchamp. At the Angevin court, William had begun to understand the importance of moving with caution, keeping one eye on the future and the pursuit of possible advantage. He had also learnt to avoid making enemies of powerful men – especially if they were your neighbours – unless strictly necessary. Thus, the fact that John's own estates and honours bordered those of Striguil, and that their respective interests overlapped in the likes of Gloucester, actually made Marshal deeply reluctant to alienate the count.

Even more than this though, William was determined to protect his claim, through Isabel of Clare, to lordship of Leinster – a valuable, semi-autonomous province in Ireland. Through Henry II's gift, John held the title 'lord of Ireland' and this made Marshal his subject in Leinster. If he wished to, the count could obstruct, even thwart any future attempt by William to assert power in his Irish lands. In the autumn of 1189, Marshal had taken the first, somewhat tentative step in this process, dispatching a certain Reginald of Quetteville to 'take possession of his holdings' in Ireland (though Quetteville evidently enjoyed little success, and was condemned by the *History* as 'treacherous' and ineffectual). In the months that followed, William formally acknowledged John's status as his overlord in Leinster, hoping to forestall any difficulties.

When Count John returned to England, William thus manoeuvred with care. By this stage, the bleak news from the front line of the Third Crusade must also have raised doubts about Richard I's prospects of survival. The European armies had already suffered grave losses. Frederick Barbarossa, the mighty German emperor, had drowned in June 1190, before he even reached the Holy Land. Elsewhere, the main campaign had become locked into one of the most devastating military engagements of the Middle Ages: the great siege of Acre. This fortified port-city – once a famous centre of commerce and pilgrim traffic – had fallen to Saladin's forces after the battle of Hattin in 1187.

A desperate, almost suicidal, attempt to retake Acre had begun in the autumn of 1189, and crusaders congregated at the siege in their thousands. Saladin arrived with a relieving army and did his best to dislodge the Latin Christian troops, but they dug defensive trenches and refused to be broken.

This investment would last twenty-two months, exacting a terrible cost in lives. It became a hellish scene of carnage, miasma, hunger and despair. Some, like Ranulf Glanville, fell prey to sickness and died within weeks of arriving. At the height of the Christians' suffering, through the winter of 1190, one eyewitness estimated that 200 crusaders lost their lives each day from illness and starvation. Archbishop Baldwin of Canterbury, who had led an advanced Angevin contingent to Acre, passed away that December; so too did Count Theobald of Blois, one of William Marshal's old friends from the tournament circuit. Acre became the graveyard of Europe's aristocracy. Given that this was known to be King Richard's destination in the summer of 1191, it was hardly surprising that many began to wonder whether he would ever return.

The Lionheart himself had equivocated on the issue of the succession, dangling strong hints that he might support his infant nephew Arthur of Brittany's claim to the throne. That summer, John moved to have his own claim formally acknowledged by the realm's leading men. At the very least, William Marshal did not step in his way. Having witnessed the chaos that followed the elevation of a boy king to the Jerusalemite throne in 1185, Marshal may have been reluctant to see Arthur's cause promoted. William was treading a difficult and dangerous path. So long as Count John made no active move to seize power or damage crown interests while King Richard lived, Marshal could maintain a politic neutrality – thus retaining John's good graces – without appearing to be complicit in treachery.

Through the summer of 1191, Count John conducted a virulent smear campaign against Longchamp, blackening his name with accusations of homosexuality, deriding his low birth and demanding his deposition. As one eyewitness put it, John 'was sharpening his teeth against the chancellor'. In October 1191, Marshal and the other co-justiciars finally bent to this pressure. Longchamp was summoned before a council of magnates and stripped of his powers, using the authority of the two sealed royal letters carried by Archbishop Walter. The exact level of William Marshal's complicity in this affair is difficult to determine. William's medieval biographer was no fan of Longchamp, but he loathed Count John far more, casting him as 'arrogant, intemperate and most treacherous'. As a result, the *History* took every possible step to distance its hero, Marshal, from the hated figure of John, at times actively concealing their dealings. But on the basis of other chronicles, such as that written by Roger of Howden, William does appear to have maintained at least the appearance of strict neutrality through the summer and early autumn of 1191.

Once removed from office, Longchamp was forced to relinquish control of the Tower of London. He then sought to escape England, travelling south to Dover, in the hope of taking a ship to the Continent. According to a particularly scurrilous story later circulated by one of John's supporters, Longchamp disguised himself as a woman to avoid detection, dressing in 'a green gown of enormous length [and] a cape of the same colour with unsightly long sleeves'. Waiting on the seashore, he was said to have attracted the attentions of a randy fisherman, and after being fondled and chased down the beach, was threatened with stoning. Saved by his servants, Longchamp eventually went into exile in Flanders.

Count John made important gains that October. His status as King Richard's primary heir was widely acknowledged and he was appointed as 'supreme governor of the realm' – tantamount to the office of regent. Crucially, John was also empowered to take control of all but three royal castles in the realm, giving him significant military power. However, not everything went his way. Walter, archbishop of Rouen, stepped into Longchamp's role as chief-justiciar, and was thus in a position to stifle some of John's broader ambitions. The *History* observed with satisfaction that Walter 'governed the land more rightfully than the chancellor had done, for there was no excess in him'.

For now at least, Marshal had managed to protect his own interests, maintaining a cordial relationship with Count John, while still discharging his responsibilities as co-justiciar. William had navigated the complex political machinations of 1191 with a measure of prudent agility, but the trace scent of self-service seems undeniable.

The return of King Philip Augustus of France

Marshal's delicate dance of allegiance could not last indefinitely, and the crisis that would ultimately draw the true extent of his loyalty to the Lionheart out into the open was set in motion in December 1191. For though King Richard remained in the Holy Land, that winter Philip Augustus returned to Europe, and was 'safe and sound and impudently boasting that he was going to devastate the king of England's lands'. The course of the Third Crusade had exacerbated the Capetian monarch's embittered antipathy for his Angevin rival. Sparks had flown even before they set sail from Europe. Philip had long been determined to force through Richard's marriage to his half-sister Alice of France, but with Queen Eleanor's encouragement, the Lionheart forged a powerful new marriage alliance with the Iberian kingdom of Navarre, in the hope of protecting his southern Aquitanian interests. Much to Philip's disgust, Richard declared his intention to marry the Navaresse heiress Princess Berengaria in February 1191, and the pair were duly wed on the island of Cyprus that May. From the Lionheart's perspective this move made strategic sense, but the Capetians deemed it a grave slur against their dynasty's honour.

In military terms, Philip and Richard enjoyed considerable success in the East. Richard reached Acre on 8 June 1191. Though he promptly fell ill less than a week later, he soon recovered. William Marshal's old associate, Philip, count of Flanders, was less fortunate, succumbing to sickness just over a month after landing in Palestine. Nonetheless, the arrival of the Angevin and Capetian kings reinvigorated the crusader siege, and Acre was finally forced to surrender on 12 July. As far as the Lionheart was concerned, the campaign had only just begun, but within weeks Philip Augustus made the shocking announcement that he intended to return to the West. With Acre conquered, Philip considered his crusading vow fulfilled. More king than holy warrior, he was understandably determined to prioritise the interests of his Capetian realm. The count of Flanders' precipitous death also left King Philip with rights to a portion of his lands – the prosperous and strategically significant region of Artois. To press home this valuable claim, the French sovereign needed to be in Western Europe. And once there, he would also be in a position to threaten the Angevin Empire.

On 29 July, Philip swore a sacred and binding oath not to attack Angevin forces or lands while Richard was still on crusade; he also promised to wait forty days before initiating any hostilities once the Lionheart returned to Europe. The Capetian king held a copy of the gospels in one hand and touched saintly relics with the other as he gave these assurances, but that did not stop him breaking these pledges at will. By year's end, Philip was back in France. The experience of the holy war seems to have left him physically and emotionally shattered. His hair fell out and, harbouring a gnawing suspicion that Richard had ordered his assassination, he surrounded himself with a permanent corps of bodyguards.

Philip's nerves may have been shot, but his political ambitions had only deepened. In early 1192 he confirmed Baldwin of Hainault as the new count of Flanders, but took possession of Artois for himself. This was a massive coup for the French crown. With direct control of towns like Arras and St Omer, and the allegiance of Boulogne and Lille, the Capetians had clear access to the Channel for the first time in the twelfth century. King Philip then trained his sights upon that most contested territory: the Vexin. This border zone, just forty miles north-west of Paris, had been an enduring bone of contention between the kings of France and the dukes of Normandy. The critical frontier followed the line of the River Epte, roughly halfway between Paris and Rouen, and was defended on the Norman side by a string of heavily fortified castles, including the redoubtable fortress of Gisors. The long-established balance of power in the Vexin had created an effective stalemate, but meant that a constant threat of invasion hung over the French realm's north-western reaches. Philip resolved to reclaim this vital territory at any cost.

Philip Augustus had used all his guile and cunning to drive a wedge between Richard and his father, the Old King, during the last years of Henry II's reign. It was only too obvious that the same frustrated ambition that had driven the Lionheart to betray his family now festered in Count John. Naturally, the French king set to work exploiting this weakness. John was invited to visit Paris, probably with the intention of drawing up a new marriage alliance that would see him wed to Alice of France, and the Norman Vexin promised to the Capetians as a dower gift. The count seems to have been more than willing to entertain such a scheme, but sensing the danger, the venerable Queen Eleanor intervened. She called John to a succession of councils, attended by William Marshal and the other justiciars, at Windsor, Oxford, London and Winchester. The position taken by William in these assemblies is unclear – though the fact that four meetings were held indicates that the discussions were extensive – but the count was eventually threatened with the confiscation of all his English lands and castles should he cross to France, and he duly relented.

In the face of this temporary setback, King Philip readied his kingdom for a more direct military incursion into Normandy, ordering 'every kind of weapon to be forged day and night' across the realm. However, his nobles were deeply reluctant to wage open war on the territory of an absent crusader, realising that it might lead to their excommunication from the Church. Philip was still trying to goad them into action in early 1193, when shocking news arrived that would reshape the history of England and France. Richard the Lionheart would not be returning. He had been taken prisoner and was even now confined under lock and key. But his captors were not Muslims; they were European Christians.

9

SERVING THE LIONHEART

While William Marshal defended the king's realm in England, Richard I had assumed overall command of the Third Crusade in the late summer of 1191. Over the next year, he waged a holy war against the Muslim Sultan Saladin; striving to recover the sacred city of Jerusalem, but ever conscious of the damage that Philip Augustus might inflict on the Angevin Empire once he returned to France. Through these long months of campaigning, the Lionheart refined his mastery of the art of war. He also proved himself to be an immensely charismatic leader, earning the adoration and loyalty of his men – many of them friends and colleagues of William Marshal. It was in this year, perhaps more than any other, that Richard's legend was forged.

The Lionheart achieved some startling military successes in the course of the expedition. In late August and early September 1191, he led some 15,000 Christian warriors on one of the most impressive fighting marches of the Middle Ages: advancing along the coast of Palestine and resisting Saladin's every attempt to halt his progress. Inspired by Richard's own bravery and sheer bloody-minded force of will, the crusaders withstood days of incessant Muslim arrow showers and skirmishing attacks – holding their tightly packed formation and trusting to the protection afforded by their armour. King Richard won the only full-scale pitched battle of his career at Arsuf on 7 September, leading his forces in a frontal assault on Saladin's position and driving the Muslim armies from the field. The following summer he spearheaded a fearless counter-attack against the Muslim army besieging the port of Jaffa. Despite being heavily outnumbered in this engagement, Richard prevailed, earning praise from Christian and Islamic chroniclers alike.

Some of William Marshal's peers lost their lives in the course of this holy war, others earned renown. One of the few Latin casualties at the battle of Arsuf was William's old acquaintance, James of Avesnes. This famed knight was isolated from his fellow crusaders when his horse was killed under him. Forced to make a desperate last stand, James felled fifteen of the enemy before being cut down, and was later found circled by Muslim dead. Another of Marshal's friends, William of Préaux, (formerly a member of Young King Henry's retinue), saved King Richard from disaster during an ill-fated reconnaissance mission in September 1191. Riding inland from Jaffa with a small party of knights, the Lionheart's force was intercepted and overrun by a Muslim patrol. Only William of Préaux's quick-thinking gallantry saved the day. Loudly declaring himself to be the king, he attracted the enemy's attention, giving Richard time to escape. William himself spent the next year in captivity before eventually being ransomed.

In spite of his undoubted martial genius, the Lionheart failed to achieve overall victory in the war for the Holy Land. In the course of the campaign, he twice led the Third Crusade to within twelve miles of Jerusalem, yet proved unable to conquer the city itself. Conscious of the desperate vulnerability of his own Angevin Empire, Richard resigned himself to returning home. The holy war thus ended in stalemate, with a thin strip of coastal territory retaken, but the Holy City left in Saladin's hands. The Lionheart agreed a three-year truce in September 1192, yet vowed to return and complete the unfinished work of conquest. The crusaders were permitted to visit Jerusalem as pilgrims, and William des Roches and Peter of Préaux were designated to organise the journey, though Richard declined to visit the city he had been unable to recapture. The king thus left the Near East – the domain of his Muslim opponents – unharmed. His problems – and the crisis that subsequently affected William Marshal in England – only began once he set foot back in Western Christendom.

King Richard set sail from the Holy Land on 9 October 1192. He deliberately avoided familiar ports like Marseille, being only too aware that Philip Augustus might seek to interfere with his journey back to Europe. Instead, the Lionheart made his way up the Adriatic – probably hoping to reach the lands of his German brother-in-law, Henry the Lion. However, when his ship was wrecked by a storm near Venice, the king was forced to continue his homeward journey over land, and this brought him into the orbit of Duke Leopold V of Austria – a veteran of the recent crusade, who had developed an abiding hatred of Richard. When Acre fell to the crusaders in July 1191, Leopold had tried to stake a claim to a portion of the city by raising his banner from its walls. However, Richard and Philip of France had already agreed to divide Acre between them, so the Lionheart simply ripped down Leopold's banner and, according to one chronicler, 'had it thrown down into the mud and trampled upon' as punishment for the duke's presumption. Leopold was left seething with anger. In the late autumn of 1192, the duke had a chance to achieve a measure of revenge.

Rumours of King Richard's whereabouts were circulating, so Leopold ordered a search to be conducted throughout his lands. The Lionheart did his best to avoid detection, travelling with only a handful of trusted knights, including Baldwin of Béthune, and posing as a simple pilgrim. But the noose tightened, and the king was eventually identified and captured in Vienna, having given himself away, according to one story, by forgetting to remove a fabulously bejewelled ring. In spite of the papal protection afforded to him as a crusader, Richard was locked away in the Austrian castle of Dürnstein, perched above the River Danube. News of the king's imprisonment reached England and France in early 1193. The tidings caused dismay across the Angevin realm, though the *History* observed that the reports 'did not grieve

[Richard's] brother' John. Not surprisingly, Philip of France was over-joyed and did everything in his power to influence and obstruct the negotiations for the Lionheart's release, hoping to prolong his rival's time in captivity. With Richard tucked away in prison, the Capetian was free to wreak havoc in France.

TREACHERY UNFOLDS

The system of governance and defence constructed by Richard I to protect the Angevin realm in his absence had proved remarkably suc-cessful. William Marshal, Eleanor and the other justiciars, had retained control over England and, in spite of the strains caused by William Longchamp's deposition, John's incessant manoeuvring and King Philip's duplicity, no territory had been lost. Pressure had cer-tainly been steadily mounting through 1192, ever since Philip Augustus returned, but had the Lionheart evaded capture that autumn, he would have returned to find his empire intact.

His imprisonment changed everything. With Richard plucked from the board, doomed to potentially indefinite incarceration, his rivals and enemies were free to act; and the full extent of their treachery was soon laid bare. When news of the Lionheart's internment reached England in January 1193, Count John immediately made cause with the Capetians. This time neither Queen Eleanor nor William Marshal could stop him. Crossing to Paris, John submitted to King Philip, paying homage to the French crown for all of the Angevins' Continental lands (including Normandy and Anjou) and, rumour had it, for the kingdom of England itself. John also agreed to marry Alice of France and cede the Norman Vexin, with the fortress of Gisors, to Philip. In return for these scandalous concessions, the Capetian monarch would help John snatch the English crown. With the alle-giance of Boulogne, Philip now had access to the Channel and could thus mount a full-scale invasion of England. A fleet was assembled at Wissant and the Capetian armies were readied for war. John was about

to welcome the Angevins' enemy on to his shores and turn his kingdom into a client state, all in pursuit of his own power.

John returned to England and immediately began fomenting an
uprising, hoping to stir up popular support for his rule. Declaring his
brother, King Richard, to be dead, the count seized the major castles
of Windsor, Nottingham and Wallingford, and looked around him for
potent allies. A moment of decision had arrived for William Marshal.
He had shown a degree of allegiance to John in the summer of 1191
safeguarding his own interests in the Welsh Marches and Ireland. The
count may well have hoped that William's loyalties could be bent to
his own advantage. Other members of the Marshal family certainly
appear to have been drawn to John's cause. Though William's biographer tried to conceal it, John Marshal seems to have declared for the
count in 1193, holding Marlborough Castle in his name. Eyewitness
testimony makes it clear that Count John was able to rally a significant
degree of support in England, with one chronicler observing that 'mul-
titudes went over to him'.

Hoping to press his case, John called Archbishop Walter, William
Marshal and the other justiciars to a council in London, demanding
'the kingdom and the fealty of its subjects', and repeating his claim
that the Lionheart had died. By this time, however, Walter of Rouen
had received a letter confirming that King Richard was still alive and
in captivity, and he staunchly refused the count's requests. With
John's blatant duplicity exposed, Geoffrey FitzPeter followed the
chief-justiciar's lead, and so too did Marshal. William proved to have
no stomach for open rebellion in 1193. He could countenance a
degree of circumspect scheming, but John had crossed the line into
treason. When the choice lay before him, Marshal remained a committed servant of the crown.

Together with Queen Eleanor and his fellow justiciars, William
moved to quell the insurrection, garrisoning the remaining 'royalist'
castles and strengthening the coastal defences against a possible
Capetian invasion. Windsor Castle was besieged on 29 March by
forces loyal to the Lionheart, and Marshal later reinforced the

investment with troops brought from the Welsh Marches, receiving a 'joyous welcome' from Queen Eleanor. Intensive efforts to negotiate Richard I's release also began. Philip Augustus called off his cross-Channel assault in light of the stalemate in England, and instead launched a major incursion into Normandy, showing scant regard for the oath he had sworn at Acre. Still doubtful of the Lionheart's return, a succession of Marcher lords transferred their allegiance to the Capetian monarch, and on 12 April 1193 the mighty castle of Gisors itself surrendered. Philip went on to seize the border fortresses of Pacy and Ivry, though his attempt to lay siege to the ducal capital Rouen faltered in the face of stern resistance.

By early summer, the persistent diplomacy of Eleanor, Walter of Rouen and the newly appointed archbishop of Canterbury, Hubert Walter, bore fruit. An astronomical ransom of 150,000 silver marks was agreed, and although it would be many months before King Richard was actually liberated, it now became apparent that his safe return was all but guaranteed. On hearing this news, King Philip was said to have sent a message to John, warning: 'Look to yourself; the devil is loose.' When two of Count John's major strongholds in England, Windsor and Wallingford, surrendered to Queen Eleanor in November, the tide finally seemed to be turning.

Terrified by the prospect of his brother's impending release, John took increasingly desperate steps to secure Philip Augustus' protection. In January 1194, the count signed away possession of all of Normandy east of the River Seine save Rouen, thus giving the Capetians rights to the likes of Neufchâtel and the port of Dieppe, as well as William Marshal's estate at Longueville. To the south and south-west of the ducal capital, John likewise ceded ownership of Verneuil, Vaudreuil and Évreux – bastions of Normandy's defensive integrity – while in the Touraine he gave up Loches and Tours. This was an act of appallingly short-sighted folly. With Normandy and the Angevin heartlands vulnerable to attack, the balance of power in northern France would shift decisively in King Philip's favour. John had frittered away the security of the realm with reckless abandon, all in the vain hope that his supposed Capetian ally would somehow shelter him from the Lionheart's wrath. Even the French king himself seems to have been shocked by the count's lack of good sense and apparently 'thought him a fool'. Philip would do little or nothing to save John's skin, but he hurriedly began snatching up the fortresses he had been granted, seeking to maximise his gains before Richard returned.

In February 1194, after the payment of 100,000 marks and the provision of hostages as surety for the remaining 50,000, King Richard was finally released into Eleanor's care at Würzburg. He had spent nearly fourteen months in captivity. Travelling via the Low Countries, the Lionheart was able to sail for Sandwich in Kent, and made landfall on 14 March. For the first time in more than four years, the king set foot on English soil and immediately began the long task of securing his realm, hoping to repair the grievous damage wrought by his perfidious brother. This monumental task would become the central focus of his remaining years, causing him to rely to an ever-greater degree on the support and counsel of William Marshal.

RECOVERY

Having recently seized Bristol Castle in the king's name, William Marshal was at Striguil when he heard that Richard had returned at last. The tidings arrived at a difficult moment, because William had just been informed of the death of his brother, John Marshal. The *History* played on the emotional turmoil caused by this jarring confluence of events, noting that, at the 'bitter news' of John's demise, William 'almost died of grief', but adding that his spirits were cheered by the fact that the Lionheart had 'arrived [back] in his own land'. Indeed, without any hint of irony, the biography stated that 'even if he had been given 10,000 marks, [William] would not have been so relieved of the sorrow that weighed on his heart'.

In reality, the *History* appears to have recorded only part of the story. It is quite likely that John Marshal – having sided with Count

John – had been seriously injured when 'royalist' forces recaptured Marlborough Castle in either late 1193 or early 1194, and died as a result of his wounds. The *History* avoided any suggestion that John Marshal had been party to the rebellion, but also gave no explanation for his sudden demise. If it was the case that John had ended his life as a traitor to the crown, then William would have found himself in a dilemma: required by social custom to mourn his brother, yet anxious that King Richard might start to doubt his own loyalty.

This probably explains why Marshal dealt with his late brother's funeral arrangements with such speed and apparent detachment. A group of household knights were sent to fetch John's body from Marlborough, so that he might be carried to the family mausoleum at Bradenstoke Priory. The funeral cortège detoured north towards Cirencester to meet William and, although his biographer was at pains to emphasise that Marshal 'showed signs of deep grief [and] very nearly fainted', he also had to admit that William then rushed off to find the king, missing John's burial. His elder brother had been marked as a turncoat and Marshal was not willing to tarnish his own name by association.

William was reunited with the king to the north of London, at Huntingdon, and was said to have been warmly received, though he must have been disturbed to discover that William Longchamp retained the king's goodwill and was also back in England. That evening, after a royal feast, Marshal and the other leading barons in attendance were summoned to the king's private chamber. Everyone was said to have been 'full of good spirits' and William was broadly praised for his fidelity and service. Though Marshal supposedly protested that he had only done his duty, he must have been deeply relieved by this public show of royal favour. His family's good name had been salvaged. But in spite of the appearance of familiarity, William was in an unusual position. He had spent more than four years faithfully defending England for Richard, yet had had virtually no time to establish a close personal bond with his monarch. It was obvious, even on that first evening, that the Lionheart had forged intimate friendships with those men who had followed him on crusade to the Holy Land – he made a point of stating that Baldwin of Béthune had been of 'greater service' to him 'than any man in this world'. For now, Marshal stood just outside this circle of comradeship, but in the protracted war to come he would have ample opportunity to demonstrate his worth and to earn his monarch's enduring affection. With John Marshal's death, William also formally inherited the ceremonial office of royal master-marshal.

Richard's experiences in the Near East had deepened his already formidable grasp of military science. Now in his mid-thirties, the Lionheart was at the height of his martial powers, both as a warrior and as a general, and had matured into an exceptionally well-rounded commander. As a meticulous logician and a cool-headed, visionary strategist, he could out-think his enemy, but he also loved front-line combat, and possessed an exuberant and inspirational self-confidence. These qualities were tempered by a grim, but arguably necessary, streak of ruthless brutality. All in all he was a fearsome opponent, unrivalled among the crown monarchs of Europe, and certainly more than a match for King Philip and John. Ten years Richard's senior, William Marshal had lost some of the vigour of youth, but as a hardened veteran, well versed in the wily arts of war, he remained a trusted lieutenant and leading field commander. Together, Marshal and his king would dedicate the next five years to reconstructing the Angevin realm, and with John having fled to Normandy, their first task was to crush the count's last outpost in England: Nottingham Castle.

William had never fought a campaign under Richard's command, but once the siege of Nottingham began on 25 March 1194, the Lionheart's qualities were immediately apparent. As an isolated outpost, Nottingham's garrison had no real hope of victory, but the king orchestrated their defeat with chilling efficiency. He arrived at the head of a sizeable military force, and had the tools to crack the castle's defences, having summoned siege machines and trebuchets from Leicester, twenty-two carpenters from Northampton, and his master engineer, Urric, from London. The garrison offered stern resistance, but on the first day of fighting the outer battlements fell. As had become his custom, Richard threw himself into the fray wearing only a 'light hauberk [and] an iron cap', but was protected from heavy crossbow fire by a number of 'strong, thick and broad' shields, borne by his bodyguards. By evening, many of the defenders were left 'wounded and crushed', which was, the *History* noted, 'a source of great pleasure to those outside', while a number of prisoners were also taken.

Having made a clear statement of intent, the Lionheart sent messengers to the garrison in the morning, instructing them to capitulate to their rightful king. At first they refused, apparently unconvinced that the long-absent Richard had indeed returned. In response, the Lionheart deployed his trebuchets, then ordered gibbets to be raised and hanged a number of his captives in full sight of the fortress. Surrender followed shortly thereafter. According to Marshal's biographer, the soldiers within were spared by the 'compassionate' king because he was 'so gentle and full of mercy'. Other sources make it clear that at least two of John's hated lackeys met their deaths soon after: one being imprisoned and starved, the other flayed alive.

With this pocket of resistance overwhelmed, Richard was able to dedicate the next month to the more refined business of royal administration, reasserting crown authority within the realm. The Lionheart was eager to direct his attention towards the Continent, but with Eleanor's encouragement, he made time for a public crown-wearing ceremony at Winchester on 17 April. After long years of absence, in which his English subjects had bankrolled his crusade and ransom, the Queen Mother rightly judged this ritual affirmation of sovereign power to be a politic move. With the kingdom returned to order, Richard appointed Archbishop Hubert Walter as his new justiciar, and empowered Geoffrey FitzPeter to serve as his deputy.

William Marshal's days as a 'co-justiciar' were over. The king needed all of his leading commanders for the coming war with the French, so William left the care of his English estates in the hands of Isabel and his household officers. In mid-May 1194, Richard I set sail for Normandy with a large fleet of a hundred ships 'laden with warriors, horses and arms'. In the course of his reign, the great warrior-king had so far spent no more than six months in England. He would never return.

THE BATTLE FOR NORMANDY

With the Capetians on the rampage, King Richard found his Continental lands in disarray. As one chronicler observed, Philip Augustus had now 'stolen the greatest and best part of Normandy', seizing Gisors and the Norman Vexin, occupying much of the duchy north-east of the Seine and threatening Rouen itself. Count John had been placed in command of the major fortress at Évreux (though his Norman county of Mortain, in the south-west, now refused to acknowledge his authority). In Touraine, Tours had declared its allegiance to the French crown and the fortress of Loches had been lost, while to the south, in Aquitaine, the counts of Angoulême and Périgord had thrown off Angevin rule.

King Philip was busying himself with the siege of Verneuil – the formidable fortress south of Rouen – that was one of the strategic lynchpins of Normandy. Its populace had been brazen in their resistance. At one point they threw open their main gates and challenged the French monarch to lead a direct attack into the castle, but he refused to take the bait. As a veteran of the great crusader investment of Acre, Philip had gained a more acute understanding of siege-craft. He brought powerful siege-machines and stone-throwing trebuchets to bear, and deployed sappers to tunnel underneath Verneuil's walls, undermining their foundations. As a result, a section of battlements collapsed and the castle looked to be on the brink of defeat.

Upon his arrival at the Norman port of Barfleur, the Lionheart was greeted by a 'great, dense, overpowering crowd of joyous folk'. Heartened by the sight of their famed crusader king, the throng was said to have chanted: 'Good has come with all his might, now the

French king will go away.' The mob may have wanted to believe that Richard's return presaged victory, but he was not so easily fooled. The monumental scale of the challenge now set before him would have paralysed many men. Even the Lionheart was not immune. William Marshal remained at the king's side throughout this turbulent period and evidently recalled Richard's disquiet, because the *History* noted that the monarch's mind was 'tormented', and added that he 'had not had a wink of untroubled sleep' for days. Nonetheless, the king recognised that Normandy's security had to be prioritised and so made haste to relieve Verneuil, travelling with Marshal and the rest of his forces through Bayeux and Caen, and on to Liseux. It was there that his brother John found him.

The Lionheart's arrival in Normandy shook John to his core. He had betrayed Richard's trust and brought ruin to the Angevin realm; now a pariah, shunned in Normandy, defeated in England, the count had nowhere to turn. His 'ally' King Philip expected him to hold Évreux, but John realised that with his brother's return, resistance was now all but futile. Rather than be captured, he abandoned his post and rode to Liseux. 'Trembling with fear', he threw himself at Richard's feet and begged for clemency. According to the *History*: 'The King lifted up by the hand his natural born brother and kissed him, saying: "John have no fear. You are a child and you had bad men looking after you. Those who thought to give you bad advice will get their just desserts!"' At twenty-seven, John was hardly a 'child', but the Lionheart pardoned John's indiscretions nonetheless, showing a remarkable lack of malice. The count was neither tried as a traitor, nor incarcerated, and though stripped of his lands and castles, he was allowed to serve in his brother's army.*

With John back in the fold, the king drove his troops on to relieve Verneuil. Once within striking distance, he readily outwitted his

---

* Other sources suggested that Queen Eleanor played a role in orchestrating a reconciliation, but the biographer seems to have been well informed on this episode because of William Marshal's presence in Richard's retinue.

Capetian foe. Rather than commit his full strength to a frontal assault, risking heavy casualties, Richard cut Philip's siege off at the legs. A heavily armed detachment of knights, infantry and crossbowmen were sent to break through French lines and reinforce Verneuil's garrison; meanwhile, a second force circled east and broke the Capetians' lines of supply. Isolated and exposed, Philip had little choice but to call off his investment on 28 May, prompting one English chronicler to proclaim that the French preferred 'to flee rather than fight, [to their] eternal shame'. A few days later, Richard and William entered Verneuil amid uproarious celebration. The king reputedly was said to have kissed each member of the garrison in turn, one by one, in recognition of the steadfast defence they had mounted.

Through speed of action and deft strategy, the Lionheart had scored an early and memorable victory. With a renewed sense of hope in the air, a massive Angevin army – reportedly numbering around 20,000 men – assembled at Verneuil in the weeks that followed, ready to march under Richard's banner. The war was far from over, but at least the tide was beginning to turn. Around the same time, another success was achieved, though by questionable means. Count John had been instructed to recover Évreux for the Angevins. He had left it in the hands of a French garrison when he fled to Liseux, and they remained in control of the fortress when he returned barely a week later. According to one version of events, John launched a swingeing assault, broke into the castle and promptly had the same troops he had himself so recently commanded, rounded up and decapitated. Their heads were then paraded on spikes. This was characterised as a 'shameful' deed, because it transgressed the norms of war. A Breton chronicler offered an even more damaging explanation for Évreux's capture. He asserted that, because the garrison remained unaware of John's reconciliation with Richard, the count was able to enter the castle in peace. Still posing as a Capetian ally, John sat down to feast with the troops, and only then had his own soldiers butcher the unsuspecting French. Both accounts convey the clear sense that the count was desperate to prove his military worth, bringing his brother a victory by any means, in the hope that he might recover some favour.

In the years to come, John did slowly regain a measure of Richard's trust, though some within the French and Angevin camps remained suspicious of his intentions and concerned by his apparent lack of judgement and integrity. Chroniclers would brand John 'a very bad man', and the *History* continued to criticise him at every turn, declaring that 'from the heart of a bad man no good can come'. But much of this condemnation was informed by later events. Perhaps the clearest view of John's rejuvenation towards the end of the 1190s was provided by the chronicler William of Newburgh, who died around 1198 and thus knew nothing of the count's subsequent career. Newburgh wrote that after 1194, John 'served Richard faithfully and valiantly in the war against the king of France, thus expiating his former errors [and] completely recovering the love of his brother'.

John remained a duplicitous schemer, but the same could be said of both his parents, and all of his brothers. Perhaps he was more prone to cruelty and casual barbarism, but the real problem was his lack of political sense and military skill. Whatever his failings, he remained the Lionheart's primary heir. After three years, Richard's marriage to Berengaria of Navarre showed no prospect of producing any issue, male or female, not least because the couple were rarely, if ever, together. Other than the boy, Arthur of Brittany, John was the king's only possible male successor.

William Marshal seems to have been deeply conscious of this fact. With John pardoned by Richard, William began, once again, to manoeuvre cautiously around the count, adopting the appearance of 'courtly' neutrality and detachment. In fact, Marshal had taken a rather slippery approach to the issue of Ireland even before John's absolution at Liseux. While still in England, Richard had asked Marshal to swear fealty to him for the Irish lordship of Leinster. But William refused, stating that because he had already paid homage to Count John for those lands, he would be 'marked by treachery' if he transferred allegiance. From one perspective Marshal was holding to the letter of custom, but that did not stop William Longchamp from openly accusing him of 'planting vines' – that is, preparing the ground for future reward.

RECLAIMING THE ANGEVIN REALM

Much of 1194 passed in a blur of fast-paced, ceaseless campaigning, as King Richard ranged through western France reclaiming Angevin territory. Like most of those serving in the Lionheart's army, William Marshal had never conducted a campaign of this scale and merciless intensity, yet in spite of his advancing years he held his own. Richard's valuable alliance with Navarre helped to secure the south, with Berengaria's brother, Sancho, leading 'a large army, including 150 crossbowmen' into Aquitaine to defend Angevin interests. This left the Lionheart free to focus on the north. The powerful host assembled at Verneuil was spilt in two, with one force sent to recover the key fortress of Montmirail, on the eastern border of Maine, while Marshal and the bulk of the army marched with Richard on Touraine. There the burghers of Tours – who had recently accepted Capetian overlordship – quickly reassessed their position, welcomed the Lionheart and offered up a payment of 2,000 silver marks by way of apology for their disloyalty. Moving south-east, Richard launched a blistering frontal assault against the castle of Loches on 13 June, seizing the fortress in just three hours and taking 220 prisoners.

By this point, Philip Augustus had regrouped and looked set to invade Maine, so as to claim the border town of Vendôme – one of those ceded by John in January 1194 – from where he would be well-placed to threaten the whole of the Loire Valley. In response Richard and William marched north into the region in early July. Vendôme itself was not fortified, so the Angevins threw up a defensive camp in front of the town. The two armies, seemingly well matched in numerical terms, were now separated by only a matter of miles. The Lionheart had gained hard-won experience of precisely this type of tense stand-off in the Holy Land, and understood the realities of military incursions and troop movements far better than his Capetian rival. In the days that followed, the extent of Richard's martial genius and the trust that he placed in William Marshal would become clear.

Philip Augustus did not realise it at first, but from the moment that the Lionheart established his defensive position before Vendôme, the Capetians were in a deadly trap. If Philip wanted to hazard a direct confrontation, he would have to march south-west along the road to Vendôme and assault the Angevin encampment – a risky proposition that would also leave him exposed to the same flanking and encircling manoeuvres that Richard had used at Verneuil. On the other hand, should the French monarch seek to cut his losses by pulling back from the front line, his retreating armies might fall prey to ravaging attacks, and be easily overrun in the relatively open landscape of this region.

King Philip thought initially to scare Richard off on 3 July, sending an envoy to declare that he was about to launch an offensive. But the Lionheart happily responded that he would await the Capetians' arrival, adding that 'should they not appear, he would pay them a visit in the morning'. Disconcerted by this brash response, Philip hesitated. When the Angevin army took to the field the following day, the French king panicked and ordered an immediate retreat back north-east, along the road to Fréteval (twelve miles from Vendôme). Richard was eager to inflict the maximum possible damage on his fleeing enemy, but he also recognised the inherent danger of a headlong pursuit. Should things go badly, his own troops might easily become disordered and prone to a counter-attack. What the Lionheart needed was a disciplined reserve force that could shadow his own advance, yet hold back from the hunt itself and thus be ready to counter any lingering Capetian resistance. The king appointed William Marshal to fulfil this challenging role, and around midday on 4 July the chase began.

Towards dusk, Richard caught up with the French rearguard and wagon train near Fréteval, and as the Angevins fell on the broken Capetian ranks, hundreds of enemy troops were slain or taken prisoner. With Philip's retreat turning into a rout, Marshal held an iron-grip over his reserve battalion as they 'rode in close formation over the countryside'. Around them they could see their compatriots seizing all manner of plunder, from 'pavilions . . . tents, cloth of scarlet and silk, plate and coin' to 'horses, palfreys, pack-horses, sumptuous garments and money', yet they kept to the task at hand. Drawing upon his long years of experience from the tournament circuit, William understood the value of this discipline and was able to command the respect and obedience of his troops.

That evening Philip Augustus suffered a desperately humiliating defeat. Much of his supply-train was lost, including many of his own possessions, and even the royal seal and a section of the Capetian royal archives; and a significant portion of his army was either captured or put to the sword. The Lionheart hunted the fleeing French king through the night, using a string of horses to speed his pursuit, but when Philip pulled off the road to hide in a small church, Richard rode by and missed his quarry. It was a shockingly narrow escape for the Capetian. The Angevins returned to Vendôme near midnight, laden with booty and leading a long line of prisoners, and William received a special commendation from his king.

The long war beside the Lionheart

King Richard made considerable gains in 1194, saving Normandy and the Angevin heartlands from full-scale French invasion. The Capetians had been bloodied and shamed. But Philip Augustus still held north-eastern Normandy and, more importantly, controlled Gisors and the Norman Vexin, which left Rouen vulnerable and the French in the ascendant. The Lionheart dedicated the next four years of his reign to a grinding war in northern France, campaigning to recover and counteract these losses; determined to reset the balance of power in the Angevin's favour. In 1196 he forged a new alliance with the count of Toulouse (through his marriage to Richard's younger sister Joanne), thus ending decades of rivalry in the south, and leaving the Lionheart free to focus on Normandy and the north. It is also notable that, after 1194, the king finally overturned the long-established ban on knightly tournaments in England, introducing a number of crown-sponsored contests – an acknowledgement of the invaluable preparation for war offered by these events.

For the vast majority of this protracted conflict, William Marshal either fought at the Lionheart's side, or served as one of his leading military commanders. Marshal can only be placed back in England on a few occasions – in the autumn of 1194, the spring of 1196 and the autumn of 1198. For the rest of the time, he had to rely on his wife and members of his household, like Master Joscelin, to oversee his English estates. Isabel does appear to have visited her husband in Normandy, outside of the summer fighting season, and she continued to conceive and bear their children (with a second son, Richard, and daughter, Matilda, being born early in this period). Some members of William's military retinue can also be placed with him in Normandy. John of Earley, who had now been knighted, probably remained with Marshal throughout; others, like Nicholas Avenel and William Waleran, may have rotated between England and service on the front line. Marshal's 'nephew', John Marshal – the bastard son of his late elder brother – had also joined the household by this point, and enjoyed considerable favour.

It was in the years following the defence of Vendôme that William developed an intimate bond of familiarity and friendship with King Richard. Marshal may have missed the Third Crusade, but in the course of the northern-French campaigns, he and the Lionheart became comrades in arms, William earning his monarch's abiding trust. In the past, Marshal had served as an envoy and ambassador for King Henry II and, in the summer of 1197, he was empowered to perform the same role for Richard: leading a delegation that also included Peter of Préaux, and his own nephew John Marshal, to the new count of Flanders, Baldwin IX. William was charged with persuading the count to break with his predecessor's policy of supporting Philip Augustus; he was also given more than £1,000 to cover expenses – a sign of the luxury and largesse that would be used to win Baldwin over. William had a vested interest in the deal, given that his former claim to the revenues of St Omer (a town previously held by the count of Flanders) must have been rescinded when King Philip took over Artois in 1193. If Flanders realigned itself with the Angevins, then the French might well be shouldered out of St Omer, and Marshal's valuable stake in the town reasserted. The lavish embassy proved fruitful, and later that summer Count Baldwin formally 'abandoned the king of France' and allied himself with Richard in return for a payment of 5,000 silver marks – a significant blow to Capetian interests in northern France.

William's increasingly close acquaintance with Richard meant that he was one of the few men with unfettered access to the king and able to treat with him in relatively frank terms. This intimacy was glimpsed after the Lionheart emerged, boiling with rage, from a meeting with the papal legate, Peter of Capua. Peter had travelled to Normandy in the hope of engineering a peace between the Angevin and Capetian dynasties, so that a new crusade could be launched. Richard was understandably indignant at the prospect of Rome's intervention; the papacy had, after all, failed to lift a finger when Philip Augustus invaded Angevin territory in 1193, even though, as a returning crusader, the Lionheart's land should have been under Rome's protection. The pope had been similarly unforthcoming during Richard's imprisonment. The *History* was utterly scathing on the issue of papal corruption, noting that any envoy to Rome needed to come bearing the relics of St Gold and St Silver, those 'worthy martyrs in the eyes of Rome'. Peter of Capua was also branded untrustworthy; said to be 'incredibly adept in the arts of trickery and subterfuge', with a face 'more yellow than a kite's claw'. After dismissing the legate from his presence, King Richard was apparently 'so furious that he was unable to utter a word; instead he huffed and puffed in anger ... like a wild boar wounded by the huntsman'. Peter hurried away, not even pausing to collect his cross, apparently convinced that 'he would lose his genitals if he did'. Retiring to his rooms, the Lionheart 'ordered the doors to be closed', but William was allowed to enter and eventually calmed Richard's rage, persuading him that any peace agreed at this point would actually be more damaging to the French.

By this time, Marshal was in his fifties, yet was still to be found in the front line of battle – commanding contingents, sometimes even jumping into the fray. Having recovered a section of Upper Normandy and much of the duchy's frontier, the Angevins were, in 1197, in a position to cross the border zone and threaten French-held territory in the region of Beauvais. In May, William was sent to capture the fortress of Milly-sur-Thérain (some five miles north-west of Beauvais). The *History*'s account of this engagement was somewhat misleading, because it indicated that Richard I actually attended the assault, while other sources make it clear that it was actually John who fought alongside Marshal that May – as ever, William's biographer seems to have been determined to gloss over any hints of association with the count.

The castle at Milly was well defended, with a dry moat, stout walls and a steely willed garrison. Nonetheless, William and John ordered a frontal assault, relying on the quick deployment of scaling ladders and sheer weight of numbers to overwhelm Capetian resistance. As the first wave of knights rushed in, the French showered them with an 'incessant rain of arrows'; then, once the Angevins reached the battlements and began trying to ascend, the defenders unleashed volleys of crossbow bolts, dropped 'huge blocks of wood' on their enemy and used 'great forks and flails' to swipe them off the walls. Even so, the onslaught continued apace. Marshal's contingent looked to be making good progress, surging up a pair of ladders, when a number of French warriors atop the parapet managed to shove one heavily laden ladder back off the wall. As it crashed to the ground, many knights were badly injured, and the Welshman Walter Scudamore broke his leg. Looking up, William realised that another knight from Flanders, Guy of la Bruyère, had crested the battlements only to find himself dangerously isolated, and when the French closed in, Guy was pinned down with 'spiked pikes'.

Marshal leapt forward and, charging at speed into the dry moat, he rushed 'full armed as he was, sword in hand, up the other side'. William mounted the remaining ladder, heaved himself over the wall and began laying about him, dealing 'so many blows right and left with the sword [that] those inside fell back'. This was a valorous act, and the sight of Marshal battling on the parapet seems to have inspired the Angevin and Flemish forces to renew their assault, but William had placed himself in a precarious position. At that moment, one of the leading members of the garrison, William of Monceaux, rushed forward, running 'straight at the Marshal with the intention of doing all within his power to do him harm'. Marshal's ageing frame was feeling the strain – the hurried climb in armour having left him 'somewhat out of breath' – but he was able to muster one mighty sword blow to Monceaux's head. The strike cut straight through the Frenchman's helm and the mail coif below, 'piercing his flesh' and stopping him in his tracks. 'Battered and stunned', he collapsed. Now more than a little unsteady on his feet, Marshal promptly 'sat on [Monceaux] to hold him firm' while Angevin troops surged around him to seize the fortress.

The *History* gave the whole incident a heroic spin and William's exploits on the day certainly seem to have been burned into the memory of his household knights – stirred by the sight of their veteran lord outlined atop the walls, still felling his enemies. Even so, Marshal's reckless bravura was more than a little foolhardy, and the episode could easily have ended in his capture or injury. The biographer admitted that King Richard later chided William for his impulsive behaviour, pointing out that 'a man of such eminence' ought not to be in the thick of the fighting, preventing other, younger men from earning renown.

Towards victory

By the end of 1198, after years of relentless campaigning and deft diplomacy, Richard had restored much of his Angevin realm's former strength. One critical step in this recovery had been the contest for control of the Vexin – the border zone seized by Philip Augustus in early 1194. Gisors had long been regarded as the key to this entire region, and the Lionheart's problem was that this fearsome stronghold could not be taken. This was not to say that the castle was somehow impervious to assault, massively imposing though its fortifications were. In truth, no medieval fortress – regardless of its size or techno-logical sophistication – was truly invulnerable. With sufficient time, resources and determination, a besieging force would always prevail: either breaking through the lines of walls and towers, or more often, simply starving the garrison into submission.

All castles in the Middle Ages relied on the support of allied field armies, and were designed to withstand assault just long enough for a relieving force to arrive. With a doughty outer wall and looming cen-tral keep, Gisors was more than capable of holding out for a week. According to the simple mathematics of medieval war, that made it impregnable in practical terms, because Gisors could expect to be relieved by French troops in a matter of days. If Richard attempted a siege he would soon find himself confronted by Philip's army and facing a desperately risky battle on two fronts.

The Lionheart adopted a masterful, two-fold solution to this seem-ingly intractable problem. First, he constructed a huge new military complex on the Seine at Les Andelys, on the Vexin's western edge, boasting a fortified island, a dock that made this site accessible to ship-ping from England and a hugely imposing fortress that was christened 'Château Gaillard' – the 'Castle of Impudence'. Built in just two years, between 1196 and 1198, the project cost an eye-watering £12,000; more than Richard spent on all the castles in England during his entire reign. This installation protected the approaches to Rouen, but per-haps more importantly, it also served as an offensive staging post for raiding attacks into the Vexin.

Richard and William Marshal then developed a novel strategy, based around the complex at Château Gaillard, to neutralise Gisors and reclaim effective control of the Vexin. The new fortifications at Les Andelys meant that, for the first time, large numbers of Angevin troops could be billeted on the fringe of the Vexin with impunity, and then deployed to police the region at will. Using Gaillard as a base, the

Lionheart's forces proceeded to dominate the surrounding area and though the French retained a number of strongholds in the Vexin, including Gisors, their emasculated garrisons were virtually unable to step out of their gates. The *History of William Marshal* proudly declared that the Capetians were so pinned down 'in the castles that they could not take anything outside them', and the French in Gisors were not even able to draw water from the nearby spring at Beaudemont.

By these steps, King Richard reasserted Angevin dominance in northern France, shifting the balance of power back in his favour. It had taken a monumental effort, but the ruinous damage wrought by John's folly had finally been repaired. Both sides were now ready for a pause in hostilities, and the young, energetic new pope, Innocent III, was trying to orchestrate another crusade. Handing over the justiciar-ship of England to Geoffrey FitzPeter, Archbishop Hubert Walter crossed over to Normandy to assist in the negotiations. In January 1199, a five-year truce was duly agreed and, though its exact terms are unknown, Richard looks to have been confirmed in possession of all the territories he had re-conquered. Nobody expected the peace to last; it served merely to formalise a lull in fighting, during which both sides could regroup ahead of the summer and the new fighting season. It also gave Richard a chance to deal with a fresh outbreak of unrest in Aquitaine.

THE CATASTROPHE AT CHÂLUS

King Richard left William Marshal to watch over Normandy and trav-elled south through Maine and Anjou to reach the Limousin in mid-March 1199. By this time, Viscount Aimery of Limoges – Young King Henry's old ally – had made cause with Philip Augustus, and the Lionheart was planning a short, sharp, punitive campaign to bludgeon Aimery into submission. Richard marched into the region around Limoges, where sixteen years earlier he had battled against his elder brother, and 'devastated the viscount's land with fire and sword'. In late March he moved on to besiege the small, relatively insignificant, castle of Châlus.

The investment proceeded at a good pace. Richard sent in sappers to undermine the stronghold's walls, while the paltry garrison was kept at bay by the Lionheart's crossbowmen. After three days, Châlus was close to collapse; only one lone defender, Peter Basilius, was perched on the battlements, popping up to take an occasional potshot at the Angevin forces below. Around dusk on 26 March, Richard left his tent having finished his supper and strode out to survey the siege. As was so often the case, he was virtually un-armoured – wearing an iron headpiece, but no mail hauberk – yet enjoyed the protection of a heavy shield, borne by one of his knights. In the half-light, Peter Basilius took aim and loosed a bolt in the king's direction and, against all expectations, the quarrel struck its mark, thumping into Richard's left shoulder. Some would later claim that this bolt had been poisoned, so that 'death was the inescapable outcome', but this does not seem to have been the case. The closest evidence indicates that a surgeon successfully removed the quarrel that same night, but the resulting wound then turned gangrenous and, from that point, there was no chance of recovery.

While still in possession of his wits, Richard dispatched a letter to Normandy, instructing William Marshal to take control of Rouen. He also sent for his mother, Queen Eleanor, then residing at Fontevraud, and she rushed south to attend his deathbed. It was said that the Lionheart pardoned the crossbowman, Peter Basilius, and declared John to be his lawful successor before he died on 6 April 1199. After his death, Richard's brain and entrails were quickly buried at a nearby abbey. His heart would later be interred at Rouen Cathedral. But his body was carried north to Fontevraud, where he was laid to rest 'at the feet of his father' Henry II, two rivals, both now consigned to the grave.

King Richard's unheralded demise seemed to contemporaries, as it still does today, a shocking and senseless waste. There had been no great feat of bravery or daring at the end; no final struggle against his nemesis, Philip. One of the greatest warrior-kings of the Middle Ages was cut down at the age of forty-one by a single crossbow bolt. Writing nearly thirty years later, William Marshal's biographer described this terrible moment as 'a source of grief to all', adding that 'everyone still mourns [Richard's] death'. The Lionheart had been, the *History* declared, a man 'who would have won all the renown in the world' had he lived. Other chroniclers were equally effusive, with one proclaiming: 'O death! Do you realise who you have snatched from us? . . . The lord of warriors, the glory of kings.'

It was perhaps Roger of Howden – a man who had followed Richard on crusade and chronicled the reigns of both the Lionheart and his father – who offered the most poignant insight into his complex character. In Howden's estimation, the king had been driven by a mixture of 'valour, avarice . . . unscrupulous pride and blind desire'; and his demise had proven that 'death was mightier than Hector'. 'Men might conquer cities', Roger declared, but 'death took men'. The Lionheart has sometimes been criticised for neglecting the kingdom of England, but such attacks ignore his far wider responsibility to govern and defend the vast Angevin Empire. In the course of his reign, this realm had almost been brought to its knees by Capetian aggression and the treachery of his brother John, yet Richard had dedicated the last five years of his life to its restoration, and through tireless effort, could bequeath a newly rejuvenated domain to his successor. The question was who that successor might be?

The choice before William Marshal

King Richard's letter describing his injury, and the expectation of his death, reached William Marshal in the Norman castle of Vaudreuil on 7 April. It had been borne in secret and, in spite of his shock and sorrow, it was essential that Marshal moved quickly to take possession of the citadel in Rouen before news spread of the terrible events at Châlus. It was there, in the great keep of the ducal city, that William received the fateful news of Richard's demise. The message arrived late at night on 10 April, when 'the Marshal was on the point of retiring and was having his boots removed', and its contents 'struck him to the quick', leaving him, in the words of the *History*, consumed with 'violent grief'.

William crossed the Seine that same night, bringing the news to Hubert Walter at the royal palace of Le Pré. Marshal had now outlived three anointed kings. One he had watched die in agony as a young man; another had had power stripped from his failing grasp. William had only been able to mourn their passing. But now, as a man of power and position, he might have some part to play in shaping the future, and seeing the Lionheart's legacy protected. No news of Richard's final wishes regarding the succession had yet circulated, so Marshal and Hubert debated their next step into the small hours. There were now two candidates for the crown: Count John and the twelve-year-old Arthur of Brittany. The archbishop argued in favour of the latter's claim. As the son of John's late elder brother, Geoffrey of Brittany, Arthur had the best claim by precepts of primogeniture, though it was far from clear that this principal was in any way binding across the Angevin world. The *History* admitted that William counselled against this choice, supposedly cautioning that 'Arthur has treacherous advisors about him and he is unapproachable and overbearing'. Instead, Marshal supported John, arguing that he was 'the nearest in line to claim the land of [the Angevins]'. Hubert eventually agreed, but was said to have warned William: 'You will never come to regret anything you did as much as what you are doing now.'

Marshal's decision was undoubtedly driven by a measure of self-interest. A man in his position could expect to reap rich rewards in return for championing John's claim. William already had a degree of association with the count through his Irish lands, and had moved with caution in his dealings with John whenever possible, though he had opposed him without reservation during the attempted coup of 1193. But Marshal's hand was also forced by the desperate predicament now facing the Angevin Empire. Having only just re-established the balance of power with France, the realm was sure to face a scouring new wave of Capetian aggression once the news of Richard's death spread. Under these conditions, the choice between an unproven boy and a fully grown man, with experience of war, was no choice at all.

Part IV

OLD AGE: ENGLAND'S GREAT MAGNATE

10

AN ENEMY OF NATURE

As dawn broke on 11 April 1199, a new era began for William Marshal. Having chosen to serve and to support John, he threw his full weight behind the count's claim to the English crown. That morning, Marshal's most trusted household knight, John of Earley, was immediately dispatched to England to bring word of King Richard's death to Marshal's old ally, Geoffrey FitzPeter, now justiciar of the realm. Earley also must have informed Geoffrey of the choice made by Marshal and Archbishop Hubert Walter at Rouen, for together these three great men would now work to ensure that the kingdom of England passed to John.

Count John appears to have been in Normandy when he himself heard the news of Richard's death, and though he evidently received some form of declaration of allegiance from William and Archbishop Walter, they are unlikely to have met in person. The count's first thought was to rush south to Chinon, to claim the Angevin treasury; meanwhile, Marshal and the archbishop were sent across the Channel to prepare the ground for John's arrival. The *History* dealt with this whole period in vague and brief terms, trying wherever possible to distance William from John's cause, but it is clear from other contemporary evidence that Marshal played a leading role in securing the support of the English nobility.

Some, like the earl of Salisbury, William Longsword, were content to back John's claim from the start. Longsword was John's half-brother, being a bastard son of King Henry II. Born around 1167, William was some twenty years younger than Marshal, and in certain respects their careers were not dissimilar. As his nickname would imply, Longsword was a distinguished knight and had fought in Normandy through the late 1190s alongside Richard the Lionheart. He also achieved power through marriage. When the earl of Salisbury (Marshal's cousin) died in 1196, his six-year-old daughter and heir, Ela of Salisbury, was betrothed to Longsword, and he duly assumed control of the prestigious Wiltshire lordship. In John's reign, the new earl would serve alongside William Marshal as a leading military commander and become a close associate of the Marshal family.

Others were not so readily persuaded during the spring of 1199, and a number of barons even prepared their castles for war. Some may have been reluctant to back John because of his treachery in 1193 and 1194, but most were simply aware that there were gains to be made in the midst of a contested succession, and now wanted a guarantee of ample reward in return for supporting their endorsement. At a council convened at Northampton, William Marshal, Geoffrey FitzPeter and Hubert Walter stood surety for John's intentions, pledging 'their word' that the magnates would receive 'their due'. As a result, some of England's greatest magnates, including Earl Richard of Clare, Ranulf, earl of Chester and David, brother of King William I of Scotland, 'swore fealty and faithful service' to John. Marshal had not acted as a 'kingmaker' in the full sense of the word, but he had certainly eased John's path to power.

Towards the end of May, John was ready to cross to England, having been invested as duke of Normandy at Rouen in late April – receiving the ducal sword and a delicately wrought golden circlet, topped with a border of roses. But Marshal did not await John's arrival; instead he crossed back to Normandy and was with John when he sailed to England from Dieppe on 25 May. This desperately solicitous attendance upon the man who would soon be king looks telling. Though no record of their dealings in this critical period survive, it is likely that Marshal applied the same wheedling pressure for reward, remarked upon by Henry II in 1188, to the new heir-apparent John – currying favour and bidding for preferment. It was certainly the case that William benefited from royal largesse in the first years of John's reign.

THE BENEFITS OF LOYALTY

On 27 May 1199, John was crowned and anointed in Westminster Abbey by Archbishop Hubert. Immediately after the ceremony, the king rewarded the three men who had helped to orchestrate his coronation. Hubert was appointed as royal chancellor, while Geoffrey and William underwent their own ritual, receiving the symbolic swords of office from John that marked them as earls – the highest title achievable among the English aristocracy, with historical roots stretching back to the Anglo-Saxon and Viking eras. Geoffrey FitzPeter thus became earl of Essex, while Marshal could now style himself 'earl of Pembroke'. In recognition of their loyalty to the crown, both men were accorded the honour of serving John at the royal feast that evening.

William and Geoffrey had attained this eminence by following strikingly different paths: Marshal was the career soldier – the knight and commander who could prove his worth in war, yet navigate the world of politics; FitzPeter, the clerk and arch-courtier, was prized for his governmental efficiency and ability to nurture Angevin power and wealth. Geoffrey's ascent reflected a broader, and deeply significant, trend – the increasing emphasis on administrative competence over martial prowess among the medieval English aristocracy. An earl's sword may have been girded to Geoffrey's side, but unlike William Marshal, he was no warrior. In times of conflict, when King John called upon FitzPeter, as earl of Essex, to uphold his ancient obligations to the crown – supplying knights for military service – Geoffrey would not lead his own war-band, but instead would pay a fixed fee into the royal coffers, which could then be used to hire troops. In the future, this increasingly popular system of payment (known as 'scutage') would have profound consequences, both for England and the institution of knighthood.

The earl of Pembroke

William Marshal was now in his early fifties and remained a distinguished military figure. His recent promotion placed him in the uppermost ranks of England's nobility – the grant of the earldom of Pembroke further enhanced his status and brought a major lordship in the far reaches of west Wales. The Clare dynasty (of Marshal's wife Isabel) held a long-standing entitlement to this region, but it had been in royal hands since the 1150s. William took possession of his new lands in 1200, gaining direct control of a territory twice the size of Striguil with claims upon the neighbouring Welsh castles of Cardigan and Cilgerran. Marshal seems to have been understandably proud of his new position. Pembroke now became the centrepiece of his ever-expanding lordship – though Striguil continued to serve as an important Marshal residence – and William immediately began to use the title 'earl of Pembroke' in official documents.

Even so, Marshal did not adopt a new seal. Many men of similar eminence had elaborate seal-dies fashioned during this period to reflect their elevated standing in society. The wax seals that these great magnates of the realm appended to documents echoed those used by the king, were replete with symbols of authority and often bore a dynasty's 'coat of arms'. One of William's peers, Robert FitzWalter (who inherited a major barony in Essex and London in 1198), commissioned a fabulously ornate, silver seal-die that showed him decked out in full armour, sword raised, astride a warhorse – and this is now on show in the British Museum. For all his ambition, William Marshal seems to have rejected such ostentatious displays of rank; for the remainder of his life, he retained the same small, simple seal that he had used as a household knight in the late 1180s. During the time of Henry the Young King, William had proudly proclaimed his promotion to the level of 'knight-banneret', sporting his own colours and war cry. Now, twenty years later, he seems to have acted with more caution. We can only speculate about what Marshal's decision to keep his diminutive seal might indicate in respect to his character – perhaps it was born out of humility or disinterest in the trappings of power, or it may have reflected a conscious, and confident attempt at understatement.

The *History of William Marshal* made no direct acknowledgement of its hero's appointment as earl of Pembroke, recording only that 'many fine gifts were made' after John's coronation. This was a staggering omission given the importance of the earldom to William's career. The *History*'s portrayal of John had always been guarded, but the text became increasingly evasive on the issue of Marshal's dealings with the new monarch. The fact that William owed his greatest honour to King John's patronage was excised; indeed, Pembroke itself was virtually written out of the *History*, being mentioned only once, and even then not in connection with Marshal.

William's biographer tried to conceal it, but there is no doubt that Marshal was showered with favours in this period. In addition to the grant of Pembroke, he was reappointed sheriff of Gloucestershire, with the keeping of the royal castles of Gloucester and Bristol. Other members of the Marshal dynasty also basked in the glow of crown benefaction, with William's 'nephew' John Marshal (the namesake and bastard son of his elder brother), receiving the guardianship of a Norfolk heiress, Aline of Rye. William himself was now, unquestionably, one of the most powerful and influential men in England. With Striguil, Pembroke and the longstanding claim to Leinster in Ireland, the new earl could begin to plot a glorious future for his dynasty – lifting the Marshal line to unimagined heights, achieving a form of immortality.

William may have seen little option but to support John's claim in April 1199 – recognising that he was the only successor likely to be accepted in England, and potentially able to save Normandy. But Marshal had benefited richly nonetheless. There were many others who likewise pursued advantage in the period, some with far more predatory determination. One of the leading 'sharks' was Marshal's northern neighbour in the Welsh Marches, William of Briouze – who had succeeded to his family's lands in the early 1190s. He had been present at Châlus when Richard I died and later verified the Lionheart's deathbed confirmation of John's status as his heir. Under the new regime, Briouze enjoyed spectacular extensions to his lands in Wales and reclaimed his family's rights to Limerick in Ireland, though most of these benefits came with the price of fixed 'fines' – monies owed to the crown – which left Briouze shouldering a mountain of debt. Like Marshal, Briouze rose high in John's favour, and both were to be found in the monarch's company almost constantly in the early years of the new century. But John would not prove to be an easy king to follow.

A 'CRUEL AND LECHEROUS' KING

King John was thirty-one years old when he assumed the English crown in 1199. He had been judged handsome, though slightly built, in his younger days, but a dissolute appetite for fine wine and rich food meant that he tended to corpulence as the years passed. Measurements taken in the late eighteenth century, when John's tomb was opened, showed that he was five-foot-six-and-a-half inches tall – around average for the time. In physical terms he may have seemed rather unimpressive when compared to Young King Henry and Richard the Lionheart, and in a real sense he had lived his life in the shadow of these elder and greater brothers. But now his time had come, just as a new century dawned.

John was one of England's most notorious and controversial kings: reviled by many in the Middle Ages and often condemned by historians today; the first of his name to rule the realm, and the last. Though another two Richards and seven Henrys would follow in the centuries to come, John's infamy was such that no other English monarch has ever borne his name. In the course of his turbulent reign, the great Angevin Empire forged by his father would be dismembered, the kingdom of England brought to its knees and the rival Capetian French left ascendant. These years of catastrophe would define the shape and course of William Marshal's later life.

Some of John's failings had been apparent even before his coronation. The betrayal of the Old King in 1189 and the attempted coup of 1193–4 proved that, like all of his brothers, he possessed a marked capacity for treachery, but in John this was fatally allied to a dearth of political judgement and an inclination to cruelty. Nonetheless, in the last years of the twelfth century he had shown some quality, loyally supporting Richard and acquiring a degree of skill in the art of war. Though he lacked the Lionheart's creative genius and vision, John was at least capable of decisive action. Concerns about his character and competence lingered, but in 1199, there was every hope that the burden of kingship would bring greater maturity and purpose to his behaviour.

The character and failings of King John

John would prove to be a troubled and troublesome monarch. Not the near-demonic, villainous figure of legend perhaps, nor the indolent fool conjured up by chroniclers in the decades after his death – the man supposedly content to lie abed with his young wife while the French ransacked the realm; but a dangerous, unpredictable king, distrustful, petty and malicious. This was the deeply flawed individual that William Marshal now had to serve, attempting to navigate his capricious nature and survive his predations. Within a year of John's coronation problems were already apparent, with the well-informed eyewitness, Ralph of Diss, declaring the new king's actions to be 'unworthy of the royal majesty'.

In some respects, John was not so dissimilar from his fêted forebears. He was born of a line of overbearing and exploitative monarchs. There had been a strong edge of tyranny and oppression to Old King Henry's reign, while the Lionheart taxed his subjects relentlessly to fund his military campaigns. Richard had also shown a capacity for brutality and sexual violence. He executed and mutilated mercenaries in the early 1180s and was said, around the same time, to have molested the women of Aquitaine; during the Third Crusade, he put thousands of Muslim captives to the sword. But crucially, Henry II's and Richard I's military and political successes had silenced most critics, and their abuses of power were directed against groups who might be deemed 'outsiders', at least in the minds of the Angevin and Anglo-Norman elite.

By contrast, John quickly developed a reputation for mistreating his own nobles, stepping beyond the boundaries of socially acceptable behaviour and alienating the very families upon whom his power depended. As one of his followers would later admit, John was a 'cruel and lecherous' man. By 1200, Western European nobles had become increasingly intolerant of arbitrary or unnecessarily vicious punishment (at least when meted out among their own ranks), so John generally refrained from open execution. Instead, his preferred method of retribution involved incarcerating enemies and then slowly starving them to death. Stories of his licentious sexual indiscretion also abounded. Kings were expected to have mistresses, but not to pursue the wives and daughters of their own nobles. Rumour had it that John tried to bed the northern baron, Eustace de Vesci's wife Margaret and, indeed, was only prevented from the act when a prostitute, dressed to resemble the noblewoman, was sent to his room. The king was also accused of attempting to force himself on Robert FitzWalter's daughter, Matilda. For the moment at least, William Marshal and his family avoided such altercations, but the earl was now operating in a dangerous and unpredictable political environment – standing alongside a monarch who was condemned as an 'enemy of nature' by contemporaries.

King John's most damaging character flaws were a marked inability to inspire confidence in others and his own profoundly suspicious nature. As the *History of William Marshal* observed: 'He who trusts no one is distrusted by all the world.' Royal records reveal the extent of John's paranoia, offering a glimpse of the incredibly elaborate system of coded communication that he instituted. By this confusing scheme, certain royal orders were supposed to be deliberately ignored by crown officials, unless accompanied by a special covert sign – a process that was not aided by the fact that John sometimes forgot his own code. The king also had a worrying tendency to promote followers to positions of power, but then seek to strip them of their lands and titles when he decided they had become over-mighty. Where King Henry II had kept his courtiers hungry, John allowed them to feed, but then ripped away their rewards without cause or warning.

Under such a capricious regime, William Marshal had to tread a cautious path. But the course of John's troubled reign would also reveal the web of interdependence that connected the Angevin dynasty to its aristocracy. Medieval kings relied on their nobles to uphold royal authority throughout the realm, but that support was not unconditional. Crown monarchs had long been expected to rule with a firm, but generally fair hand; but there was an increasing sense that they also ought to adhere to the same chivalric notions of honour and justice implicit in 'knightly' conduct. Kings who were more minded towards tyrannical exploitation needed access to an ample supply of lands and honours with which to buy acquiescence. But unfortunately for John, his reign coincided with a period of grave contraction, not fresh conquest. Under these conditions, William Marshal's well-attested reputation for unflinching loyalty would be put to the ultimate test.

THE COLLAPSE OF THE ANGEVIN EMPIRE

John's reign would be marred by a succession of crises, but not all of the blame for these calamities can be laid at his feet. At the moment of his accession, the new king faced challenges that would have tested the mettle of any ruler. From the beginning, John's claim to power was contested outside of Normandy and England. In other areas of the Angevin realm, such as Anjou, Maine and Brittany – where the system of primogeniture predominated – Duke Arthur of Brittany's claim (as the son of John's elder brother) was upheld, in spite of the fact that he was still only twelve years old. Naturally, the Capetian King Philip Augustus was happy to encourage a damaging succession dispute among the Angevins and recognised that the young Breton might be easily manipulated. The French monarch thus declared his support for Arthur's cause and duly received his homage for the Angevin lands on the Continent.

While John gained the support of the English and Norman aristocracy after Richard I's death – thanks in part to William Marshal – elsewhere, many well-established servants of the crown, like Andrew of Chauvigny, sided with Duke Arthur. The most influential of these supporters was William des Roches, a skilled knight similar to William Marshal, who had prospered under King Richard. After the Third Crusade, des Roches had also fought alongside the Lionheart during the wars with Capetian France, earning the hand in marriage of Marguerite of Sablé, heiress to estates in Anjou and Maine. But in 1199, des Roches backed Arthur of Brittany's claim and, in return, was appointed seneschal of Anjou, with control of Le Mans.

This schism among the Angevin aristocracy was inevitable, given the lack of clarity surrounding the succession in the late 1190s. Before the disaster at Châlus, Richard must have expected that he would have many years in which to finalise his choice of heir, and probably still hoped to produce a son of his own. Nonetheless, John initially made some progress towards a reconciliation. William des Roches began to question Philip Augustus' underlying intentions in the autumn of 1199, when the French king invaded Angevin territory and laid waste to the fortress of Ballon. Des Roches protested that Philip had overstepped his authority, given that this region belonged to Duke Arthur, but the Capetian remained unrepentant. King John managed to exploit this estrangement, winning des Roches to his side (and confirmed the seneschal's hereditary right to his office as part of the bargain). This was a major coup. Like William Marshal, des Roches had the power and influence to shift 'public' opinion in the Angevin heartlands. He duly delivered Le Mans into John's hands and brokered a peace with young Arthur. When the boy and his mother, Constance of Brittany, travelled to Le Mans to discuss a settlement, John looked to be on the brink of reunifying the empire. Unfortunately, John's unsavoury reputation cost him dearly. Almost as soon as he set foot in Le Mans, Arthur heard rumours that the king 'intended to take him captive and throw him into prison'. That same night, the young duke and his mother fled, along with a number of Angevin nobles. The chance had been missed.

King John also had the misfortune to come to power just as his main rival, Philip Augustus, was reaching the height of his strength. After twenty years on the throne, the French king had grown in stature and experience. At thirty-four, he was only marginally older than John, but in real terms, he was already one of the elder statesmen of Western Europe. Contemporaries were only too aware of this shift, with the esteemed English prelate Hugh, bishop of Lincoln, declaring that 'as the ox eats the grass down to its roots, so shall Philip of France entirely destroy this people'. Through Philip's dutiful husbandry, the Capetian realm was enjoying a period of significant territorial growth, and the wealth of the French crown could at last match, even eclipse, that of the Angevins. In the early thirteenth century, Philip was able to amass a war chest of more than 85,000 marks; financial reserves that allowed him to win the arms race by recruiting large numbers of mercenaries and developing the most advanced siege weaponry. Richard I had found the Capetian king to be an implacable and determined enemy, but the Lionheart had been able to match, and usually exceed, Philip's skills in the arts of war and diplomacy. John lacked this quality when he came to power and had little or no time to hone his abilities. In the years that followed, he would be outplayed by King Philip at almost every turn. As the *History* wistfully observed, the Capetian monarch 'turned [John] upside down'. William Marshal was now following a king who was plainly incapable of matching his opponent.

The first significant move came with the Treaty of Le Goulet, agreed between John and Philip on 22 May 1200. On the face of it, this two-year truce favoured the Angevins. By its terms, John was recognised as Richard I's rightful heir, and Arthur was required to pay him homage for Brittany. The question of the succession appeared settled. But the French king had learnt in 1194 that John had a tendency to make short-sighted concessions, and he now exploited that weakness. The price he extracted through the Treaty of Le Goulet was emasculating. First, and most importantly, Philip asserted his feudal rights over the Angevin realm when John agreed to pay homage to the Capetian monarch for all of his Continental French lands. Henry II and Richard had both performed similar submissions, but their subservience had always been symbolic. Philip cannily drove home the harder reality of John's sub-ordinate status by requiring him to pay 20,000 marks as the fee for succeeding to these lands. Such a demand would have been unthink-able in the past, yet John acquiesced, reinforcing the powerful sense that the French king was indeed his overlord; and if John owed his power to the Capetians – as the terms of Le Goulet implied – any 'mis-behaviour' on his part in France might legally be punished.

Alongside this reassertion of Capetian royal rights, Philip negotiated three additional stipulations that, by increments, undermined John's position. Territory in the Norman Vexin and the region around Évreux was conceded, leaving Normandy dangerously exposed to future aggression. John also agreed to sever the valuable alliance with Flanders that William Marshal had helped to engineer in 1197 (and the king later broke with Boulogne in a similar fashion), thus shifting the balance of power in northern France back in Philip's favour. The treaty was sealed by a final condition: a new marriage alliance between the French king's son and heir-apparent, Louis, who was then twelve, and John's eleven-year-old niece, Blanche of Castile (the daughter of his sister Eleanor, who had married into the Castilian dynasty thirty years earlier). This union promised to further strengthen Capetian claims to Angevin territory and would come to have deep significance in the latter stages of William Marshal's career.

Through this complex array of provisions, King Philip subtly out-manoeuvred his rival, carefully preparing the ground for the more open and decisive confrontation to come. John seems to have been largely oblivious to these dangers, but the Treaty of Le Goulet marked an important turning point. Chroniclers later recognised its signifi-cance and began to mark John with a humiliating new nickname. As a young man, without territory of his own, he had been known as 'Lackland'. Now he was branded with another moniker – the ultimate put-down for the Lionheart's little brother – John 'Softsword'.

An uneasy peace held in the wake of Le Goulet, but steps were soon being taken to prepare Normandy for the onset of war. William Marshal's lordship of Longueville lay in the far north-eastern reaches of the duchy, and he assumed a broader responsibility for this area of Upper Normandy in the early thirteenth century. This region, to the west of Dieppe and the River Béthune, effectively constituted the duchy's second line of defence, lying some twenty miles back from the main frontier of the River Bresle. Marshal held two small castles at Longueville and Meleurs, but the main stone fortress protecting the Béthune valley was at Arques (just south of Dieppe). In the early spring of 1201, Marshal sent Jordan of Sauqueville – a recently recruited member of his military retinue – to oversee the strengthening of Arques' already formidable battlements. Then in May, William him-self crossed over to Normandy with a force of 100 knights, furnished by the king. By this stage, an invasion of Normandy was looming, because King John had been lured into making another significant diplomatic blunder.

The allure of Isabella of Angoulême

In the first years of his reign, John benefited from the support and guid-ance of his elderly mother, Eleanor of Aquitaine. Before Richard I's death, she had been living in semi-reclusion at Fontevraud Abbey, but the succession crisis brought her back on to the political stage and, despite being in her mid-seventies, she had retained much of her vigour and mental acuity. It was Eleanor who helped to enforce John's authority in Aquitaine in 1199, and then deftly secured the support of the Lusignan dynasty by granting them the disputed county of La Marche in early 1200. She even found the energy to cross the Pyrenees and fetch her young granddaughter, Blanche of Castile, from Spain, so as to seal the terms of Le Goulet – though she had been unable to prevent John from agreeing to such damaging concessions. Understandably exhausted by this grand excursion, and suffering from illness, Eleanor returned to Fontevraud to rest and recover.

In her absence, John suddenly decided to take a new wife. His union with Isabella of Gloucester had been annulled on the grounds of consanguinity soon after his coronation, and he now alighted upon the daughter of Audemar, count of Angoulême, as a suitable bride. This girl, Isabella of Angoulême, was perhaps twelve years old (and possibly as young as eight), and though some suggested that John was driven to marry her by a 'mad infatuation', he was perhaps equally attracted by the prospect of confirming Angoulême's support, a step that would secure the region between Poitiers and Bordeaux. So it was that the couple were duly wed on 24 August 1200. At first glance this appeared to be a rather shrewd political match, but there was an underlying problem. Isabella had already been betrothed to Hugh of Lusignan (Geoffrey of Lusignan's nephew), and he now went into open rebellion. William Marshal was with the king at this point, but it is not clear whether he offered any counsel on the issue of the marriage. However, according to two well-informed contemporaries, John decided to wed Isabella 'on the advice of his lord, Philip, king of France', so it may well be that the Capetian monarch had deliberately primed a trap for his enemy and then watched contentedly as it snapped shut.

After John's and Isabella's wedding, Hugh of Lusignan protested vehemently at the grave offence caused to his honour, arguing that his binding betrothal had been illegally overturned. Ultimately, he brought his grievance to the Capetian royal court in Paris, and not surprisingly, Philip Augustus offered Hugh a sympathetic ear. Whether by devious design or simple fortune, Philip now had the perfect excuse to move against his Angevin opponent. After John's submission in the Treaty of Le Goulet, the French king had every right to summon his Angevin vassal to answer the Lusignans' charges. John wriggled, evaded and ultimately refused to appear in the Capetian court. This left King Philip free to formally declare the confiscation of John's Continental lands in April 1202. The Capetian monarch later knighted Arthur of Brittany (who was now fifteen) with his own hand, and accepted his oath of homage for all of the Angevin lands; the sole exception being Normandy, which Philip now claimed as a crown possession. The French king had been gifted a legal cause to drive John out of France.

The crisis of 1202

Philip Augustus launched an immediate invasion of eastern Normandy, alongside Baldwin of Flanders. Together, they quickly pushed over the first line of defence in the Eu valley, taking the fortresses of Eu and Aumale, and marched on to seize Neufchâtel. A more sustained siege of Gournay followed, but that too fell in July. Upper Normandy was thus on the brink of collapse when Philip turned north to assault the major royal castle of Arques, in the territory guarded by William Marshal and the earl of Salisbury, William Longsword.

Marshal had been hard at work bolstering the stronghold's defences: financial records show that in the middle weeks of June alone, he spent 1,600 Angevin pounds (drawn from the crown treasury) on improving its fortifications and strengthening its garrison. This level of frantic expenditure gives a clear sense of the alarm now felt throughout eastern Normandy. William Marshal seems to have recognised that he was likely to be badly outnumbered in the conflict ahead. When the Capetians marched on Arques, around 20 July, the fortress itself was left under the command of King John's castellan, William Mortimer, while Marshal and Longsword pulled back west. Together, they held a sizeable mobile force in the field, and launched a succession of skirmishing attacks against the French forces investing Arques. This was a sound strategy, but ranged against the full force of Philip Augustus' army, their cause still looked hopeless.

Then in early August, news of an extraordinary Angevin victory reached Upper Normandy. While King Philip attacked in the north, Duke Arthur of Brittany had opened up a second front to the south, invading Anjou with an army of Breton knights and other supporters, including Andrew of Chauvigny. The aged Queen Eleanor had been trying to maintain a grip over the region, but soon found herself besieged in the castle of Mirebeau. When King John heard of this attack, he took decisive action – prosecuting a lightning-quick forced march south from Le Mans, alongside nobles such as William des Roches and William of Briouze. Together they covered eighty miles in just two days, and fell on Arthur of Brittany's unsuspecting troops at dawn on 1 August 1202. Briouze captured the young duke, and another 252 knights were taken prisoner. Eleanor was saved and Mirebeau secured; it was the greatest triumph of John's reign.

The king immediately dispatched a messenger north to inform William Marshal of this success. Philip Augustus also heard the tidings from Mirebeau and broke off his siege of Arques, fearing that John would now be able to pour an overwhelming concentration of forces into Upper Normandy. The Capetians had still made important gains along the eastern frontier, but the duchy had been saved. The *History* described, in gleeful terms, how Marshal and Longsword withdrew with their troops to Rouen and enjoyed a lavish feast of celebration that included no small quantity of fine wine.

It seemed that King John had regained the initiative. His mother, Eleanor, had been left drained by the effort of holding Mirebeau, and now went into permanent retirement in Fontevraud Abbey. But in all other respects, John's position had been transformed. He had affirmed his military competence; he now held more than 250 valuable hostages, each of whom could be ransomed either for money or strategic advantage; and he had his rival Arthur of Brittany in captivity. If John took the right steps, moving with shrewd caution, the fortunes of the Angevin

Empire might be restored. At this moment, perhaps more than any other, he had a chance to steer his reign back on to a steady course.

As it was, the king squandered this crucial opportunity, and a dreadful corner was turned in his career, from which there would be no return. Even as William Marshal rejoiced in Normandy, John began to mistreat the hundreds of captives taken at Mirebeau. Under normal circumstances, these nobles would have been kept in confinement, but treated with respect and allowed to live in relative comfort, while the terms of their release were negotiated. In 1202, the vast majority of John's prisoners – including Arthur of Brittany – simply disappeared. Many were sent to castles in Normandy and southern England, and starved to death. Andrew of Chauvigny's exact fate is uncertain, but he was dead by 1203.

The king's merciless behaviour caused a serious scandal. The *History* recorded that John treated his captives 'so vilely and in such evil distress that it seemed shameful and ugly to all those who were with him and who saw this cruelty'. William des Roches had been a friend, and even kinsman, to scores of the knights seized at Mirebeau, and a former supporter of young Duke Arthur. At first, des Roches entreated the king to observe the normal conventions, and report on prisoners' whereabouts and well-being, but his requests met with a stony silence. The king seems to have assumed that he could flout accepted custom with impunity, but he was mistaken. As one chronicler noted, his 'pride and arrogance . . . so blurred his vision that he could not see reason'.

William des Roches was so disgusted by John's behaviour that he abandoned him – transferring his allegiance to Philip of France – and the leading nobles in the Angevin heartlands soon followed suit. Through late 1202 and early 1203, the thin veneer of support that John had enjoyed in the south shattered, and he rapidly lost control of Maine, Anjou and Touraine. Even in Normandy, nobles began to question the king's judgement and reconsider their positions. In January 1203, the lord of Alençon (on the southern border with Maine) declared for the Capetians; many others would follow. William

Marshal's biographer loathed King John, but he also despised turn-coats, and he now likened these renegade Norman nobles to stinking pieces of rotten fruit, infecting all around them. For now, Marshal remained loyal and returned to defend Upper Normandy, but the crisis had barely begun.

The fate of Arthur

After his capture at Mirebeau, Duke Arthur of Brittany – John's fifteen-year-old nephew – was held in confinement in Normandy. He seems to have been taken first to the castle of Falaise (in the centre of the duchy), and probably remained there at least until early 1203. The king appears to have been unsure of how to deal with this young prisoner, the rival claimant to the English crown and wider Angevin realm. With the benefit of hindsight, it is clear that the wise choice would have been either to commit Arthur to lifelong imprisonment in England, but afford him a relatively comfortable existence, or to use him as a powerful bargaining chip in negotiations with Philip Augustus over the fate of Normandy. But John's suspicious nature trumped reason. He did not trust his servants to hold the duke in indefinite captivity, and he seems to have doubted his own ability to secure advantageous terms from the Capetians.

According to the chronicler Ralph of Coggeshall, unnamed 'counsellors' initially advised the king to have Arthur blinded and castrated, 'thus rendering him incapable of rule'. Three men were sent to Falaise 'to perform this detestable act', but John's chamberlain, Hubert of Burgh, intervened at the last moment to save the duke, 'having regard for the king's honesty and reputation'. Through the early months of 1203, the questions being asked about Arthur's treatment became increasingly voluble, and dark rumours began to circulate. At some point before the start of April, he seems to have been moved to the citadel at Rouen, probably by William of Briouze, who would later claim that he could 'no longer answer' for Arthur's safety once he had been delivered into custody.

The duke's exact fate from this point forward remains a mystery. Two contemporary accounts, seemingly based on the oral testimony of Briouze, indicated that, on 3 April, John confronted his prisoner in a drunken rage, and 'possessed by the Devil', proceeded to crush his skull with a rock. Arthur's body was weighted down and thrown into the Seine, only to be later found by a fisherman, and discreetly buried at the nearby priory of Notre-Dame-des-Pré. The king may have committed this act of murder, with Briouze as an eyewitness; or it could be that Briouze did the terrible deed himself, following John's orders, and only later sought to transfer the blame. The truth will never be known, but Duke Arthur of Brittany was not seen again.

William of Briouze certainly appears to have been complicit in Arthur's disappearance, and was evidently told to remain silent on the matter. In the years that followed, John continued to promote Briouze's interests and add to his lands, keeping him close to the crown. But William was carrying a dangerous secret – one that would ultimately lead to his ruin. The king would also be haunted by the rumours surrounding Arthur's death for the remainder of his reign, with accusations of treachery and foul play multiplying. He had handed his enemies a significant advantage. From this point forward, Philip Augustus was able to respond to any overtures towards diplomacy with the damaging demand that John must produce Duke Arthur – alive and well – before any talks could begin. The *History* remained silent on this whole episode, but given the course of later events, it is possible that William Marshal eventually came to know the truth of the matter.

The loss of Normandy

By the early summer of 1203, a mounting number of nobles were defecting to the Capetian cause. All the hopes of renewal briefly entertained after Mirebeau had been dashed, and to many it seemed that the battle for Normandy was already a lost cause. Nonetheless, a defence was mounted. Longsword was sent to hold the western frontier against the Bretons, while William Marshal joined King John in patrolling the duchy's central and eastern reaches, ahead of an expected French offensive.

When the final blows came, they were shockingly effective. Philip Augustus launched a massive incursion from the region around Évreux in June, marching on Vaudreuil in the Seine valley – the fortress standing guard over the western approaches to Rouen. The castle was under the command of Robert FitzWalter, but its garrison surrendered to the French without offering any resistance. This gave Philip control of the left bank of the Seine, and critically, a position downstream from Les Andelys and the great stronghold of Château Gaillard. The Capetians were now in a position to hamper any attempts to resupply Richard the Lionheart's famous military complex.

King Philip began to tighten the noose in August, laying siege to Gaillard and Les Andelys, along with his renowned military commander William des Barres. Here at least, the Angevin troops put up a hard-fought stand, with Gaillard's garrison led by the formidable Roger of Lacy. King John and William Marshal began to plan an offensive of their own in September, hoping to break the French siege. This disastrous operation was not recorded in the *History*, and was only described in detail by a single Breton account. The plan called for a coordinated attack, with Marshal leading a land-based force (alongside John's mercenary commander Lupescar), linking up with a second body of troops that had sailed up the Seine, thereby enveloping Philip's army. Unfortunately, the French hold on Vaudreuil made it difficult to navigate the river in daylight, so the assault was timed for the early hours, just before dawn. It proved to be a depressing shambles. The sailors transporting the water-borne contingent misjudged the strength of the Seine's currents, and their ships failed to arrive as planned. Isolated and outnumbered, Marshal's division was badly mauled by William des Barres' men, and soon driven off, and when the second force finally arrived on the river it was quickly decimated. It was one of the most humiliating reversals of William Marshal's military career.

The failure to relieve Les Andelys and Gaillard delivered a crushing blow to Angevin morale. King John's position in Normandy was now collapsing at a desperate rate. Sections of Upper Normandy around Arques and Marshal's own estate at Longueville still held, but elsewhere losses were mounting. According to the *History*, William Marshal was sent on an embassy to discuss terms of truce with King Philip Augustus, but this was not mentioned in any other source and, in any case, met with no success. The Capetian knew full well that he was closing in on overall victory, so 'there was no question of peace'. John's deepening paranoia also left him increasingly fearful of treachery. He began to suspect that his own Norman vassals would take him prisoner and hand him over to the French and, according to one contemporary, refused to make any further attempt to save Château Gaillard, 'through fear of treason of his men'.

With the approach of winter, John decided to return to England. The official line was that he was leaving 'to seek advice and help from his barons [and would] then make a speedy return', but according to the *History*, his decision to take Queen Isabella with him from Rouen meant that many 'feared his stay would be a long one'. The great ducal city was left under the guardianship of William Marshal's old associate, Peter of Préaux. By this point, Les Andelys had fallen to the French, but Gaillard remained under Roger of Lacy's command, holding out against a close siege. Outside of a few remaining outposts, such as Arques in Upper Normandy and Verneuil on the southern frontier, the duchy had been overrun. On 5 December 1203, John set sail from Cherbourg with Marshal at his side. William's biographer afforded this voyage only the briefest mention, but the atmosphere on board must have been desperately sombre, for the king's departure was a tacit admission that Normandy was now lost.

II

A LORD IN THE WEST

William Marshal failed to turn the tide of the war in 1203, serving a king who could not command the loyalty of his Norman subjects, and who lacked the requisite vision and determination to face Philip Augustus. The final axe fell in 1204. Château Gaillard – the Lionheart's grand 'Castle of Impudence' – surrendered on 6 March, the pitiful remnants of its garrison having been starved into submission. With no possible hope of holding out against the Capetians, Peter of Préaux opened the gates of Rouen on 24 June and returned to England. Philip swept up the rest of the duchy with ease.

The news from the south was equally grim. Queen Eleanor died at Fontevraud on 1 April, and with her demise, the last link to the glory days of Angevin authority was broken. The barons of Aquitaine paid homage to Philip Augustus, leaving him free to occupy Poitiers in August, while Iberian forces from Iberian Castile crossed the Pyrenees to claim Gascony. By year's end, only a string of ports on the Atlantic Coast, running north from Bayonne to La Rochelle, remained in Angevin hands. The garrisons of Chinon (under Hubert of Burgh) and Loches made brave efforts to stave off defeat, but were eventually overrun. Barely a shadow remained of the once mighty empire forged by

King Henry II. His youngest son – the 'Softsword' – had presided over a period of catastrophic decline.

A REALM DIVIDED

King John's personal prestige and reputation now lay in tatters, and the disastrous events of 1202 to 1204 would hang over the remainder of his reign. The collapse of the Angevin realm, and the previously unimaginable loss of Normandy, would also have far-reaching consequences for the history of England. But in the immediate wake of these events, William Marshal, and his fellow barons, had to face an unsettling new reality. The vast majority of the 'Angevin' English nobility was Anglo-Norman by birth. When the duchy fell to the French, their Norman 'homeland' was effectively lost, and this heralded a crisis of identity and allegiance. As many magnates held land on both sides of the Channel, they now had to decide where their loyalties lay. Most followed the preponderance of their estates. The Préaux family was a case in point. The elder brother, John of Préaux, relinquished his English lands and remained in Normandy, retaining control of his family's major lordship (north-east of Rouen) and becoming a vassal of Philip Augustus. His sibling Peter gave up the small parcels of property he held in Normandy and lived out the rest of his life in semi-retirement on his far larger estates in southern England. King John made some attempt to soften the blow of this partition by reapportioning English territory to barons such as Baldwin of Béthune (who now lost the honour of Aumale), but a significant level of disruption to long-established patterns of landholding was unavoidable.

A *step too far*

The sudden contraction of the Angevin realm forced William Marshal to reconsider his own position and the future of his nascent dynasty.

It was now obvious that any hopes of strengthening and extending the Marshal power base would have to be redirected, away from the Continent. But William was also one of the few magnates who sought to resist the forfeiture of his Norman estates. Like so many of his peers, Marshal felt a strong affinity for Normandy – the land of his adolescence and a region in which he had spent much of his adult life, and unlike Peter of Préaux and Baldwin of Béthune, William was not willing to relinquish his valuable lordship at Longueville, in Upper Normandy.

In May 1204, Marshal was sent, along with Earl Robert of Leicester (who also held major estates in Normandy), across the Channel by King John to discuss terms of peace with Philip Augustus. The French monarch remained disinterested in negotiation, but he saw a valuable opportunity to sow seeds of discord within the Angevin ranks. William and Earl Robert were given a chance to salvage their Norman estates, but had to agree to the strict provisions laid out by King Philip. The terms settled upon were described in the *History*, but were also preserved in a copy of the contract, lodged in the French royal archive. Marshal and the earl of Leicester were to surrender their property to Capetian forces, on the understanding that it would be returned, so long as they 'paid homage' to Philip Augustus for these lands within the space of a year. For the privilege of this period of grace, both men had to pay the sum of 500 silver marks.

By giving 'homage', William and Robert would formally acknowledge King Philip's overlordship in Normandy – and hold their Continental lands from him – yet remain servants of King John in England. There was some precedent for this type of arrangement. In the past, a small number of nobles who held lands on either side of the Norman-French border had paid homage to both the Capetians and the Angevins; but crucially they had always identified only one king as their primary 'liege-lord' – the monarch alongside whom they would fight at times of war. This might seem like an arcane, legalistic argument, but for medieval noblemen like William Marshal, the traditions surrounding feudal obligations could be of critical importance. They offered a mechanism for reconciling the day-to-day realities of landholding, with the more ephemeral notions of allegiance. In May 1204, Marshal seemed to have found a way to retain the estate of Longueville, and he had twelve months in which to persuade King John to accede to this arrangement.

An undercurrent of hubris appears to have blinded William to the inherent danger of these dealings. He evidently believed that he could manipulate 'feudal' custom, and exploit his eminent position, to achieve what others could not, and thereby maintain his foothold in Normandy. The extent of his fidelity to John must also be questioned, because it is clear that Marshal put his own interests ahead of those of the crown in this period. William had not followed others into open acts of 'treachery' by disavowing the Anegvin king, but his dedication to the capricious 'Softsword' seems to have wavered.

It looked, at first, as though the plan to retain Longueville would pass without a hitch. Marshal and Robert of Leicester returned to England, and when the latter died in late 1204, the task of convincing John to sanction the bargain fell to William alone. According to the *History*, he succeeded, receiving official letters of authorisation from the king in the spring of 1205. Marshal apparently pleaded, saying: 'You can see that the time is nearly up as regards my land in Normandy. I do not know what to say: if I don't pay [King Philip] homage, I will sustain [a] heavy loss' of land. John supposedly replied: 'I know you to be ... a loyal man [and] I am very willing for you to pay him homage, [for] the more you have, the greater will be your services to me.' No official record of this endorsement survives, though Marshal's heirs would later testify to the existence of a formal royal licence. It is unlikely that William would have been foolish enough to take the next step without permission, but he had failed to account for John's changeable nature and the guile of Philip Augustus.

In April, William Marshal travelled to France with the intention of giving his oath to the Capetian king. But when they met at Anet (the scene of some of Marshal's most famous tournament triumphs) Philip insisted upon a more binding promise – one that went far beyond a mere acknowledgement of overlordship. William was required to recognise the French monarch as his liege-lord 'on this side of the sea' (in France), or else forfeit Longueville. This would be tantamount to Marshal declaring that he had two masters: one, King Philip, whom he would serve on the Continent; the other, John, who would remain his liege-lord in England. When looked at in the cold light of day, there was no escaping the fact that this represented a grave division of loyalty – not least because the Capetians remained the arch-enemies of the Angevin dynasty. Yet backed into a corner, William agreed nonetheless. By this act, Marshal preserved his hold over the valuable lordship of Longueville – an estate that he would now be able to pass on to his heirs. He had defended the rights of his dynasty, but he had also made a serious miscalculation.

Sailing back to England, William seems to have convinced himself that any difficulties with King John could be smoothed over, not least because he had carried the monarch's letter of licence. On arrival, however, he discovered that one of the archbishop of Canterbury's representatives (who had also been in France) had returned ahead of him, and had informed the king of the specific terms of Marshal's oath. John was understandably furious and accused William of 'acting against me and against my interests'. Not surprisingly, the *History* sought to defend William's reputation, condemning those who spoke against him at this point as 'base flatterers and traitors', and maintaining that Marshal had not 'committed the slightest crime'.

Standing before his incensed king, William reputedly protested: 'My lord, I can tell you straight out that I did nothing against you, and what I did, so it please you, I did with your leave.' In one respect Marshal was right – John had consented to an act of homage. But he had not condoned the far more serious liege-oath demanded by the wily Philip Augustus. William also was foolish to think that a man of King John's unpredictable and suspicious nature would easily be persuaded to see reason. As it was, the English monarch flatly denied ever issuing 'this permission of mine you speak of' and the *History* observed that from this point onwards 'the Marshal was on bad terms with the king for a long time'.

Into the cold

William Marshal's fall from royal favour was sealed in June 1205. By this time, King John had laid plans for a major military offensive, hoping to recover ground in the Angevin heartlands by sailing with a large fleet to Poitou, and then launching a full-scale invasion inland. This was a bold scheme, and the king had taken careful steps to assemble ships, supplies and arms, but it was also deeply unpopular with a large section of John's leading barons. According to the contemporary chronicler Ralph of Coggeshall, the proposed campaign was seen as an act of folly that would leave England exposed to invasion, and it was feared that John 'would lose what he held, by trying to recover what he had lost'. Many also doubted that the king could actually defeat Philip Augustus in the field.

As the expedition was being debated, the king confronted Marshal. According to the *History*, he commanded William to follow him to Aquitaine and join in the 'fight against the king of France'. But the earl demurred, stating that to do so would be both 'wicked' and a 'crime', because outside of England he was now King Philip's 'liegeman'. A bitter and protracted argument ensued, in which both parties sought to defend their positions in front of a crowd of nobles. John accused Marshal of being 'the king of France's man', while William offered to defend his honour in a trial by combat. The *History* suggested that Marshal prevailed in this argument: his old ally Baldwin of Béthune spoke in his favour, and no one was willing to take up William's challenge. But the biographer could not conceal the underlying equivocation of the assembled knights and magnates. Most had no desire to sail to Poitou, but they also had good cause to question William's motives and his claim that he had never intended to be 'disloyal' to the crown. Tellingly, the *History* described how 'the barons looked at one another, and then drew back' in silence, shocked by the spectacle of such a quarrel. No one, it seems, quite knew how to react to this public confrontation between the king and one of the greatest magnates in England – a man so long esteemed as a paragon of fidelity.

The dispute ended in stalemate, with Marshal maintaining his innocence and John nursing a cold fury. William was said to have warned his peers: 'Be on your alert against the king: what he thinks to do with me, he will do to each and every one of you.' Archbishop Hubert of Canterbury later implored the king to 'abandon the expedition' to Poitou 'lest the whole kingdom be thrown into confusion by his departure', and lacking the general support of his nobles, John reluctantly agreed to cancel the offensive – much to the dismay of the thousands of sailors who had assembled at Portsmouth.

Marshal had been able to stand behind the shield of his reputation when confronted by the king, but in real terms, the balance of power remained with John. And, as the *History* observed, he now sought to 'exact his revenge'. His first step was to request that William hand over Young William Marshal – 'the eldest son who was most dear to him' – so that he might be taken into the care of the crown. The boy was now around fifteen, so this could be passed off as a form of royal wardship, but it was obvious that he would be held as a hostage – as surety for Earl William's reformed behaviour. Perhaps this awoke painful memories of Marshal's own time as a child captive in the early 1150s, but he was in no position to refuse this request. To do so would have been tantamount to declaring himself a traitor – thereby allowing the king to confiscate his lands, and subject him, and perhaps the rest of his family, to imprisonment. The biographer admitted that William 'surrendered [his son] readily to the king', adding that he did so because 'he was a man who would have nothing to do with evil-doing, or ever thought of such' – a clear indication of the type of accusations that would have been levelled against Marshal had he declined. Nonetheless, the grim rumours circulating about John's treatment of Duke Arthur, and the other prisoners taken at Mirebeau in 1202, must have caused William to feel a degree of anxiety about his son's safety.

In the months that followed, King John gradually edged Marshal out of the Anegvin court. There appears to have been no grand ostracism, just the slow, but unmistakeable, withdrawal of royal favour and support. The rewards of land and office ceased and were replaced by blank disregard. For the first time in more than twenty years, William experienced the powerful effects of this type of estrangement. He had flourished under Henry II and Richard I, and enjoyed manifold rewards at the start of John's reign. Now he was pushed out into the cold. In 1206, Marshal disappeared from royal records altogether, having withdrawn to Striguil. With the collapse of the Angevin realm on the Continent, and his rift with the king, there would be no prospect of advancement in France or England. If William wished to strengthen his position, and secure the future of his dynasty, he would have to look to the west.

THE PURSUIT OF POWER IN PEMBROKE AND LEINSTER

Marshal re-orientated his career after 1206. Up to this point, the clear focus of his activities and ambitions had been in England and France, but his life now shifted away from the north-south axis – running from the English realm, through Normandy and the Angevin heartlands to Aquitaine – that had defined his earlier years. From his powerbase at Striguil, on the Welsh March, Marshal began instead to channel his energies westwards into Wales itself, and even further afield into Ireland. These regions, on the fringes of Angevin royal authority, were almost akin to the medieval Wild West. They offered the prospect of fresh conquests and opportunities to forge a semi-autonomous earldom. As William approached his sixtieth year, he became increasingly intent upon the need to secure the future of the Marshal dynasty by constructing a grand lordship that could be bequeathed to his heirs. He also looked to reward his faithful retainers with lands and honours. These were objectives that could be best fulfilled in Wales and Ireland.

After more than two decades of regular attendance at the Angevin court, in royal service, William withdrew from the front line of politics and war. This was a direct response to his estrangement from King John, but the earl seems to have embraced the prospect of stepping back from the crown, severing his close association with a dangerously unpredictable and predatory monarch. Marshal may well have made a conscious decision to extract himself from the maelstrom of John's court, judging this detachment to be the safest course and best hope of surviving the capricious king's reign. William was not the only magnate to pursue this course of action. Though only in his mid-thirties, Marshal's northern neighbour, Earl Ranulf III of Chester – who ruled over a mighty lordship on the northern March – already had a long track record of faithful service to the Angevin cause. He had fought to recover Normandy alongside Richard the Lionheart in the late 1190s, and supported John on the Continent in the early years of the new century. After the fall of Normandy, however, Ranulf dedicated an increasing amount of his time to the needs of his own earldom, securing Chester's status as north-west England's leading port, and a centre of trade and commerce.

In the course of his own long career, William Marshal had made his fortune as a knight and royal servant, and though he had been a landed baron since the late 1180s, he had never truly dedicated himself to the business of local governance, administration and territorial consolidation within the Marshal lands. He had served the king first, and dealt with the needs of his lordship and then earldom second. But in this new phase of his career, after 1206, William sought to assert himself as a fully fledged Marcher baron in his own right. This brought Marshal face to face with the fresh challenges of direct rule – forcing him to rely to an even greater extent upon the support of his household and his wife, Countess Isabel – and meant that he had to grapple with issues of military confrontation and conquest as a leader of men, not merely a follower of the crown. This was a critical transformation: Earl

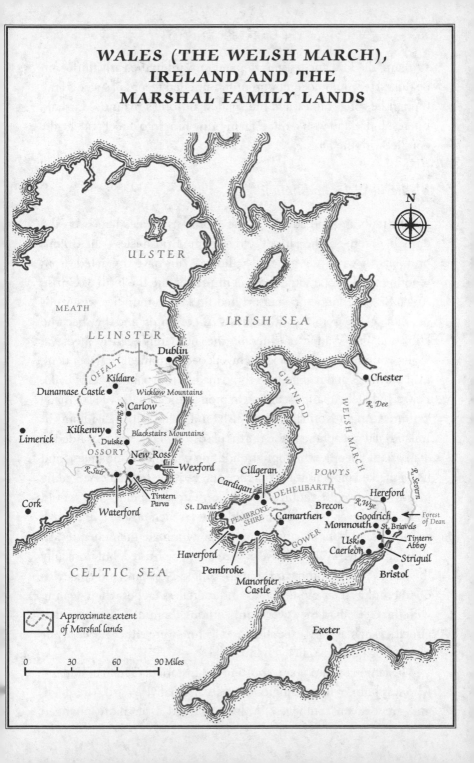

William, the lord and master, stepped forward in the early thirteenth century. He would not enjoy an untrammelled record of success and, though he sought to escape the shadow of John's regime, Marshal's interest in Ireland would once again bring him into direct and deadly conflict with the king.

Medieval Wales and Ireland

Before 1066 and the advent of the Normans, Wales had been the domain of some of the earliest settlers of the British Isles – the Britons or Celts – who are generally thought to have migrated from Continental Europe some three centuries before the birth of Christ. Anglo-Saxon conquerors had pushed these communities westwards out of England from the fifth century AD onwards, and they became known as the 'Wallenses' (literally the 'borderers'). Early medieval Wales consisted of a complex patchwork of determinedly independent, rival provinces and realms, with three major principalities – Gwynedd, Powys and Deheubarth – coming to prominence. In the view of many 'cultured' Anglo-Normans, the Welsh (and their Celtic neighbours in Ireland) did not adhere to the norms of society. They were regarded as 'barbarians': people who thought nothing of adultery and incest, and had a marked propensity for violence and extreme brutality. According to one mid-twelfth century Anglo-Norman chronicler, they would 'fight against each other like animals', murder their prisoners and make routine use of blinding and castration to eliminate their enemies. In short, the native Welsh and Irish were not to be trusted, but ironically this jaded perception meant that the Anglo-Normans and Angevins often employed far more vicious and merciless tactics when dealing with the Celts than they ever would among themselves, arguing that atrocities such as mass execution and torture were either necessary or justified against this 'alien' enemy.

The famous churchman, courtier and historian, Gerald of Wales – who was born of mixed Anglo-Norman and native Welsh parentage, and grew up in south-west Wales – offered a far more nuanced appraisal of the country's indigenous inhabitants. He acknowledged that they could be hot tempered, quarrelsome and 'fierce', but also noted that 'the Welsh are very sharp and intelligent'. Theirs was a land of 'generosity and hospitality', he contended, where 'no one begs'; rich in culture, and filled with the sounds of harmonious singing and the music of the harp, pipe and 'crowder' (an early stringed instrument). Gerald also maintained that the Welsh were marked out by their distinct physical appearance, noting that both men and women cut their hair short and 'shape it round their ears and eyes', men shave their beards, but keep moustaches and 'both sexes take great care of their teeth, more than I have seen in any country ... constantly cleaning them with green hazel-shoots and then rubbing them with woollen cloths until they shine like ivory'.

Few Anglo-Normans shared Gerald's interest in, or respect for, the customs of the Welsh. Most simply saw Wales as a valuable prize – a region replete with abundant natural resources, 'a land of wood and pasture, abounding in deer and fish, milk and herds', and thus a natural target of conquest. Under the thin pretext of bringing peace and law to the supposedly savage Welsh, territory along the Welsh March, including Striguil itself, was forcibly settled after 1066. The rugged inland terrain of Wales, especially in the mountainous north, proved virtually impossible to suppress, so most Anglo-Norman settlements beyond the supposed 'border of the March (at the River Wye in the south and along the Dee in the north) were either on the coast – at sites like Pembroke and the new town of Cardiff – or accessible via easily navigable rivers, such as at Brecon. Many of these sites were essentially isolated outposts of 'foreign' rule, connected only by waterborne communication links, with much of the surrounding inland territory still under the control of the indigenous Welsh.

During the twelfth century, this frontier environment gave birth to a number of powerful, independent-minded dynasties, including the Clare family into which William Marshal married. It also led to a degree of social and cultural interaction, and intermarriage, between the Anglo-Norman settlers and the native population. By the second or third generation, many of the great 'Anglo-Norman' colonising dynasties of this area had native Welsh ancestors in their bloodlines, and thus viewed themselves as a breed apart – hence Gerald of Wales' own mixed heritage.

This process of intermingling was further complicated by the Anglo-Norman/Angevin conquest of Ireland. One of the first colonisers was Countess Isabel's father, Richard Strongbow, a member of the Clare dynasty who sought new territories across the Irish Sea and joined forces with King Henry II in the early 1170s when the Angevin monarch descended on Ireland with a massive fleet of 400 ships. At the same moment that a youthful William Marshal was serving the recently crowned Henry the Young King in England, Strongbow was busy conquering eastern Ireland.

Most of these invaders held deeply disparaging views of the sup-posedly 'primitive' and 'savage' native Irish; a people who showed little interest in building towns or engaging in trade (though in reality, parts of Ireland enjoyed long-established links with regions such as Brittany). Gerald of Wales visited Ireland, and wrote detailed accounts of its topography, natural history and conquest, but he proved far less cautious or sympathetic in his appraisal of its inhabitants, branding them as treacherous and claiming that they were 'the most jealous people on earth'. In terms of military technology, the mail-clad, mounted knights of Henry II and his followers were light years ahead of the Irish, many of whom still rode bareback and un-armoured. As a result, the conquerors easily achieved dominance over a swathe of territory. Henry II proclaimed himself ruler of Ireland, taking the major ports of Wexford, Waterford and Dublin for the crown. His youngest son, John, was designated as 'lord of Ireland' in 1177, and the future king led his own, largely ineffective expedition to the region in 1185.

Other territories were either seized or apportioned to Marcher lords. Strongbow asserted his rights to the region of Leinster, in south-east Ireland, and as part of this process married Isabel's mother, Aoife, princess of Leinster (daughter of Dermot MacMurrough). Other

Marcher lords, like Hugh of Lacy in Meath (north of Leinster), followed suit – claiming lands, marrying native Irish heiresses – creating a dizzying web of marital connections and nuanced, hybrid identity. Later, the Lacy family also took hold of Ulster in the far north-east, while the Briouzes gained rights to Limerick in the south-west. During the last decades of the twelfth century, Anglo-Norman conquerors pushed much of the native Irish ruling elite to the fringes of Ireland, while the colonists set about developing new towns, roads and bridges, and built a network of castles (often of the basic timber and earthwork form). Feeling themselves to be largely detached from the direct control of the Angevin crown, these hard-nosed frontier settlers came to expect, and to enjoy, a high degree of autonomy.

It was these waves of Anglo-Norman conquest that brought William Marshal his claims – through marriage to Richard Strongbow's half-Irish daughter and heir, Isabel of Clare – to both Pembroke and Leinster. Both were valuable territories, boasting expanses of richly fertile lands and promising opportunities to harness trade. But neither region would be easy to dominate. West Wales was threatened by the rising power of the native Welsh, especially that of Llewellyn ap Iorwerth (later known as Llewellyn the Great), prince of Gywnedd in the north; while Leinster was ruled over by a mixture of first- and second-generation colonists, most of whom were fiercely independent and promised to be little impressed by a soft-born Angevin courtier. Marshal might be regarded as a great tournament champion, warrior and paragon of chivalry in England and France, but that storied reputation would count for little in the Wild West.

Marshal's first steps in the west

William Marshal made some attempt to pursue his claims in west Wales and Ireland at the start of King John's reign. A brief tour of these territories was conducted at some point between the autumn of 1200 and the spring of 1201, and it was probably no accident that Countess Isabel accompanied her husband during this journey. She was the heiress through whom Marshal's rights to Pembroke, and particularly Leinster, were derived – the symbol of legitimacy, with a bloodline connection to the Celtic world. William and his wife probably sailed from Striguil itself, hugging the coastline of south Wales to reach the peninsula of Pembrokeshire.

Here a rugged, majestic coastal landscape shielded rolling, verdant inland terrain. Gerald of Wales painted a vivid picture of this region, his homeland. He considered it to be 'particularly attractive because of its flat lands and long sea-coast' and claimed that 'of all the different parts of Wales [this] is at once the most beautiful and the most productive', being 'rich in wheat [and] fish from the sea'. Its capital was the town of Pembroke, 'built high on an oblong plateau of rock', above 'an inlet of the sea which runs down from [the estuary of] Milford Haven', thus offering a well-sheltered, natural harbour.

Through his connection to the Clare dynasty and the grant awarded by King John, Marshal could stake a claim to the full extent of this peninsula, but the northern half had been lost to the native Welsh. William took possession of Pembroke itself, and may have initiated work on a major new stone fortification: the great round tower that now lies at the heart of the larger late medieval castle at Pembroke. This is a tremendously impressive structure, rising through four storeys to a height of almost eighty feet, with twenty-foot-thick walls at its base and topped by a domed, stone roof. It was designed to dominate the landscape and send an inescapable message about the earl of Pembroke's might.

Given the significant threat of native Welsh attack and invasion, Pembrokeshire was also defended by a network of royal fortresses, such as Haverford and Manorbier. In the early years of the thirteenth century, William Marshal managed to strengthen his hold over the region, gaining custody of the royal fortress at Cardigan in 1202, and retaking the neighbouring castle of Cilgerran (with King John's permission and military support) two years later. Pembrokeshire was undoubtedly an extremely valuable territory in its own right, but it was also subject to an extensive degree of crown control and exposed to aggression on the part of the indigenous Welsh. On the whole, Earl William seems to have viewed Pembroke as a stepping stone to Ireland, and what he came to regard as the more promising Irish territory of Leinster.

Pembrokeshire was the main point of embarkation for the journey across the Irish Sea. Gerald of Wales described how one could look out from the peninsula's south coast and see a stream of passing traffic, as 'boats [made] their way to Ireland from almost any part of Britain'. He also claimed (rightly) that 'in clear weather the mountains of Ireland can be seen from St David's', on Pembrokeshire's north-western coast. From Pembroke itself, the crossing could usually be made 'in one short day', but the waters were 'nearly always tempestuous' according to Gerald, because they were 'surging with currents'.

Though the *History* made no record of the journey, it seems certain from other contemporary evidence that William and Isabel sailed from Pembroke to Ireland, probably in the first months of 1201. Marshal had made a half-hearted attempt to assert rights to Leinster soon after his marriage in 1189, but it was not until the early thirteenth century that William began to take a more direct and active interest in Ireland. His first crossing of the Irish Sea was a desperately unpleasant experience – caught in a severe storm, Marshal seems to have feared for his life – but safe landfall was eventually made, probably at the royal port of Wexford.

The lordship of Leinster lay to the south of Dublin (which was held by the English crown) and extended in an arc inland, seventy miles deep at its apex, to enclose the regions of Ossory and Offaly, the fortresses of Kildare and Carlow, and the major castle at Kilkenny. In comparison to the surrounding territories, such as Meath, Leinster was relatively mountainous, rising beyond the rolling lowlands along the coast to the Blackstair range and the broken hill country beyond, and enclosed to the north by the looming Wicklow Mountains.

Gerald of Wales described Ireland as the 'the most temperate of countries', where 'you will seldom see snow' and 'the grass is green in the fields in winter, just the same as in summer'. He wrote that 'the land is fruitful and rich in its fertile soil and plentiful harvests. Crops abound in the fields, flocks on the mountains and wild animals in the woods', and boasted that the province was replete with lush 'pastures and meadows, honey and milk'. He was particularly enamoured of its 'healthy' and 'sweet-smelling' air – which, he asserted, imbued residents with almost miraculous physical well-being – but less impressed by the 'ever-present over hanging of clouds and fog' and frequent 'storms of wind and rain', complaining that 'you will scarcely see even in summer three consecutive days of really fine weather' in Ireland.

William Marshal seems to have received a rather frosty reception upon his arrival in 1201. The long-established Anglo-Norman/Irish nobles of Leinster were proud, hard-bitten warlords, accustomed to self-governance. William made some limited progress in asserting his authority: the local landholder Adam of Hereford appears to have recognised his overlordship; friendly relations were also established with the Anglo-Norman bishop of Ossory. It was probably also at this point that the first steps were taken to establish a new settlement and port on the River Barrow – the main waterway that wound its way inland through Leinster – that was christened Newtown (almost certainly on the site of modern New Ross). This would be a major development, designed to offer Leinster its own centre of communication and trade, independent of the local crown-held ports of Wexford and Waterford.

Marshal also set in motion plans to establish two new Cistercian monasteries in Leinster: one, a colony of Tintern (on the Welsh March) named Tintern Parva, was founded in thanks to God for surviving the recent crossing from Wales; and another was initiated at Duiske. All in all, it was hardly a disastrous first venture on to Irish soil, but in the main William's appearance was greeted with grudging acknowledgement, not open welcome. During the spring of 1201, the bulk of the Marshal party returned to the mainland. William's well-established household knight Geoffrey FitzRobert was left behind to oversee his lord's interests in Leinster, serving as seneschal (or steward). Geoffrey's marriage to Strongbow's illegitimate daughter Basilia may have enhanced the legitimacy of his position in the eyes of the established colonists. William took the further step of sending his nephew John Marshal to assist in the governance of Leinster in 1204, probably for the term of one year.

In reality, all of these measures represented somewhat desultory or intermittent attempts to engage with affairs in his western lands, at a time when the main focus of Marshal's energy and ambition remained in England and France. Even so, these forays must have opened William's eyes both to the rich potential of a region like Leinster and to the significant commitment of time and resources required to bring the province to heel. After the fall of Normandy and his withdrawal from court, Marshal was at last willing to make that determined effort.

THE LORD OF LEINSTER

William Marshal spent much of late 1206 laying plans for a full-scale expedition to Ireland. He would once again be accompanied by Countess Isabel, but their party would also be bolstered by a large portion of the Marshal household. Geoffrey FitzRobert remained in Leinster, but William now decided to bring many of his most trusted and able knights and retainers on this journey westwards. These included his kinsman John Marshal, the ever-faithful John of Earley and Jordan of Sauqueville, the knight who helped to defend Upper Normandy. All of these men were becoming established landholders in their own right, having been granted estates by King John, yet they chose to remain in Earl William's service.

Some prominent members of Marshal's retinue had moved on to fresh ventures by this time. William Waleran married and took possession of lands in Gloucestershire. Alan of St-Georges returned to Sussex to take up his inheritance, but he was replaced in the earl's entourage by a near neighbour from the Rother Valley, Henry Hose, who hailed from the village of Harting, at the foot of the South Downs. Another notable recruit was Stephen of Évreux, a well-established knight whose family held lands in Herefordshire (on the Welsh

March) from the Lacy dynasty, and who came to be trusted for his cool-headed judgement. Both would play significant roles in the Leinster campaign. Two other familiar faces also made the journey to Ireland: William's devoted counsellor and clerk, Master Michael of London, and the knight Philip of Prendergast. The latter had a close connection to Ireland, as his father Maurice had fought in Leinster alongside Richard Strongbow in the 1170s, and Philip himself was of mixed Norman-Irish birth.

William Marshal was by no means abandoning his lordship in Striguil after 1206, but the decision to employ so many of his leading supporters on the coming expedition suggests a clear recognition of the challenges that would be faced, and a determination to see them overcome. As was customary, Earl William also sought official licence from King John to travel to Leinster, and this was duly issued on 19 February 1207. Final arrangements were made for the departure from the southern Welsh March. Less than ten days later, however, a crown messenger arrived at Striguil with disturbing news. The capricious monarch had reconsidered his position, and was no longer happy for Marshal to make his journey to Ireland.

King John perhaps failed to give sufficient consideration to William's initial request, or it may be that this change of heart was simply a product of his notoriously inconsistent nature. In any case, the king now sought to restrict Marshal's movements. At one level, John appears to have been concerned by Earl William's growing influence and independence, but the monarch also had a more direct and self-serving reason to interfere in the proposed Leinster campaign. As 'lord of Ireland', John had his own ambitions there and, in many respects, saw the province as his own pet project – a region that had resisted his will in 1185, but would now, in the new century, be curbed by his royal might. From 1200 onwards, the king had been sponsoring the forcible imposition of his own rights in Ireland, happily trampling over the claims of other lords (including those of William Marshal in Leinster). At the same time, John sought to destabilise potential opponents by encouraging infighting between the native Irish and Anglo-Norman colonists, and power struggles among the settler barons themselves. The crown's representatives had enjoyed considerable success, so John was not enamoured by the prospect of Earl William making a bold and determined entry into the Irish world.

Marshal now faced a difficult decision. He still possessed a formal royal licence for his expedition that had not been rescinded, but according to the *History*, the king's envoy made it clear that John's 'sole wish is that you should not go to Ireland.'* Any journey to Leinster would not be illegal as such, yet there could be little doubt that failure to back down would result in a measure of punishment. William took time to consult in private with 'the countess and some of his closest retainers'. Having weighed up the prospects awaiting in Ireland – plus the time and resources already expended in preparation for the venture – against the penalties that might be exacted by the crown, Marshal made a bold choice. The royal envoy was informed that 'whether for good or ill' William still intended to sail to Ireland. King John soon made his displeasure apparent. Marshal's rights to the fortresses of Carmarthen and Cardigan in west Wales were rescinded on 9 April 1207; four days later he lost the custody of Gloucester Castle, the Forest of Dean and St Briavels Castle. But by that stage, Earl William and Countess Isabel had arrived in Ireland.

William Marshal's return to Leinster

Earl William enjoyed a somewhat warmer reception from many of Leinster's nobles in March 1207 – including Adam of Hereford and another local landholder, David de la Roche – largely because he was seen as a potential counter to King John's overbearing influence. The

---

* The *History of William Marshal* suggests that King John demanded another hostage from William Marshal at this point – his second son Richard Marshal, who was then around twelve years old. However, royal records indicate that Richard was not placed into the custody of the crown for more than a year (4 June 1208), so this appears to have been an error on the biographer's part.

monarch's leading representative and justiciar in Ireland since 1199, Meiler FitzHenry, had become increasingly unpopular, having adopted an acquisitive and predatory approach to governance. Meiler was a formidable figure – a grizzled veteran of the first wave of Anglo-Norman conquest in Ireland, he was only marginally younger than Marshal himself. Gerald of Wales painted a vivid picture of Meiler from first-hand experience, describing him as a broad-chested man of below medium height, with strong muscular limbs, 'a dark complexion, with black eyes and a stern, piercing look'; and characterised him as a skilled warrior who relished combat, but loved glory even more. Meiler was undoubtedly a canny, ambitious and unscrupulous figure, with long experience of warfare. He would prove to be a dangerous enemy. He also boasted an impressive familial heritage – his father having been one of King Henry I of England's many bastards, his mother a Welsh princess of near-legendary beauty – so was hardly over-awed by Earl William's own status and pedigree.

Meiler was opposed to William Marshal's plan to assert his authority in Leinster on a number of levels. As justiciar of Ireland, Meiler regarded himself as the king's right hand and leading power in the province, and like John, he was hardly minded to welcome the advent of a forceful Anglo-Norman rival, especially one who had fallen from the crown's favour. Meiler also held lands in Leinster itself, most notably the imposing stone castle of Dunamase, and was trying to press his own claim to rule over the region of Offaly in the north-west, which he argued had been confiscated by royal order. All of this guaranteed that the justiciar would seek to thwart William at every step.

Nonetheless, it seemed initially that Meiler had overplayed his hand. Upon his arrival in Ireland, Marshal was quickly able to build a coalition of disgruntled local lords in Leinster and neighbouring Meath (to the north), where Walter of Lacy held the reins of power. In May 1207, the 'barons of Leinster and Meath' sent a formal letter of complaint to King John, demanding that Meiler FitzHenry relinquish his hold over Offaly and return the territory to its rightful lord. Earl William was not directly named in this missive, but the implication

William Marshal served at the right hand of five English kings in the course of his long career: Henry the Young King (shown above, between his father and brother, as 'Henr.Iunior', in the mid-thirteenth century illustration by Matthew Paris); Henry II; Richard the Lionheart; John and Henry III. As such, Marshal was both a witness to, and leading participant in, many of the events that shaped English and European history in this formative period.

After marrying the heiress Isabel of Clare in 1189, William Marshal took possession of the stone fortress of Striguil (Chepstow), perched above the Wye River, on the Welsh March (above left). He set about improving this stronghold (which initially consisted of a single-storey stone keep and a timber palisade), constructing a double-towered stone gatehouse (foreground right) – which can be dated to 1189–90 through the age of its original ironclad, oak gates (shown right) – and later adding an inner wall (between the keep and gatehouse), with a pair of the three-storey towers.

William Marshal was appointed as earl of Pembroke in 1199, after supporting John's claim to the English crown, and probably took possession of Pembroke itself in late 1200. The imposing four-storey, eighty-foot-tall great tower that now lies in the heart of the later medieval castle (above) can been dated to this period and can probably be associated with Marshal's rule.

Strongholds and sieges featured prominently in William Marshal's career. He probably marched to the defence of the desert fortress of Kerak (above) during his pilgrimage to the Holy Land in the mid-1180s. William fought to defend the circuit of Roman battlements at Le Mans in 1189 (right) and made a failed attempt to relieve the mighty Château Gaillard, positioned above the River Seine (below), in 1203.

William Marshal was reputedly the only man who ever bested the famed warrior-king, Richard the Lionheart (above, shown in his tomb effigy at Fontevraud), in single combat. Nonetheless, after Richard's coronation in 1189, Marshal emerged as one of his most trusted and influential supporters. William also championed King John's cause (below, in a detail from his tomb effigy in Worcester Cathedral), though the latter proved to be a dangerously unpredictable monarch. John presided over the collapse of the once-mighty Angevin Empire, faced a baronial rebellion and was forced to concede the terms of Magna Carta in 1215.

By contrast, William Marshal seems to have always retained the diminutive seal of a household knight, seen here (small green seal on the bottom right) appended to the 1217 version of Magna Carta that he re-issued with the papal legate Guala of Bichierri.

n William Marshal's lifetime, t became customary to uthenticate and empower fficial documents by attaching vax seals imprinted with listinctive text and images. Leading nobles, like Robert FitzWalter, often adopted elaborate and ornate designs n their seal-dies (as seen bove, bearing the inscription: *IGILLUM ROBERTI ILI WALTERI*). Note the epresentation of FitzWalter's oat of arms upon his shield nd the caparison cover on his orse, and the heraldic device of is ally, Saer of Quincy, on the nield to the left.

After King John's death in 1216, William Marshal championed the cause of the young King Henry III. In May 1217, Marshal sought to defeat the combined forces of the baronial rebels and the French at Lincoln (above), and the resultant battle reached its climax in front of the cathedral.

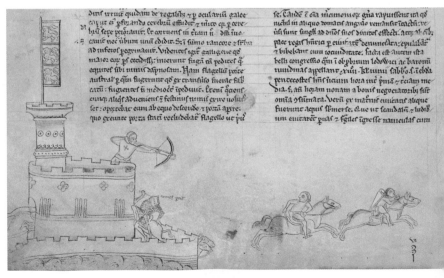

Crossbowmen positioned in Lincoln Castle helped to rout the French and baronial forces, driving them from the town. The victory was later depicted in this illustration by Matthew Paris, which also shows the mortally wounded figure of the count of Perche.

After an extraordinary career spanning more than seven decades, William Marshal died on 14 May 1219. His body was laid to rest in the Round Temple Church in London on 20 May, where this effigy (now generally considered to be a representation of the earl) can still be seen today. The precise location of his remains is unknown as the effigy has been moved over the centuries and badly damaged, most recently during a Second World War bombing raid.

A rare photograph of the mid-nineteenth century statue of William Marshal erected in the House of Lords, to the left of the royal throne, at a time when Marshal remained a notable, yet shadowy figure of history.

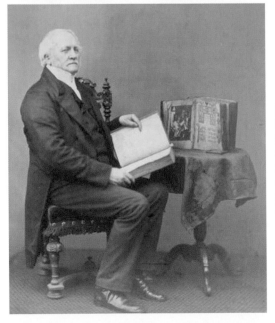

It was only after the discovery of the *History of William Marshal* that the full scale and scope of the earl's achievements began to become apparent, though the sole surviving copy of this work was almost lost in the vast library of Sir Thomas Phillipps (left).

was clear. Marshal must have imagined that the sheer volume of Anglo-Irish support for his cause might force John to reprimand his justiciar, but he was badly mistaken. The king's letter of response was full of embittered rage at the 'unheard of' affront to his majesty, and declared in decisive terms that 'what you ask is neither right, nor has any precedent'. William had overstepped the mark, and would now have to pay the price.

In the months that followed, Meiler appears to have been in direct communication with John, plotting Marshal's downfall. It was probably at the justiciar's urging that the king issued an official royal summons in late summer 1207, instructing the earl in strict terms 'not to fail for any reason to come to him' in England. William was to attend an audience, along with Meiler and the leading Leinster lords who had complained about the issue of Offaly. These included men such as Adam of Hereford, David de la Roche and Marshal's retainer, Philip of Prendergast, to whom he had granted land in County Wexford. In this meeting, John would pass fair judgement over the disputed territory.

At first glance, this might have appeared to be an act of conciliation, but according to the *History*, when William, Isabel and their leading retainers met in council to debate this message, all 'greatly feared [that] the king's sending for him was a trick, designed more for harming him than for his good', and the countess expressed grave doubts about 'the king's word'. Just as when John asked in 1205 to take custody of his eldest son, Earl William now found himself facing an ominous choice. Any refusal to respond to a crown command of this type would expose him to accusations of treachery, yet Marshal 'had no doubt that once he left the land there would be strife and war between those men he left behind' and Meiler's forces. The earl's absence in England would offer a perfect opportunity for the justiciar's men to attempt the seizure of key fortresses like Kilkenny, driving the Marshal dynasty from Leinster.

William might have considered a full withdrawal from Ireland at this point, essentially forsaking his claim to Leinster, but this would have been a severe blow to his prestige and a massive concession of rights. Countess Isabel was pregnant once again, and thus not well disposed to the perilous voyage across the Irish Sea. Marshal resolved instead to stand his ground, attending the meeting in England along with two of his most trusted knights – his nephew John Marshal and retainer Henry Hose – while making detailed preparations for Leinster's defence. Like King Richard the Lionheart before the start of the Third Crusade, Earl William had to devise a system of governance and defence that could function in his absence. At this moment of looming crisis, William looked to bulwarks of his household. Jordan of Sauqueville was appointed as guardian of the north-eastern half of Leinster, covering Carlow, Wicklow and Kildare, while John of Earley would protect Ossory in the south-west, holding the likes of Kilkenny and Wexford, with Stephen of Évreux serving as his advisor.

With autumn approaching, William Marshal called all of the knights and barons of Leinster to a major assembly at the great stronghold of Kilkenny. The earl arrived at the meeting, hand in hand with his wife, Countess Isabel, and according to the *History*, delivered an impassioned speech to his Anglo-Irish subjects, imploring them to show continued loyalty in his absence. The recorded wording of his declaration cannot be taken as precise, but the central tenets of Marshal's appeal may well be accurate. The most telling feature was his repeated emphasis on Isabel, the Anglo-Irish heiress. She was described as 'your lady by birth; the daughter of the earl [Strongbow]' – the man who had given them their lands – a woman who 'by birthright' deserved their 'protection'. William shrewdly downplayed his own claim to Leinster, stating that 'I have nothing but through her', while emphasising Isabel's delicate state, noting that 'she remains amongst you pregnant'. By stressing the legitimacy of the Clare/Marshal rights and his wife's abject vulnerability, William evidently hoped to secure the fidelity of his subjects 'until such time as God brings me back here'. Marshal trusted the power of his words, rejecting John of Earley's suggestion that he demand hostages from his Anglo-Irish barons. This would prove to be a dreadful miscalculation.

A *trap is set*

After the meeting at Kilkenny, 'the earl took leave of his men and quickly crossed the Irish Sea', arriving back in west Wales on 27 September 1207. Meiler FitzHenry travelled separately, but duly appeared in November, when the audience with King John was convened at Woodstock – one of the grandest of all of the Angevins' royal residences (and today the site of Blenheim Palace). It was here that Earl William was betrayed. John was supposed to adjudicate on the issue of Offaly, but he immediately treated Marshal in a 'hostile and unpleasant' manner, and proceeded to teach his once loyal servant a potent lesson about the depth of a king's power and the weakness of men's hearts.

The *History* passed over the close and humiliating detail of this assembly, but an outline of the proceedings has survived in official crown records. King John and Meiler had laid a trap for Marshal. He had been drawn away from Ireland, leaving his lands exposed, coming to Woodstock in the company of his Leinster subjects – the barons who had protested the unlawful confiscation of Offaly. Now, William had to watch as his monarch bought these same men – the likes of Adam of Hereford and David de la Roche – with grants of land, winning their silent acquiescence to Meiler's claim. Worse was to follow. Two members of Marshal's own retinue turned against him: Philip of Prendergast was endowed with territory near Cork (south of Leinster); while John Marshal – the earl's own kinsman – was appointed as marshal of Ireland. As earl of Pembroke, lord of Striguil and Leinster, William Marshal could offer his knights and vassals largesse, but his rewards paled in comparison to those proffered at the font of royal favour. Roundly outbid, William was forsaken by men who saw more profit in direct service to the crown. After the gathering at Woodstock, only Henry Hose remained steadfast beside the earl.

With Earl William stripped of support, Meiler FitzHenry went on the offensive. King John granted his justiciar leave to return to Ireland, and he duly departed in early January 1208. Meiler was also furnished with three letters demanding that John of Earley, Jordan of Sauqueville and Stephen of Évreux all quit their posts in Ireland, and appear before their monarch within fifteen days or forfeit their own estates. Not surprisingly, William Marshal's request to return to Leinster was flatly denied. Meiler and the treacherous Philip of Prendergast managed to make a successful winter crossing to Ireland, in one of the only ships to do so that season, while Marshal was forced to remain at court, travelling 'the length and breadth of England' with the itinerant royal entourage. Throughout this period, John was said to have 'treated him with such coolness that it was a wonder to behold and all the court marvelled at it', and no one would speak to the earl.

Throughout the early weeks of 1208, William was left in a state of desperate apprehension, with 'no knowledge at all' of events across the Irish Sea. He managed to maintain his implacable veneer of calm, conscious that any public display of fear, worry or emotion would be seized upon as a sign of weakness and exploited. Any attempt to leave the court without the king's permission would also invite terrible retribution, not least because John still had Young William Marshal in custody as a hostage. Earl William had to force himself to wait for news from Leinster with every ounce of patience he could muster.

Then, on 25 January, as the royal party rode out from Guildford (south of London), King John brought his horse up beside William's. 'Marshal, tell me, have you heard any news from Ireland,' the monarch reputedly demanded. When William replied that he had not, the king said 'with a laugh': 'I can give you news from there.' As the earl rode on in deepening shock, John proceeded to tell him that Meiler had launched an attack on Marshal's lands. Countess Isabel had been besieged in Kilkenny and a bloody battle was fought outside the castle, in which 'Stephen of Évreux was killed', while 'John of Earley [had] died from a wound sustained that very day'. At these terrible tidings, William somehow held his composure, but the *History* admitted that he was 'greatly aggrieved at heart'.

12

THE FALTERING CROWN

William Marshal had been right to fear that an offensive would be launched against Leinster during his absence from Ireland. According to the *History*, Meiler FitzHenry had instructed his kinsmen and followers to 'wage war on the Marshal's men as soon as they knew that the others had arrived in England', with a view to doing 'harm and damage to the Marshal's lands'. In the early autumn of 1207, Meiler's forces attacked the key settlement of New Ross, setting 'fire to the earl's barns ... reducing them to ashes' and seizing plunder. Twenty of William's men were slain in the course of this destructive assault. This marked the start of a period of 'upheaval and war on a grand scale [fought] throughout that land'.

THE DEFENCE OF LEINSTER

Countess Isabel and the earl's leading knights held their own through the winter of 1207. Cut off from the outside world by the closing of the sea-lanes, they had to fend for themselves, and appear to have done a commendable job of defending Leinster in Earl William's absence. They sustained no major losses of territory and captured a number of

Meiler's troops, including one of the justiciar's leading knights and lieutenants. Up until the early weeks of 1208, the measures put in place by William proved effective. This meant that when Meiler and Philip Prendergast crossed the Irish Sea, they discovered that 'the land was not so free of the Marshal's men as [they] thought it would be'.

Nonetheless, Meiler had one crucial weapon in his arsenal: the royal summons issued to John of Earley, Jordan of Sauqueville and Stephen of Évreux, demanding their attendance at royal court within fifteen days. These orders were delivered soon after the justiciar made landfall in Ireland, and immediately threatened to undermine the Marshal dynasty's hold over Leinster. According to the biographer, all three knights met 'in secret conclave to consult privately' about their response to King John's demand and the prospect of forfeiting their own lands should they demur. The underlying intention of the summons was obvious. Even if immediate travel back to the mainland proved impossible because of the stormy seas, the three warriors could only hope to avoid crown punishment by submitting to Meiler, the king's representative. John, Jordan and Stephen now faced a test of loyalty. By this point, they must have heard that Earl William had been betrayed at Woodstock; that Philip Prendergast and even John Marshal had turned against him. The question was whether they would now follow this example, salvaging their own fortunes?

Their response to this dilemma revealed the depth of their dedication to William Marshal, and underlined the intimate bonds of allegiance that united military retinues in this period. John of Earley was said to have told his compatriots that he had no desire to 'lose the love of our lord', the man who had 'committed [his estate] to us to guard', and Stephen and Jordan likewise refused to '[abandon] the earl's land'. These same ties of affection and fidelity had linked Marshal himself to the Young King Henry, and his father Henry II. But the events of 1208 also suggest that the ideal of chivalry – and in particular, the intertwined notions of shame and honour – exerted an increasingly profound influence over knightly conduct.

According to the *History*, Earley made 'a magnificent speech that was full of wisdom' in the course of this meeting. This indicates that his recorded words were intended to represent a praiseworthy example of chivalric reasoning. His declaration is particularly fascinating because it did not simply trade in abstract notions of emotion or fidelity. Instead, John suggested that he and his peers should be moved by personal interest. Two distinct forms of loss or reward hung in the balance: land and reputation. Should they follow the king's orders, the knights would preserve their material wealth, but suffer public shame as a result – for, as Earley reputedly argued, it would be a 'most disgraceful thing to leave the earl's land' and to do so would mean that 'our own honour would be diminished'. Arguing that a knight should 'be concerned with his honour, so that no tale of our wrongdoing can be told', Earley concluded that enduring a loss of territory was preferable, as 'shame lasts longer than destitution'.

This was obviously an idealised reconstruction of the debate, and the recent actions of Philip of Prendergast and John Marshal demonstrate that not all members of the warrior class prioritised honour over power and wealth. Even so, it was the case that John, Jordan and Stephen decided to reject the king's orders and defend Leinster in early 1208, and this choice does not seem to have been rationalised simply as an act of selfless altruism, but rather as a form of chivalric self-preservation.

Having chosen to stand their ground, the three knights went on to consider what strategy could be employed to defeat Meiler FitzHenry. A crucial decision was made to seek an alliance with the Lacy dynasty, who held power to the north of Leinster, and Jordan of Sauqueville duly travelled to Ulster in the hope of forging a pact with Earl Hugh of Lacy. No record of their dealings survives, so it is not clear what arguments or enticements Jordan used, but his mission proved a success. Hugh marched into Leinster in support of the Marshal family with some sixty-five knights, all 'well armed and riding chargers', 200 men-at-arms and around 1,000 lightly equipped infantry. These significant reinforcements shifted the balance of the conflict, allowing Earl William and Countess Isabel's men to move on to the offensive.

There was a decisive confrontation between Meiler and Marshal's men in early 1208, but not in the way that King John reported to William Marshal outside Guildford. The monarch's claim that both Stephen of Évreux and John of Earley had died was a barefaced, malicious lie, designed to torment Marshal and elicit an un-courtly loss of composure. In reality, the combined might of the Marshal and Lacy forces prevailed in the Leinster war, such that, in the words of the biographer, 'the damage that Meiler sought to do to the earl's lands was done to him by the earl's men, for they devastated his own property'. The justiciar was captured, along with the turncoat Philip Prendergast, whose property was also seized. Both men were forced to make peace with Countess Isabel and had to give their sons into custody as hostages, while a number of other opponents had likewise to hand over kinsmen, 'for the earl's men would not accept other pledges'.

News of the actual course and outcome of this conflict finally reached England in late February or early March. Unsurprisingly, the king was apparently 'not amused at all' by these tidings, while William Marshal was said to have been 'overjoyed at heart'. On 5 March, King John summoned the earl to a formal audience at Bristol, but Marshal still had to tread with exceptional care. Any attempt to shame the king over the spiteful lies spoken outside Guildford, or hint of gloating over the victory in Leinster, might alienate and enrage John. As a result, William decided to feign ignorance of the events in Ireland. In their meeting the king showed no flicker of remorse for his recent ill-treatment of Marshal, but was said to have declared: 'I shall give you good and welcome news – your men are in fine health and spirits [as is] the countess herself.' According to the *History*:

> The Marshal paid great attention to his words, as if he knew nothing about the matter, and replied in a wise and moderate manner: 'Sire, thanks be to the Lord our God, but not for a moment did I think, on the day I left my land, that I had an enemy who would wage war on me.'

This feat of control permitted King John to save face and draw back from continued confrontation. Official records confirm that a reconciliation was achieved later that month. In return for royal recognition of his full rights to Leinster, Marshal reaffirmed his status as John's subject in Ireland, and conceded some powers over the appointment of bishops and legal jurisdiction to the crown. This compromise curbed Earl William's independence in Leinster to an extent, but still left him with far more autonomy than most barons enjoyed in England. The king also wrote to Meiler, instructing him to return Offaly to Marshal without delay or argument.

William had survived the storm. He was granted permission to return to Ireland in April 1208, but a barely submerged current of tension still coloured his relationship with John. It was probably at this point that the monarch demanded that a second hostage – Marshal's son, Richard – be given into custody. The biographer intimated that Countess Isabel was disquieted by this 'villainous request', but as always, the foreboding threat of retribution forced William to comply. The wisdom of that choice would soon be made clear in the starkest terms.

The lord of Leinster triumphant

William Marshal returned to Ireland that spring to secure control of Leinster. Upon his arrival, the earl was greeted by John of Earley and Jordan of Sauqueville, though the former was still wearing a mail hauberk – a clear sign that the region had yet to be wholly pacified. On the following day, William was reunited with his wife Isabel at Kilkenny, who must by this stage have given birth to the child she had been carrying. The biographer recorded that the countess was intent upon exacting 'savage revenge' against the barons and knights who had supported Meiler, but Marshal insisted on pursuing a more measured approach. Perhaps imitating the magnanimity shown by King Henry II after the rebellions of his eldest son had been quelled in 1174 and 1183, William resisted the temptation to take direct and violent retribution, relying instead upon the force of his presence and reputation to impose order.

He seems to have been aware that 'there were many who greeted him' upon his return 'whose hearts belied their smiling countenances', but most of the hostages held from these lords were returned. There is no record of John Marshal's treatment in the immediate aftermath these events, but he seems to have been swiftly forgiven for his moment of disloyalty, probably because he had not actively gone to war alongside Meiler. Some of those who betrayed the earl at Woodstock, or fought against his men in Leinster, received somewhat harsher treatment. They were said to have come before Marshal 'in fear and trembling', begging him for mercy 'with tears in their eyes'. David de la Roche and Philip of Prendergast tried to declare their enduring loyalty, but John of Earley openly testified to their treachery. Though William agreed to give them the kiss of peace, both men were publicly shamed. Prendergast's son remained a hostage for at least the next seven years, while de la Roche became a social pariah. He was shunned by his peers and, in future, knights refused to sit next to him at social gatherings.

The most severe punishment was meted out to Meiler FitzHenry, but restraint was shown even here. Meiler had to relinquish control of his major stone castle at Dunamase and concede that all of his lands would pass to Marshal on his own death. Hostages taken from his family were also kept for years to come. The failed plot of 1208 marked a decisive fall from royal favour for the justiciar, who was now branded a 'cruel and savage man' and the 'root of all the evil done'. By early 1209, Meiler had been replaced in Ireland by a new royal justiciar – John of Gray, bishop of Norwich – and the disgraced baron lived out his remaining years in Ireland (until 1220) in abject impotence, looking on from the sidelines.

With peace restored, William Marshal was free to continue the work of strengthening his power base in Leinster. Well-earned rewards were apportioned to his steadfast retainers. John of Earley was given land in County Kilkenny, thus establishing a settlement that still bears his name to this day – Earlytown. Jordan of Sauqueville, Stephen of Évreux and Henry Hose likewise received territories of their own. Earl William dedicated much of the next four years to the management of his Leinster estates, constructing a secure, prosperous and enduring satellite of Marshal authority in Ireland. A limited range of evidence survives for this period, but William appears to have been firm, yet fair minded, in the treatment of his own vassals, but a scourge to the neighbouring native Irish and their churchmen.* Marshal also became increasingly focused upon the need to secure advantageous marriage alliances for his children. His eldest son had already been betrothed to Alice, the daughter of Baldwin of Béthune – a long-standing ally of the family. A union between the earl's eldest daughter Matilda and Hugh Bigod, heir to the earldom of Norfolk, was also arranged. This process of dynastic and territorial consolidation was briefly interrupted and threatened, however, in 1210, when King John sought once again to assert his will in Ireland. But on this occasion the monarch came in pursuit of a different quarry.

A KING'S VENGEANCE

The grim fate suffered by William of Briouze and his family offers an apposite lesson in the dangers of opposing a monarch like John. It also goes some way to highlight the mixture of astute judgement, deft skill and pure luck that had so far enabled William Marshal to negotiate a path through this most tumultuous of reigns. Briouze was Marshal's social peer, his neighbour in Ireland and on the Welsh March, and a relatively close associate and friend. A notable royal favourite from the start of John's reign and an unfaltering supporter of the king, Briouze had also played some part in the disappearance and likely murder of

---

* A particularly ugly dispute broke out with the native Irish prelate, Albinus, bishop of Ferns, over lands that Marshal claimed as his own, and this caused the earl to be condemned by the Irish Church.

Duke Arthur of Brittany, John's nephew, in April 1203. As time went on, Briouze also amassed a burdensome array of debts to the crown from fines owing for the lands and honours he had received. By 1208, in Ireland alone he still had 5,000 marks to pay for rights to the lordship of Munster, and £2,865 outstanding on the fine related to Limerick. This financial liability was manageable so long as one retained the king's favour, but if John suddenly insisted on all of these monies being repaid in short order, Briouze would be placed in an impossible position.

In the spring of 1208, William of Briouze suddenly lost his monarch's trust and support. One cause of this estrangement may have been tangentially related to William Marshal. In March of that year the Leinster dispute was resolved, but John remained suspicious and thus seems to have requested that Marshal place another hostage into the custody of the crown. Around the same time, the king asked William of Briouze to hand over his own eldest son, perhaps as a precautionary measure, given Briouze's known connection to Marshal. Had Briouze followed Marshal's example in acceding to this demand, the whole incident might have passed unnoticed. But, according to the chronicler Roger of Wendover, when the king's men arrived at the family's estate, Briouze's wife Matilda openly declared that she would never hand over her own sons to the man who had 'murdered Arthur, his own nephew'. When this desperately incautious remark was reported to John, a calamitous rift opened.

William Briouze tried to recover his position, agreeing by way of atonement to return the Marcher castles of Hay, Brecon and Radnor to the crown, but he was later accused of attacking these same fortresses and burning half of Leominster in open defiance of the king – charges that may well have been invented in order to cover John's subsequent actions. The Briouze family's lands were summarily confiscated and their arrests ordered. With the world fast crumbling around him, William of Briouze fled with his wife and two of his sons to Ireland, hoping to escape the king's wrath and find refuge with Walter of Lacy, his son-in-law (through marriage to one of Briouze's daughters).

In the course of this flight, the Briouzes sailed to Leinster, probably in early 1209, narrowly avoiding shipwreck during a terrible winter crossing of the Irish Sea. They remained in Marshal territory for twenty days. The *History* acknowledged that King John 'conceived such hatred for [Briouze]' that 'no peace could ever be made between them', but the biographer refused to explain the precise cause of this enmity, stating bluntly that, 'I do not know the reason for the banishment, nor would it be wise for me, even if I did, to speak of it or even undertake to do so.' This wording suggests that the author of the *History* did at least know that a dark scandal lay at the bottom of this whole affair. Briouze must have offered some explanation to William Marshal for his sudden appearance, though it is not certain that he confessed any involvement in Duke Arthur's disappearance at this point.

King John's envoys soon tracked the Briouzes to Ireland, and informed the new justiciar, John of Gray, of the order for their arrests. William Marshal was subsequently instructed to hand over Briouze and his family, and accused of having 'housed a traitor to the king', but Earl William tried to cover his tracks. He flatly denied all knowledge of the fact that charges had been levelled against Briouze, and stated that as the family was under the protection of his hospitality he would escort them safely beyond the boundaries of his lands. Marshal took a significant risk in refusing the justiciar's official request, but the earl found himself in a compromising position and could hardly have guessed what would follow. The Briouzes were ushered out of Leinster with polite haste and took sanctuary with Walter of Lacy in Meath. Earl William must have hoped that he had extricated himself from this dispute without undue penalty.

King John descends on Ireland

In fact, King John was utterly determined to pursue the Briouze family and also intent upon demonstrating the full force of his royal authority in Ireland. Over the course of the next year, John made extensive preparations for a massive military campaign, and in the late spring of 1210, mustered a 700-ship armada in west Wales, ready to transport no less than 800 knights and an army of Flemish mercenaries across the Irish Sea. Judging that this expedition posed an irresistible threat, William Marshal hastily sailed to Pembrokeshire to offer a renewed submission to the king, thereby making it clear that he had no intention of lending any further support to the Briouze family or their allies. In some respects, there was an unpleasant edge of self-serving treachery to this decision. Marshal had turned his back on a former friend to safeguard his own position and family, but having already endured one period of conflict with the king, he seems to have had a better understanding of exactly what was at stake than many of his peers in Ireland. William's bond of allegiance to the Briouzes did not extend to dynastic suicide.

The king's mighty host landed near Waterford on 20 June 1210, and proceeded to march through Leinster. William Marshal was obliged to feed and entertain John and his troops at massive personal expense, until the army finally moved on to the royal city of Dublin. Walter of Lacy quickly recognised that he was facing impossible odds and submitted to the king's mercy, but was stripped of all of his estates in Meath (and these were not returned for another five years). His brother, Hugh of Lacy, earl of Ulster, made the mistake of trying to resist the crown, but his own forces were no match for those assembled by John. Hugh eventually retreated with the Briouze family to his fortress at Carrickfergus, and later fled to Scotland, leaving the king free to confiscate Ulster.

William of Briouze fled to France, where he died in exile in 1211 (but not, it would seem, before telling the story of Duke Arthur's murder). His wife Matilda and eldest son were less fortunate. Taken prisoner by King John, they were thrown into a cell in Windsor Castle and slowly starved to death. Chroniclers later reported that their bodies were found in a chillingly gruesome pose: Matilda kneeling before the corpse of her son, having been driven by unbearable hunger to gnaw upon the flesh of his cheeks.

The merciless pursuit and cruel mistreatment of the Briouze family, and the associated ruination of the Lacys, caused widespread outrage across the realm. This singular act of royal retribution alienated many barons in England, igniting deep resentment of an already unpopular monarch. William Marshal had escaped the worst, but there was still a price to be paid for having harboured the 'traitorous' Briouzes in early 1209. He was summoned before John in Dublin to answer for this indiscretion in August 1210. Just as he had in 1205, when confronted over the issue of Normandy, Marshal offered to undergo trial by combat to prove his innocence, but even though he was now in his early sixties, no courtier was willing to meet his challenge. William also repeated the excuse that he had originally offered to the justiciar John of Gray, arguing that he had been ignorant of the dispute and noting that the king had still been 'on very good terms' with Briouze when Marshal left England in April 1208.

This evasion was only partially successful. King John forced Earl William to relinquish control of Dunamase Castle, and required him to place a number of his most valued knights in crown custody. John of Earley was sent to Nottingham Castle, 'where he suffered much hardship and tribulation', while Jordan of Sauqueville was confined in Gloucester. They emerged after one year, but Geoffrey FitzRobert, who was sent to Hereford, fell ill and died towards the end of his imprisonment.* William Marshal had managed to avoid being caught in open defiance of the king and thus saved his own dynasty from decimation, though his eldest sons remained as royal hostages. Earl William was now in his twilight years – an elderly man by the standards of the time. Many of his contemporaries had already withdrawn from public life or passed away. In the aftermath of this

---

* Marshal's well-established ally, Geoffrey FitzPeter, earl of Essex, offered a pledge in support of Earl William's loyalty around this time (and stood as surety for Marshal's willingness to surrender his castles to the crown, if called upon to do so). This pledge may have been connected to the release of John of Earley and Jordan of Sauqueville from custody.

fraught period of disruption between 1207 and 1210, William appears to have made a conscious decision to step back from the front line, entering retirement. He still sought to engineer the release of his children, but otherwise the earl remained in Leinster, looking to preserve the Marshal estates and secure the best future possible for his dynasty. It seemed that Earl William's days as a great magnate of the realm were drawing to a close.

THE DOWNWARD SPIRAL

William Marshal had little cause to love King John. If bonds of affection had ever linked the two men, they had surely been grievously eroded by recent events in Ireland and beyond. Yet, although William may have distrusted, disliked and perhaps even feared his monarch, it turned out – somewhat ironically – that he was still the closest thing to a friend that John had among the English nobility. This meant that, as the king's reign entered its second decade and spiralled into an ever-deepening crisis, Marshal was inevitably drawn back into the centre of events.

By 1212, John had accumulated a long list of embittered enemies. The king's heavy-handed and unpredictable treatment of the aristocracy had earned him the abiding antipathy of many English nobles, especially those in the north. After the fall of Normandy and most of the other Angevin territories on the Continent, John had also promoted a number of his 'French' supporters from these regions to positions of power within England. Many of these 'outsiders' gained unsavoury reputations. Peter des Roches, from the Touraine, was an able administrator, closely involved with the work of the royal 'chamber' (with oversight of the king's money) and a loyal crown servant. But his appointment as the new bishop of Winchester raised eyebrows, not least because the prelate had a distinct fondness for the battlefield. In spite of the Church's official prohibition against the shedding of blood by clerics, Peter was often to be seen, clad in armour, leading military expeditions, and contemporaries mockingly proclaimed him the 'warrior [of] Winchester', noting that he was 'keen on finance', but 'slack at the scriptures'.*

One of King John's leading military commanders, Faulkes of Bréauté, also became a figure of hate. Faulkes' origins are obscure. He appears to have been the bastard son of a Norman knight, and it was said that his unusual first name had been earned when he used a scythe (or '*faux*' in French) to kill a man in his younger days. The king's patronage lifted this low-born 'foreigner' to prominence in England, and Faulkes proved himself to be a fearsomely effective warrior, emerging as the crown's leading enforcer. But his ruthless approach to war and a marked penchant for the systematic despoliation of enemy lands also caused him to be branded as the 'scourge of the earth' and the 'most evil robber'.

After 1206, John's increasingly exploitative approach to the governance of the realm also inspired wider discontent. The king was determined to refill the royal treasury, hoping to finance a grand campaign of re-conquest on the Continent. Victory in France would silence his critics – he would be the 'Softsword' no longer. Fixated upon this goal, John was willing to use every conceivable means to bleed England dry. A swingeing wave of taxation was imposed, money was squeezed from the Jewish moneylenders (which in turn impacted upon their debtors) and exorbitant fines were extracted from the nobility at every possible turn (whether for rights to inherit, marry or hold office). A mighty war chest of some 200,000 marks was amassed by this relentless drive, but the cost to John's standing and reputation in the realm was ruinous. The monarch, already regarded by many as cruel and untrustworthy, was now cast as a tyrant. After 1210, increasing numbers of nobles demonstrated their deep dissatisfaction by refusing to participate in the king's military campaigns or to pay scutage (the 'shield price' owed in lieu of military service).

---

* Peter des Roches hailed from the same dynasty as the knight William des Roches, though their precise familial relationship is unclear.

King John was also embroiled in a damaging dispute with the Roman Church. In common with most medieval crown monarchs, he wished to influence, if not directly control, appointments to key ecclesiastical offices within his realm. After all, prelates were not just spiritual figureheads – they exercised political and military power. However, the current pope, Innocent III, was an ardent reformer and determined to uphold the rights of Rome. When Hubert Walter died in 1205, a prolonged quarrel erupted over the choice of the next archbishop of Canterbury. Innocent's preferred candidate was Stephen Langton – an esteemed theologian and ardent supporter of papal authority. But John regarded Langton with suspicion, in part because the churchman had spent years studying in the Capetian capital, Paris (at what would become one of Europe's first universities). This raised understandable doubts about Langton's loyalties and his potential sympathy for the cause of the French crown.

King John's relations with Rome deteriorated to such an extent that, in March 1208 – just as William Marshal was returning to Ireland after the dispute over Leinster – England was placed under papal interdict, a sanction that would remain in place for the next six years. Church bells fell silent across the kingdom, no burials on consecrated ground were performed, nor was Sunday Mass celebrated. In November 1209, John was himself formally excommunicated. In official terms, this meant that he had been expelled from the body of the Church. With their king exiled from the Christian community, the English were free, in theory at least, to select a new ruler – their bonds of allegiance to John having been dissolved. The actual effect of the interdict and royal excommunication should not be overstated. Christian England did not grind to a halt in 1208, nor was there immediate or wholesale rebellion against royal authority in 1209. In part this was because, in the course of the last century-and-a-half, the Roman Church had made over-frequent use of these penalties, such that their sting and impact became blunted. Nonetheless, John's ostracism gifted ammunition to his opponents.

Outside of England, the king faced outbursts of aggressive militancy from the native Welsh, largely inspired by Llewellyn ap Iorwerth, but Philip Augustus remained John's most troublesome rival. The Capetian monarch had achieved spectacular success on the Continent between 1202 and 1205, but his ambitions were by no means sated. By 1212, Philip was training his gaze upon England itself, only too aware of the discontent within the realm, and happy to exploit John's schism with Rome. The French king was particularly keen to pursue fresh conquests because his eldest son and heir, Prince Louis, was now in his twenties and hungry for power. Louis' marriage to Blanche of Castile – King Henry II's granddaughter and thus John's niece – gave the Capetian prince a tenuous claim to the English crown. Such was the depth of antipathy for King John's rule that in some quarters an idea that would once have been unthinkable now began to gain real traction. Perhaps a Capetian overthrow of the despised Angevin regime might actually be acceptable.

William Marshal's return to the fold

All of these pressures and threats – which had been gradually building during William Marshal's extended absence from royal court – combined to spark a crisis in August 1212. King John had gathered an army that summer with the intention of attacking France, but an outburst of native Welsh insurrection forced him to redirect his resources. In retribution, he hanged twenty-eight Welsh hostages at Nottingham Castle and then initiated preparations for a full-scale invasion of north Wales. In mid-August, however, John caught wind of disturbing rumours. A conspiracy had been hatched to overthrow his reign. According to one chronicler, he was told of a plan 'to drive him and his family from the kingdom and choose someone else as king in his place', while another account suggested that his murder had been plotted, such that, in the course of the coming expedition 'he would either be slain by his own nobles, or given over to the enemy for destruction'. Long paranoid about precisely this type of threat, John took these reports seriously. The incursion into Wales was called off. The king's eldest son and heir, Henry (who had been born in 1207), was placed under close protection and John surrounded himself with a sizeable armed guard.

It is impossible to know the extent to which this supposed 'plot' was a reality. It was certainly the case that two leading nobles immediately fled the country, which may indicate a measure of guilt. The northern baron, Eustace of Vesci, crossed the border into Scotland, while Robert FitzWalter escaped to France, and John ordered two of the latter's strongholds to be demolished, including Baynard's Castle in London. The king also arrested and imprisoned three royal administrators, and demanded hostages from many of his magnates. Isolated and fearful, John now 'had almost as many enemies as barons' according to one chronicler.

It is clear that the king suspected William Marshal of being involved in this conspiracy, as one royal commander was specifically warned to watch for an attack launched from Leinster. But, in fact, Marshal chose to extend a hand of friendship to his monarch at this point, making a clear show of support. William somehow convinced twenty-six Anglo-Irish barons to renew their oaths of allegiance to the crown, and wrote to John himself, offering to travel to England in all haste so as to lend his assistance, while also recommending that the king agree terms of peace with the pope. The text of John's letter of reply offers a remarkably candid insight into the sudden thawing of his relationship with Earl William. Its conciliatory tone indicates that the king was now desperate to secure Marshal's loyalty. John wrote of his 'eternal gratitude' to the earl, acknowledging that it was William's 'counsel and encouragement' that had persuaded the Irish to affirm their fidelity. He also thanked Marshal for his willingness 'to come to England', though he asked him to remain in Ireland for now, assisting the justiciar, John of Gray.

More surprising still was John's attempt to engender a sense of warm familiarity and amity with William, a man whom he had so recently hounded and harassed. The king's letter made repeated references to his dutiful, almost avuncular, stewardship of Marshal's son, Young

William – now a knight in his early twenties, yet still described as a 'boy'. John noted that Young William needed 'horses and a robe', but wrote that he would furnish these himself for now, casually adding that Marshal could pay him back at a later date. The missive also stated, in almost nonchalant manner, that the king was happy to 'hand [Young William] over to one of your knights, perhaps John of Earley, or one of his men', adding that 'if you want it otherwise, let me know by letter that he is to stay with the court'. Taken as a whole, the message represented an impressive feat of dissimulation. To all appearances, this was a relaxed exchange between two intimate friends, not a delicately worded olive branch, extended to a former opponent.

The underlying motive behind John's placatory approach is readily apparent. The steadfast support of a man of Earl William's stature and renown was a massive boon for the faltering monarch, so the king had every reason to mollify Marshal. William's reasoning is more difficult to divine. It is likely that, at first, his overwhelming priority was to secure the release of his two sons. This was achieved in relatively short order. By early 1213, John of Earley had taken custody of Young William, and Richard Marshal had also been freed. Marshal's heirs had been pried from John's clutches at last. Had that been Earl William's sole objective, he might perhaps have withdrawn back into retirement, seeking to maintain a studied neutrality through the troubled years that lay ahead.

Instead, he allowed himself to be pulled back into the world of politics and war; indeed, in some respects he pushed himself to the fore. William must have entertained hopes that a renewal of royal favour might bring rewards – the return of lost lands and rescinded honours – and these were indeed forthcoming. In the years that followed, Marshal recouped many of his losses. King John took particular care to bolster the earl's position in Wales, hoping to enlist his aid in suppressing the Welsh. William regained control of Cardigan, but was also granted custody of the major Pembrokeshire port and stronghold of Haverford, and command of Carmarthen and the Gower peninsula. Other members of Marshal's circle also benefited: John Marshal was appointed as custodian of the Welsh March in Shropshire; while John of Earley was confirmed in the office of hereditary royal chamberlain and given care of the county of Devon.

But it is likely that William Marshal was also driven by an authentic sense of duty to the crown (regardless of its incumbent) and devotion to the Angevin dynasty, the family to whom he had dedicated his adult life. Like John of Earley in 1208, he may have wished to avoid the shame of disloyalty. Marshal certainly demonstrated a remarkable capacity to overlook King John's shortcomings and his recent attempts to seize Leinster. As the *History* noted, William now seemed to forget 'the king's cruel conduct towards him', and the biographer sought to explain this by stating that the earl 'was ever a man to espouse the cause of loyalty'. In fact, Marshal would prove to be one of John's most important allies and unflinching servants from this point onwards, even as almost all others fell away and the tide turned irrevocably against the king.

To the brink

By the early spring of 1213, King John's position had become so precarious that he deemed it necessary to summon William Marshal from Leinster. By this stage, Pope Innocent III had authorised the Capetian French to cross the Channel, depose John and take possession of the realm. Philip Augustus had even formalised an agreement with his son, whereby Prince Louis would rule England, but be subject to his father's supervision and authority. That April, a large French force was assembled at Bruges in Flanders, and a sizeable fleet readied. An invasion was about to be launched.

Earl William brought a sizeable force from Ireland to Kent, joining a general muster of those forces still loyal to the king. John's half-brother, William Longsword, earl of Salisbury, and the earl of Essex, Geoffrey FitzPeter, were also present. The king was persuaded that the only way to avert this dire threat was to forge a settlement with Rome. John duly met with Pandulf, the papal legate, on 15 May near Dover.

Marshal may have played a role in orchestrating this meeting, as it was held in a Templar house. He had established a link with the Order when he visited the Holy Land in the 1180s and then developed a close friendship with the Master of the Templars in England, Aimery of St Maur, in the early part of John's reign. William also appointed a Templar named Geoffrey to serve as his personal almoner in this period, who distributed the earl's charitable donations to the poor.

In the course of this assembly, King John took the massive, but necessary, step of submitting the kingdom of England to the authority of the papacy. John formally acknowledged Innocent III to be his liege-lord, declaring his 'homage and sworn allegiance' to the pope and his successors. He also agreed to an annual tribute of 1,000 marks to Rome as a token of obedience. These terms were confirmed in a charter, witnessed by William Marshal among others. On that day, the king turned his realm into the equivalent of a papal state.* This was a grievous concession of sovereignty, but it also signalled an immediate transformation in Pope Innocent's attitude. At a stroke, John was turned from Rome's arch-enemy into its most favoured son. The king's sentence of excommunication was lifted by none other than Stephen Langton on 20 July. More importantly, the pope rescinded his support for the imminent French invasion. An enraged Philip Augustus was forced to back down, grumbling that he had already spent 60,000 marks preparing for war.

This diplomatic coup was followed by a military victory. On the advice of Marshal and Longsword, John ordered a swift naval strike against the assembled French fleet, then harboured at Damme. Longsword led the attack on 30 May and managed to torch many of the Capetians' ships. According to one contemporary, 'it was a very bitter thing for the king of France to see his vessels . . . burning and belching forth smoke, as if the very sea were on fire'. With William Marshal's help, the kingdom had been brought back from the brink of disaster.

---

* This step was not unprecedented elsewhere in Europe, as a number of other realms, including Sicily, Portugal and Denmark, had previously accepted papal overlordship.

THE CATASTROPHE AT BOUVINES

It must have been obvious to all, nonetheless, that this only represented a stay of execution. The threat from France had been
forestalled, but not extinguished. And as part of his submission to the
papacy, King John was forced to accept Stephen Langton's appointment as archbishop of Canterbury. His arrival in England was followed
by the return of the 'conspirators' Robert FitzWalter and Eustace of
Vesci, emboldening the many barons who nursed a deep resentment
of the king. John's position was also weakened by the death of
Marshal's old ally Geoffrey FitzPeter, in October 1213. He was replaced
as justiciar of England by the unpopular Peter des Roches, further
alienating the Anglo-Norman aristocracy.

King John had one final chance for success. Drawing upon his
remaining financial resources and military support, he sought yet
again to launch a grand campaign of re-conquest on the Continent,
hoping to recover the Angevin realm. John was able to exploit the
growing sense of disquiet among the potentates of north-western
Europe over King Philip Augustus' seemingly inexorable rise to a position of pre-eminence. An alliance was patched together with Otto IV,
emperor of Germany, and the counts of Boulogne and Flanders –
England's established trading partners. The coalition's strategy called
for a two-pronged offensive. John was to sail to Aquitaine and lead an
invasion force out of Poitou (mirroring the scheme thwarted in 1205).
At the same time, William Longsword, earl of Salisbury, would prosecute a forceful invasion of Normandy, alongside the massed ranks of
England's northern allies. Meanwhile, William Marshal was to remain
in England, defending the March against a Welsh counter-attack.

The basic idea of stretching Capetian resources by attacking on two
fronts was sound, but it required careful coordination. Unfortunately for
John and his allies, the slow muster and advance of Otto IV's German
forces undermined the entire plan. The English king enjoyed some initial success in the south, after landing at La Rochelle in mid-February

1214, with gains made in Aquitaine and parts of Anjou. By early summer, John was able to enter the city of Angers, but his advance was arrested by the need to capture the neighbouring castle of La Roche-aux-Moine, recently constructed by William des Roches. A siege began on 19 June, but the French garrison refused to buckle, and when a Capetian relief force approached under the command of Prince Louis, John wrongly assumed that he was facing the full force of the French army and thus ordered a hasty retreat on 2 July.

With the English king stymied in the south, Philip Augustus was able to focus his attention upon Normandy, where the northern coalition's tardy incursion was not launched for another four weeks. On Sunday 27 July, the two sides clashed in a rare pitched battle at Bouvines, just south of Lille (in north-eastern France). Both armies were relatively evenly matched in numerical terms, but the Capetian troops seem to have been more disciplined and effective, benefiting from the presence in their ranks of both William des Barres – a storied champion, whose skills and reputation equalled those of Marshal himself – and the renowned William des Roches.

A vicious and bloody confrontation played out over the course of some three hours, with the French gradually gaining the upper hand. Longsword was taken captive, as were the counts of Boulogne and Flanders, while Emperor Otto was driven from the field by a contingent of knights led by William des Barres. Philip Augustus was left in control of the field, having scored a resounding victory. This was the crowning glory of his reign – one that confirmed Capetian ascendancy in Europe. The battle of Bouvines heralded an end to Otto IV's reign in Germany and proved an utter catastrophe for King John in England. Having been forced to agree to the punitive terms of a five-year peace (including a payment of damages to the French, rumoured to total 60,000 marks), John returned to England in October a broken king. His war chest had been squandered. There was no famous victory with which to quell dissent at home, only humiliation. After Bouvines, a historic reckoning in England was unavoidable, and its course and outcome would reshape William Marshal's career.

13

A ROYAL RECKONING

In the aftermath of the battle of Bouvines, a tide of rebellious unrest swept across the kingdom of England. An increasingly vocal and cohesive party of discontented barons began to call for concessions from the crown and, through the autumn of 1214, their demands became more coherent, even as their ranks swelled beyond the core of northern magnates to include many major landholders from the south of England. The movement was spearheaded by the likes of Robert FitzWalter – who began, in 1215, to style himself as the 'Marshal of the Army of God' – and Eustace of Vesci, and enjoyed some veiled support from the archbishop of Canterbury, Stephen Langton.

With his coffers all but empty and his reputation in tatters, King John was too weak to simply ignore or overthrow the emerging baronial faction. The ranks of his steadfast supporters diminished with each passing month, as the nascent rebellion gathered momentum. William Marshal remained loyal, as did John's half-brother William Longsword (after he had been ransomed from the French) and Ranulf, earl of Chester, but the balance of power was tilting away from the crown. As both sides readied themselves for civil war, attempts to broker a settlement began in January 1215. William

Marshal found himself at the heart of these convoluted negotiations between the king and his nobles and, after five months, this process culminated in the sealing of a peace treaty containing sixty-three clauses – a document that became known as the Great Charter or Magna Carta.

THE GREAT CHARTER

Magna Carta has come to be regarded as one of the most significant documents in world history, achieving a near-mythical status. It is often described as a cornerstone of Western democracy: characterised as the 'first written constitution in European history', a 'charter of liberties' or 'bill of rights' that curbed royal power, paving the way for the English Parliamentary system of government and the template for the Constitution of the United States of America. Magna Carta changed the balance of power, and the nature of kingship, in England. It also impacted upon the expectations and experiences of knights and nobles for decades, even centuries, to come. At first glance, then, it would seem that William Marshal's close involvement in the forging of the Great Charter of 1215 merits an especially honoured place in the catalogue of his many storied achievements.

The accord was perhaps the ultimate expression of a transformation that reshaped medieval England – a tectonic shift away from the age of conquest towards that of settlement. This gradual process of evolution had been percolating, almost unseen, in the background of William Marshal's life and would continue after his death. It was marked by the increasing emphasis placed upon the rule of law within society, and the determined dissection of the reciprocal bonds of service and obligation that linked lords, knights and their subjects. But can Earl William really be regarded as one of the architects of Magna Carta, and does this document actually deserve its vaunted reputation?

Marshal's role in the forging of Magna Carta

William Marshal served as King John's leading lay negotiator through-out the first half of 1215, as the settlement enshrined in Magna Carta was deliberated. William was now perhaps sixty-seven years old – one of the great, established figures of the English aristocracy – trusted by his king and respected by the barons. While the latter group might have detested many of John's other supporters, such as Peter des Roches and Faulkes of Bréauté, they knew only too well that Marshal had endured his own difficulties with the king, and as such might har-bour some sympathy for the baronial cause. All of this made Earl William an ideal intermediary. His connection with the Templars may also have proven useful, given that the Order played a supporting role in these events.

For much of the time, Marshal worked in tandem with Stephen Langton. The archbishop may have offered some early inspiration to the baronial party, perhaps encouraging them to consult archived doc-uments such as the 'Coronation Charter' of King Henry I dating from 1100 – a text which seemed to offer a historic framework of precedents around which they could shape their otherwise nebulous demands for royal reform. For much of 1215, however, Langton sought to present himself as a neutral mediator and servant of the realm.

The first significant meeting between John and the barons took place in January 1215, in London's New Temple (the Templars' centre of operations in the city). It proved to be an ill-tempered encounter, with the magnates arriving clad in armour and determined to demand that the terms of governance established in Henry I's 'Coronation Charter' be reinstituted. King John equivocated, requesting a pause in discussions until April so that he could consider this request, but assured them that he would satisfy their demands in due course. William Marshal and Archbishop Stephen both made pledges con-firming that the king would hold to his word and meet the barons on the agreed date. As a result, a truce was settled until after Easter (which fell on 19 April).

In reality, John was simply looking for time to seek the support of Rome and hopefully raise a military force with which to defeat the barons. By the end of April, the patience of Robert FitzWalter, Eustace of Vesci and their allies was running thin. They assembled at Brackley in Northamptonshire, with an eye to launching armed rebellion. The baronial party had grown considerably. Two notable converts to the cause were Saer of Quincy, earl of Winchester (FitzWalter's close friend and associate), and the new earl of Essex, Geoffrey FitzPeter's son and heir, Geoffrey of Mandeville – who turned against the crown after John demanded the vast sum of 20,000 marks in return for a marriage licence.

Marshal and Langton were sent by the king to placate the barons at Brackley. At a meeting on 27 April, FitzWalter's party issued a further list of demands. These were relayed back to John and declined out of hand. As a result, the barons laid siege to Northampton Castle, and the king's position then deteriorated rapidly. On 17 May, the rebels seized control of London – now widely recognised as 'the capital of the crown and realm' – and the city became a centre of dissent. This setback to John's fortunes promoted a fresh wave of defections to the baronial party, forcing the king to re-engage with the process of arbitration, if only as a stalling tactic, so that he could use money borrowed from the Templars to hire mercenaries.

A period of intense negotiation followed. According to one version of events, William Marshal was sent to London to inform the barons that John was ready to agree terms, though in reality the process appears to have been more convoluted (involving numerous meetings, exchanges and emissaries). As the king was now residing in Windsor, some eighteen miles west of London, a halfway meeting point was chosen; an obscure spot in the countryside known as Runnymede. It was here – on 15 June 1215 – that the provisions of peace were finally settled and laid out in a long and detailed document. The sheer scale and scope of this agreement meant that it was later described as 'the Great Charter'. No signatures were appended to this original version of Magna Carta. Constructed as a royal charter, it was validated by the king's seal, with at least thirteen copies subsequently produced by the chancery. William Marshal was afforded a prominent position in the text, appearing as the first named English magnate, said to have given 'advice' to the king on the terms agreed and to be one of those who remained a 'loyal subject'. The names of a further fifteen barons followed, including William Longsword, William of Warenne, earl of Surrey, Hubert of Burgh and John Marshal.

In the past, historians have suggested that William Marshal may have been one of the main authors of the 1215 Magna Carta. In 1933, the American academic Sidney Painter claimed that Marshal 'was probably perfectly capable of inspiring the Great Charter' – possessing 'the necessary administrative experience ... wisdom and statesmanship' – and thus, 'should share the honour' due for having 'procured for England her beloved charter'. In fact, at best, we can suggest that Earl William may have encouraged continued discussion and moderation on both sides in the months that led up to Runnymede, but beyond this it is impossible to gauge the exact degree of Marshal's input. Elsewhere, it has been argued that the learned Stephen Langton must have been the Great Charter's primary originator, but although he does seem to have inserted a number of key clauses relating to the Church, in other respects the archbishop's impact appears to have been quite limited. In fact, no one knows precisely who drafted the terms set out on 15 June and, given that the final document was the product of forceful debate and argument, its contents could not truly be said to have been conceived by a single mind.

A number of northern barons were dissatisfied with the agreement from the start, believing that it had not gone far enough, but most of the rebels laid down their arms on 19 June. With a limited peace in place, William Marshal was sent to hold the Welsh March. Yet even though this treaty had been the subject of prolonged negotiation, its terms were soon disregarded, and the truce it engendered proved to be desperately short-lived. This may explain why William Marshal's seemingly historic involvement in the sealing of Magna Carta was completely ignored in the *History*. The swift pace of events meant that the 1215 version of Magna Carta was quickly superseded and largely forgotten in the 1220s, when the biographer was writing his account. It is also possible that the *History*'s silence was more studied, being a deliberate attempt to skirt over potential embarrassment. Other sources make it clear that Earl William's eldest son and heir, Young William Marshal, had joined the baronial party in May 1215. Given that it was Young William who later commissioned the *History of William Marshal*, it would not be surprising if its author deemed it politic to ignore his patron's complicity in the rebellion – an uprising that was later viewed, at best, with ambivalence.

The significance of Magna Carta in 1215

The Great Charter sealed at Runnymede is one of the most famous, treasured and widely misrepresented documents of the Middle Ages. Four copies of this version of Magna Carta are known to have survived into the modern era: two reside in the British Library in London, one is held in the archives of Salisbury Cathedral, another in Lincoln Cathedral. They are regarded as priceless heirlooms of the English nation. Yet for all its renown, the charter actually had a surprisingly limited impact upon the course of events in 1215. As a political tool it was defunct within three months, and by the end of the year its terms were regarded as null and void by all parties. This does not mean that the text should now be dismissed or discounted, merely that it must be assessed in its proper context.

The 1215 Magna Carta was not intended to serve as a universal bill of rights. In the first instance, it was expressly designed as a peace treaty and thus contained a series of conditions, conceded by the crown in response to intense baronial pressure, that were supposed to lead, in the words of the charter, to the 'better ordering' of the kingdom. Robert FitzWalter and his allies did not view their demands as either revolutionary or even innovative. Over successive generations, their families had endured the predatory exploitation of the Angevin dynasty, and these abuses – and the blatant profiteering from feudal law – had now become intolerable under King John's failing regime. The barons thus wished to restore the 'ancient liberties' they had enjoyed before the advent of the Angevins; to return to the supposed golden age of justice evoked in King Henry I's Coronation Charter, when established customs were upheld.

In fact, they were trying to recreate a fantasy. This Coronation Charter, listing fulsome promises of fair governance, had been issued when Henry I came to power in 1100 and he was desperate to secure support against his brother and rival for the crown, Duke Robert of Normandy. Once his position was assured, King Henry chose to ignore most of his pledges, so the notional period in which barons and land-holders received fair treatment from the crown never actually existed. They did not know it at the time, but in 1215 the barons were asking for more than any English monarch since the Norman Conquest had ever been willing to grant.

The barons' primary concerns were decidedly self-serving. They wished to safeguard their own welfare and ensure better treatment from the king. As a result, many of Magna Carta's clauses dealt with issues of inheritance, landholding and military service, and sought to limit the fees and fines exacted by the crown, and to reduce the rate of scutage (the money owed, per knight, in lieu of military service). Clause forty-nine addressed John's habitual seizure of hostages from his nobles and demanded the immediate release of persons currently held in this manner. At a fundamental level, the aristocrats who nego-tiated the terms of Magna Carta were not driven by egalitarian impulses; nor did they set out, in the first instance, to secure basic human liberty and equality for all.

Nonetheless, the rebel barons and King John were contending for supporters in 1215, both hoping to secure popular backing for their respective causes. To that end, the baronial party introduced some pro-visions to Magna Carta that appealed to the interests of the knightly class and the wider population. Clause twenty-nine, for example, guar-anteed knights fair terms of service and treatment, while clause eight specified that widows could not be compelled to marry against their will. Aspects of the document related more broadly to 'the community of the whole land'. The charter's most famous clauses, thirty-nine and forty, stated that 'no free man shall be seized or imprisoned' or suffer other forms of persecution, losing 'rights' or 'standing' in society, 'except by the lawful judgement of his peers, or by the law of the land'. They went on to enshrine a far-reaching royal proclamation: 'To no one will we sell, to no one will we deny or delay right or justice.' It was these passages, tucked away in the middle of the document, which gave rise to the idea that Magna Carta affirmed the basic and universal human rights to justice and liberty, later inspiring such phenomena as trial by jury.

Unfortunately, the document's precise terms and stipulations also made it all but inevitable that the king would soon disown and disregard the accord finalised at Runnymede. Clause one seemed to render the treaty inviolate, with John stating clearly: 'To all free men of our kingdom we have also granted, for us and our heirs forever, all the liberties written out below.' But the barons overstepped the mark towards the end of Magna Carta, in clause sixty-one, by imposing excessively punitive conditions and controls upon the crown. A self-elected group of twenty-five barons were to supervise the enactment of the charter's terms and to judge the king's actions. Crucially, should John or any of his supporters 'offend in any respect against any man, or transgress any articles of the peace', the twenty-five were empowered to 'assail [the king] in every way possible, with the support of the whole community of the land, by seizing [his] castles, lands [and] possessions'. This represented a massive infringement on royal power. John was prepared to concede clause sixty-one on 15 June, but only to secure a temporary cessation of hostilities, during which he could retrench his position. Such a grievous derogation of crown authority could never have been endured by a medieval monarch of the early thirteenth century. This provision alone ensured that John would seek to overturn Magna Carta at the first possible opportunity. Indeed, by the middle of July he had already secretly contacted the pope, requesting that Rome condemn the document.

The treaty agreed on 15 June would form the essential blueprint for far more enduring and significant settlements in the future, and William Marshal would play a leading role in this process. But the direct force of the 1215 Magna Carta was undermined in early September, when a damning papal pronouncement arrived in England. Pope Innocent III offered his unflinching support for King John – Rome's new vassal – and condemned the Runnymede accord as 'shameful and base, but also illegal and unjust'. Innocent stated that the charter 'dishonours the Apostolic See (Rome), injures the king's rights and shames the English nation', and as a result, declared it 'null and void'. John now had a formal mandate to ignore the terms of Magna Carta, but elsewhere, few in the baronial party heeded the pope's scorching rhetoric. Indeed, even the Latin Church's leading representative in England, Stephen Langton, archbishop of Canterbury, staunchly refused to renounce the charter. He was formally suspended from his office by Rome as a result. With both sides assuming such entrenched positions, a full-scale civil war was inevitable.

STANDING WITH THE KING

William Marshal spent much of the summer of 1215 overseeing the defence of Wales, but proved unable to prevent significant losses to the native Welsh in northern Pembrokeshire, Carmarthen and the Gower. He remained on the sidelines through the autumn, as King John tried to mount a counter-attack against rebels, using Flemish mercenaries to bolster his military forces. In the south, at least, the barons were confined to London, and John managed to seize Rochester Castle – which had been held in the name of Stephen Langton – after a gruelling seven-week siege.

In December, the king initiated a brutal campaign of destructive raiding across England, ravaging rebel-held territory. One chronicler described how John's men were 'running about with drawn swords and open knives', ransacking 'towns, houses, cemeteries and churches, robbing everyone, and sparing neither women nor children'. Alongside this indiscriminate violence John also tortured captives seized during these months, seemingly in a calculated attempt to intimidate his opponents. As a result, the royalist armies were described as 'the limbs of the devil' and likened to a plague of locusts covering the Earth. Such savagery had not been seen in the realm since the dark, anarchic days of King Stephen's reign, seventy years earlier.

A few barons buckled under this pressure, but most only became hardened in their resolve to resist the king's hated regime. Pushed into a corner, the rebels now took the dramatic step of sending Saer of Quincy across the Channel, bearing an offer of the English crown to Prince Louis of France. The legitimacy of the Capetian's claim – through right of marriage to King Henry II's granddaughter – was questionable, but in the face of John's loathsome predations, any lingering doubts over the wisdom or legality of this choice were discounted. Many leading members of the baronial faction also expected Louis to grant them additional lands in England in return for their support. The French prince duly declared that he would sail with the full might of his armies in the spring of 1216, but he also sent an advanced detachment of troops to London, and these men arrived in the capital in January.

Some contemporaries welcomed the prospect of Capetian intervention. Gerald of Wales promoted Louis of France as 'a new light' that would banish the dark clouds of Angevin tyranny. Not surprisingly, the *History* was far less sympathetic, characterising the invitation to the prince as 'a highly foolish course of action', and declaring that the French forces billeted in London spent their time drinking 'many a barrel and cask of fine wine'. King John recognised that Louis' arrival would transform the balance of power in England. He therefore sent William Marshal and Peter des Roches, bishop of Winchester, on an embassy to France, in the vain hope that they might somehow convince Philip Augustus to abandon the invasion, but the Capetian monarch remained resolute.

The arrival of a new papal legate – the Italian churchman, Guala of Bicchieri – in Paris on 25 April gave Philip greater pause. Guala expressed his entrenched scepticism regarding Louis' supposed entitlement to the English crown, and then promptly sailed across the Channel to support King John's cause. The French would now be wading into a war in which they stood to be branded enemies of the Church. Nonetheless, Prince Louis followed through with his invasion plan, landing at Sandwich, in Kent, on 22 May 1216. King John had contemplated meeting him head on in the field, but at the last moment he chose instead to retreat. This decision may have been influenced by the advice of William Marshal, who apparently warned the king not to gamble the fate of the realm on another pitched battle, though in truth, the earl's precise movements throughout this period are unclear. It is likely that John also doubted the continued loyalty of his mercenaries, many of whom were waiting to be paid and had familial ties to France.

King John ordered his eldest son, Henry, to be placed under close guard in Devizes Castle (in Wiltshire) and withdrew to Corfe Castle in Dorset, seemingly at a loss as to how he might defend his kingdom. This gifted Louis of France a free hand. He advanced through Kent, seizing Canterbury and later Winchester. The mighty fortress at Dover held out against attack under the command of the redoubtable Hubert of Burgh, as did Windsor and Lincoln Castle in the north-eastern Midlands. The defence of the latter stronghold was organised by Lady Nicola de la Haye, a remarkably formidable woman who had assumed the role of castellan after the death of her husband and son. But the Capetians' triumphant arrival sparked a fresh surge of desertions from the royalist camp. These included the earls of Arundel, York and Surrey and, most shockingly, King John's own half-brother, William Longsword. One chronicler suggested that this betrayal was inspired by the discovery that the king had used the opportunity afforded by Longsword's brief captivity after Bouvines to seduce his wife, Ela of Salisbury. It is more likely that Longsword simply made a pragmatic decision to move with the tide, having determined that John's day was done.

By the summer of 1216 a vast swathe of northern and eastern England supported the French prince. As the *History* observed, 'the king ran out of resources' and thus 'very few of the men stayed with him'. Some two-thirds of England's aristocracy renounced John, and even a sizeable portion of the king's own household knights turned against him, including Robert of Roppesley, who had been named in Magna Carta as one of his leading advisors. The collapse of Angevin rule now seemed inevitable.

William Marshal remained on the southern Welsh March through much of this period, defending the border and holding the west of England for the royalists alongside Ranulf, earl of Chester. In spite of his engrained antipathy towards King John, William's biographer painted a vivid and admiring picture of his hero's unfailing fidelity to the broken monarch, writing that as 'a man of loyal and noble heart, [Marshal] stayed with him in hard and difficult circumstances'. The *History* had persistently downplayed William's proximity to John's regime, but at this stage, its author could not hold back from commending the earl's 'steadfast' behaviour and the 'good faith' he showed to 'his lord and king'.

Even so, Marshal may have paused to consider his position in the early spring of 1216. Royal records show that, on 10 April, a grant of safe conduct was provided so that Aimery of St Maur, the Master of the Templars in England, could escort Young William Marshal to a meeting with his father. No record has survived to indicate the nature of their discussion (as with so much of Young William's activities in this period, the episode was ignored in the *History*). It is possible that Earl William tried to persuade his eldest-born to return to the royalist side, or it may be that he encouraged him to maintain close contact with the French – hedging the Marshal family's bets, so as to protect the dynasty's long-term interests. Young William certainly pursued advantage under the Capetian claimant: rushing to declare his allegiance to Louis and then receiving confirmation of his right to act as marshal of the prince's court in England. However, Young William's attempts to assert rights to Marlborough Castle were blocked.

If Earl William entertained thoughts of desertion, he certainly did not act upon them. It must have been apparent that John's cause was lost, yet just as he had done with King Henry II in 1189, Marshal refused to forsake his royal master. This was all the more remarkable because he found himself in a distinctly different position in 1216. William was no longer simply a household knight. He was now a great magnate of the realm: a man of power and responsibility, with a vast lordship and a large family to protect. His relationship with John had also been troubled and tempestuous. Marshal had good reason to dislike, perhaps even to detest, his monarch, yet as the biographer remarked, 'whatever the king had done to him, [William] never abandoned him for anyone'. Even the author of the *History* seems to have been perplexed by this unswerving devotion, but the greatest test of Marshal's fidelity was yet to come.

King John's reign reached its bitter end in the autumn of 1216. He had marched north in the hope of mounting one last campaign and bringing aid to Nicola de la Haye at Lincoln, but he contracted 'a violent fever' in early October. With his body already weakened, the king's 'pernicious gluttony' supposedly prompted him to gorge himself on peaches and freshly brewed cider, and as a result he became afflicted with dysentery. As his illness took hold, John seems also to have been gripped by a sense of guilt and remorse. On 10 October he made a grant to one of William of Briouze's surviving daughters, Margaret, for the 'sake of the souls' of her parents and brother. The king limped on to Newark, south of Lincoln, but there his condition worsened. On 18 October, he was said to have made a deathbed confession of his many sins, and to have spoken of the hope that William Marshal might 'forgive the harm and wrongs which I have unjustly done to him'. Later that night he 'lost his strength [and] his mind', and at some point in the small hours he died – a man of forty-eight years, who had presided over the disintegration of the great Angevin Empire and brought the kingdom of England to its knees. A number of chroniclers confidently predicted that the late king would be condemned to Hell. One even added that: 'Foul as it is, Hell itself is made fouler by the presence of John.'

In accordance with his last wishes, the king's body was carried south-west to Worcester Cathedral – a site dedicated to one of his favoured saints, Wulfstan. William Marshal heard the news of John's demise and came north from Gloucester with the papal legate Guala to bury yet another king. The earl had now served, and survived, four crowned and anointed monarchs. It seemed that the days of the Angevins were at an end. A new era would surely dawn, with a French prince wearing the English crown.

THE GREATEST CHOICE

In spite of his ignominious end, King John was afforded a regal funeral. His body had been arrayed 'in royal robes', and William Marshal and Guala ensured that he was honoured with 'a service befiting a monarch', before he was laid to rest. The earl even sent John Marshal to fetch precious silks with which the king's tomb could be covered. Once this ceremony was complete, however, the beleaguered remnants of the royalist party had to face a stark reality. Their prospects were dreadfully bleak. More than half of the kingdom lay in the hands of the baronial rebels and their French allies, including the city of London, while the crown's treasury lay all but empty. And the heir to this sundered realm was a nine-year-old boy, John's son, Henry; a figure seemingly bereft of support.

With King John dead and buried, William Marshal faced the most momentous decision of his entire career, a choice that, in many ways, would define his life, and the fate of England. As a young household knight, William had fought alongside the Young King Henry; now another Angevin of that same name lay in desperate need of his aid. But would Marshal champion Henry's claim, or turn aside and watch him fall as Louis of France swept to victory? In terms of cold-blooded, political calculus, the correct path was blindingly apparent: William should abandon the royalist camp and forsake Henry. The earl was now perhaps sixty-nine years old. The time was ripe to withdraw from the front line and hope to weather the storm of dynastic revolution, ensconced on the Welsh March or in Ireland. William's established link to the Capetian dynasty, through the oath of homage sworn for his Norman estate at Longueville, made subjection to Prince Louis a natural step. William Longsword had understood, like so many others, that the wind of change was blowing. It was clear that Marshal should follow his lead.

The stakes set before William could not have been higher. All the labour of his life – the pursuit of power, wealth and office; the long path forged from anonymous knight to earl of the realm – now stood to be squandered. Should Marshal falter, the future of his wife and children, of the dynasty he had established, might well be shattered. The prospects of the faithful household knights he had sheltered and nurtured also hung in the balance. And William was no self-sacrificing saint. Without the drive of ambition and some willingness to plot, scheme and manipulate, he could never have achieved such glittering eminence amidst the cut-throat world of the Angevin court. Nor would he have survived the predations of King John's reign. Marshal's careful manoeuvring around John during the 1190s and his equivocation on the issue of his Norman lands proved him to be a political animal.

But William Marshal was not merely a politician. He was also a warrior and a knight; a man who had lived his long life in accordance with the ideals of chivalry, pursuing and preserving honour. The earl had cultivated a well-earned reputation for steadfast loyalty. It seems clear that the royalist faction expected Earl William to defend the late king's heir. Indeed, John appears to have placed Henry into William's care before his death. According to the *History*, John asked his knights 'to see that [Earl William] takes charge of my son and always keeps him under his protection, for my son will never govern these lands of mine with the help of anyone but Marshal', and this bequest was confirmed in another contemporary source. William had never turned his back on a lord or king; could he bear to do so now? Could he countenance the public shame, reflected in the eyes of his own closest retainers, of renouncing this charge; the muddying of his cherished good name and, perhaps, the fracturing of his own conception of himself. Something of the same dilemma had lain before John of Earley in 1208, and he had chosen to lose land and power, but avoid dishonour. Perhaps William had already made his choice as he rode to attend John's funeral; certainly he must have understood that the decision could not be long postponed.

William Marshal's decision

In the immediate aftermath of King John's burial, Marshal returned to Gloucester, and an armed force was sent south to Devizes, with strict instructions to take possession of the young heir, and to 'let nobody prevent them from coming [north] with him'. Earl William then set out to meet the boy on the road near Malmesbury (in Wiltshire). Their encounter in the open countryside was charged with emotion. According to the *History*, Henry was so small that he had to be carried in the arms of one of his knights. Coming before William Marshal, he declared, 'I give myself over to God and to you, so that in the Lord's name you may take charge of me.' The earl was said to have replied: 'I will be yours in good faith [and] there is nothing I will not do to serve you while I have the strength.' Young Henry reportedly wept, and so too did Marshal and those gathered around them.

William Marshal thus placed the full weight of his support behind Henry's claim. The earl would now face the ultimate challenge of his life – the battle to rekindle the fortunes of the Angevin dynasty, defeat the barons and the French, and save his boy-king. Other historians have suggested that Earl William leapt at the chance to support King John's young heir, seeing it as one more opportunity to achieve yet greater advancement. But this view seems to be conditioned by hindsight, and misrepresents the reality of the moment. In October 1216, most considered young Henry's cause to be hopeless. Victory, and any rewards it might bring, would have seemed like distant dreams to all involved, including the nearly seventy-year-old Marshal. William might expect to hold the leading position within the royalist faction, but given the monumental struggle that lay ahead, that was cold comfort. The motives behind his fateful decision remain open to debate. Perhaps he could not resist the chance to lead one last campaign or was determined to preserve his own reputation. It may even be that he acted out of pure, selfless dedication to the dynasty that he had served for the last five decades.

14

THE GUARDIAN OF THE REALM

William Marshal's decision to support young Henry's claim to the English crown was critical to the fortunes of the royalist cause. A handful of other magnates might have championed the boy-heir, had William stepped back from the fray or decamped to the baronial faction, but none possessed Marshal's breadth of experience or his illustrious reputation. Yet, having bound himself to Henry on the road near Malmesbury and escorted him to Gloucester, the earl had to make a swift and determined effort to uphold the boy's interests. In these first days, speed of action was paramount. Henry was only nine years old, but his rights to the English crown had to be asserted immediately, for fear that Prince Louis of France might seek to have himself proclaimed king – not least because the rebels and their French allies controlled access to Westminster Abbey, outside the walls of the city of London, the traditional venue for royal coronations.

THE ADVENT OF KING HENRY III

The royalists did enjoy one significant advantage: the unswerving support of the papal legate Guala of Bicchieri, and the bishop of Winchester, Peter des Roches – a rather disreputable, but nonetheless formidable, character. With the backing of the Church, a coronation was hurriedly arranged for 28 October 1216, and regal robes were cut down in size to fit the diminutive Henry. Custom dictated that only a dubbed knight could become king, so Marshal duly performed the ceremony. The boy was then crowned and anointed as King Henry III by Bishop Peter, with Guala presiding over the ceremony in Gloucester Cathedral, and affirming the young monarch's status as the pope's 'vassal and ward'.

With the new king proclaimed, all thoughts turned to the impending civil war, and the question of who should lead the royalist faction. As a churchman, Guala was in no position to command military forces, and while Peter des Roches was more than happy to engage in combat, he remained a divisive figure. The only obvious candidates for the office were William Marshal and Ranulf of Chester, who had yet to reach Gloucester. Earl William made no move to snatch power that day, despite vocal calls raised in the immediate aftermath of the coronation for him to step forward and 'protect the king and the kingdom' as overall leader. Marshal recognised that consensus would be crucial in the struggle ahead, and he understood that he could ill afford to alienate a key ally of Ranulf's standing, but he also appears to have been unsure of his own position. Begging for time to consider his next step, and await the imminent arrival of the earl of Chester, William retired to his rooms.

The role of William Marshal

That evening, Marshal sought the advice of his closest confidants, seemingly plagued by real doubts over which course to follow. Probably drawing upon the testimony of John of Earley, the *History* recalled the heated debate that followed. John Marshal apparently emphasised the great 'honour' that might be earned from leading the new king's armies. It was also suggested that, as leader, Marshal would 'be in a position to make all your men – rich if it so please you'. This might seem like an astonishingly mercenary sentiment, but it simply reflected the well-established notion that a lord was obliged to reward his knights – indeed, William Marshal may have mobilised precisely the same argument himself some four decades earlier as a member of Henry the Young King's retinue.

As the discussion continued, only John of Earley was said to have objected, concerned that his beloved master – the man he had served for more than thirty years – might be broken by the looming conflagration. Marshal was now nearly seventy: a remarkably advanced age in an era when most men were fortunate to live past their forties. Earley cautioned the earl, saying 'your body is in decline, both through your exertions and old age', and pointing out the stark fact that 'the king has barely any resources'. He concluded with a blunt warning: 'I fear greatly the pain and great trouble involved will be difficult for you to endure.'

This scene, as portrayed in the *History*, cannot necessarily be taken at face value. Earley was an eyewitness, but he also seems to have been at pains to emphasise his own role in offering sage counsel. Perhaps William Marshal did harbour serious misgivings about shouldering the onerous burden of leadership on the night of 28 October, or was suddenly struck by a wave of apprehension, once the stark reality of his position alongside Henry III hit home. The account could also reflect the memory of a broader discussion that actually began once news of King John's death was received. Of course, it may be that the biographer constructed the whole debate to counter any suggestion that Marshal pursued power out of self-interest; playing on the age-old theme of the great man reluctant to accept office and honour.

On the following day, Ranulf of Chester rode into Gloucester. Some members of his retinue complained that the coronation should have been postponed until he arrived, but Ranulf himself ignored these jibes, and seems to have openly encouraged Marshal to accept the position of regent. At this stage, Ranulf appears to have been understandably wary of becoming the figurehead of such an embattled party, though he would later make a brief and fruitless attempt to convince Guala to divide the responsibility of leadership between himself and Earl

William. On 29 October 1216, however, it was agreed 'by common counsel', that Marshal should be appointed as the secular leader of the royalist cause. As papal legate, Guala offered William a hugely compelling reward in return for this service – a full 'remission and pardon of his sins'. As a result, the earl agreed, and was said to have declared himself ready 'to take on this role as regent... whatever it may cost me'.

Marshal thus assumed the position of 'guardian of the realm'. Together with Guala, he now bore full responsibility for the royalist cause and the defence of King Henry III's rights, though the day-to-day care and custody of the young monarch was apportioned to Peter des Roches, because William himself needed to be free to move through the realm as regent. Marshal's willingness to assume this office later earned him high praise in a royal letter authorised by Guala. His 'devotion and constancy' was applauded, and he was commended above 'all other magnates of our kingdom, since in our necessity he has proved himself like gold in the furnace' – seemingly a scriptural allusion to the testing of men's hearts.

Later that day, William met once again with Earley and John Marshal. According to the *History*, the earl confessed himself to be daunted by the task now set before him, saying: 'I have embarked upon the open sea' like a sailor who has no hope of finding the 'bottom or shore, and from which it is a miracle if he reaches port and a safe haven.' John of Earley comforted his lord, and together they resolved to remain steadfast. Should England fall to Louis of France, Earley argued, they could retreat to Ireland, gaining 'high honour' for their resolute loyalty. At this, William was said to have declared: 'If everyone abandons the boy but me, do you know what I shall do? I will carry him on my back, and if I can hold him up, I will hop from island to island, from country to country, even if I have to beg for my bread.'

William Marshal had risen to an unimaginable height. The landless younger son was now effectively ruler of England. It was an unprecedented ascent; the apogee of his career. But this honour also meant that William's fate, and that of his dynasty and leading knights, was irrevocably interwoven with that of the young King Henry III.

RESTORING THE FORTUNES OF THE CROWN

William Marshal, Guala and the other leading members of the royalist faction travelled south to Bristol in early November 1216, convening a major council of all those loyal to King Henry III and the Angevin cause. To have any hope of guiding this party to victory, Marshal would have to draw upon the many skills he had acquired in the course of his life: the intimate knowledge of warfare and astute grasp of generalship, honed alongside Richard the Lionheart; and the political acuity, diplomatic sense and tempered judgement, proven in the royal court and tested on the international stage.

William also possessed a finely tuned appreciation of the baronial mindset and the power of chivalric ideals. He understood the system of patronage, the potent allure of land and office, and the importance of honour and knightly service – and thus knew how to harness these forces and impulses to secure the new king's position and, with luck, prise away supporters from the rebel faction. In this regard, Earl William's near-legendary status as a renowned warrior and paragon of virtue lent a compelling, totemic power to his leadership. He was a living relic of the bygone age of Angevin glory; a man who could readily command respect and allegiance.

In the course of the assembly at Bristol, Marshal's pre-eminent position within the royalist faction was confirmed and his formal title agreed. There was no legal precedent for his office. Regents were customarily expected to possess a hereditary or familial link to the crown, but William could boast no such connection. As a result, he adopted the more ephemeral title of 'guardian', and thereafter was described within documents issued in Henry III's name as 'rector nostri et regni nostri' ('our guardian and the guardian of our realm'). With this formality attended to, the council turned to the more pressing business – the king's prospects in the civil war.

The baronial faction had suffered some notable losses in recent months. Geoffrey Mandeville, earl of Essex, was slain during a sporting joust with the French, while Eustace of Vesci had died after being shot through the head by an arrow during an attack on Durham, in northern England. Nonetheless, the rebels still clearly held the balance of power and resources. They continued to dominate much of northern, eastern and south-eastern England, including London; and they enjoyed the backing of the Scots. Most importantly of all, the barons' alliance with Prince Louis of France meant that the internecine conflict had assumed an international character, with the might of the Capetian dynasty brought to bear in England.

The royalists' strategy

Henry III's supporters retained control of a number of significant castles embedded in enemy-held territory – most notably Dover, Windsor and Lincoln – and had a relatively firm grasp over west and south-west England, with Bristol as an administrative centre. They could also call upon the services of some notable military commanders, such as Hubert of Burgh and Faulkes of Bréauté. But in other respects, William Marshal and his allies were in a desperately weak position, short of money and manpower, and bereft of allies. Earl William and Guala now set out to address these deficiencies, taking a number of carefully considered steps designed to spark a renewal of the royalists' fortunes.

To assert the legitimacy of Henry III's reign, they made a calculated effort to distance the boy-king from his late father's detested regime. A royal letter was distributed, in which Henry mentioned the 'quarrel' of the past, but stated in clear terms that 'we wish to remove it for ever since it has nothing to do with us'. Most importantly, Marshal and Guala issued a redrafted version of Magna Carta in Henry III's name on 12 November 1216. This document was the equivalent of a political manifesto – a statement of intent, declaring Henry's willingness to rule with a fair and even hand, for the 'common utility of all'. This new Magna Carta restated many of the key principles of the 1215 charter – with promises to uphold justice and ancient custom, and rebalance the relationship between the king and his subjects – but it was shorter and more focused, with just forty clauses, rather than sixty-three. A number of the more controversial terms agreed at Runnymede were excised, including the panel of twenty-five barons, and the text also made it clear that the stated terms would be open to further negotiation.

The 1216 Magna Carta was distinctive in two further regards. It was not a mere peace treaty, extracted under duress from an embattled monarch, but a freely given assurance of rights. Crucially, the document was also issued with the full and unequivocal support of the papal legate, Guala. It bore his seal and that of William Marshal, the 'guardian of the realm'. As such, it was imbued with a far greater sense of permanence. Its text could no longer be casually nullified by Rome. It was this document, validated by Guala and Marshal, which resurrected Magna Carta – the discarded pact of 1215. This development represented a critical step in English history, for without this reissue and those that followed in later years, the Great Charter would have been forgotten.

The 1216 Magna Carta was published in the hope of broadening Henry III's base of support and winning over members of the baronial party to the royalist cause. In pursuit of this goal, William Marshal followed the same approach to reconciliation that he had employed in Leinster in 1208. Rebels who returned to the king were to be shown leniency, not punished out of hand. They were offered guarantees of safe conduct to discuss terms, and the restitution of lost lands. This was a sound policy, but as yet it elicited little or no response. Most advocates of the baronial cause still believed that Prince Louis of France would eventually be proclaimed as the rightful king of England, and expected to receive ample rewards of lands and offices from the new monarch. While these ingrained, vested interests remained in place, there would be few converts to the royalist faction.

William Marshal also made a concerted effort to address Henry III's dire lack of financial resources. Outstanding debts to King John's mercenaries had to be paid and the defence of royalist outposts funded. William took the bold step of liquidating John's royal treasures, then stored in Corfe Castle and the stronghold at Devizes. The latter fortress alone produced a bewildering array of rings set with precious and semi-precious stones – fifteen with diamonds, twenty-eight with rubies and no less than 218 set with either emeralds or sapphires. Much of this haul went to Hubert of Burgh at Dover Castle, the lynchpin of royalist resistance in the south-east. Marshal likewise made further attempts to call for taxes and other forms of royal revenue, but the system of crown administration lay in ruins, so these measures proved largely ineffective. The issue of liquidity was of critical importance. Earl William recognised that the royalists could not afford to wage a prolonged military campaign against the baronial rebels and their French allies for the simple reason that Henry III would soon be penniless. This meant that the only viable course of action was to seek a swift and decisive confrontation.

The sparks of hope

The royalists limped on through December in a forlorn state, but with the dawning of the New Year their prospects began to improve. Prince Louis had a firm hold over eastern England and retained control of London, but he believed that, to press home his advantage and complete the conquest of England, a fresh influx of manpower and resources would be needed. As a result, the Capetian agreed a truce with the royalists in January 1217 and promptly sailed back to France to raise reinforcements. During the subsequent lull in hostilities, a number of rebel barons finally responded to William Marshal's overtures and declared their allegiance to King Henry.

Some appear to have been disenchanted with their ill-mannered French allies. Others had become understandably concerned that Louis was planning to distribute the lion's share of any forthcoming conquests to his Capetian followers, thus depriving the English nobles of their expected rewards. Under these circumstances, backing the royalist camp seemed to offer the best chance of advancement. The 'reversi', or 'returners' as they were described in royal records, were welcomed without punishment. The most important convert, William Longsword, earl of Salisbury – King Henry III's half-uncle – came back into the fold on 5 March, and he brought his close friend and ally, Young William Marshal, with him.

In this same period, Guala of Bicchieri took the extraordinary step of proclaiming the war in support of Henry III to be the equivalent of a crusade. The pope had declared, in somewhat vague terms, that this struggle 'earned glory in the eyes of men and merits in the eyes of God', but his legate went further. Guala permitted the royalists to bear the cross of a crusader on their clothes and promised them a remission of their sins. William Marshal would now be leading a holy war in England, sanctioned by the papacy. This was a remarkable transformation. As one contemporary observed: 'Those who once called themselves the army of God, and boasted that they fought for the liberties of the Church and the kingdom, were [thereafter] reputed to be the sons of the Devil and compared to infidels.' Even so, when Louis of France returned to England in late April with fresh troops, and the civil war drew towards its climax, it seemed that Marshal and his allies would need a miracle if they were to prevail.

THE BATTLE OF LINCOLN

In the late spring of 1217, it fell to William Marshal – now some seventy years old – to fight for King Henry III's right to rule England. The earl understood that only a clear-cut victory against the French would cement the young monarch's legitimacy and snuff out the baronial rebellion. William drew up his forces at Northampton, in the centre of the country, waiting for any opportunity to strike. Then suddenly, in early May, a slim chance presented itself. Prince Louis was determined to sweep up the remaining pockets of royalist resistance in eastern England before driving westwards. With this objective in mind, he divided his army in two, leading a force to besiege Dover Castle on 12 May, while a second contingent was sent north.

This Anglo-French host contained many prominent rebels, including Robert FitzWalter and Saer of Quincy, along with more than 500 English knights, and around seventy Capetian knights alongside a large detachment of infantry, under the French commander Count Thomas of Perche. Together, these allies marched north to the walled town of Lincoln – a royalist stronghold that had already endured a long siege at the hands of the northern rebels and a sizeable party of Capetian troops.* Lincoln's outer battlements had fallen, but Lady Nicola de la Haye retained control of its heavily fortified castle. The Anglo-French army now intended to bludgeon her garrison into submission.

The renewed assault on Lincoln posed a grave threat, but William Marshal also saw it as an opportunity to confront, and hopefully defeat, the allies when their army was not at full strength. Assembling every available ounce of fighting manpower, William mustered the royalist forces at Newark, the site of King John's death, twenty-five miles southwest of Lincoln. Troops started to arrive on 17 May, and a number of contemporary sources offer quite precise estimates of their numbers. The biographer claimed to have access to an array of written sources at this point, so it is quite possible that he was working from an official muster list. The royalist army appears to have been made up of 406 knights, 317 crossbowmen and a large mixed force of 'followers', some of whom were non-combatant supporters and servants. Earl William held overall command, but other leading figures were also present, such as the armour-clad bishop Peter des Roches, Ranulf of Chester, William Longsword, Faulkes of Bréauté, John Marshal and Young William Marshal.

Earl William probably guessed that he would be heavily outnumbered in the fight ahead. Once the Anglo-French host joined up with the existing besiegers, Thomas of Perche and Robert FitzWalter must

---

* This Anglo-French army initially marched north to relieve Mountsorrel, which had been besieged by Ranulf of Chester, but when he retreated, they quickly moved on to Lincoln.

have had well in excess of 600 knights and several thousand infantry at their disposal. Marshal was only too aware of the dangers posed by a direct military engagement, but he judged that a gamble had to be taken, for if this enemy force could be confronted and defeated, it might tip the balance of the entire civil war. William resolved to risk the future of the Angevin dynasty, and his own career and life, on a pitched battle at Lincoln. In the words of the *History*, he was ready to 'play for the highest stakes'.

The preparations for battle

The royalists made careful preparations in these final days, girding themselves for war. Guala proclaimed the excommunication of the French army and their allies, and performed the ritual of Mass for the supporters of Henry III's cause, absolving them of their sins. In their own minds at least, Marshal's troops would take to arms as holy warriors, bearing white crosses on their surcoats. According to the *History*, Earl William delivered a number of rousing speeches to his troops in this period, and while these cannot be taken as verbatim records, the terms and imagery used are revealing.

He was said to have exhorted his men to fight, 'in order to defend our name, for ourselves and for the sake of our loved ones, our wives and our children', but also 'to defend our land and win for ourselves the highest honour'. This powerful appeal played upon notions of chivalry, sovereign allegiance and familial obligation. But William also warned that the French had come 'to take for themselves the lands of our men' and stated that 'they seek our total destruction', phrases that emphasised both the threat to personal property and the enemy's supposed savagery.

Marshal then seems to have made an effort to stiffen the royalists' resolve. 'Let us make sure there is no coward amongst us,' he reputedly declared, for 'it is God's wish that we defend ourselves' – a clear evocation of the army's sanctified status. Finally, he cautioned his troops to ready themselves for a bloody mêlée. 'The road that lies ahead' must be freed 'with blades of iron and steel', he argued, but 'nobody should hold back [because] a man takes full revenge for the wrong and shame done to him'. The speech, as recorded by the biographer, was a model of inspirational battlefield rhetoric, leading the audience from the justification of conflict, through to potent appeals for steadfast courage and ruthless ferocity.

By 19 May, the royalists were ready to march on Lincoln. The shrewd strategy employed by Earl William in planning his advance was shaped by the nature of local topography – knowledge of which was probably gleaned from Peter des Roches, who had been attached to Lincoln Cathedral earlier in his career – and informed by Marshal's own rich military experience. Lincoln was built on the northern banks of the River Witham, with a circuit of ancient Roman walls running in an extended rectangle from the lower town, north up a steep slope – rising 175 feet in less than three-quarters of a mile – to a long ridge. Here the battlements enclosed an imposing twelfth-century Norman castle in the west and a towering cathedral to the east. The outer ring of defences was punctuated by at least five major gateways. The French and the rebel barons were stationed inside the town walls, and were trying to break through the castle's inner defences using siege engines and stone-throwing machines.

William Marshal recognised that any attempt to march directly on Lincoln from Newark would be fraught with danger. Should they arrive from the south, the royalists would be forced to confront the enemy across the bridge spanning the River Witham, and would then have to make an exhausting climb up a sharp incline from the lower town, fighting as they went. The earl decided to negate these obstacles by circling around from the west in a wide arc, and then ascending the main ridge, to advance on Lincoln from the north-west. This would allow his men to attack from the north, giving them the benefit of fighting downhill once they pushed through the upper town. It might also enable the royalists to link up with the castle's garrison before the Anglo-French could mount a counter-attack. Given that William's

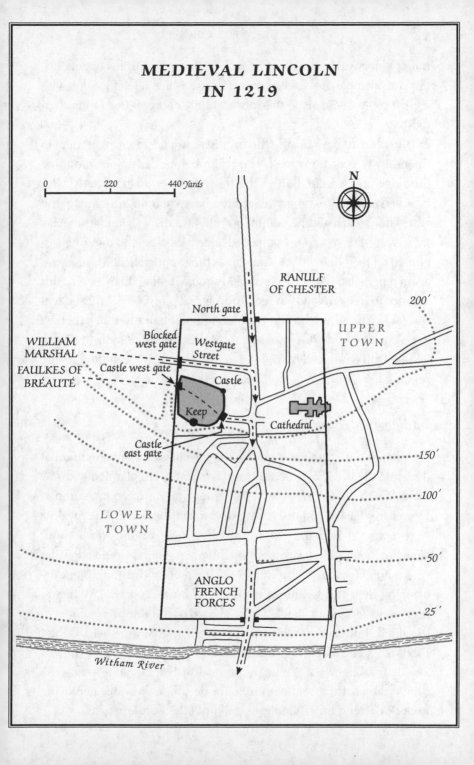

MEDIEVAL LINCOLN
IN 1219

0 220 440 Yards

N

RANULF
OF CHESTER

200′

North gate

UPPER
TOWN

Blocked
west gate

Westgate
Street

WILLIAM
MARSHAL

Castle west gate

Castle

FAULKES OF
BRÉAUTÉ

Keep

Cathedral

Castle
east gate

150′

100′

LOWER
TOWN

50′

ANGLO
FRENCH
FORCES

25′

Witham River

major objective was to inflict a crushing blow against his opponents, the one potential drawback of this strategy was that it left the allies with a clear route of escape to the south, if they chose to flee rather than fight.

After the first day's march, the royalists camped about eight miles to the north-west of Lincoln. Then, rising before dawn, they mounted the ridge and marched on to the town in seven detachments, with crossbowmen in the vanguard and the baggage train bringing up the rear. They arrived at Lincoln not long after 6 a.m. on Saturday, 20 May 1217. According to a song composed after the battle, the morning sun glinted off their helmets and armour as they approached. Marshal was again reported to have called out to his troops, telling them to seize this 'chance to free our land', to seek the 'eternal glory' of victory and feel no fear because any who fell would soon find themselves 'in paradise'. 'God knows who are his loyal servants', William supposedly declared, 'of that I am completely certain'. He would reward the faithful, while sending the French 'down to Hell'.

Battle joined – 20 May 1217

Despite his remarkable old age, William Marshal had no intention of directing the battle of Lincoln from a distance. He planned to throw himself into the thick of the fighting, leading his force by example. However, Marshal had first to engineer a confrontation. The royalists were ready to face the enemy on the ridge running north from Lincoln, though an engagement on this open ground would allow the Anglo-French allies to capitalise on their numerical advantage by bringing their full weight of numbers to bear. As it was, William's opponents refused to attack. Once alerted to the royalists' approach, the allied commanders rode out of Lincoln to survey the field. Robert FitzWalter and Saer of Quincy argued for an immediate frontal assault, but Thomas of Perche (not unreasonably) saw no reason to risk such a direct strike, and withdrew inside the town walls, deploying troops to defend the battlements and hold the northern gate.

Earl William now had to find a way to force an entry into Lincoln. The royalists had not come equipped with heavy siege machinery; nor could they afford to settle in for a prolonged investment of the town walls, as the resultant delay might allow Prince Louis time to march north and bolster the Anglo-French position. The castle, held by Lady Nicola de la Haye, could be entered through a gate from the west, where its ramparts abutted the main town wall, but the idea of leading the entire royalist army into this fortress was rejected. This was probably because the stronghold's east gate, which gave access to the upper town and the area in front of the cathedral, was heavily guarded by the besieging allied forces.

Marshal therefore dispatched a number of reconnaissance parties to search out other points of access. One of these was led by John Marshal, but it seems to have been Peter des Roches' group who made a crucial discovery: a sizeable gate, in the north-western quadrant, that had been blocked by masonry and rubble. The Anglo-French had evidently judged this entryway to be securely barricaded, but when des Roches reported back to Earl William, he argued that, with enough men, it could be cleared and a path into Lincoln opened. This would allow the royalists to launch an unheralded and deadly strike into the heart of the upper town.

William Marshal set about creating a diversion, so that this work could begin unseen. Ranulf of Chester was keen to lead the first charge of the day, so he was sent to attack the northern gate. At the same time, Faulkes of Bréauté led a large contingent of crossbowmen into the castle, positioned them on the walls facing into the town and began peppering the Anglo-French troops within, inflicting terrible damage. The task of clearing the north-western gate proved laborious, and perhaps took a number of hours, but this effort escaped the notice of the allies within – as fighting continued in front of the castle and the north gate – and the work was eventually completed around midday.

The royalists now had a route into Lincoln. As a large force of knights mounted their warhorses in advance of launching a blistering charge, the excitement of the moment seems to have overwhelmed

Earl William. According to the *History*, he pushed to the front and, bellowing 'Ride on!', spurred his mount forward through the newly opened gate. But in his eagerness to enter the fray, the elderly Marshal had forgotten to don his helmet – a potentially lethal mistake. A young squire rushed forward to rein him in and politely pointed out this over-sight. Once William and all of his comrades were fully armoured, they poured through the north-west gate and the assault began.

Earl William led the way, along with his son Young William Marshal, Longsword and Peter des Roches. Riding together, they raced down Westgate Street and then turned right (to the south), to emerge in front of the castle. Here Faulkes of Bréauté's crossbowmen were still wreaking havoc among the enemy – one chronicler noting that the horses of the rebel barons were being 'mown down and slaughtered like pigs'. Marshal's force suddenly burst on to this chaotic scene, charging at full pace into the Anglo-French ranks. William was said to have 'plunged into the very thick of them', surging forward to the depth of three spear lengths. Amid this first cacophonous crush of combat, des Roches apparently shouted, 'This way! God is with the Marshal', and battle was joined.

The dramatic arrival of William Marshal's contingent shocked the allied forces stationed in front of the castle, as they were wholly unaware that Lincoln's outer defences had been breached. One of their engineers, who was busily operating a stone-throwing machine, mistook the earl's men for his own troops and turned back to his siege engine. He was just preparing to unleash another missile on the castle, when the royalist knights raced past and 'cut off his head with-out any further ceremony'. In the aftermath of the initial charge, the fighting inside Lincoln quickly dissolved into a frenzied mêlée. This was the same frantic, close-quarter combat on crowded streets that Marshal had mastered in his younger days at the likes of Neufchâtel and Le Mans, but as a seventy-year-old, he was hard-pressed to hold his own.

According to the *History*, the aged William Marshal did muster one mighty attack. Robert of Roppesley – one of King John's former household knights who had joined the baronial party – drove forward, delivering a 'savage' lance strike to William Longsword's body (though his armour saved the earl of Salisbury from major injury). Roppesley's weapon shattered on impact, but as he charged through and wheeled his horse, Marshal rode up and 'dealt him such a fierce blow between the shoulders that he almost knocked him to the ground'. The battered rebel knight reportedly crawled to a nearby house, where 'out of fear, [he] went to hide in an upper room as quickly as he could'.

As the intense fracas raged in the area between the castle and the cathedral, the outcome of the battle hung in the balance. The French commander, Count Thomas of Perche, rallied his troops in the court-yard directly in front of Lincoln Cathedral and made a hard-bitten stand. It was here that the fighting reached a crescendo. Many were said to have been 'wounded and maimed, trampled on and beaten'. Count Thomas 'put up a very stern defence' and began to regain some ground. The biographer claimed that Earl William was still in the very heart of the fray, and took three shuddering blows to the head from Thomas of Perche himself, that left his helmet badly dented. But this detail was not mentioned in other sources, so it may have been added for dramatic effect.

Nonetheless, it is clear that Count Thomas came to a sudden, grisly end, there in the great cathedral's shadow. One of Faulkes of Bréauté's knights – a former mercenary named Reginald Croc – pressed forward to assail the count of Perche. Croc delivered a deadly lunge that went 'through [the] visor' of Thomas' helmet and, as 'the point of the sword' pierced the count's eye it drove straight into his brain. 'Mortally wounded', Thomas fell from his horse, though Reginald Croc also seems to have been severely injured during this bold attack, and died later that same day.

The sight of Count Thomas' collapse caused shock on both sides. The Anglo-French forces were 'greatly dismayed', and began to make a panicked retreat south, down the steep hill into the lower town. At first, the royalists were also uncertain of what had occurred. It was thought that Thomas of Perche may simply have been knocked unconscious. William Marshal ordered the count's helm to be carefully removed, and only then did it become clear that 'he was stone dead'. The violent demise of such a prominent figure was unusual, even in the heat of full battle – a testament to the effectiveness of medieval armour and the general practice of seizing high-value captives for ransom. Even the biographer conceded that 'it was a great pity that [Count Thomas] died in this manner'.

The battle of Lincoln was not yet over, but its momentum was swinging definitively in the royalists' favour. Earl William's forces pursued the fleeing Anglo-French troops downhill and the earl of Chester, who had managed to break through the north gate, joined the fight. With the slope in their favour, the royalists were able to beat back the allies' forlorn attempt to mount a counter-attack, and a full-scale rout began. Many of the fleeing Anglo-French were caught in the bottleneck of the southern gate and the bridge over the Witham. Others were pursued for many miles to the south of Lincoln. Some were butchered, especially among the infantry, but most were taken as prisoners. Around 200 knights managed to escape, and the *History* mockingly likened them to rats, scuttling all the way to London.

William Marshal had led the royalists to a stunning victory. Robert FitzWalter, Saer of Quincy and many other leading rebel barons were taken captive, along with a large portion of Prince Louis' forces. Earl William had taken a huge, yet arguably necessary, risk, but the gamble had paid off. He survived the fearsome encounter, somewhat battered, yet otherwise unscathed, but the heart of the Anglo-French army had been crushed. The English historian David Carpenter has rightly described Lincoln as 'one of the most decisive [battles] in English history', concluding that its outcome 'meant that England would be ruled by the Angevin, not the Capetian dynasty'. With such glorious news to relate, it is little wonder that Marshal rode off to Northampton that same day, even 'before [taking] any food' according to Roger of Wendover – determined to tell young King Henry III and Guala that the tide of the civil war had been turned.

WAR'S END

Louis of France learnt of the disastrous defeat at Lincoln on 25 May and immediately broke off his siege of Dover, retreating north to London. William Marshal could perhaps have sought to encircle the great city and capture the Capetian prince, but the earl recognised that the royalists' resources remained meagre, in spite of their recent triumph. It was now critical that the war be drawn to a swift end, as efficiently as possible, and the key step in this process was to usher Louis out of England.

Negotiations over a settlement began almost immediately, and initial terms were agreed on 13 June. Marshal's demands were far from punitive. In return for Prince Louis' immediate departure, the sentences of excommunication levelled against the French and the rebel baronial allies would be lifted, and the latter would recover their English lands. Prisoners on both sides were to be released, and the 'liberties and customs of the kingdom of England' set out in the 1216 re-issue of Magna Carta would henceforth be 'enjoyed across the realm'. Even so, a stumbling block was hit when the papal legate Guala insisted that the churchmen who had ignored Rome's express orders by continuing to support Louis of France must remain excommunicate. The Capetian prince refused, quite admirably, to abandon these faithful allies, declaring that 'there was no way that he would make peace without them', and the talks thus broke down on 15 June.

The baronial party now began to fracture at a precipitous rate. Over the next eight days, more than sixty nobles returned to the king's camp, and close to another hundred followed suit in the course of that summer. As before, the vast majority of these *reversi* received equitable treatment. The Capetians made a last-ditch attempt to snatch victory in late August, when a large army of French reinforcements set sail from Calais. The fleet of ships carrying them across the Channel was commanded by the infamous mercenary sea captain Eustace the

Monk – a man who had renounced his holy orders to become a pirate, and was thus derided with particular vitriol by clerical chroniclers.

On 24 August 1217, a makeshift English fleet set sail from Sandwich to repel this invasion force. For once, William Marshal agreed not to place himself in the front line, allowing Hubert of Burgh to lead the defence in his stead. Earl William watched from the shore, alongside King Henry, and they seem to have enjoyed a clear view of events, as the biographer noted 'it was a fine day and [thus] possible to see far out to sea'. The battle of Sandwich was a vicious affair that left an esti-mated 4,000 men dead or drowned. A number of heavily loaded French ships, including Eustace the Monk's own lead vessel, were rammed and boarded. Hubert of Burgh's men threw pots of lime powder crashing down on to the enemy decks and, with the acrid air blinding the French, they managed to overcome any resistance with relative ease. The English scored a second historic victory that day, and the remnants of the Capetian fleet beat a hasty retreat. William des Barres, the famed Capetian champion, was captured, as was the count of Blois. Eustace the Monk was apparently found cowering below decks, but was dragged up into the light and summarily beheaded.

After this reversal, Prince Louis' position in England became unten-able. As one chronicler put it, he found himself 'destitute of present aid and despairing of the future'. William Marshal now moved to encircle London, and peace negotiations began anew on 28 August. It took two weeks of wrangling to finalise terms, but a treaty, closely mir-roring that tabled on 13 June, was eventually agreed at Kingston, to the south-west of London. By late September, Earl William was able to escort Louis to Dover and watch, with satisfaction, as the Capetian invader set sail for France.

William Marshal has sometimes been criticised for not forcing more injurious and humiliating conditions upon his vanquished enemy. Indeed, within a generation, rancorous and uncharitable chroniclers such as Matthew Paris would suggest that William had somehow betrayed England in 1217 by not punishing Louis of France with suf-ficient venom. Marshal does seem to have placed too much trust in the

French prince. Louis promised to convince his father, Philip Augustus, to restore the Continental Angevin lands seized from King John to Henry III. Earl William took Louis at his word, rather than requiring him to seal a binding assurance, and the prince subsequently reneged on his oath. But critics like Matthew Paris ignored the continued weakness and instability of the royalists' position in England during the late summer of 1217. The realm had been broken by the civil war, its finances and systems of governance lay in ruins and its king was barely ten years old. Just as it had been in the immediate aftermath of Lincoln, Marshal's overriding priority in September 1217 was to secure peace and herd the French out of England before the whole kingdom ground to a halt.

In that aim, William Marshal succeeded. Against all the odds, the 'guardian of the realm' had quelled the baronial rebellion and thwarted the most threatening invasion of England since 1066. To contemporaries, the swift defeat of the French seemed to be nothing less than 'a miracle'. Marshal had made the hardest of choices after John's death, endangering the fortunes of his dynasty and supporters, by backing the forlorn boy-king, Henry III. But in steering the royalists to victory in 1217, Earl William had secured Henry's right to rule and saved the kingdom.

EPILOGUE

William Marshal was afforded little time to savour the victories of 1217. With Louis of France's departure, the immediate threat of Capetian aggression was at an end, but the huge challenge of restoring England to a state of peace and order remained. The kingdom had been ravaged by years of baronial insurrection. Crown authority had collapsed, and the Royal Exchequer, the main organ of financial administration, had not sat since 1214. The Welsh and the Scots had also capitalised upon the English civil war and French invasion by clawing back lost territory. Stabilising the kingdom would have been a monumental task even for a vigorous adult monarch, yet Henry III remained a minor, and his 'guardian', Earl William, was entering his seventies.

WILLIAM MARSHAL AS 'REGENT'

Marshal held the office of 'guardian of the realm' – serving to all intents and purposes as Henry III's regent – for another nineteen months, dedicating himself to the unforgiving and unglamorous business of governance, striving all the while to secure the best possible future for his young king's regime. The ills of the realm were not cured at a stroke – Marshal was no magician. But given the staggering scale of the problems faced, and his own advanced age and limited previous experience of wielding executive power, the progress made was remarkable. Belying his years, William set to work with enormous energy. Much of his time was spent in London and Westminster, but he also moved between Striguil and one of his favoured manor houses at Caversham, on the banks of the River Thames, across from Reading.

As the elder statesmen of the realm, Marshal proved to be an effective figurehead – his peerless reputation as a paragon of chivalry helping to legitimise the 'regency' government. It also enabled him to arbitrate in disputes over land (which were legion), and to oversee the restitution of hostages and payment of ransoms. There was no scent of overbearing tyranny, and only the barest hint of partisan self-service, to Earl William's rule. He shared authority with Guala of Bicchieri until the late autumn of 1218, when the papal legate returned to Rome (complaining of exhaustion) and was replaced by Pandulf, who had recently held the office of papal chamberlain. Peter des Roches, the bishop of Winchester, and Hubert of Burgh also played leading roles in the administration. Through the collaborative efforts of these men and others, William's term of office witnessed a gradual restoration of the systems of royal justice and crown finance. A new version of Magna Carta was issued on 6 November 1217, under the seal of the papal legate and William Marshal (who, in spite of his status as regent, continued to employ the same diminutive die he had used as a knight). The document had been further reworked to restore some aspects of royal authority, but it still contained critical clauses dealing with rights to justice, fair trial and freedom from tyranny.

Earl William enjoyed some success restoring England's borders in the north, as the Scots agreed to return the lands they had seized during the baronial uprising. The native Welsh were another matter. Wales continued to be beset by insurrection, with Llewellyn ap Iorwerth in resurgent mood, and Marshal's neighbours on the southern Welsh March in Caerleon going on the rampage. Significant losses were sustained across the province, including the fall of Carmarthen and Cardigan in west Wales. The entire region would remain a troublesome thorn in the side of the English monarchy for much of the thirteenth century.

Earl William did show some favour to the members of his dynasty and household in the course of his regency, but his actions were generally restrained and far from predatory. Young William Marshal was granted rights to Marlborough Castle – the fortress he had sought during the rebellion – and a valuable slice of the profits from royal exchanges (in centres such as London, Winchester and York). John Marshal was given oversight of the royal forests throughout the realm, while John of Earley and Jordan of Sauqueville received handsome rewards of land. The earl also appointed his long-standing advisor, Master Michael of London, as royal procurator (or legal representative) in the papal court in Rome. William took relatively little for himself, save the custody of Gloucester Castle and the right of free passage for ships to New Ross in Leinster.

Marshal's resignation from office

By the start of 1219, William had done what he could to consolidate King Henry III's position, rebuilding the crown's relationship with the aristocracy and resurrecting the framework of government. But the incessant demands of office eventually took their toll. In January of that year, he travelled from Marlborough to Westminster, but fell ill on his arrival. Marshal had always been extraordinarily healthy throughout his long life, but according to the biographer, he was 'plagued by illness and pain' in the weeks that followed, and it gradually became clear that, after some seventy-two years, his body was finally failing him.

The earl was joined by his wife, Lady Isabel, and a number of doctors sought to minister to him, but with little effect. On 7 March, he was able to ride to the Tower of London, but was said to be 'suffering much pain and discomfort', and by the middle of that month he recognised that his end was approaching. William decided to leave London, for 'if death was to be his lot', the History noted, 'he preferred to die at home [rather] than elsewhere'. Young William Marshal and John of Earley made the necessary arrangements, and Isabel and the earl were taken up the Thames in a pair of boats, travelling at a measured pace, to reach the manor house at Caversham on 20 March. Marshal seems to have yearned for the clean air of the countryside and a calm space where he could be surrounded by his family and closest retainers. The estate also boasted its own chapel, presided over by Augustinian monks from Notley (in Buckinghamshire), who could tend to the earl's spiritual well-being. Yet first, he needed to free himself from the responsibilities of office.

William continued to manage the affairs of state from his bed for a number of weeks, while King Henry III took up residence across the river at Reading, along with Peter des Roches. But the earl was wracked by intense pain and had no appetite for food, so he took the final steps to relinquish his authority as regent. On 8 April 1219, the eleven-year-old monarch and his leading counsellors all crowded into Marshal's bedchamber to begin two days of debate. Peter des Roches sought to press his own claim to the regency, arguing that he had been appointed as a form of guardian in October 1217, but William's mind was still sharp enough to see through this ruse. Des Roche had been a competent ally, but William seems to have distrusted his insatiable ambition and doubted that he could command the loyalty of the barons. As a result, Marshal placed Henry III into the care of the papal legate, Pandulf, and even took the precautionary step of sending his son, Young William, to watch the public proclamation of this act so that des Roche could not intervene.

Before the meeting broke up, Earl William called the young king to his bedside. According to the *History*, Marshal offered one last piece of advice to the monarch whose cause he had done so much to champion. William spoke of his hopes that Henry would 'grow up to be a worthy man', but he also issued a stark warning. If the king were to follow 'in the footsteps of some wicked ancestor' then Marshal prayed that God 'does not give you long life'. There was no more that William could do, but hope that young Henry would not repeat the sins of his father. With that, power passed from Marshal's hands, and he was said to have felt that he had been 'delivered of a great burden'.

THE LAST DAYS

Over the course of the next month, William Marshal's life slowly ebbed away, until his days finally came to an end. This famed knight – the veteran of so much war and turmoil – was granted a peaceful death, secure in the comforts of his Caversham manor. His wife, Isabel, was present throughout, as was his son, Young William. The earl's daughters arrived, and the youngest of them sang to him, bringing gentle comfort through his hours of pain. The leading members of Marshal's retinue also gathered at Caversham, John of Earley chief among them. Their enduring fidelity through these last days laid bare the deep sense of affection and loyalty that they felt for their great lord. They stood in constant vigil over the earl, with never less than three knights in attendance, while Young William insisted on staying by his side through the dark hours of the night. In this way, Marshal was loved and honoured to the last.

The kings that William served had all suffered tortured, or sudden, deaths. Young Henry's final, agonising days had been passed as a rebellious son, denied succour by his father. Old King Henry himself had been hounded to his grave, while the Lionheart fell to a tragically wasteful wound and John met his end as a reviled figure of hate. Earl William was not spared the pain of death – the debilitating disease that snatched away his strength, left him often in agony, and he was barely able to consume food in his last twenty days. But he was afforded the time to prepare for his demise. The *History* recorded an intensely detailed account of these last weeks, describing how Marshal sought to set his affairs in order, and it is perhaps these closing sections of the biography that offer the clearest picture of the inner man, as we learn what mattered most to William in his dying days.

The care of Marshal's dynasty and men

The future of the Marshal dynasty weighed heavily on William's mind. His last will and testament was prepared with the utmost care, so as to ensure the preservation of his legacy. As a younger son, William had inherited nothing from his own father, but over seven decades Marshal had amassed an extraordinary assortment of lands and honours. At a personal level, this was perhaps the greatest achievement of his life. He had lifted his family's name to unimagined heights and was now determined that these efforts should not be wasted. All of the provisions of his will were recorded by William's personal almoner, Geoffrey the Templar. John of Earley was named as one of Marshal's executors, and the written terms were formally confirmed by Pandulf, the papal legate, and Stephen Langton, archbishop of Canterbury. Nothing was to be left to chance. The first thought, of course, was given to Isabel. She would retain rights to all of the lands he had gained through her hand in marriage thirty years earlier until the time of her own death, after which point the territories would be divided according to Earl William's wishes.

Young William was to receive the core estates of the Marshal dynasty – the lordships of Striguil, Pembroke and Leinster – as well as the lands held by the Marshal family elsewhere in England, including Hamstead Marshall. As second son, Richard Marshal was granted Longueville in Normandy, but instead of confining his holdings to France, William also allotted him the Buckinghamshire manor of Crendon. Gilbert Marshal was destined for a career in the Church and thus received no estates, but the earl's fourth son, Walter, was promised custody of Goodrich Castle, on the Welsh March. The earl's initial instinct was to leave nothing to his youngest son, Ancel, who was still but a child. Not, it would seem, for lack of love, for Marshal was said to have declared that '[he] is very dear to me', but because William believed Ancel should make his own way in the world, as he himself had done – finding 'someone who will love and honour him greatly'. Yet, in the end, John of Earley intervened on the boy's behalf, and he was apportioned Irish land worth £140. Four of Earl William's daughters were already married, but he granted a small income to the fifth, Joan, in anticipation that she would soon be wed.

With the safety of his family secured, Marshal's mind turned to the well-being of his knights. He had spent the first forty years of his own life in service, and cherished the intimate bonds of friendship and trust forged with the members of his own *mesnie*. Most of William's closest retainers had already been well rewarded with lands and offices, but the obligation to provide for his warriors remained a pressing concern. In these final weeks, one of Marshal's clerks suggested that the store of eighty fine, fur-trimmed scarlet robes held in the manor house might be sold off. He apparently told the earl that the money raised could be used 'to deliver you from your sins', but William was appalled by this suggestion. 'Hold your tongue you wretch,' he reputedly countered, 'I have had enough of your advice.' Marshal's firmly held view was that these robes should be distributed to his men, as a last token of his duty to provide for their needs, and he bid John of Earley to commend him to all the household knights to whom he had been unable to speak in person. Beyond the inner circle of his family, the *mesnie* had been the cradle of William's life – a priceless sanctuary – and it remained so to the very end.

The fate of William's soul

As Marshal's time drew to a close, thoughts of the afterlife and the judgement of souls spoken of by the Church began to press in upon his mind. With death approaching, he was said to have declared: '[I must] take great thought for the salvation of my soul, for my body is now in peril.' Earl William revealed that he had prepared carefully for this moment decades earlier. The ever-faithful John of Earley was sent on a special mission to the southern March. William told him to bring 'the two lengths of silk cloth which I gave to Stephen [of Évreux] to look after [and] make haste to return here'. Earley duly performed this task, and the *History* detailed the intimate scene that played out upon his return.

The long-hidden silks were presented, but at first one of the earl's knights seemed unimpressed, saying: 'I find them a little faded, unless my eyesight is blurred.' William ordered the cloths unfolded. Perhaps in that moment he wondered if his memory of this treasured fabric had been at fault. But once they were laid out, Marshal was relieved to see that 'they looked very fine and valuable' and were obviously 'choice cloth of good workmanship'. The earl called in his son and then explained: 'I have had these lengths of cloth for thirty years; I had them brought back with me from the Holy Land [so that they might] be draped over my body when I am laid in the earth.' William then charged Earley with performing this task and even instructed him to use coarse cloth to protect the silk in case of bad weather, so that it would not become 'damaged or dirtied'. This was how Marshal had long envisaged the honouring of his corpse, and he was determined that this ritualised union with a relic of sacred Jerusalem be performed to the letter.

Towards the middle of May, a messenger arrived at Caversham bearing the news that the papal legate, Pandulf, had granted Marshal a special reward. He was told that the 'legate absolves you of all the sins you have committed in your lifetime and which you have truly confessed', and as the *History* pointedly observed, William wisely made sure to offer confession throughout this period. The earl also made additional donations to religious houses in his last days and was said to have asked that alms be given to the needy, and food, drink and clothing be set aside for 'one hundred of the poor' after his death.

When viewed from a distance, these elaborate preparations might seem to suggest that Marshal was fanatically obsessed with the fate of his soul – or, at least, that the biographer wished to present him as such. But in truth, William was merely following the established customs of his day; taking due precautions for what all Western Christians then believed would be the moment of ultimate judgement before their God. One further incident, reported by the *History*, seems to reveal that, as a knight, Marshal held a distinct view of Christian doctrine and his own spiritual well-being. While confined to his bed, William apparently struck up a conversation with some of his household knights. One of them recalled that he had heard clergymen claim that 'no man will find salvation on any account if he does not return what he has taken', and thus wondered if the earl intended to renounce all his worldly goods.

Marshal's fascinating response, as described by the biographer, is worth quoting in full, for even if it was not a precise record of his words, it offers a unique insight into the knightly mindset – exposing the ways in which medieval warriors sought to reconcile the essential needs of their profession with the teachings of the Latin Church. This, then, was Earl William's reported reply:

> 'Churchmen are too hard on us, shaving us too closely. If, simply because I've taken 500 knights and kept their arms, horses and all their equipment, the kingdom of heaven is closed in my face, then there is no way for me to enter in, for I am unable to return these things. I believe I can do no more as regards God but surrender myself up to him as a penitent for all the sins I have committed and all the wrongs I have done. They might well wish to push me, but they can push me no further; either their argument is false on this score or no man can find salvation.'

Death and burial

In William Marshal's last days 'he was unable to eat or drink', and though his servants tried to feed him with mushrooms, and a few crumbs of white bread, 'his heart became weak and his natural functions stopped'. Around this time, the earl divulged his secret agreement with the Templars. Back in the 1180s, he had decided to enter the ranks of that Order before his death and wished to receive a burial at the brethren's hands. In return for this service, he would be leaving the Templars a 'fine manor in Upleadon to enjoy in perpetuity'. In

William's mind, induction into this esteemed knightly Order must have seemed a fitting end to a warrior's life. His friend Aimery of St Maur, the master of the Templars in England, travelled to Caversham to perform the rite in person. One year earlier, Marshal had issued instructions for a special white Templar robe, emblazoned with a red cross, to be prepared 'without anyone knowing of its existence'. The garment was now produced, but William then called for Isabel to come to his room. The biographer described how:

> The earl, who was generous, gentle and kind towards his wife the countess, said to her: 'Fair lady, kiss me now, for you will never be able to do it again.' She stepped forwards and kissed him, and both of them wept.

His daughters, who were also present, were said to have 'stood round him in deep grief', and eventually had to be ushered outside. Once the ritual was complete, Aimery apparently offered William some parting words of comfort, saying: 'you have known higher honour in this world than ever any other knight had, both in respect of your valour [and] your wisdom and loyalty.' He then went on to assure the earl that God 'wishes to have you for his own'.

The end came near midday, on Tuesday 14 May 1219. John of Earley had been trying to ease Marshal's position in his bed, when 'the final throes of death, against which he had no defence, took him in their grip'. William implored Earley to open the doors and windows of his room, and to call his family. John 'took the earl in his arms' and watched as his 'face grew paler, and became livid because death was pressing him and wounding him to the heart'.

Young William, Isabel and Marshal's knights arrived, and the earl spoke his last words, saying: 'I am dying, and commend you to God. I am no longer able to think of your needs, for I cannot fight against death.' Young William then took his father in his arms and 'wept tears of pity, as was natural, quietly and openly'. A cross was brought to the bed and placed before the earl and then, as the abbot of Notley performed a final rite of absolution, William Marshal set his eyes upon the crucifix, 'joined his hands together' and died. The author of the *History* confidently declared that: 'we believe he is saved and sits with God and His company [because] he was a good man in death as in life.'

Later that day, the earl's body was embalmed, prepared for burial and covered in Marshal's treasured silken cloths. On 15 May, his corpse was transported to Reading Abbey, where it was carried in solemn procession and the ritual of full Mass was sung. Lady Isabel followed the remains of her late husband, but it was said that her grief rendered her unable to walk. Marshal's body was then carried towards London. On 18 May a large crowd of barons escorted the funeral procession to Westminster Abbey for a further vigil and Mass, performed amid a 'magnificent display of candles'. Finally on 20 May 1219, two years after his famous victory at Lincoln, the earl was laid to rest in the round Temple Church in London – the space that evoked Christ's own Holy Sepulchre in Jerusalem. The archbishop of Canterbury presided over the funeral, alongside the bishop of London, and in his oration, Stephen Langton was said to have described William Marshal as 'the greatest knight to be found in all the world'. And there, the tomb effigy of this peerless warrior – the architect of England's salvation – can still be seen to this day.

AFTERMATH

Lady Isabel did not long survive her husband. She died in 1220, in her mid-forties, and was buried at Tintern Abbey, north of Striguil. Together, she and Earl William had established the Marshal dynasty as one of the leading baronial families in England. Yet for all their efforts and dedication, the fortunes of the Marshal house were broken within a quarter of a century. In part, the dynasty fell prey to the upheavals of King Henry III's tumultuous reign. England was saved from the immediate renewal of French aggression by King Philip

Augustus' own demise in 1220. When his son and successor, Louis VIII, passed away just six years later, his young son and namesake acceded to the Capetian crown, leaving France to endure its own period of regency government. Even so, under Henry III, England continued to struggle with the consequences and aftershocks of the baronial rebellion. Magna Carta was re-issued once again in 1225 (achieving its definitive form) and the young king's minority finally came to an end in 1227. But the early years of Henry III's reign were disrupted by power struggles as Hubert of Burgh and then Peter des Roches sought to exploit their influence over the crown for personal gain.

The fall of the Marshals

Responsibility for the collapse of the Marshal dynasty cannot be laid solely at the feet of any one family member, nor can it be explained by grave deficiencies of character. William Marshal's heirs were neither indolent, nor foolish, but they did lack their father's inimitable ability to navigate the fractious world of medieval politics. Most crucially of all, they proved unable to sire heirs. The earl's first successor, his eldest son, William II, enjoyed considerable success and continued to benefit from John of Earley's loyal service to the Marshal family, until the latter's death in 1229. William II was responsible for commissioning the *History of William Marshal* in celebration of his father's extraordinary career. An Anglo-French scribe working in England, named John, wrote this account – the first known biography of a medieval knight. He drew upon written evidence and the oral testimony of those who had known Earl William in life, including most notably John of Earley, and the text was completed soon after 1226.

William II recovered territory in west Wales, consolidated his family's hold over Leinster and presided over a significant period of castle-building in the Marshal domains, with major extensions made to fortresses such as Striguil and Cilgerran. Following the precipitous death of his first wife Alice (the daughter of Baldwin of Béthune) after barely a year of marriage, William II wed King Henry III's own younger sister, Eleanor, in 1224, but their union proved childless. On 6 April 1231, while in London to attend the second marriage of his widowed sister Isabella, William II died suddenly of unknown causes in his early forties. He left no heir, and was buried in Temple Church alongside his father.

The earldom of Pembroke thus passed to his younger brother Richard, who had inherited the Marshal estates in Normandy in 1219 and spent twelve years serving as a noble in the French court. After returning to England to lead the Marshal dynasty, Richard gained renown as a warrior – being described by one contemporary as 'the flower of chivalry in our time' – but he also became embroiled in an armed insurrection against Henry III's increasingly unpopular regime. Richard fought on the March in alliance with the Welsh Prince Llewellyn ap Iorwerth, then sailed to Ireland, where the king's justiciar had sought to seize Leinster, with the connivance of the Lacys.

Earl William Marshal had survived just such an attack, but his son proved less fortunate. Richard was persuaded to a parley with the justiciar near Kildare, on 1 April 1234, but this turned out to be a trap. Rather than discuss terms of peace, the justiciar launched an attack with 140 knights, and Richard's Irish vassals betrayed him by refusing to fight in his defence. Forced to mount a hopeless last stand alongside fifteen loyal members of his household, Richard fell beneath a torrent of blows. He was carried to Kilkenny Castle and died of his wounds two weeks later, like his brother before him, leaving no heir.

As a result, Gilbert Marshal was forced to renounce his clerical orders and take up leadership of the Marshal dynasty, but he never prospered at royal court. Ironically, he met his end during a tournament held at Hertford in 1241, trying to emulate his father's legendary feats of prowess. Gilbert lacked skill as a horseman and found himself struggling to control his spirited warhorse. Unfortunately, the members of his retinue had ridden off in pursuit of glory and plunder, so there was no one to assist him. Gilbert was thrown from his mount, but his foot became stuck in a stirrup, and he was dragged along the ground for a considerable distance, sustaining mortal injuries. He was succeeded by his two remaining brothers. Walter was appointed as earl of Pembroke in 1242, and briefly fought in a royal campaign in southern France, but passed away in 1245. The youngest brother, Ancel, died barely one month later. Neither left legitimate heirs.

As a result, the Marshal estates – so carefully accumulated during Earl William's career – were broken up and parcelled out among the heirs of his daughters. In 1246, the title of Marshal of England passed to Roger Bigod, the son of William Marshal's eldest daughter Matilda. Through lack of luck, long life and fertility, the male line of the Marshal dynasty was brought to a desperately premature end.

Medieval England and knighthood

The English monarchy remained enfeebled through much of the thirteenth century. Henry III faced a second full-scale baronial revolt after 1258 and was forced to accept the imposition of consultative, parliamentary government. This was one of the most significant consequences of King John's reign and William Marshal's involvement in Magna Carta: nobles and knights were no longer the mere agents of royal will, they now served as the check and balance against crown authority.

The loss of Normandy and the other Angevin territories on the Continent, and Earl William's defeat of the French in 1217, also contributed to the emergence of a far more pronounced and pervasive sense of English identity in the course of the thirteenth century. By the end of Marshal's life, English was already emerging as the dominant language of the aristocracy. The days of the hybrid, cross-Channel society drew to a close. The ruling elite no longer regarded themselves as Anglo-Normans, or Angevins, but as English – not least because they continued to find themselves pitted against the Capetian French.

The kings of England and their leading nobles remained haunted by memories of the 'glorious' Angevin realm throughout the Middle

Ages. Little progress was made on the Continent in the thirteenth century, but the obsession with re-conquering France proved inescapable and eventually prompted the outbreak of the Hundred Years' War in 1339. While locked into this seemingly perpetual struggle, the 'Plantagenet' dynasty founded by Henry II and Eleanor of Aquitaine finally came to an end with the overthrow and death of King Richard II in 1399.

The knightly class, which William Marshal had come to epitomise, endured throughout this period, yet its ideals and practices underwent dramatic changes. Many facets of chivalric culture were increasingly defined. Knightly training became more sophisticated and regimented, and the ritual of dubbing was formalised. Technological advances in metallurgy and smithcraft also meant that the mail hauberks worn by William Marshal and his contemporaries were first augmented, and then wholly superseded, by plate armour – giving rise to the burnished suits of elaborate, full-plate worn by knights from the mid-fourteenth century onwards. The extraordinary level of protection afforded by later medieval armour meant that the type of slashing or concussive weaponry popular in Earl William's heyday as a tournament champion came to be replaced by sharper-pointed swords, daggers and spears, capable of targeting and piercing vulnerable joints. Heavier armour, in turn, produced the need for larger and stronger warhorses.

All of this changed the way in which knights fought, but it also significantly increased the cost of equipment. Even towards the end of William Marshal's life, the expense associated with becoming a knight and then maintaining that station was prohibitive. This process of inflation, combined with the gradual shift in emphasis from the warrior aristocracy of the eleventh and twelfth centuries to the landholding nobility of the thirteenth (of which Earl William was himself a part), made knighthood an increasingly rarefied profession. Before long, the expenditure and responsibilities involved left many wondering why they should bother to become knights when they could be better served by holding and administering estates as members of what would later be termed the 'gentry'.

In the decades that followed Marshal's death, England faced an increasingly severe shortage of knights. The crown took to imposing fines (known as 'distraint') upon aristocrats who refused to join the warrior class, but it also had to lower the numbers of knights that lords and barons were expected to put into the field at times of war. Estimates indicate that there were approximately 4,000 knights in England in the later twelfth century; this total had fallen to 1,250 by the end of the thirteenth. This drastic reduction was partially reversed under Henry III's militaristic son and heir, King Edward I – known to history as the 'Hammer of the Scots' – but even he was forced to use a system of direct payment for knightly service by contract.

Yet, though the number of knights fell, aristocratic culture harkened back to the supposed 'golden age of chivalry' witnessed during William Marshal's lifetime. Notions of shame and honour came to hold even greater importance, while the lavish pageantry of tournaments and jousts reached its apogee in the fourteenth century, under King Edward III. His famous son, Edward the Black Prince, sought to rejuvenate the ideals of chivalry by introducing a new elite cadre of knights – the Order of the Garter – and the French followed suit with their Order of the Star. But this could not arrest the slow decline and eventual disappearance of the knightly class in the centuries that followed. The mounted, armour-clad warriors like William Marshal, who had done so much to mould the history of medieval Europe, would have no part to play in the dawn of modernity.

WILLIAM MARSHAL: IN LIFE AND LEGEND

In many respects, William Marshal was the archetypal medieval knight. His qualities epitomised, perhaps even defined, those valued in late twelfth- and early- thirteenth-century Western European aristocratic culture. His storied career stood as testament to what knights could achieve: the heights to which they could rise and the extent to which they could shape history. In spite of Archbishop Stephen's reputed pronouncement at his funeral, Marshal was not the only great knight of his generation. Other warriors, such as William des Barres and William des Roches, could match his prowess and reputation. Yet they never reached such astonishing heights. William Marshal's life represents both a model of knightly experience and a unique example of unparalleled success, for in the end, his story transcended the normal boundaries of his warrior class.

William's remarkable achievements can be explained, to an extent, by his personal qualities. In the military arena, his unusual physical strength and resilience lent him a natural advantage. Masterful horsemanship helped him to dominate the tournament circuit, while the experience of war gleaned under leaders such as Henry II and Richard the Lionheart enabled Marshal to emerge as a highly skilled battlefield commander and strategist. Unlike many of his knightly contemporaries, William was able to temper his martial ferocity in the setting of the royal court. He possessed a rare ability to exercise ironclad emotional restraint and knew enough of politics to avoid confrontation, and engage in a measure of calculated machination.

William's behaviour was also informed (and, at times, conditioned) by the precepts of chivalry. But his actions did not always conform to our modern fantasies of knightly gallantry. Marshal lived in an age when the public display of prowess and the acquisition of honourable reputation were paramount. He was naturally materialistic – especially in his younger days – because visible wealth served to affirm status in his society. Similarly, his decision to pursue an honourable course of action was often grounded in an acute sense of social expectation. William's capacity for steadfast loyalty might be laudable, but it was also self-serving, in that it safeguarded his good name and allowed him to avoid the potent stigma of public shame.

Marshal was a driven and deeply ambitious individual. At certain moments, the surviving evidence allows us glimpses of his abiding appetite for wealth and power, or his capacity to promote his own interests. Before the summer of 1188, William lobbied King Henry II incessantly for rewards. During Richard the Lionheart's reign, he danced around the issue of his relationship with John so as to preserve his claim to Leinster. And in 1205 Marshal equivocated over the oath of homage to King Philip Augustus, hoping to protect his rights to the Norman lordship of Longueville. Even so, these moments have to be balanced against William's unusual willingness to risk his own fortunes in service to the crown: most notably, the faithfulness shown to Henry II in 1189; and his defining decision to support the future King Henry III in 1216.

By the end of his long life, contemporaries recognised the scope of William's achievements – not least his defence of the Angevin dynasty and defeat of the French. For many, he was the peerless knight; Lancelot brought to life. Marshal seems to have served as an inspiration for writers of medieval Arthurian literature. Indeed, the Comte Guillaume (Count William) to whom the elusive, but highly influential, Marie de France dedicated her translation of Aesop's *Fables* may well have been William Marshal. It is little wonder that, while grounded in fact, his biography, the *History of William Marshal*, was fashioned in Anglo-French verse to resemble an Arthurian epic. With the fracturing of the Marshal dynasty, however, that text fell out of circulation, and the associated celebration of his exploits gradually subsided. By the end of the Middle Ages, the *History* had been forgotten and William became merely another name in the dusty annals of the distant past.

William Marshal never dropped out of memory entirely. He appeared in Shakespeare's play *King John* as the minor figure Pembroke – though the text borrowed little from historical fact. In the early modern era, he was recalled as a leading figure behind the forging of Magna Carta and a champion of the royalist cause. When the Palace of Westminster was rebuilt after the Great Fire of 1834, a special Fine Arts Commission (chaired by Queen Victoria's husband, Prince Albert) was established to coordinate its decoration. A series of statues of those involved in the drafting of Magna Carta were commissioned for use in the House of Lords, and on the advice of the historian Henry Hallam, William Marshal – as a 'a very eminent man' – was given a prominent place, to the left of the royal throne: quite literally represented as the figure behind the crown.

Yet even then, only the bones of William's career were known from references in medieval chronicles and royal documents. The human story – his rise from obscurity to the highest office in the land, the ideals that conditioned his behaviour, and the bonds of service and friendship that defined his life – had been lost. The wheel only began to turn when Paul Meyer walked into Sotheby's on 6 February 1861 and stumbled upon the intriguing 'Norman-French chronicle on English Affairs (in Verse)'. The rediscovery of the biography brought its hero back into the light, but still today he remains largely unknown outside academic circles. With the 800th anniversaries of the great battle of Lincoln and William Marshal's death approaching, this once fêted figure surely deserves wider recognition.

William died in a different England to the one in which he had been born, but it was a country that he had been instrumental in shaping. For centuries thereafter, England would be ruled by kings supported, but also checked, by a warrior aristocracy. And the ideals that they hammered out on the tournament field, in the politics of the court, in the blood of civil war and, ultimately, in Magna Carta, form the basis of the principles by which much of the world is now governed.

CHRONOLOGY

1187	Saladin wins the battle of Hattin and conquers Jerusalem, sparking the Third Crusade
1189	William fights to defend Le Mans and unhorses Richard the Lionheart
	Henry II succeeded by Richard I
	William marries Isabel of Clare, becoming lord of Striguil
1190–4	King Richard absent on crusade and in captivity
	William serves as co-justiciar of England
1194–9	William fights alongside King Richard to restore the Angevin realm
1199	Richard the Lionheart slain at Châlus; succeeded by John
	William appointed as earl of Pembroke
1200	Treaty of Le Goulet agreed between John and Philip II Augustus
1200–1	William's first visit Pembroke and Ireland
1202	William seeks to defend Normandy from French invasion
	John successfully relieves Mirebeau
1203	Probable murder of Arthur of Brittany; the Angevin realm starts to collapse
1204	Rouen and Château Gaillard fall to the French; Normandy is lost
1205	William quarrels with King John
1207–8	William returns to Ireland
	Crisis in Leinster
1210	King John leads an expedition to Ireland in pursuit of William of Briouze
1212	'Plot' to kill King John uncovered
	William returns to royal favour
1213	King John reconciled with the papacy
1214	Battle of Bouvines
1215	Start of the Baronial Rebellion
	Sealing of Magna Carta
1216	Prince Louis of France invades England
	Death of King John and coronation of Henry III
	William appointed as 'guardian of the realm'
1217	Battle of Lincoln
1219	William dies and is buried at the Temple Church in London
c. 1226	The *History of William Marshal* completed
1861	Paul Meyer examines a copy of the *History of William Marshal* at Sotheby's

CAST OF CHARACTERS

Marshal Dynasty

John Marshal	William Marshal's father (with Sybil of Salisbury); an Anglo-Norman noble of middling rank who held the office of royal master marshal
John II Marshal	William Marshal's elder brother (d. 1194)
William Marshal	Tournament champion, royal servant, lord of Striguil (from 1189), earl of Pembroke (from 1199) and ultimately regent of England
Isabel of Clare	Wealthy heiress who married William Marshal in 1189
Young William Marshal	Eldest son and heir of William Marshal and Isabel of Clare

Angevin Dynasty

Henry II	King of England (1154–89) and founder of the mighty Angevin realm
Eleanor of Aquitaine	Heiress to the duchy of Aquitaine and wife of Henry II
Henry the Young King	Eldest son and heir of Henry II and Eleanor, crowned as associate king in 1170; William Marshal's lord and patron
Richard the Lionheart	Duke of Aquitaine, count of Poitou and king of England (1189–99); one of the great warriors of his generation

John	Count of Mortain and king of England (1199–1216); Henry II's and Eleanor's youngest son – a divisive figure
Arthur of Brittany	Son of Geoffrey of Brittany and claimant to the Angevin realm in 1199
Henry III	Imperilled son and heir of King John (with Isabella of Angoulême); king of England (1216–72)

Capetian Dynasty

Philip II Augustus	King of France (1180–1223); son and heir of Louis VII; an able and ambitious monarch and the Angevins' arch-rival
Marguerite of France	Louis VII of France's daughter and wife of Henry the Young King
Prince Louis	Eldest son and heir of Philip II Augustus

Nobles, Knights & Courtiers

Patrick, earl of Salisbury	William Marshal's uncle (d. 1168)
William of Tancarville	Lord of the castle in Upper Normandy where William Marshal underwent his knightly training
Philip, count of Flanders	Powerful and unscrupulous nobleman, and noted devotee of the tournament circuit
William des Barres	Renowned French knight and servant of the Capetian dynasty
Baldwin of Béthune	William Marshal's peer and associate in the entourage of Henry the Young King and at the Angevin court
William des Roches	Servant of the Angevin dynasty who rose through the ranks, but ultimately switched allegiance under King John
Geoffrey FitzPeter	Administrator in the Angevin court who rose to become earl of Essex
John of Earley	William Marshal's loyal squire and knightly retainer

William Longchamp	Loyal servant to Richard the Lionheart and justiciar of England (for a time) during the king's absence on the Third Crusade
William FitzPatrick	Earl of Salisbury and William Marshal's cousin (d. 1196)
William Longsword	Illegitimate son of King Henry II and earl of Salisbury through marriage to the heiress Ela
Meiler FitzHenry	Justiciar of Ireland for King John
Robert FitzWalter	Prominent nobleman in England and leading scion of the baronial rebellion
William of Briouze	Prominent Marcher lord who found favour and then suffered ruination under King John

Churchmen

Hubert Walter	Bishop of Salisbury (from 1189), archbishop of Canterbury (from 1193 to 1205) and justiciar of England
Stephen Langton	Renowned theologian who became archbishop of Canterbury in 1213
Peter des Roches	Administrator, warrior and bishop of Winchester (from 1206)
Pandulf	Papal legate to England from 1211 and again from 1218
Guala of Bicchieri	Papal legate to England from 1216 to 1218

MARSHAL FAMILY TREE

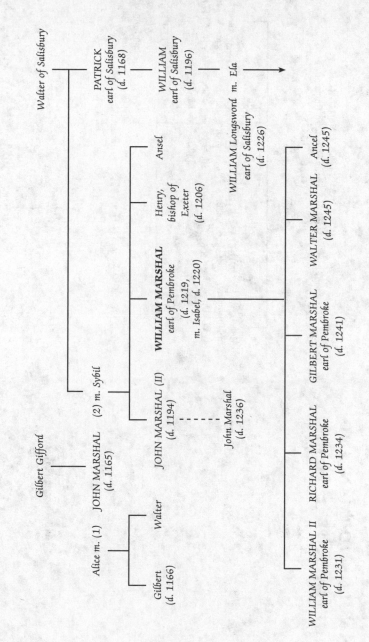

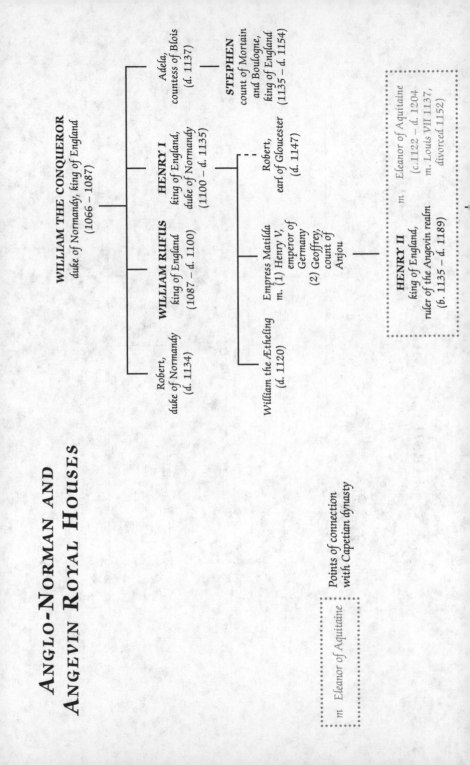

ANGLO-NORMAN AND ANGEVIN ROYAL HOUSES

WILLIAM THE CONQUEROR
duke of Normandy, king of England
(1066 – 1087)

Robert,
duke of Normandy
(d. 1134)

WILLIAM RUFUS
king of England
(1087 – d. 1100)

HENRY I
king of England,
duke of Normandy
(1100 – d. 1135)

Adela,
countess of Blois
(d. 1137)

STEPHEN
count of Mortain
and Boulogne,
king of England
(1135 – d. 1154)

William the Ætheling
(d. 1120)

Empress Matilda
m. (1) Henry V,
emperor of
Germany
(2) Geoffrey,
count of
Anjou

Robert,
earl of Gloucester
(d. 1147)

HENRY II
king of England,
ruler of the Angevin realm
(b. 1135 – d. 1189)

m. Eleanor of Aquitaine
(c.1122 – d. 1204
m. Louis VII 1137,
divorced 1152)

Points of connection
with Capetian dynasty

m. *Eleanor of Aquitaine*

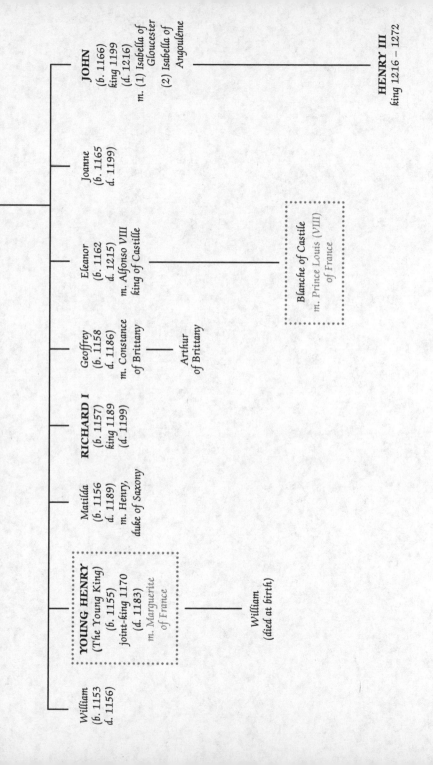

William
(b. 1153
d. 1156)

YOUNG HENRY
(The Young King)
(b. 1155)
joint-king 1170
(d. 1183)
m. Marguerite
of France

Matilda
(b. 1156
d. 1189)
m. Henry,
duke of Saxony

RICHARD I
(b. 1157)
king 1189
(d. 1199)

Geoffrey
(b. 1158
d. 1186)
m. Constance
of Brittany

Eleanor
(b. 1162
d. 1215)
m. Alfonso VIII
king of Castile

Joanne
(b. 1165
d. 1199)

JOHN
(b. 1166)
king 1199
(d. 1216)
m. (1) Isabella of
Gloucester
(2) Isabella of
Angoulême

William
(died at birth)

Arthur
of Brittany

Blanche of Castile
m. Prince Louis (VIII)
of France

HENRY III
king 1216 – 1272

END NOTES

Abbreviations

HWM   *History of William Marshal*, ed. & trans. A.J. Holden, S. Gregory & D. Crouch, 3 vols (2002–6).

ODNB   *Oxford Dictionary of National Biography*, ed. H.G.C. Mathew & B. Harrison (Oxford, 2004).

PREFACE

spoken in France in barbarian times (fifth to ninth centuries)'. Paul Meyer described his visit to Sotheby's and subsequent hunt for the mysterious 'Norman-French chronicle on English Affairs (in Verse)' in the article: 'L'Histoire de Guillaume le Maréchal, comte de Striguil et de Pembroke, régent d'Angleterre', *Romania*, vol. 12 (1883), pp. 22–74.

comte de Striguil et de Pembroke. P. Meyer (ed.), *L'Histoire de Guillaume le Maréchal, comte de Striguil et de Pembroke, régent d'Angleterre de 1216 à 1219*, 3 vols (Paris, 1891–1901).

Marshal had himself been fond of recounting. The manuscript of the *History of William Marshal* purchased by Thomas Phillipps and studied by Paul Meyer was eventually acquired by the Morgan Library in 1958 (where it is catalogued as M.888). This manuscript was used as the basis for the excellent modern edition and translation: *History of William*

Marshal, ed. & trans. A.J. Holden, S. Gregory & D. Crouch, 3 vols (2002–6). It is to this edition, hereafter cited as *HWM*, with line number(s) specified, to which all subsequent references to this source refer. See vol. 3, pp. 23–41, for David Crouch's illuminating discussion of the value and nature of this primary source.

Sidney Painter and David Crouch. The most important and authoritative accounts of William Marshal's life remain: S. Painter, *William Marshal: Knight Errant, Baron and Regent of England* (Baltimore, 1933); D. Crouch, *William Marshal: Knighthood, War and Chivalry, 1147–1219*, 2nd Edition (London, 2002). Crouch's work is particularly valuable because it was underpinned by the painstaking collation and analysis of all the primary source material relating to William Marshal's career, much of it in unedited form. There can be no doubt that, in academic terms, Crouch established the foundation (and set the bar) for all modern study of Marshal's life and influence. By contrast, George Duby's fanciful *Guillaume le Maréchal ou le meilleur chevalier du monde* (Paris, 1940) cannot be recommended.

PART I
CHILDHOOD & YOUTH: BECOMING A KNIGHT

young William was duly led away to face his fate. *HWM*, lines 513–16, 519–20. This book is divided into four parts, each reflecting a different stage of William Marshal's life. It should be noted that a number of methods for delineating the 'ages of man' were current in the Middle Ages, and not all conformed to the stages employed here.

that Christ and his saints were asleep'. *Gesta Stephani*, ed. & trans. K.R. Potter (Oxford, 1976), pp. 2–4; *Anglo-Saxon Chronicle*, ed. D. Whitelock, Revised Edition (London, 1965), p. 200.

William Rufus (1087–1100) and Henry I (1100–35). Among the most valuable overviews of this period are: R. Bartlett, *England under the Norman and Angevin Kings* (1075–1225) (Oxford, 2000); D. Carpenter, *The Struggle for Mastery: Britain 1066–1284* (London, 2004); N. Vincent, *A Brief History of Britain: The Birth of the Nation (1066–1485)* (London, 2011). D. Danziger & J. Gillingham, *1215: The Year of Magna*

Carta (London, 2003), is more focused, but illuminating and entertaining.

notorious in the history of the world'. William of Malmesbury, *Gesta Regum Anglorum*, ed. & trans. R.A.B. Mynors, R.M. Thomson & M. Winterbottom, vol. 1 (Oxford, 1998), pp. 758–62.

'enslaved by female seduction'. Henry of Huntingdon, *Historia Anglorum*, ed. & trans. D. Greenway (Oxford, 1996), p. 700.

his forceful and ambitious daughter Matilda. The seminal study of Matilda's career remains: M. Chibnall, *Empress Matilda* (Oxford, 1991). See also: M. Chibnall, 'Matilda', *Oxford Dictionary of National Biography*, ed. H.G.C. Mathew & B. Harrison (Oxford, 2004); H. Castor, *She-Wolves: The Women Who Ruled England Before Elizabeth* (London, 2010), pp. 39–126.

acknowledge Stephen as the new monarch. On King Stephen's reign and civil war see: R.H.C. Davis, *King Stephen (1135–54)*, 3rd Edition (London, 1990); J. Bradbury, *Stephen and Matilda: The Civil War of 1139–53* (Stroud, 1996); D. Matthew, *King Stephen* (London, 2002).

Stephen could manage neither. Walter Map, *De Nugis Curialium*, ed. & trans. M.R. James, rev. C.N.L. Brooke & R.A.B. Mynors (Oxford, 1983), p. 474; William of Malmesbury, *Historia Novella*, ed. E. King, trans. K.R. Potter (Oxford, 1998), p. 28.

the full penalties of the law'. J.A. Green, *The Government of England under Henry I* (Cambridge, 1986), p. 95; *Anglo-Saxon Chronicle*, pp. 197–203.

before things were settled'. *HWM*, lines 44–51.

managed to walk to safety. *HWM*, lines 167–276; Crouch, *William Marshal*, pp. 16–17.

extorting money and property from the Church. *HWM*, lines 316–18, 326–8; *Gesta Stephani*, p. 168; Painter, *William* Marshal, pp. 3–12; Crouch, *William Marshal*, pp. 12–23; D. Crouch, 'John Marshal', *ODNB*.

church in Flanders burned to death. *Gesta Stephani*, p. 92; William of Malmesbury, *Historia Novella*, pp. 74–6.

'a man of surprising subtlety'. *Gesta Stephani*, pp. 104–8; William of Malmesbury, *Historia Novella*, pp. 74–6.

He was given the name William. Painter, *William Marshal*, p. 9; Crouch, *William Marshal*, pp. 17–19.

these emotions were widely experienced. On medieval childhood see: S. Shahar, *Childhood in the Middle Ages* (London, 1990).

that, supposedly, was still standing. Gerald of Wales, *The Journey Through Wales and the Description of Wales*, trans. L. Thorpe (London, 1978), pp. 142–3; Crouch, *William Marshal*, pp. 20–1. On Gerald's career see: R. Bartlett, *Gerald of Wales: A Voice of the Middle Ages* (Oxford, 1982).

John's existing castle at Hamstead Marshall. D.J. Bonney & C.J. Dunn, 'Earthwork Castles & Settlement at Hamstead Marshall, Berkshire', *Cornwall to Caithness, Some Aspects of British Field Archaeology*, vol. 209 (1989), pp. 173–82.

a lull in the fighting followed. *HWM*, lines 399–466.

taken to the gallows for hanging'. *HWM*, lines 467–524; Painter, *William Marshal*, pp. 13–16; Crouch, *William Marshal*, pp. 20–1.

no reference to John Marshal's reaction. *HWM*, lines 525–710.

when his temper [was] aroused'. Peter of Blois, *'Epistolae'*, *Patrologia Latina*, ed. J.P. Migne, 221 vols. (Paris, 1844–64), vol. 207, pp. 48–9. On King Henry II and his accession see: W.L. Warren, *Henry II* (London, 1973); T.K. Keefe, 'Henry II', *ODNB*; E. Amt, *The Accession of Henry II in England: Royal Government Restored, 1149–1159* (Woodbridge, 1993); G.J. White, *Restoration and Reform, 1153–65: Recovery from Civil War in England* (Cambridge, 2000); C. Harper-Bill & N. Vincent (eds.), *Henry II: New Interpretations* (Woodbridge, 2007).

Marshal as a much older man. *HWM*, lines 712–36.

performed by a paid administrator). *Collectanea Topographica et Genealogica*, vol. 2 (London, 1835), pp. 163–4; Crouch, *William Marshal*, pp. 21–2.

was reapportioned in 1158. Crouch, *William Marshal*, p. 22.

as did his siblings. *HWM*, lines 737–68.

the land of his forefathers. On Normandy in this period see: D. Power, *The Norman Frontier in the Twelfth and Early Thirteenth Centuries* (Cambridge, 2004); D. Power, 'Henry duke of the Normans (1149/50–1189)', *Henry II: New Interpretations*, ed. C. Harper-Bill & N. Vincent (Woodbridge, 2007), pp. 85–128.

a very death to the envious'. Walter Map, p. 488.

to mould this warrior class. On the concept and practice of medieval knighthood, and the development of the aristocratic class see: M.H. Keen, *Chivalry* (New Haven & London, 1984); P. Coss, *The Knight in Medieval England, 1000–1400* (Stroud, 1993); R. Barber, *The Knight and Chivalry*, 2nd Edition (Woodbridge, 1995); D. Crouch, *The Image of the Aristocracy in Britain, 1000–1300* (London, 1992); D. Crouch, *The Birth of the Nobility: Constructing Aristocracy in England and France, 900–1300* (Harlow, 2005); D. Crouch, *The English Aristocracy, 1070–1272: A Social Transformation* (New Haven & London, 2011); N. Saul, *For Honour and Fame: Chivalry in England, 1066–1500* (London, 2011).

hold on to valiant knights'. *HWM*, lines 28–58.

a near-miraculous victory in 1099. On the First Crusade see: J.S.C. Riley-Smith, *The First Crusade and the Idea of Crusading* (London, 1986); J. France, *Victory in the East: A Military History of the First Crusade* (Cambridge, 1994); T. Asbridge, *The First Crusade: A New History* (London, 2004).

at Rockley, in Wilshire, in 1157. Crouch, *William Marshal*, p. 24. On the

Templar knights see: M. Barber, *The New Knighthood. A History of the Order of the Templars* (Cambridge, 1994); H. Nicholson, *The Knights Templar* (London, 2001)

to conquer Iberia from the Moors. For accessible translations of these two works see: *The Song of Roland*, trans. G. Burgess (London, 1990); *The Chanson d'Antioche*, trans. S.B. Edgington & C. Sweetenham (Aldershot, 2011).

tomb at Glastonbury in 1191. Geoffrey of Monmouth, *The History of the Kings of Britain*, trans. L. Thorpe (London, 1966); N.J. Higham, *King Arthur: Myth Making and History* (London, 2002), pp. 218–32; Saul, *For Honour and Fame*, pp. 39–59; M. Aurell, 'Henry II and Arthurian Legend', *Henry II: New Interpretations*, ed. C. Harper-Bill & N. Vincent (Woodbridge, 2007), pp. 362–94.

polish an otherwise underwhelming image. *HWM*, lines 769–804.

mistaken for bearded-Turks and accidently butchered. *HWM*, line 796; Daniel of Beccles, *Urbanus Magnus Danielis Becclesiensis*, ed. J. Gilbart Smyly (Dublin, 1939); Bartlett, *England under the Norman and Angevin Kings*, pp. 582–8; Danziger & Gillingham, *1215*, pp. 26–8; R. Bartlett, 'Symbolic Meanings of Hair in the Middle Ages', *Transactions of the Royal Historical Society*, vol. 4 (1994), pp. 43–60.

because he feared becoming fat. Walter Map, p. 476.

could 'engage in battle confidently'. Roger of Howden, *Chronica*, ed. W. Stubbs, 4 vols (London, 1868–71), II, pp. 166–7.

or a staggering 4,500 sheep. R.H.C. Davis, *The Medieval Warhorse* (London, 1989); A. Hyland, *The Medieval Warhorse: From Byzantium to the Crusades* (Stroud, 1994); P. Latimer, 'Early Thirteenth-Century Prices', *King John: New Interpretations*, ed. S.D. Church (Woodbridge, 1999), pp. 41–73.

like a blacksmith on iron'. *HWM*, lines 1002–3; E. Oakeshott, *The Sword in the Age of Chivalry*, 2nd Edition (London, 1981); E. Oakeshott, *Records of the Medieval Sword* (Woodbridge, 1991). I am also indebted to

Dr Tobias Capwell at the Wallace Collection, London, for his observations on medieval swords.

'crafted by that master Wayland'. John of Marmoutier, *'Historia Gaufredi ducis Normannorum et comitis Andegavorum'*, *Chroniques des Comtes d'Anjou et des Seigneurs d'Amboise*, ed. L. Halphen & R. Poupardin (Paris, 1913), pp. 179–80.

a first taste of real battle. *HWM*, lines 815–26; Keen, *Chivalry*, pp. 64–82; Crouch, *William Marshal*, p. 28.

as the real fighting began. *HWM*, lines 827–908; Painter, *William Marshal*, pp. 19–22; Crouch, *William Marshal*, pp. 32–6.

everyone broke into laughter. *HWM*, lines 909–1160.

prepared to seek his fortune. *HWM*, lines 1163–200.

PART II
ADULTHOOD: A KNIGHT IN SERVICE

the great craze of the day. On the history of medieval tournaments see: Keen, *Chivalry*, pp. 83–101; D. Crouch, *Tournament* (London, 2005); Crouch, *William Marshal*, pp. 192–9; R. Barber & J. Barker, *Tournaments: Jousts, Chivalry and Pageants in the Middle Ages* (Woodbridge, 1989).

it could not be tamed'. *HWM*, lines 1201–302. The story of the seemingly untameable mount may well be a literary topos.

'the handsomest knight of all'. *HWM*, lines 1303–28.

even the notion of celebrity. *HWM*, lines 2928–30; Crouch, *Tournament*, pp. 19–56.

('Go get them Châtillon'). Crouch, *William Marshal*, p. 48; Crouch, *Tournament*, pp. 74–5.

and no more than that.' *HWM*, lines 1329–80.

cannot be summoned when necessary'. Roger of Howden, *Chronica*, II, p. 166.

William 'let him go'. *HWM*, lines 1339–41.

like Lancelot fighting at tournaments. Keen, *Chivalry*, pp. 1–63, 102–24; C.S. Jaeger, *The Origins of Courtliness: Civilising Trends and the Formation of Courtly Ideals, 939–1210* (Philadelphia, 1985); M. Strickland, *War and Chivalry: The Conduct and Perception of War in England and Normandy, 1066–1217* (Cambridge, 1996); R.W. Kaeuper, *Chivalry and Violence in Medieval Europe* (Oxford, 1999); M. Aurell, *Le chevalier lettré: Savoir et conduite de l'aristocratie aux XIIe et XIIIe sieclès*, (Paris, 2006); Saul, *For Honour and Fame*, pp. 7–59.

fourteenth-century knight Geoffrey of Charny. R.W. Kaeuper & E. Kennedy, *The Book of Chivalry of Geoffroi de Charny: Text, Context and Translation* (Philadelphia, 1996); Geoffrey de Charny, *A Knight's Own Book of Chivalry*, trans. R.W. Kaeuper & E. Kennedy (Philadelphia, 2005).

began to spread through France. *HWM*, lines 1381–525.

tournament champions of his day'. Crouch, *Tournament*, p. 22; Painter, *William* Marshal, pp. 24–5; Crouch, *William Marshal*, pp. 36–7.

to see his worthy kin'. *HWM*, lines 1526–9.

another remarkable woman: Eleanor of Aquitaine. J. Martindale, 'Eleanor of Aquitaine', *ODNB*; B. Wheeler & J.C. Parsons (eds.), *Eleanor of Aquitaine: Lord and Lady* (Basingstoke, 2003); M. Bull & C. Léglu (eds.), *The World of Eleanor of Aquitaine* (Woodbridge, 2005); Castor, *She-Wolves*, pp. 131–222.

many of his supposed vassals. On King Louis VII of France and the Capetians see: R. Fawtier, *The Capetian Kings of France: Monarchy and Nation, 987–1328*, trans. L. Butler & R.J. Adam (London, 1960); E. Hallam, *Capetian France, 987–1328*, 2nd Edition (London, 2001);

J. Bradbury, *The Capetians: The History of a Dynasty* (London, 2007).

journey by horse or ship'. Peter of Blois, '*Epistolae*', *Patrologia Latina*, ed. J.P. Migne, 221 vols (Paris, 1844–64), vol 207, col. 197; Herbert of Bosham, '*Liber Melorum*', *Patrologia Latina*, ed. J.P. Migne, 221 vols (Paris, 1844–64), vol. 190, col. 1322; Ralph of Diss, *Opera Historica*, ed. W. Stubbs, 2 vols (London, 1876), I, p. 351. The Angevin realm was never formally constituted as an empire, but in light of its power and geographical extent, many modern historians having taken to describing it as such. J. Gillingham, *The Angevin Empire*, 2nd Edition (London, 2001); M Aurell, *The Plantagenet Empire*, 1154–1224, trans. D. Crouch (Harlow, 2007).

the dispute remained unresolved. On the career of Thomas Becket see: F. Barlow, 'Thomas Becket', *ODNB*; F. Barlow, *Thomas Becket* (London, 1986); A. Duggan, *Thomas Becket* (London, 2004).

pillaging as they went. *HWM*, lines 1568–76; J. Gillingham, *Richard I* (New Haven & London, 1999), pp. 30–8.

to a semblance of order. Robert of Torigni, 'The Chronicle of Robert of Torigni', *Chronicles of the Reigns of Stephen, Henry II and Richard I*, ed. R. Howlett, vol. 4 (London, 1889), pp. 235–6; *HWM*, lines 665–7. On the role and practice of raiding and *chevauchées* see: J. Gillingham, 'War and Chivalry in the History of William Marshal', *Thirteenth–Century England II*, ed. P. Coss & S. Lloyd (Woodbridge, 1988), p. 1–13; J. Gillingham, 'Richard I and the Science of War', *War and Government in the Middle Ages*, ed. J. Gillingham & J.C. Holt (Woodbridge, 1984), pp. 78–91; M. Strickland, *War and Chivalry*, pp. 258–90.

covered in blood'. *HWM*, lines 1619–720; Painter, *William Marshal*, pp. 26–7; Crouch, *William Marshal*, pp. 37–8.

for them in any spot'. *HWM*, lines 1741–6.

he was now 'in the gold'. *HWM*, lines 1721–888.

Henry II's fawning courtiers. *HWM*, lines 1893–4, 1905–22; Gerald of Wales, '*Topographica Hibernica*', *Opera*, vol. 5, ed. J.F. Dimock (London,

1867), p. 194. On the career of Henry the Young King see: O.H. Moore, *The Young King, Henry Plantagenet* (Ohio, 1925); E.Hallam, 'Henry the Young King', *ODNB*; M. Strickland, 'On the Instruction of a Prince: The Upbringing of Henry, the Young King', *Henry II: New Interpretations*, ed. C. Harper-Bill & N. Vincent (Woodbridge, 2007), pp. 184–214.

held without his daughter. *HWM*, lines 1910–22; A. Heslin [Duggan], 'The Coronation of the Young King in 1170', *Studies in Church History*, vol. 2 (London, 1965), pp. 165–78.

be they pagan or Christian'. *HWM*, lines 1950–8.

where Marshal's loyalties really lay. *HWM*, lines 1935–48; Gillingham, *Richard I*, pp. 24–51; Painter, *William* Marshal, pp. 31–2; Crouch, *William Marshal*, pp. 41–2.

to the business of state. E. Mason, '"Rocamadour in Quercy above all other churches": The Healing of Henry II', *Studies in Church History*, vol. 19 (Oxford, 1982), pp. 39–54.

He is England's forgotten king. Warren, *Henry II*, p. 580; Crouch, *William Marshal*, pp. 41–2, offered a similarly damning appraisal of Young Henry's character and capabilities.

Marshal presumably among them. *HWM*, lines 1967–74; Robert of Torigni, p. 253. King Henry II did pass through ports in England and Wales in this period, but did not return to England in any real sense.

reward for their loyal service. Roger of Howden, *Gesta Regis Henrici Secundi et Ricardi Primi*, ed. W. Stubbs, 2 vols. (London, 1867), I, p. 177; Strickland, 'On the Instruction of a Prince', pp. 194–5, 206–7.

his son's 'counsel and household'. William of Newburgh, 'Historia Rerum Anglicarum', *Chronicles of the Reigns of Stephen, Henry II and Richard I*, ed. R. Howlett, 2 vols. (London, 1884), I, p. 170; Robert of Torigni, pp. 255–6.

might turn on his master. Walter Map, p. 478.

the Old King's beloved empire. Roger of Howden, *Gesta Regis*, I, pp. 35–6, 41; Robert of Torigni, pp. 255–6; Geoffrey of Vigeois, *Chronique*, trans. F. Bonnélye (Tulle, 1864), p. 117.

an enemy of the state. M. Strickland, 'On the Instruction of a Prince', pp. 207–8; Roger of Howden, *Gesta Regis*, I, pp. 41–6; T.M. Jones, *War of the Generations: The Revolt of 1173–4* (Ann Arbor, 1980).

mere puppet manipulated by others. Warren, *Henry II*, pp. 118–21; Gillingham, *Richard I*, pp. 42–7.

seeds of a pitiless war. Jordan Fantosme, *Chronicle*, ed. R.C. Johnston (Oxford, 1981), lines 17–22.

anything else, just his chivalry'. *HWM*, lines 1975–2122; Painter, *William Marshal*, pp. 33–5; Crouch, *William Marshal*, p. 46.

in veneration of St Thomas. Ralph of Diss, I, pp. 382–3.

more in captivity in England. On the progress of the 1173–4 war see: Roger of Howden, *Gesta Regis*, I, pp. 41–79; Roger of Howden, *Chronica*, II, pp. 45–69; Ralph of Diss, I, pp. 355–87, 393–5; Robert of Torigni, pp. 255–65; William of Newburgh, 'Historia', I, pp. 172–97; *HWM*, lines 2123–384; Warren, *Henry II*, pp. 117–41.

tournament world, even in 1176. *HWM*, lines 2385–438; Roger of Howden, *Gesta Regis*, I, pp. 81–4, 91–9, 101–11; Painter, *William Marshal*, pp. 37–8; Crouch, *William Marshal*, pp. 44–6.

packing him off to Normandy. Roger of Howden, *Gesta Regis*, I, pp. 114–15, 120–3.

for it on his return. *HWM*, lines 2471–576; Painter, *William Marshal*, pp. 39–44; Crouch, *William Marshal*, pp. 192–9.

dishonesty was fair game. *HWM*, lines 2443–70, 2577–772.

drawn from the military household. R.J. Smith, 'Henry II's Heir: The *Acta* and the Seal of Henry the Young King, 1170–1183', *English*

Historical Review, vol. 116 (2001), pp. 297–326; Crouch, *William Marshal*, p. 42.

with Young Henry – seems authentic. *HWM*, lines 2773–874.

he accepted it nonetheless. *HWM*, lines 2875–3164.

the wretch had 'suffered enough'. *HWM*, lines 3180–380, 4319–430.

must have made a fortune. *HWM*, lines 3007–9, 3381–424, 6677–864. It has previously been suggested that Roger of Jouy fought in opposing tournament teams, but the *History of William Marshal* clearly stated that 'he belonged to the young king's household'. Crouch, *William Marshal*, pp. 193–4; Crouch, *Tournament*, p. 98.

in a rather unscrupulous manner. *HWM*, lines 3888–4284.

refusing anything to any man'. *HWM*, lines 2637–95, 3572–96, 5051–9.

that he had taken away. *HWM*, line 3603; Ralph of Diss, I, pp. 428; M. Strickland, 'On the Instruction of a Prince', pp. 187, 211–3; Crouch, *Tournament*, p. 23.

for the rest of his career. Crouch, *William Marshal*, p. 47.

this death in September 1180. On the career of Philip II Augustus see: J. Bradbury, *Philip Augustus: King of France, 1180–1223* (London, 1988).

clear for all to see. Robert of Torigni, p. 287; *HWM*, lines 4750–76; Crouch, *Tournament*, p. 24–5.

3,000 charging, battling knights. *HWM*, lines 4457–970; Painter, *William Marshal*, pp. 44–6; Crouch, *William Marshal*, p. 47, Crouch, *Tournament*, pp. 24, 36–7, 51, 76–7.

an additional 100 knights. Roger of Howden, *Chronica*, II, p. 266.

which Young Henry held rights. *Itinerarium Peregrinorum et Gesta Regis Ricardi, Chronicles and Memorials of the Reign of Richard I*, vol. 1, ed. W. Stubbs (London, 1864), p. 143. The seminal study of Richard the Lionheart's career remains: J. Gillingham, *Richard I* (New Haven & London, 1999). See also: Turner & R. Heiser, *The Reign of Richard the Lionheart: Ruler of the Angevin Empire* (London, 2000); J. Flori, *Richard the Lionheart: Knight and King* (London, 2007).

to his men to enjoy. Ralph of Diss, II, p. 19; Gervase of Canterbury, *Opera Historica*, ed. W. Stubbs, 2 vols. (London, 1879–80) I, p. 303; Roger of Howden, *Gesta Regis*, I, p. 292; Gillingham, *Richard I*, pp. 62–7. On the background to crusading history and events in the Holy Land see: T. Asbridge, *The Crusades: The War for the Holy Land* (London, 2010).

***Rex Henricus* – King Henry.** Geoffrey of Vigeois, 'Chronicon Lemovicense', *Recueil des Historiens des Gaules et de la France*, vol. 18, ed. M. Brial (Paris, 1879), p. 212.

may be the third man. HWM, lines 5109–60; Crouch, *William Marshal*, pp. 47–50; Smith, 'Henry II's Heir', pp. 300, 317–8, 323, 325,

him with all his heart'. HWM, lines 5161–434.

not caused an earlier rift. R.W. Kaeuper, 'William Marshal, Lancelot and the Issue of Chivalric Identity', *Essays in Medieval Studies*, vol. 22 (2005), pp. 1–19; L. Ashe, 'William Marshal, Lancelot and Arthur: Chivalry and Kingship', *Anglo–Norman Studies*, vol. 30 (2007), pp. 19–40. I am grateful to Laura Ashe for her insights and comments on the representation of William Marshal during this episode in the *History of William Marshal*; I. Short, 'Literary Culture at the Court of Henry II', *Henry II: New Interpretations*, ed. C. Harper–Bill & N. Vincent (Woodbridge, 2007), pp. 335–61.

he was man or no'. Danziger & Gillingham, *1215*, pp. 30, 89–93; Walter Map, pp. 210–14.

of these events remains hidden. HWM, lines 5435–90; Roger of Howden, *Chronica*, II, pp. 82–3; Ralph of Diss, I, p. 402; Crouch, *Tournament*, pp. 105–9; Crouch, *William Marshal*, pp. 48–50.

King's household had been reordered. HWM, lines 5491–652;

Smith, 'Henry II's Heir', pp. 321–2; Crouch, *William Marshal*, p. 50.

His exile had begun. *HWM*, lines 5693–848; Walter Map, pp. 488–90; R. Bartlett, *Trial by Fire and Water: The Medieval Judicial Ordeal* (Oxford, 1988).

a bloody war in Aquitaine. *HWM*, lines 5849–6305, 6527–606; Painter, *William Marshal*, pp. 49–51; Crouch, *William Marshal*, p. 52.

playing a dangerous, unpredictable game. Roger of Howden, *Gesta Regis*, I, p. 294; Warren, *Henry II*, pp. 580–7; Gillingham, *Richard I*, pp. 69–72.

brother as his liege lord'. Ralph of Diss, II, pp. 18–19; Roger of Howden, *Gesta Regis*, I, p. 295; Roger of Howden, *Chronica*, II, pp. 273–5; William of Newburgh, '*Historia*', I, p. 233; *HWM*, lines 6309–52.

was not to be trusted. Gerald of Wales, '*Topographica Hibernica*', p. 200. Roger of Howden, *Gesta Regis*, I, p. 297, described Geoffrey as the 'son of perdition'.

would now back the Lionheart. Roger of Howden, *Gesta Regis*, I, p. 296; Roger of Howden, *Chronica*, II, p. 275; Warren, *Henry II*, pp. 590–3; Gillingham, *Richard I*, pp. 72–3.

Marshal with all possible haste. *HWM*, lines 6353–552; Painter, *William Marshal*, p. 50; Crouch, *William Marshal*, p. 52.

unconscious and died soon thereafter. *HWM*, lines 6607–988; Roger of Howden, *Gesta Regis*, I, pp. 297–301; Roger of Howden, *Chronica*, II, pp. 276–9; Geoffrey of Vigeois, '*Chronicon Lemovicense*', pp. 214–7; Robert of Torigni, pp. 305–6; Ralph of Diss, II, p. 19; William of Newburgh, '*Historia*', I, pp. 233–4; Painter, *William Marshal*, pp. 53–4; Crouch, *William Marshal*, pp. 52–3.

Henry II later settled the arrears. *HWM*, lines 6989–7155; Roger of Howden, *Gesta Regis*, I, pp. 301–2; Roger of Howden, *Chronica*, II, pp. 279–80. Howden reworked the representation of King Henry II's reaction to his eldest son's death between the writing of the *Gesta* and the *Chronica*.

It would not be his last. Ralph of Diss, II, pp. 20; Robert of Torigni, p. 306; William of Newburgh, '*Historia*', I, p. 234; *HWM*, lines 7157–84.

all the world went begging'. Walter Map, pp. 278–82; Gerald of Wales, '*Topographica Hibernica*', pp. 194–5; Bertrand of Born, *The Poems of the Troubadour Bertan de Born*, ed. W.D. Padern, T. Sankovitch & P.H. Stabelin (Berkeley, 1986), pp. 215–23; Gervasc of Tilbury, *Otia Imperialia*, ed. & trans. S.E. Banks & J.W. Binns (Oxford, 2002), pp. 486–7; M. Strickland, 'On the Instruction of a Prince', pp. 186–7, 214; Crouch, *William Marshal*, pp. 53–5.

prolonged, perhaps even permanent, absence. *HWM*, lines 7233–74; Crouch, *William Marshal*, pp. 55–6.

thoughts of a Levantine future. For the history of the crusader states in this period see: B. Hamilton, *The Leper King and his heirs: Baldwin IV and the crusader kingdom of Jerusalem* (2000); B. Hamilton, 'The Elephant of Christ: Reynald of Châtillon', *Studies in Church History*, vol. 15 (1978), pp. 97–108; R.C. Smail, 'The predicaments of Guy of Lusignan, 1183–87', *Outremer*, ed. B.Z. Kedar, H.E. Mayer & R.C. Smail (Jerusalem, 1982), pp. 159–76.

their midst, victory was assured. *HWM*, lines 7292–4; A.J. Boas, *Jerusalem in the Time of the Crusades* (London, 2001); Asbridge, *The Crusades*, pp. 104, 120–1.

the destructive storm of 1187 broke. *HWM*, lines 7275–99; Painter, *William Marshal*, pp. 55–6; Crouch, *William Marshal*, pp. 55–6.

of inciting a massive reprisal. Hamilton, *The Leper King*, pp. 186–217; Asbridge, *The Crusades*, pp. 285–336.

to this rather disreputable raid. Hamilton, *The Leper King*, pp. 198–204; *HWM*, line 7290; Crouch, *William Marshal*, p. 57, n. 1.

mounting evidence of imminent collapse. Hamilton, *The Leper King*, pp. 211–4; William of Tyre, *Chronicon*, ed. R.B.C. Huygens, 2 vols. (Turnhout, 1986), pp. 1061–2.

his own day of judgement. *HWM*, lines 18184, 18201–26, 18231–6.

which the Angevins could not ignore. On the background to, and launching of, the Third Crusade see: Asbridge, *The Crusades*, pp. 337–80.

PART III
MIDDLE AGE: A LORD OF THE REALM

and access to crown favour. *HWM*, lines 7302–11; Painter, *William Marshal*, p. 61; Crouch, *William Marshal*, p. 57.

feared again in the future'. Walter Map, p. 374; N. Vincent, 'The Court of Henry II', *Henry II: New Interpretations*, ed. C. Harper-Bill & N. Vincent (Woodbridge, 2007), pp. 278–334.

a total cost of some £6,500. Danziger & Gillingham, *1215*, pp. 16–19; Warren, *Henry II*, p. 234.

leave nothing untouched and untried'. Vincent, 'The Court of Henry II', pp. 319–33; Walter Map, pp. 2, 12–26.

remember everyone's name and station. Walter Map, pp. 2, 25.

implied and nothing said openly. *HWM*, lines 525–654, 2875–3173; Crouch, *William Marshal*, pp. 183–92.

and dependence upon, these retainers. Crouch, *William Marshal*, pp. 57–8, 167–8; F.J. West, 'Geoffrey fitz Peter', *ODNB*; R.V. Turner, *Men Raised from the Dust: Administrative Service and Upward Mobility in Angevin England* (Philadelphia, 1988).

hand to secure other advantages. *HWM*, lines 7312–18; Painter, *William Marshal*, p. 61; Crouch, *William Marshal*, p. 59.

prominent feature of William's life. *HWM*, lines 7948–50; Crouch, *William Marshal*, pp. 59, 161–3; D. Crouch, 'John of Earley', *ODNB*.

by way of recompense. *HWM*, lines 7304–18; Crouch, *William Marshal*, pp. 59–61; N. Vincent, 'William Marshal, King Henry II and the Honour of Châteauroux', *Archives*, vol. 25 (2000), pp. 1–15.

the Lionheart in his place. Gillingham, *Richard I*, pp. 76–82.

only be secured at a price. Gillingham, *Richard I*, pp. 82–5.

children to become a crusader'. *HWM*, lines 7319–40; Asbridge, *The Crusades*, pp. 337–64.

back to the French heartlands. *HWM*, lines 7348–67.

have been 'full of grief'. Roger of Howden, *Gesta Regis*, II, pp. 45–6; *HWM*, lines 7782–840.

grim feature of medieval warfare. Jordan Fantosme, lines 439–50; *HWM*, lines 7882–910; Gillingham, *Richard I*, pp. 93–4; Gillingham, 'War and Chivalry in the History of William Marshal', pp. 5–6.

the Angevin realm by force. *HWM*, lines 8065–188. This is a simplification of a more convoluted period of intrigue and negotiation. For a fuller outline see: Warren, *Henry II*, pp. 619–22; Gillingham, *Richard I*, pp. 94–8.

this] cruel act of treachery'. *HWM*, lines 8189–261.

and had to return empty–handed. *HWM*, lines 8262–332.

Marshal remained at Henry's side. *HWM*, lines 8303–10; Painter, *William Marshal*, pp. 66–7; Crouch, *William Marshal*, pp. 62–3.

'they withdrew as enemies'. *HWM*, lines 8345–58; Ralph of Diss, II, p. 62.

would never abandon the city. *HWM*, lines 8361–82; Roger of Howden, *Chronica*, II, pp. 363–4; A. Bouton, *Le Maine: Histoire économique et sociale* (Le Mans, 1962), pp. 444–7.

heading 'straight for Le Mans'. *HWM*, lines 8383–473.

his arm in the process. *HWM*, lines 8475–712; Roger of Howden, *Chronica*, II, pp. 363–4; Painter, *William Marshal*, pp. 68–70; Warren, *Henry II*, p. 623; Crouch, *William Marshal*, pp. 63–4.

ordered William to return to his side. *HWM*, lines 8713–914; Gerald of Wales, 'De Principis Instructione Liber', *Opera*, vol. 8, ed. G.F. Warner (London, 1891), p. 286; Gillingham, *Richard I*, pp. 98–9; Crouch, *William Marshal*, pp. 64–5. It should be noted that William Marshal removed his own hauberk before riding from Le Mans and thus was himself unarmoured by the time of his confrontation with Richard the Lionheart [*HWM*, lines 8791–5].

then became a livid colour'. *HWM*, lines 8915–80.

a shroud and sing Mass. *HWM*, lines 8981–9290; Roger of Howden, *Gesta Regis*, II, pp. 69–71; Roger of Howden, *Chronica*, II, pp. 365–7; Ralph of Diss, II, p. 64–5; Warren, *Henry II*, pp. 625–6; Gillingham, *Richard I*, pp. 99–100; Crouch, *William Marshal*, pp. 65–6.

with you over that matter.' *HWM*, lines 9291–346.

for the north almost immediately. *HWM*, lines 9347–409; Gillingham, *Richard I*, p. 101.

made plans for their wedding. *HWM*, lines 9439–522; Painter, *William Marshal*, pp. 73–6; Crouch, *William Marshal*, pp. 66–8.

quacks, belly dancers [and] sorcerers'. Danziger & Gillingham, 1215, pp. 57–64.

the maelstrom of power politics. *HWM*, lines 9523–50; Painter, *William Marshal*, pp. 76–9; Crouch, *William Marshal*, pp. 68–71.

were bought for this occasion. Roger of Howden, *Gesta Regis*, II, pp. 78–83; Gillingham, *Richard I*, pp. 107–9.

precursor to the white feather. Roger of Howden, *Gesta Regis*, II, pp. 155–6; Roger of Howden, *Chronica*, III, pp. 93–4; *HWM*, lines 9699–710; Gillingham, *Richard I*, p. 140; Asbridge, *The Crusades*, pp. 368–88.

kingdom to rule on his return. *HWM*, lines 9551–736. This account represents a significant simplification of the process by which justiciars and co-justiciars were appointed. For a more detailed examination of these events see: Gillingham, *Richard I*, pp. 109–22; J.T. Appleby, *England Without Richard, 1189–99* (London, 1965), pp. 1–55.

a close association with the abbey. On the Cistercians see: J. Burton & J. Kerr, *The Cistercians in the Middle Ages* (Woodbridge, 2011).

creating a truly impressive fortification. R. Avent, 'William Marshal's building works at Chepstow Castle, Monmouthshire, 1189–1291', *The Medieval Castle in Ireland and Wales*, ed. J.R. Kenyon & Kieran O'Conor (Dublin, 2003), pp. 50–71; R. Turner & A. Johnson (eds.), *Chepstow Castle: Its History and Buildings* (Almeley, 2006).

a few would betray his trust. Crouch, *William Marshal*, pp. 143–58, 217–25.

more than a decade earlier. Crouch, *William* Marshal, pp. 88, 175, argued that this Basilia was Strongbow's sister (born in 1116), but she appears to have been her namesake, Strongbow's illegitimate daughter.

amassed a considerable fortune. Painter, *William Marshal*, p. 49; Crouch, *William Marshal*, pp. 52, 66, 152–7.

on William's heart and soul. Crouch, *William Marshal*, pp. 72–3, 211–12.

Longchamp should the need arise. *HWM*, lines 9766–76.

whether he would ever return. Asbridge, *The Crusades*, pp. 398–445.

summer and early autumn of 1191. Richard of Devizes, *Chronicon*, ed. & trans. J.T. Appleby (London, 1963), pp. 44–6; *HWM*, lines 9784–5; Roger of Howden, *Gesta Regis*, II, pp. 207–15.

of self-service seems undeniable. Roger of Howden, *Gesta Regis*, II, pp. 219–20; *HWM*, lines 9859–76; Gillingham, *Richard I*, pp. 227–9; Crouch, *William Marshal*, pp. 76–80.

a permanent corps of bodyguards. Gillingham, *Richard I*, pp. 226–9; Asbridge, *The Crusades*, pp. 446–9.

they were European Christians. Roger of Howden, *Gesta Regis*, II, pp. 235–7; Gillingham, *Richard I*, pp. 222–35; Appleby, *England Without Richard*, pp. 99–106.

free to wreak havoc in France. *HWM*, lines 9807–23; Richard of Devizes, pp. 46–7; Asbridge, *The Crusades*, pp. 444–516. For the detail of King Richard's period in captivity and the process by which he was transferred into the hands of Emperor Henry VI of Germany see: Gillingham, *Richard I*, pp. 222–53.

servant of the crown. Roger of Howden, *Chronica*, III, pp. 204–5; *HWM*, lines 9877–10011; Appleby, *England Without Richard*, pp. 107–11.

finally seemed to be turning. *HWM*, lines 9883–964; Roger of Howden, *Chronica*, III, pp. 216–17.

'thought him a fool'. *HWM*, lines 10168–70.

his own name by association. *HWM*, lines 10020–80; Painter, *William Marshal*, pp. 101–5; Crouch, *William Marshal*, pp. 80–2.

office of royal master–marshal. *HWM*, lines 10081–152; Painter, *William Marshal*, pp. 102–3.

the other flayed alive. *HWM*, lines 10153–288; Gillingham, *Richard I*, pp. 269–70.

He would never return. *HWM*, lines 10289–354; Roger of Howden, *Chronica*, III, p. 251.

his brother John found him. *HWM*, lines 10355–72, 10432–52.

serve in his brother's army. *HWM*, lines 10373–425.

steadfast defence they had mounted. *HWM*, lines 10453–508; Ralph of Diss, II, pp. 114–15.

he might recover some favour. Rigord, 'Gesta Philippi Augusti', *Oeuvres de Rigord et Guillaume le Breton, historiens de Philippe Auguste*, ed. H–F. Delaborde, vol. 1 (Paris, 1882), p. 127; William the Breton, 'Gesta Philippi Augusti', *Oeuvres de Rigord et Guillaume le Breton, historiens de Philippe Auguste*, ed. H–F. Delaborde, vol. 1 (Paris, 1882), p. 196; M. Powicke, *The Loss of Normandy, 1189–1204* (Manchester, 1913), p.101; Strickland, *War and Chivalry*, p. 223.

the love of his brother'. *HWM*, lines 10423–5; William of Newburgh, 'Historia', II, p. 424.

the ground for future reward. *HWM*, lines 10289–340; Painter, *William Marshal*, pp. 106–7; Crouch, *William Marshal*, pp. 78–80.

and taking 220 prisoners. Ralph of Diss, II, pp. 116–17; Roger of Howden, *Chronica*, III, pp. 252–3.

special commendation from his king. *HWM*, lines 10581–676.

and enjoyed considerable favour. Painter, *William Marshal*, pp. 116–17; Crouch, *William Marshal*, pp. 82–4.

Capetian interests in northern France. *HWM*, lines 10745–72; Roger of Howden, *Chronica*, IV, pp. 19–20; Ralph of Diss, II, pp. 152–3; Crouch, *William Marshal*, p. 84.

more damaging to the French. *HWM*, lines 11351–688.

younger men from earning renown. *HWM*, lines 11117–286; Roger of Howden, *Chronica*, IV, p. 16; Ralph of Diss, II, p. 152.

outbreak of unrest in Aquitaine. *HWM*, lines 10579–80, 11680–6, 11727–45; Gillingham, *Richard I*, pp. 301–20.

who that successor might be? *HWM*, lines 11751–832; Roger of Howden, *Chronica*, IV, pp. 82–5; Gillingham, *Richard I*, pp. 321–34.

what you are doing now'. *HWM*, lines 11776–908; Crouch, *William Marshal*, p. 85.

PART IV
OLD AGE: ENGLAND'S GREAT MAGNATE

support of the English nobility. *HWM*, lines 11908–45; Roger of Howden, *Chronica*, IV, pp. 86–8.

associate of the Marshal family. M. Strickland, 'William Longspée', *ODNB*.

eased John's path to power. Roger of Howden, *Chronica*, IV, p. 88.

first years of John's reign. *HWM*, lines 11943–5; Crouch, *William Marshal*, pp. 85–6.

the royal feast that evening. Roger of Howden, *Chronica*, IV, p. 90.

confident, attempt at understatement. Crouch, *William Marshal*, p. 200.

achieving a form of immortality. *HWM*, line 11944; Painter, *William Marshal*, pp. 122–4; Crouch, *William Marshal*, pp. 86–8, 94.

to be an easy king to follow. R.V. Turner, 'William (III) de Briouze', *ODNB*.

and purpose to his behaviour. On the reign of King John see: W.L. Warren, *King John*, 2nd Edition (New Haven & London, 1978); R.V. Turner, *King John* (London, 1994); S.D. Church (ed.), *King John: New Interpretations* (Woodbridge, 1999); J. Gillingham, 'John', *ODNB*.

'enemy of nature' by contemporaries. Ralph of Diss, II, pp. 170–4; William of Newburgh, '*Historia*', p. 402; Warren, *King John*, pp. 1–16; Danziger & Gillingham, *1215*, pp. 103–5.

rewards without cause or warning. *HWM*, lines 12582–4.

The chance had been missed. Roger of Howden, *Chronica*, IV, pp. 96–7.

incapable of matching his opponent. Adam of Eynsham, *Magna Vita Sancti Hugonis*, ed. J.F. Dimock (London, 1864), p. 332; *HWM*, lines 12027–30.

little brother – John 'Softsword'. On the Treaty of Le Goulet see: Warren, *King John*, pp. 54–63.

making another significant diplomatic blunder. Painter, *William Marshal*, pp. 125–8; Crouch, *William Marshal*, pp. 90–1.

contentedly as it snapped shut. Roger of Howden, *Chronica*, IV, p. 119; Ralph of Diss, II, p. 170; N. Vincent, 'Isabella of Angoulême: John's Jezebel', *King John: New Interpretations*, ed. S.D. Church (Woodbridge, 1999), pp. 165–219.

no small quantity of fine wine. *HWM*, lines 12059–404; Warren, *King John*, pp. 76–80.

the crisis had barely begun. *HWM*, lines 12500–12.

Arthur of Brittany was not seen again. Ralph of Coggeshall, *Radulphi de Coggeshall Chronicon Anglicanum*, ed. J. Stevenson (London, 1875), pp. 139–41; 'Annals of Margam', *Annales Monastici*, vol. I, ed. H.R Luard (London, 1864), p. 27.

William Marshal's military career. William the Breton, '*Gesta Philippi Augusti*', pp. 213–6; Painter, *William Marshal*, pp. 133–5; Crouch, *William Marshal*, pp. 91–2.

that Normandy was now lost. *HWM*, lines 12674–704, 12783–92; Ralph of Coggeshall, p. 144; Painter, *William Marshal*, pp. 135–6.

of landholding was unavoidable. Warren, *King John*, pp. 93–9; M. Powicke, *The Loss of Normandy, 1189–1204* (Manchester, 1913).

'Softsword' seems to have waivered. *HWM*, lines 12854–904; Ralph of Coggeshall, pp. 144–5; Painter, *William Marshal*, pp. 137–8; Crouch, *William Marshal*, p. 93.

the king for a long time'. *HWM*, lines 12944–13090; *Layettes du Trésor des Chartes*, ed. M.A. Teulet (Paris, 1863), p. 499, n. 1397; Painter, *William Marshal*, pp. 138–41; Crouch, *William Marshal*, pp. 94–6.

who had assembled at Portsmouth. Ralph of Coggeshall, pp. 152–4; *HWM*, lines 13091–270; Painter, *William Marshal*, pp. 141–3; Crouch, *William Marshal*, p. 96.

to look to the west. *HWM*, lines 13271–8; Painter, *William Marshal*, pp. 143–4; Crouch, *William Marshal*, pp. 97–100.

centre of trade and commerce. R. Eales, 'Ranulf (III) of Chester', *ODNB*.

Gerald of Wales' own mixed heritage. *Gesta Stephani*, p. 14; Gerald of Wales, *The Journey Through Wales*, pp. 233–44, 255–64. On the history of medieval Wales see: D. Walker, *Medieval Wales* (Cambridge, 1990); R.R. Davies, *The Age of Conquest: Wales, 1063–1415*, 2nd Edition (Oxford, 2000).

little in the Wild West. Gerald of Wales, *The Journey Through Wales*, p. 236. On medieval Ireland see: S. Duffy, *Ireland in the Middle Ages* (London, 1997).

they were 'surging with currents'. Gerald of Wales, *The Journey Through Wales*, pp. 147–56, 168–9; Gerald of Wales, *The History and Topography of Ireland*, trans. J.J. O'Meara (London, 1982), p. 58; Crouch, *William Marshal*, pp. 86–7, 93–4.

for the term of one year. Gerald of Wales, *The History and Topography of Ireland*, pp. 34–5, 53–5; Crouch, *William Marshal*, pp. 87–9.

of mixed Norman-Irish birth. Crouch, *William Marshal*, pp. 100–3, 218, 222–3.

Isabel had arrived in Ireland. *HWM*, lines 13311–422; Painter, *William Marshal*, pp. 145–8; Crouch, *William Marshal*, pp. 102–3.

thwart William at every step. M.T. Flanagan, 'Meiler fitz Henry', *ODNB*; Crouch, *William Marshal*, pp. 102–4.

judgement over the disputed territory. *Rotuli Litterarum Patentium in turri Londinensi asservati*, ed. T.D. Hardy (London, 1835), p. 72; Crouch, *William Marshal*, pp. 104–5.

the Marshal dynasty from Leinster. *HWM*, lines 13429–61; Painter, *William Marshal*, pp. 154–5; Crouch, *William Marshal*, p. 105.

to be a dreadful miscalculation. *HWM*, lines 13462–550.

remained steadfast beside the earl. *HWM*, lines 13551–4, 13575–84; *Rotuli Chartarum*, ed. T.D. Hardy (London, 1837), pp. 171–3; Painter, *William Marshal*, p. 156; Crouch, *William Marshal*, pp. 105–6.

was 'greatly aggrieved at heart'. *HWM*, lines 13585–675, 13787–866.

scale [fought] throughout that land'. *HWM*, lines 13555–74.

'shame lasts longer than destitution'. *HWM*, lines 13676–762.

would not accept other pledges'. *HWM*, lines 13763–86, 13867–88; Painter, *William Marshal*, p. 157; Crouch, *William Marshal*, pp. 106–11.

clear in the starkest terms. *HWM*, lines 13889–937; *Rotuli Chartarum*, p. 176; *Rotuli Litterarum Patentium*, p. 80; Crouch, *William Marshal*, pp. 111–12.

looking on from the sidelines. *HWM*, lines 13941–14116, 14433–46. Crouch, *William Marshal*, pp. 112–14, offered a more damning appraisal of Marshal's treatment of Meiler.

in pursuit of a different quarry. Painter, *William Marshal*, pp. 167–8; Crouch, *William Marshal*, pp. 113–15.

a calamitous rift opened. *HWM*, lines 13585–98; Roger of Wendover, *Chronica Rogeri de Wendover liber qui dicitur Flores Historiarum*, ed. H.G. Hewlett, 3 vols. (London, 1886–9), II, pp. 48–9.

this dispute without undue penalty. *HWM*, lines 14136–232.

the flesh of his cheeks. Turner, 'William (III) de Briouze', *ODNB*; S. Duffy, 'John and Ireland', *King John: New Interpretations*, ed. S.D. Church (Woodbridge, 1999), pp. 221–45.

were drawing to a close. *HWM*, lines 14233–484; *Rotuli Litterarum Patentium*, p. 98; Painter, *William Marshal*, pp. 161–70; Crouch, *William Marshal*, pp. 115–16.

and the 'most evil robber'. N. Vincent, 'Peter des Roches', *ODNB*; N. Vincent, *Peter des Roches: An Alien in English Politics, 1205–1238* (Cambridge, 1996); D. Power, 'Falkes de Bréauté', *ODNB*.

gifted ammunition to his opponents. Warren, *King John*, pp. 154–73. On the pontificate of Innocent III see: J. Sayers, *Innocent III: Leader of Europe* (London, 1994); J.M. Powell (ed.), *Pope Inncoent III: Vicar of Christ or Lord of the World?* (Washington, DC, 1994).

according to one chronicler. 'Annals of Barnwell Priory', *Memoriae Walteri de Coventria*, vol. II, ed. W. Stubbs (London, 1873), p. 207; Roger of Wendover, II, pp. 61, 63. The classic study of the Baronial rebellion remains: J.C. Holt, *The Northerners: A Study in the Reign of King John* (Cambridge, 1961).

extended to a former opponent. *Rotuli Litterarum Clausarum, 1204–27*, vol. I, ed. T.D. Hardy (London, 1833), p. 132; Crouch, *William Marshal*, pp. 116–18.

turned irrevocably against the king. *HWM*, lines 14588–90; Painter, *William Marshal*, pp. 172–4, 176–7; Crouch, *William Marshal*, pp. 118–19.

from the brink of disaster. *HWM*, lines 14629–32; Painter, *William Marshal*, pp. 174–6; Crouch, *William Marshal*, p. 119.

would reshape William Marshal's career. Warren, *King John*, pp. 217–24; Brabury, *Philip Augustus*, pp. 279–315; Holt, *The Northerners*, p. 100.

the Great Charter or Magna Carta. J.C. Holt, *Magna Carta*, 2nd Edition (Cambridge, 1992); N. Vincent, *Magna Carta: A Very Short Introduction* (Oxford, 2012).

Hubert of Burgh and John Marshal. Holt, *Magna Carta*, pp. 448–73.

conceived by a single mind. Painter, *William Marshal*, pp. 119–21; Crouch, *William Marshal*, pp. 178–82.

at best, with ambivalence. Matthew Paris, *Chronica Majora*, ed. H.R. Luard, 7 vols. (London, 1872–84), II, pp. 604–5; Painter, *William Marshal*, p. 180; Crouch, *William Marshal*, p. 122.

civil war was inevitable. Holt, *Magna Carta*, pp. 448–73; Vincent, *Magna Carta*, pp. 58–84.

Stephen's reign, seventy years earlier. Roger of Wendover, II, pp. 170–2.

the Capetian monarch remained resolute. Gerald of Wales, '*De Principis Instructione*', pp. 326–9; *HWM*, lines 15061–70, 15097–108; Painter, *William Marshal*, pp. 185–6; Crouch, *William Marshal*, pp. 122–3; D. Carpenter, *The Minority of Henry III* (London, 1990), pp. 5–12.

had familial ties to France. Painter, *William Marshal*, pp. 186–7; Crouch, *William Marshal*, p. 123.

to 'his lord and king'. *HWM*, lines 15117–28.

to Marlborough Castle were blocked. *Rotuli Litterarum Patentium*, p. 175; Painter, *William Marshal*, pp. 185–6; Crouch, *William Marshal*, pp. 121–2.

Marshal's fidelity was yet to come. *HWM*, lines 15135–8; Painter, *William Marshal*, pp. 188–9.

by the presence of John'. *HWM*, lines 15143–206; Matthew Paris, *Chronica Majora*, II, p. 669; Crouch, *William Marshal*, pp. 123–4.

could not be long postponed. *HWM*, lines 15185–91, 15207–28; S.D. Church, 'King John's Testament and the Last Days of his Reign', *English Historical Review*, vol. 125 (2010), pp. 505–28.

for the last five decades. *HWM*, lines 15229–84; Painter, *William Marshal*, p. 192; Crouch, *William Marshal*, p. 192.

William retired to his rooms. *HWM*, lines 15287–397; Painter, *William Marshal*, pp. 192–5; Crouch, *William Marshal*, pp. 125–6; Carpenter, *The Minority of Henry III*, pp. 13–14.

difficult for you to endure'. *HWM*, lines 15398–464.

whatever it may cost me'. *HWM*, lines 15465–561; Painter, *William Marshal*, pp. 195–6; Crouch, *William Marshal*, p. 126.

to beg for my bread.' *Patent Rolls of the Reign of Henry III* (London, 1901), p. 10; *HWM*, lines 15562–708; Painter, *William Marshal*, pp. 196–7; Crouch, *William Marshal*, pp. 126–7; Carpenter, *The Minority of Henry III*, pp. 15–17, 32.

prospects in the civil war. Painter, *William Marshal*, pp. 197–8; Crouch, *William Marshal*, p. 127; Carpenter, *The Minority of Henry III*, pp. 17–22.

a swift and decisive confrontation. Carpenter, *The Minority of Henry III*, pp. 22–6; Painter, *William Marshal*, pp. 198–205; Crouch, *William Marshal*, pp. 127–8; Vincent, *Magna Carta*, pp. 82–6.

if they were to prevail. 'Annals of Barnwell Priory', p. 236; Carpenter, *The Minority of Henry III*, pp. 26–35; Crouch, *William Marshal*, pp. 128–9; C. Tyerman, *England and the Crusades* (Chicago, 1988), pp. 133–42.

'play for the highest stakes'. *HWM*, lines 16085–130, 16168; Painter, *William Marshal*, pp. 211–13; Crouch, *William Marshal*, pp. 128–9; Carpenter, *The Minority of Henry III*, pp. 35–6.

steadfast courage and ruthless ferocity. *HWM*, lines 16131–235.

the French 'down to Hell'. *HWM*, lines 16236–304; Crouch, *William Marshal*, pp. 129–30; Carpenter, *The Minority of Henry III*, pp. 36–7; F. Hill, *Medieval Lincoln* (Cambridge, 1965).

and the assault began. *HWM*, lines 16305–604; Carpenter, *The Minority of Henry III*, pp. 37–9; Crouch, *William Marshal*, pp. 131–2.

hard-pressed to hold his own. Roger of Wendover, II, pp. 215–16; *HWM*, lines 16605–85.

Thomas] died in this manner'. *HWM*, lines 16686–768; Painter, *William Marshal*, p. 218; Crouch, *William Marshal*, p. 133. Thomas of Perche was William Marshal's distant cousin, as Thomas' great grandmother had been Hawise of Salisbury, William's aunt.

civil war had been turned. *HWM*, lines 16769–17068; Roger of Wendover, II, pp. 216–19; Carpenter, *The Minority of Henry III*, p. 40.

invader set sail for France. *HWM*, lines 17069–726; Carpenter, *The Minority of Henry III*, pp. 40–9; Painter, *William Marshal*, pp. 219–25; Crouch, *William Marshal*, pp. 133–4; S. McGlynn, *Blood Cries Afar: The Forgotten Invasion of England, 1216* (Stroud, 2011), pp. 217–34.

rule and saved the kingdom. 'Annals of Barnwell Priory', p. 239; Painter, *William Marshal*, pp. 225–7; Crouch, *William Marshal*, pp. 134–5. William Marshal probably was over–generous (or simply naive) in agreeing to pay Louis of France 10,000 marks to secure peace, on the expectation (confirmed by oath, but subsequently broken) that Louis would do all in his power to persuade his father, King Philip, to return the continental Angevin territory lost by John to Henry III.

EPILOGUE

to New Ross in Leinster. *HWM*, lines 17727–876; Carpenter, *The Minority of Henry III*, pp. 50–127; Painter, *William Marshal*, pp. 228–74; Crouch, *William Marshal*, pp. 135–8.

the responsibilities of office. *HWM*, lines 17877–936; Painter, *William Marshal*, pp. 275–6; Crouch, *William Marshal*, p. 138.

'delivered of a great burden'. *HWM*, lines 17937–18135; Painter, *William Marshal*, pp. 276–9; Crouch, *William Marshal*, p. 139.

William in his dying days. *HWM*, lines 18136–982; Painter, *William Marshal*, pp. 279–89; Crouch, *William Marshal*, pp. 139–40, 214–16.

remained so to the very end. *HWM*, lines 18136–78, 18675–734.

be performed to the letter. *HWM*, lines 18124–35, 18180–225, 18243–60.

no man can find salvation. *HWM*, lines 18459–96, 18591–674, 18905–60.

have you for his own'. *HWM*, lines 18227–42, 18323–6, 18351–412, 18443–458. Ironically, Aimery of St Maur fell ill on his return to London and died even before William Marshal.

still be seen to this day. *HWM*, lines 18797–9215; Painter, *William Marshal*, p. 289; Crouch, *William Marshal*, p. 141.

the crown for personal gain. Carpenter, *The Struggle for Mastery*, pp. 300–37.

to a desperately premature end. R.F. Walker, 'William (II) Marshal', *ODNB*; D. Power, 'Richard Marshal', *ODNB*.

of King Richard II in 1399. Carpenter, *The Struggle for Mastery*, pp. 338–530; C. Allmand, *The Hundred Years War: England and France at War, c. 1300–c.1450* (Cambridge, 2001).

in the dawn of modernity. Keen, *Chivalry*, pp. 102–253; Saul, *For Honour and Fame*, pp. 60–370; M. Prestwich, *Armies and Warfare in the Middle Ages: The English Experience* (New Haven & London, 1996).

annals of the distant past. Aurell, 'Henry II and Arthurian Legend', p. 376; Kaeuper, 'William Marshal, Lancelot and the Issue of Chivalric Identity', pp. 1–19.

the figure behind the crown. *The Fine Arts Commission Reports*, vol. 4 (1845), vol. 7 (1847) vol. 8 (1849). I am very grateful to James Ford at the Palace of Westminster for his assistance on the issue of the redecoration of the House of Lords.

PICTURE CREDITS

All images are copyright of the author, other than those stated below.

Section one:

p.1   Portrait of Paul Meyer: © L. Sabattier in George Bonnamour, *Le Procès Zola – Impressions d'audience*/Wikicommons.

p.2   Aerial view of Old Sarum: © Jason Hawkes/Corbis.

p.3   Bayeux Tapestry: © Myrabella/Wikicommons.
Double-edged sword: © by kind permission of the Trustees of the Wallace Collection.
Mail hauberk © Richard T. Nowitz/Corbis.

p.5   Eleanor of Aquitaine, Codex Manesse: © Andreas Praefcke/Wikicommons.
Young Henry's coronation, The Becket Leaves: © Wormsley Library.

p.6   Morgan Picture Bible: © Pierpont Morgan Library/Art Resource/Scala, Florence.
Kneeling knight: © The British Library.

p.7   Casket depicting Tristan and Isolde: © The British Museum.
Casket depicting the 'Siege of the Castle of Love': © The Walters Art Museum.

p.8   Roll of Arms: © The British Library.

Section two:

p.1   Depiction of five English kings: © The British Library.

p.2   Chepstow Castle: © Skyscan.

p.3   Roman defences at Le Mans: © Guiziou Franck/Hemis/Corbis.
Château Gaillard: © Julia Waterlow/Eye Ubiquitous/Corbis.

p.5   Seal of Robert FitzWalter: © The British Museum.
Magna Carta: © Bodleian Library.

p.6   Lincoln: © Richard Klune/Corbis.
Wounding of the count of Perche: © The Parker Library, Corpus Christi College.

p.8   Portrait of Sir Thomas Phillipps: courtesy of Wikicommons.

ACKNOWLEDGEMENTS

I am grateful to all those who supported me through the researching and writing of this book. My thanks to Hilary Redmon at Ecco and Mike Jones at Simon & Schuster for their patience and editorial insight, and to Jo Whitford for overseeing the final stages of production. I am also indebted to my agents, Andrew Gordon and George Lucas, for their guidance.

William Voelkle, at the Morgan Library, kindly granted me access to the sole surviving manuscript of the History of William Marshal, and James Ford, at the Palace of Westminster, offered valuable guidance on the positioning of William's statue in the House of Lords. I am also grateful to Peter Robinson, Amanda Vickery and Andrew Buck for their contributions.

In the midst of writing, I filmed a documentary about William Marshal's life for the BBC – an experience which proved to be both hugely enjoyable and inspirational (even if it did keep me from my desk). I would like to thank John Farren, Martin Davidson and James Hayes for that rare opportunity, and my production team – Jack MacInnes, Catherine Stefanini, Fred Fabre and Katalina Echeverria–Valda – for their hard work.

I owe a huge debt to my friend and colleague, James Ellison, for the role he played in the genesis of this book – commenting on countless drafts, proffering sage advice and generous encouragement. As always, I am grateful to my family for their forbearance and kindness, and must thank my parents, Camilla and Jamie Smith, Jane Campbell, Margaret Williams and Craig Campbell. I have dedicated this work to Per Asbridge. William Marshal may have been the 'greatest knight', but Per has always been the finest brother.

Lastly, and most importantly, I am thankful for the love and patient understanding of my daughters, Ella and Violet, and immeasurably grateful to my wife, Christine – my first reader, without whom no word would be written.

Thomas Asbridge
September 2014
West Sussex

INDEX